STRATEGIC ASIA 2015–16

STRATEGIC ASIA 2015–16

FOUNDATIONS OF NATIONAL POWER

in the Asia-Pacific

Edited by

Ashley J. Tellis with Alison Szalwinski and Michael Wills

With contributions from

Michael Auslin, Dennis C. Blair, Andrew C. Kuchins, Chung Min Lee, Vikram Nehru, Rajesh Rajagopalan, Nadège Rolland, and Ashley J. Tellis

 THE NATIONAL BUREAU *of* **ASIAN RESEARCH**
Seattle and Washington, D.C.

THE NATIONAL BUREAU *of* ASIAN RESEARCH

Published in the United States of America by
The National Bureau of Asian Research, Seattle, WA, and Washington, D.C.
www.nbr.org

ISBN (print): 978-1-939131-41-6
ISBN (electronic): 978-1-939131-42-3

Cover images

Front: Silhouette person working on construction frame © Getty Images

Back (left to right): Cargo ship in the harbor at sunset © iStock; Medical student doing experiment in laboratory © Getty Images; The development of Shanghai © Getty Images; Military port in Kure, Hiroshima, Japan © iStock

Design and publishing services by The National Bureau of Asian Research

Cover design by Stefanie Choi

Publisher's Cataloging-In-Publication Data
(Prepared by The Donohue Group, Inc.)

Foundations of national power in the Asia-Pacific / edited by Ashley J.
 Tellis with Alison Szalwinski and Michael Wills ; with contributions
 from Michael Auslin [and 7 others].
  pages : illustrations, maps ; cm. -- (Strategic Asia, 1933-6462 ; 2015-16)
 Issued also as an ebook.
 Includes bibliographical references and index.
 ISBN: 978-1-939131-41-6
  1. Asia--Military policy--History--21st century. 2. Asia--Defenses--History--21st century. 3. Natural resources--Asia--History--21st century. 4. Asia--Economic conditions--21st century. 5. Asia--Politics and government--21st century. 6. Asia--Foreign relations--United States. 7. United States--Foreign relations--Asia. I. Tellis, Ashley J. II. Szalwinski, Alison. III. Wills, Michael, 1970- IV. Auslin, Michael R., 1967- V. National Bureau of Asian Research (U.S.) VI. Series: Strategic Asia ; 2015-16.

UA830 .F68 2015

355.02/17/095

Printed in Canada

The paper used in this publication meets the minimum requirement of the American National Standard for Information Sciences—Permanence of Paper for Printed Library Materials, ANSI Z39.48-1992.

Contents

Preface

Richard J. Ellings

For practitioners and observers alike, the starting point for understanding international relations, and indeed the sweep of history, is apprehending a hazy, fluid milieu. I am referring to the constantly changing structure of power, tracked by relative growth and diminishment plus the geography of states. Because of its complexity, obscured elements, and constant motion, the structure of power is terribly difficult to measure. Strategists require assessments to make decisions, however, and historians need to explain the human experience, from its triumphs to its tragedies, marked by the rise and fall of the most influential states.

As we are all aware, states in similar structural circumstances do not necessarily behave similarly. The second most important set of variables for the analysis of state behavior is strategic culture. How states strive to accumulate and use power is shaped by their particular values, domestic affairs, and legacies of past events, both real and mythologized.

Applying these approaches to the post–World War II era, we need to understand Pax Americana. In 1945 the United States had amassed enormous power through its extraordinary economic success and military victory and prowess, and it had a clear set of purposes. What ensued reflected American power, values, and historical experience. Top priorities were an inclusive United Nations and the disassembly of empires. Economics received equal attention. In the wake of the Bretton Woods Conference, every U.S. president pushed a free trade agenda focused on lowering trade barriers and urging liberal economic reform overseas. Building on Bretton Woods in the early years of the Cold War, the United States greatly expanded the notion and practice of foreign economic aid and led efforts to institutionalize international aid. The human condition was revolutionized by the growth of markets, unprecedented accumulation of wealth, alleviation of poverty, and extraordinary improvements in health and longevity. Disappointed in the effectiveness of the United Nations and at tremendous cost, the United States led efforts to contain or defeat a wide array of threats to international peace—by aggressive regimes mostly in Eastern Europe, Asia, and the Middle East and by terrorist organizations worldwide. Under U.S. leadership, the world avoided war among the major powers. In parallel, the United States promoted democracy, which spread from its outposts in North America and Western Europe across parts of Asia, Eastern Europe, Latin America, and Africa, bringing to these states stronger rule of law, respect for human rights, environmental protection, and political legitimacy and stability. In all of history, this period stands out as the most successful by far for human progress. It is hard to imagine these monumental achievements if the United States had been defeated in World War II.

Is this period ending? The success of U.S. leadership is judged in part by the grand accomplishments of other states, whose success has ironically contributed to the relative diminishment of U.S. leadership capacity. Seventy years into the post–World War II era, we are now living in a time of extremely complex and fluid international relations, with enormous implications for prosperity, peace, and justice. It is certainly not the bipolar world of the Cold War. I use the term "skewed multipolarity" to describe today's power structure: power is distributed widely around the globe, but unevenly and skewed toward the United States, Western Europe (less in recent years), and increasingly Asia, particularly China.

Commentators often emphasize that today's complexity stems from high economic interdependence, but to get a clearer handle on things it is wise to review the basics. We live in a period of rapidly dispersing power, both globally and in certain regions, leading to heightened strategic ambiguity and fear. Driving much of the structural change is the rapid rise of China, an authoritarian, world-leading industrial powerhouse, and in this great civilization, nationalism is rising. The United States' advantages are ebbing. Its economy now accounts for less than 20% of world product, the lowest point in a century. Strategic cultures clash in Europe between the West and Russia, in Asia between many states and China, and in the Middle East between the West and a variety of actors. The result is tumult, and it is broad and deep: weakness in international institutions; weakness in Europe; the resurgence of Russian ambition and military power; the combination of growing Iranian power, the fracturing of key states, and spreading violence in the Middle East; initiatives by China for expanding territory and influence; and responses by the United States that suggest war weariness, difficulty in assessing and prioritizing its interests, and signs of ambivalence about its leadership.

These developments need to be viewed through a historical lens. In last year's *Strategic Asia* preface I looked at the years running up to World Wars I and II for precedents. As in one or both of those periods, we again see rapid changes and ambiguities in the balance of power, heightened nationalism, greater strategic opportunities for rising and dissatisfied regimes, mercurial economic performance, and greater opportunities for aggressive political movements. Add to these factors serious questions about current domestic affairs in major states—especially in China but also in Japan and the United States itself. My conclusion in that essay was that two variables in the current cycle make world war a less likely outcome this time: (1) the United States' continued, albeit weakening, capacity and commitment to leadership and (2) nuclear proliferation.

Today, the single biggest challenge to—and opportunity for—the international system is integrating China peacefully and otherwise successfully. In the 37 short years since Deng Xiaoping introduced its early reforms, China has grown from playing an insignificant role in international trade to ranking first among all nations. China's exports to the United States are enormous and four times U.S. exports to China. The United States' trans-Pacific trade has grown to twice the value of its trans-Atlantic trade. China's industrial sector is the world's largest, 50% bigger than the second-ranked United States. As with any new major actor industrializing and gaining relative power, China has evidenced rising nationalism and exerted greater influence in regional and global affairs. The United States and the world have supported China's development and integration into international affairs through open markets, World Bank support, aid (especially from Japan), the country's inclusion in the World Trade Organization, and stability in East Asia guaranteed by U.S. forces and alliances. The positive consequences for the world have been low inflation and a sustained source of growth even in bad times elsewhere. In this trading era, when China reforms, opportunity for other countries expands.

Today China's commitment to further economic reform is unclear, and there is no indication of impending political reform other than an anticorruption campaign that is aimed at strengthening the hand of the Chinese Communist Party (CCP). Moreover, the values, historical legacies, political structures, industrial polices, and people behind China's foray into international affairs frequently conflict with the values and arrangements of the prevailing liberal order. With China's success and its actions overseas more impactful, frictions are growing. Indeed, the enormity of the challenge for U.S. policymakers is hard to understate, coming at a time of diminished capacity and will and as an authoritarian China seems on its way to constituting a peer competitor, more so than the Soviet Union ever was.

The purposes to which China will apply its power are not clear. Even as Russian aggression in Eastern Europe and the horrific actions of the Islamic State in the Middle East capture public attention, it is crucial to remember that the greatest potential for large-scale conflict or economic warfare resides where power has concentrated—in the Asia-Pacific.

China's policies, political opaqueness, and uncertain future only serve to foster greater ambivalence in the region. How should policymakers in the region interpret China's actions in the South China Sea, its "One Belt, One Road" initiative, or its establishment of the Asian Infrastructure Investment Bank? The latter two could be contributions to economic development in Asia, while the former appears ominous, spurring neighboring states to hedge more than ever, and mostly with the United States. The past year, for instance, saw updated U.S.-Japan defense guidelines and increased defense cooperation between New Delhi and Washington. The Trans-Pacific Partnership, for which preliminary agreement was reached in early fall 2015, is not just a mechanism for liberalizing regional trade. It is a strategic grouping providing the region with an alternative driver of economic growth and a means to dilute economic dependence on China.

Competition between the United States and China is, in fact, unavoidable and multifaceted, occurring across political, economic, military, and ideological arenas. The challenge for U.S. policymakers is the toughest the United States has faced since World War II—simultaneously preserving the international liberal order and balancing China as unambiguously as possible to avoid war, while accepting China's sharing of international responsibilities commensurate with that country's capacities. Key will be the United States' ability to lead coalitions to accomplish these goals and successfully rejuvenate its own economy and sustain the will to lead. Will U.S. innovation be enough to balance China's scale and industrial might? Will domestic priorities overwhelm international ones?

The United States will not determine the future alone, of course. To the contrary, China will determine most of what it does, and much of that may be beyond state control. Whether or not an authoritarian Chinese state can remain viable in the face of an increasingly educated and prosperous Chinese citizenry, and given the ramifications of globalization, remains to be seen. Among the many plausible outcomes are both positive ones in which China reforms politically as well as economically and negative ones in which China falls into chaos, or worse in which the CCP responds to domestic threats by taking a super-nationalist course.

The function of the Strategic Asia Program is to provide U.S. leaders with the very best and most useful data and analysis. With this imperative in mind, this year's volume marks the first of a three-part series designed to assess the future character of geopolitical competition in the Asia-Pacific. It seeks to closely examine the foundations underlying the national power of key states: China, Japan, South Korea, Russia, India, Indonesia, and the United States. The next two volumes will build on this base to explore each country's strategic culture, before moving to examine power in the regional context. It is our intention that the valuable insights provided in each of these chapters, and in the forthcoming volumes, will enable decision-makers to better understand the complexities of the rapidly changing geopolitical context in which we currently operate, thus equipping them with the knowledge necessary to guide U.S. policy during this turbulent time.

Acknowledgements

The strength of this year's *Strategic Asia* volume is a reflection of the exceptional work and dedication of the many individuals who helped make the publication a reality. This marks the twelfth year in which Ashley Tellis has provided his guidance as the research director of the Strategic Asia Program. The contributions he has made over the course of his tenure are immeasurable. Former NBR senior vice president and *Strategic Asia* editor Abraham Denmark played an essential role in the early stages of this year's volume before transitioning to government service. Abe deserves special acknowledgement for his tireless contributions to the series over the past three years, and we wish him the very best. Alison Szalwinski and Michael Wills also played central roles in ensuring that the work contained in this volume reflects the highest standard of academic rigor and quality. Their leadership over the course of this year has been exceptional.

NBR's publications team, led by Joshua Ziemkowski with the assistance of Jessica Keough, Craig Scanlan, Adam Kahn, and Maya Kuhns, performed the essential services of formatting, technical editing, and proofreading. *Strategic Asia* would also not have been possible without the assistance of Kyle Churchman, Jessica Drun, Xiaodon Liang, Deep Pal, Louis Ritzinger, and John Ryan, who not only contributed valuable research support but helped plan and organize critical events surrounding the project.

Of course, *Strategic Asia* would be nothing were it not for this year's exceptionally talented and knowledgeable scholars, who dedicated countless hours of research and writing to ensure that the publication continues its long tradition of including only the highest caliber of academic work within its pages. Their accomplishments are made more impressive by their adherence to a strict and rigorous timetable, which made it possible to publish their findings in a timely manner. The prompt and detailed work of anonymous reviewers further improved the chapters by ensuring their relevance and factual accuracy.

Finally, I would like to extend a special thanks to the Lynde and Harry Bradley Foundation, whose continued support is absolutely vital to the Strategic Asia Program. The foundation's recognition of the importance of this work is both gratifying and a testament to the value it places on an informed and principled foreign policy. I look forward to continuing to work with the Bradley Foundation as we examine the insights set forward in this volume.

As always, the goal of our work here at NBR is to provide policymakers and idea leaders with the highest-quality, most objective information possible. While the challenges that face the United States and its partners around the world are indeed formidable, I am confident that the insights found in these pages fulfill this mission.

Richard J. Ellings
President
The National Bureau of Asian Research

STRATEGIC ASIA 2015–16

EXECUTIVE SUMMARY

This chapter explains how three distinct conceptions of power—as resources, ability, and outcomes—informed the framework of this study and presents an overview of each chapter in the volume.

MAIN ARGUMENT

The many diverse expressions of power can be compressed into three broad conceptions: power as resources, power as ability, and power as outcomes. Framing national power in terms of resources, ability, and outcomes is a useful means of evaluating the countries of the Asia-Pacific region. Resources are the dominant consideration in competitive social environments, but solely examining resources can be deceptive. Almost as important is national performance, which accounts for variance in converting raw materials into physical and social products. This broad conception of power provides a better baseline for understanding strategic competition than a narrow focus on military metrics because disruptive scientific and technological advances can allow dynamic nations to rapidly overtake their competitors in future capabilities. By examining the resources of the major countries in the Asia-Pacific and their ability to convert these resources into national performance, this volume in the *Strategic Asia* series lays the foundation for a three-year study of each nation's likelihood of achieving its desired outcomes in international relations.

POLICY IMPLICATIONS

- Political realism emphasizes national power as the most important determinant of whether a state can achieve its strategic objectives.

- National performance, which encompasses state-society relations and the capacity for rationality in strategic action, determines whether a nation can effectively convert material resources into elements of national power.

- Military capability must necessarily be included in any portrait of national power even if it is not by itself an effective predictor of regional outcomes.

Assessing National Power in Asia

Ashley J. Tellis

In a competitive international environment, material power represents the necessary, though not sufficient, condition for a country to achieve its desired strategic objectives, whatever those may be. The fundamental importance of tangible capabilities for success has endured over time, irrespective of what kind of human collectives dominate at any given point in history. Consequently, all entities involved in contestational politics seek to maximize their power, even though there are considerable variations in the skill with which this resource is accumulated, organized, or deployed. The rise of the modern state signaled the intensification of power accumulation in ways previously unknown in history: social mobilization, technological innovation, bureaucratic organization, institutional design, and ideological promotion came together on a grand scale to stimulate the production of material capabilities for such diverse ends as national consolidation, internal development, and external security. But regardless of the character or the aims of various constituent entities, or the depth or scale of their mutual antagonisms, power has remained fundamental to success in every political system.

Hence, it may seem surprising that despite its pivotal standing in sociopolitical life, power still remains an "essentially contested concept."[1] The vast literature on the subject in fact suggests that what makes countries "powerful" in international politics is often hard to articulate precisely or

---

Ashley J. Tellis is a Senior Associate at the Carnegie Endowment for International Peace and Research Director of the Strategic Asia Program at The National Bureau of Asian Research. He can be reached at <atellis@carnegieendowment.org>.

[1] W. B. Gallie, "Essentially Contested Concepts," *Proceedings of the Aristotelian Society* 56 (1955): 167–98.

universally, even when there is an intuitive consensus about their relative strength. Contemporary social science actually abounds with different, often incommensurable, notions of power, and modern international relations theory is not much different: sometimes power is treated as the property of an entity, or as a resource; sometimes it is viewed as the characterization of relationships between entities, or as the attribute of particular systems or social structures; sometimes it is presumed to be a product of inequality, and at other times it is presumed to derive from shared values; and sometimes it is judged to be zero-sum, reflexive, or transitive, and at other times the exact opposite.[2]

Relating Power to National Power

The notion of national power explored in this *Strategic Asia* volume is grounded broadly in political realism. Political realism here refers to the tradition of understanding human behavior as part of the permanent struggle for security. It views the units of analysis, whether they be individuals, fiefdoms, or states, as largely self-regarding political entities that are locked into competition with one another, where each remains the principal limitation on the security, freedom, and ambitions of the others. As a result of such rivalry, all entities are propelled to enlarge their material capabilities in order to advance their own interests. The resulting maximization at the national level is driven primarily by the desire to minimize the prospect of harm arising from one's own relative weakness in what is overall a pervasively competitive environment that sometimes resembles the Hobbesian state of nature.

Because power alone protects its possessors in such a milieu, with greater power offering greater degrees of protection, it is possible to compress many diverse expressions of power into three broad conceptions. As the French sociologists Raymond Boudon and Francois Bourricaud summarized, power may be treated in the first instance as simply an "*allocation of resources*, of whatever nature these might be."[3] This notion of power, which refers to the sum total of the capabilities available to any entity for influencing others, is an old one and goes back to Thomas Hobbes, who

---

[2] Dennis H. Wrong, *Power: Its Forms, Bases, and Uses* (Piscataway: Transaction Publishers, 1980). It may well be that these conflicting notions are indeed irreconcilable because every analytical concept, including power, is ultimately theory-dependent, as Karl Popper demonstrated in the early 1930s in *The Logic of Scientific Discovery*. If all concepts are thus by definition theory-laden, then both the idea of power and any disputes over its characteristics can only be articulated and resolved within the context of a specific theory. This constraint implies that even a crucial organizing variable such as power cannot really be understood either a-theoretically or meta-theoretically. Specifying its provenance, therefore, remains essential for intellectual clarity and explanatory utility.

[3] Raymond Boudon and Francois Bourricaud, *A Critical Dictionary of Sociology* (London: Routledge, 1989), 267.

defined it as "man's present means to any future apparent good."[4] Power, in this conception, is dispositional. It refers not to actual performance but merely to the capacities or assets possessed by any given entity, resources that either may enable certain outcomes to be produced by the very fact of their existence or could be utilized subsequently to produce particular outcomes through intentional action.

The view of power as resources is particularly appealing to theorists of international relations who often treat countries as "bordered power-containers":[5] the country is akin to a receptacle and the resources it possesses are akin to stock, allowing the latter to be measured, quantified, and compared with the holdings possessed by others. Although there may be disputes about which particular resources, such as population, natural wealth, productive capabilities, and military strength, are best suited to describe a country's national power, the utility of having a standardized set of measurable variables allows for cross-country comparisons and the global rank ordering of nations. Because material endowments matter in competitive social environments and because superior assets help their possessors secure advantageous outcomes—even if this causality does not hold in every instance—the tradition of viewing power as resources continues to remain attractive and cannot be easily discarded, no matter what its limitations may be.

The second conception of power highlighted by Boudon and Bourricaud is the "*ability* to use…resources," which in turn implies, among other things, "a *plan of use* and [the necessity of] minimal information about the conditions and consequences of this use."[6] This notion of power as ability is a valuable complement to the conceptualization of power as resources because it emphasizes intentionality and the active dimension of the actual-potential dichotomy that inheres in any notion of power centered on brute capabilities. This approach, by focusing on the idea of the power "to do" something, as opposed to the notion of power emanating from a stock of resources, opens the door to thinking about power as strategy in which the processes, relationships, and situations that shape purposeful action all play an important role.

This shift in focus from objects, which remain central to the idea of power as resources, to deliberate action in a certain context, which constitutes the cornerstone anchoring the idea of power as ability, is extremely useful for conceptualizing national power as understood within the framework of

---

[4] Thomas Hobbes, *Leviathan* (London: Oxford University Press, 1996), chap. 10.

[5] Anthony Giddens, *The Nation-State and Violence* (Oakland: University of California Press, 1985).

[6] Boudon and Bourricaud, *A Critical Dictionary of Sociology*, 267.

international relations theory. By highlighting the importance of calculated activity against the backdrop of certain structured relationships as well as specific forms of interaction between particular entities within or outside the nation, resources can be treated not simply as mute facts of nature but rather as products created as a result of willful state or societal action—outcomes that owe their existence to negotiation, bargaining, and even coercion between different entities within a given country or beyond it. Specifically, the idea of power as ability allows state-society relations to be restored to a pivotal position in the understanding of how national power comes to be produced by or in a given country; it also opens the door to incorporating various transnational activities into the production of national power. Both of these elements, in turn, highlight the fact that resources, which ordinarily define the relative power of various countries, do not exist in usable form *ex ante* but rather are brought into being *ex post* through conscious action for certain political ends.

The third notion discussed by Boudon and Bourricaud centers on "the *strategic* character of power," namely that "ultimately it is exercised not only against the inertia of things, but against the *resistance of opposing wills*."[7] This conception of power, which focuses fundamentally on the consequences of a given action, comports with the common human intuition of what it means to be powerful: getting one's way.[8] In its strongest form, this understanding of power incorporates the simple question of whether an agent is able to influence the targeted entity to act in a desired way, even if that entails undermining the target's own interests—an idea that was later encapsulated in Robert Dahl's now classic definition of power as the ability of A to get B to do something B would otherwise not do.[9]

Many kinds of historical explanation employ such an understanding of power when explaining the success of political action. This notion of power as outcomes is also immensely appealing to many theories of international relations, especially political realism. By incorporating both power as resources and power as ability into the singular conception of power as outcomes, most realist approaches ordinarily seek to explain a country's ability to attain its desired ends—despite possible resistance by others—as a logical function of its possessing greater resources, which in turn derive

---

[7] Boudon and Bourricaud, *A Critical Dictionary of Sociology*, 267.

[8] In social theory, Max Weber was perhaps the first among classical theorists to not only systematically reflect on power as an outcome but actually embed it in an analysis of human interaction (while also allowing for the possibility of treating it as an emergent property of various aggregated interactions) when he described power as "the probability that one actor within a social relationship will be in a position to carry out his own will despite resistance, regardless of the basis on which this probability rests." See Max Weber, *The Theory Of Social And Economic Organization* (New York: Simon and Schuster, 2009).

[9] Robert A. Dahl, "The Concept of Power," *Behavioral Science* 2, no. 3 (1957): 201–15.

ultimately from its superior ability to mobilize these assets through concerted state and societal actions.

The attempt to explain success, particularly in conflicts, purely through the availability of superior resources, even with military capabilities as the relevant proxy, has unfortunately not fared too well analytically. Numerous studies have suggested that "the international distribution of capabilities" seems to correlate poorly with getting one's way consistently in international wars or disputes—and numerous explanations have, in turn, been adduced to "save" the presumption that superior resources are necessary for the production of favorable outcomes.[10] Given the discomfiting fact that poorly endowed entities are often able to win tests of will in international politics, Kenneth Waltz attempted in his celebrated *Theory of International Politics* to restate the case for the relevance of power as resources and ability by arguing that even if superior capabilities cannot produce success in every instance, they do enlarge their possessors' autonomy—undoubtedly a more defensible notion, but one that also runs into evidentiary difficulties of other kinds.[11]

The Framework of the Volume

Despite whatever their inherent limitations may be, each of the three conceptions of power elaborated above offers important insights that are of value to any analysis of national power. The studies gathered in this 2015–16 volume of the *Strategic Asia* series, *Foundations of National Power in the Asia-Pacific*, are envisaged as the first phase of a three-year effort aimed at understanding the future character of geopolitical competition in the Asia-Pacific region. The success of such an evaluation hinges considerably on the ability to judge the capacities of the key political entities involved, because national power serves as the foundation that enables them to secure their geopolitical and geostrategic aims.

The very first volume in the *Strategic Asia* series, *Strategic Asia 2001–02: Power and Purpose*, assessed the national power of key Asian states in the context of their grand strategies.[12] The chapters in this volume revisit that earlier discussion, aiming to investigate the national power of critical states in the Strategic Asia Program's arc of focus more systematically, using a schema developed at the RAND Corporation at the turn of the century. This framework was developed primarily for the intelligence community and was originally

---

[10] Ashley J. Tellis, Janice Bially, Christopher Layne, Melissa McPherson, and Jerry M. Sollinger, *Measuring National Power in the Postindustrial Age: Analyst's Handbook* (Santa Monica: RAND, 2000).

[11] Kenneth N. Waltz, *Theory of International Politics* (Long Grove: Waveland Press, 2010).

[12] Richard J. Ellings and Aaron L. Friedberg, eds., *Strategic Asia 2001–02: Power and Purpose* (Seattle: National Bureau of Asian Research [NBR], 2001).

intended to help country specialists assess the capacities of potential great powers in depth.[13] It was consciously designed to enable the close scrutiny of a few significant countries, one at a time, and hence required the integration of significant quantities of raw data as well as specialized knowledge.

Single-author assessments of the kind gathered in this volume cannot match the collaborative work undertaken by large teams of intelligence analysts with access to classified information—an issue that becomes particularly relevant when evaluations of military capabilities are concerned. Yet although the chapters that follow deviate somewhat from the analytical template described in the next section with respect to scope of coverage and level of detail, the broad framework is nonetheless consistently followed in every chapter. This framework uses several traditional measures of national power, while incorporating the notion of state capacity to describe how a country might produce—in absolute terms—both the material resources and the military power necessary to influence regional and global events. Toward that end, all these studies are anchored primarily in the tradition of power as resources, but they also draw substantially from the notion of power as ability. Each country is investigated intensively in order to assess the extent and the depth of its capabilities beyond the basic yardsticks of physical size, natural resources, economic growth rates, and military inventories. Because national power here is conceived simply as the capacity of a country to pursue strategic goals through purposeful action, each chapter attempts to engage both the external dimension, which consists of how a nation is affected by its wider environment, and the internal dimension, which consists of a nation's capacity to mold and transform the resources of its society into actionable knowledge that produces the best civilian and military capabilities possible.

By thus analyzing a country's material capabilities as well as its ability to produce those assets, this volume aims to establish a baseline for describing the absolute power of a given country, while also illuminating how each stacks up relative to its Asian neighbors when all the chapters are read synoptically. It is important to note that these studies do not make any attempt to assess whether the national capabilities of the countries examined suffice to advance their specific political aims in the Asian or the global context. That examination—of power as outcomes—will be the focus of the third-year product of this research effort. The third volume will integrate the analysis of capabilities published here—which draws from the notion of power as resources and the notion of power as ability—with next year's volume on the strategic culture of various Asian states in order to assess how resources and worldviews come together to produce the warfighting capabilities that each

---

[13] Tellis et al., *Measuring National Power in the Postindustrial Age.*

country believes are required for success in the face of concrete regional and global threats. The next three volumes of the *Strategic Asia* series, beginning with the current book, are thus conceived as an integrated effort, even though each particular one addresses a different but related topic.

Thinking about National Capabilities

Creating a useful national power profile that incorporates notions of both power as resources and power as ability requires not simply judging certain attributes of the country in question, such as population size or GNP, but unpacking the concept of the "country" itself in order to look within that which is often treated as a black box.

Such reconstruction is justified on the assumption that the real sinews of national power are manifested not merely by the visible military assets brandished during ceremonies or parades but rather by deeper capacities such as the aptitude for innovation, the fecundity of social institutions, and the quality of the knowledge base—all of which profoundly bear on a country's capacity to produce the *ultima ratio regum* in international politics: effective military power.[14] The validity of this assumption, in turn, derives from three specific premises.

The first premise is that the international system has witnessed for some time now something resembling a science-based "knowledge revolution," most clearly manifested by the current breakthroughs in information processing, technology, and management; biotechnology; advanced materials; robotics; renewable energy and energy storage; and the "Internet of things"—disruptive innovations that promise consequential transformations in society at large with major implications in both the civilian and the military realms.[15]

The second premise is that the performance of the state (understood specifically as the governing institutions that steer a nation's political direction) and the character of state-society relations (understood specifically as the character of the interdependence between the rulers and the ruled) are critical to a country's success in the evolving international system for two reasons. The first is that no matter how successful a given society may be in developing or exploiting the science-based knowledge revolution currently underway, a minimally efficient state is required if these societal advances are to be transformed into national power. The second is that societal vitality is

---

[14] Tellis et al., *Measuring National Power in the Postindustrial Age*, 12.

[15] Ibid., 6.

indispensable for a state's success, even as an effective state is critical for the success of collective action in society.[16]

The third premise is that national power in a rivalrous international system will continue to find its most potent expression in terms of warfighting capabilities, and that the best forces will be those that can better exploit emerging militarily critical technologies, such as those relating to information and communications, energetic materials, electronics, optics and sensors, signature control, cyber, and space, to nurture the highest forms of combat proficiency in order to sustain projectable power against opposition at the greatest distance necessary.[17]

Articulating a conception of national power that satisfactorily accommodates these three premises requires unpacking the term "country" in order that its constituent entities—population, state structures, state-society relations, constitutional arrangements, culture, and worldview—may be conceived as active social artifacts that, in interaction, make up the entity that looks from the outside as a geographic representation. Such disaggregation, then, allows national power to be seen as a product that ensues from the synergy of three distinct realms, every one of which is as important as the other for the generation of usable power in international politics. The first realm encompasses the level of resources either available to or produced by a country. The second realm encompasses national performance deriving from the security pressures facing a country; from the efficiency of its governing institutions, nominally labeled "the state," as well as society at large; and from its capacity for rational maximization of material power. Finally, the third realm encompasses military capability, which is understood in terms of operational proficiency or effectiveness produced as a result of both the strategic resources available to a military organization and its ability to convert those resources into effective coercive power. These three realms together describe national power (see **Figure 1**).

The first realm depicts the national resources that a country must possess if it is to achieve its aims in international politics. These capacities could be crudely considered the raw materials that enable successful national action in any political realm—diplomatic, economic, or military—and they remain the foundation from which effective military forces are produced. Since the beginning of the modern international system, this dimension has been the focus of most comparisons of national power, which has been measured by variables such as population, size of territory, economic strength (frequently in terms of GNP or GDP), and natural resources.

---

[16] Tellis et al., *Measuring National Power in the Postindustrial Age*, 22.

[17] Ibid., 27–28.

FIGURE 1   The three realms of national power

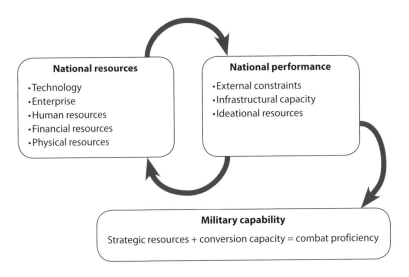

National resources

- Technology
- Enterprise
- Human resources
- Financial resources
- Physical resources

National performance

- External constraints
- Infrastructural capacity
- Ideational resources

Military capability

Strategic resources + conversion capacity = combat proficiency

SOURCE: Ashley J. Tellis et al., *Measuring National Power in the Postindustrial Age: Analyst's Handbook* (Santa Monica: RAND, 2000), 5.

In neoclassical economics, these variables are generally captured by the locution "factors of production," which encompass land, labor, capital, and enterprise, thereby including all the elements that combine to make up the productive system and, by implication, the material foundations of national power. Because these elements have enduring significance, they cannot simply be jettisoned; hence, they are incorporated into the framework above in the context of other, newer qualitative variables that speak to a country's wider ability to incorporate the science-based knowledge revolution into its political, economic, and social spheres.

Thus, for instance, the authors in this volume examine how the countries on which they focus are positioned with respect to cutting-edge technology: the priority placed on it, the achievements or absence thereof, and the level of resources committed to the acquisition of new technology as well as the strategies pursued toward that end. Because the capacity to shift the technological production frontier outward has a critical bearing on national power, the analyses here also consider, under the rubric of enterprise, each given country's aptitude for innovation and how this might be diffused within its society. Quantifying technological vitality is often a difficult enterprise, but examining the levels of R&D expenditures as well as patent performance might offer useful clues. Given that the size and quality of the labor force are vital ingredients of economic growth and technological change, the chapters perforce consider population trends and educational achievements in both the formal and informal realms. The category of financial resources attempts to capture the accumulation of capital and the effectiveness of that accumulation. Hence, it considers broadly domestic savings and investment (including foreign contributions), aggregate GDP growth, and the performance of particular sectors relevant to the country examined. Finally, the realm of national resources includes physical assets, and special attention is paid to energy and critical materials. In an interdependent global economy, physical resources should be the least significant factor of production so long as markets operate efficiently and without political constraints. Since this still remains an ideal, assessing physical resources is important because they are crucial sources of revenue or external dependency for several Asian nations.

The realm of national resources analyzed in this way is obviously important because it represents a society's tangible and intangible assets. As the causal arrow on the top of Figure 1 indicates, however, they are significant not simply as raw materials but rather as valuables that permit an organized state to sustain itself and, hence, are intimately linked to the second realm of national performance. The cyclic character of this relationship is equally important: as the causal arrow on the bottom linking the resources and performance boxes indicates, even raw materials—the truly brute gifts of nature—often have little economic or political value unless actualized as a result of conscious human action at the state and societal levels. This leads to the insight that national performance—the arena of state-society interactions, the values that shape them, and the constraints that channel them—is critical for the "production" of all the components identified under the rubric of resources, which, even if they exist as such in nature, require human artifice to realize their economic and political worth.

National performance, accordingly, becomes critical. In the framework above, this second realm seeks to capture the mechanisms that enable countries to create or convert national resources, which represent latent power, into tangible forms of usable power. The objective of incorporating this transformative dimension of national power is to move beyond the traditional view of countries as resource containers to one that scrutinizes them as active social structures consisting of state and societal actors and institutions, all of which exist in an environment populated by many similar entities abroad. Introducing this dimension permits an analysis of national power that goes beyond most traditional measures: understanding a state's relationship both to its external security environment (and its internal security environment, if appropriate) and to its own society and the consequences thereof for national power capability.

To achieve these aims, the chapters that follow address to the degree possible three separate but related components. First, they locate the given country's production of national power in the context of its security environment, on the assumption that nations that face acute external or internal security challenges would in principle be motivated to maximize power generation in order to equip their rulers with the wherewithal required to neutralize these hazards. Alternatively stated, these countries' rulers would be motivated to maximize the production of national power in order to entrench their own internal domination while parrying external threats.

Framing the problem in this way leads to the second task: considering what Michael Mann once described in a pathbreaking study as "infrastructural power."[18] In this context, infrastructural power refers to the capacity of the state to penetrate its own society, regulate its activities, and extract its resources, while at the same time permitting those ruled sufficient ordered freedom to engage in private activities that maximize the production of the assets previously treated as natural resources. Attaining these ends involves two broad kinds of activities: the capacity to set goals in the face of competing societal interests, and the capacity to attain those goals through the mechanisms of penetration, extraction, and regulation of social relations. These diverse activities constitute the warp and woof of domestic politics and yet are fundamental to a country's capacity to produce national power.

Finally, the ideational component is critical as well. Does the state encode the logic of instrumental rationality in its policies and institutions, while also being substantively rational in the sense mandated by political realism, namely, possessing the conscious desire to enlarge material power?

The maximization of national power in this framework, then, derives from an effective state nurturing the production of high levels of national resources. These in turn contribute toward the maintenance and enlargement of state capacity that, interacting in a virtuous cycle, can produce the military capabilities required to underwrite the internal and external security or ambitions of the country writ large.

Because the analyses in this volume are embedded in the tradition of understanding power as resources and power as ability, rather than power as outcomes, the treatments of military capabilities do not focus on analyzing whether the combat forces in a given country would be capable of successfully prosecuting various missions against its adversaries. As noted

---

[18] Michael Mann, "The Autonomous Power of the State: Its Origins, Mechanisms and Results," *European Journal of Sociology/Archives Européennes de Sociologie* 25, no. 2 (1984): 185–213.

earlier, that analysis will have to await the third volume of this research effort. What is undertaken in the chapters that follow is a broad analysis of military power, primarily in terms of the resources available and, whenever possible, supplemented by a discussion of conversion capability. Military resources here refer mainly to manpower under arms, equipment inventory, defense budgets, and the defense industrial base. Conversion capability refers to the type of military strategy pursued; the character of civil-military relations; the doctrine, training, and organization of the forces; and their capacity for innovation—the critical variables that condition how the available military resources are converted into combat proficiency in different warfighting domains.

The country studies all conclude with a discussion of military capability, but not necessarily at the level of detail denoted in the graphical depiction of national power earlier. There are two reasons for this, both practical. Assessing combat proficiency in terms of various operational competencies is an exceptionally involved enterprise and requires access to enormous amounts of information (especially in regard to training and operations) that is often not available in the open literature, and which even when available may require military experience to interpret. Moreover, the *Strategic Asia* series has examined the military capabilities of various Asian states at high levels of granularity before.[19] Given the need to limit the scope of each chapter for the purposes of this volume, concentrating on the important realms of national resources and performance, with just enough focus on military power to complete the story, was deemed sufficient. The discussions of military capability in the chapters that follow are, therefore, more in the nature of broad surveys, anchored importantly in the analysis of national resources as well as state aims and performance, than detailed assessments of operational competency.

Surveying National Power in Asia: Key Insights

It is appropriate that a volume dedicated to surveying national power in Asia lead with a chapter on China because it not only is a vast country of almost subcontinental proportions but, more importantly, has been the most noteworthy example of rapidly expanding power in recent history. Thanks to its large size, China has been blessed with a vast reservoir of natural resources. Nadège Rolland's survey captures in fine detail the fact that China has been one of the few states to consciously pursue the

---

[19] Ashley J. Tellis and Michael Wills, eds., *Strategic Asia 2005–06: Military Modernization in an Era of Uncertainty* (Seattle: NBR, 2005); and Ashley J. Tellis and Travis Tanner, eds., *Strategic Asia 2012–13: China's Military Challenge* (Seattle: NBR, 2012).

expansion of national power with almost fanatical zeal, bringing several consequences, not all beneficial. China's rise has led to the dramatic expansion of many national resources in the last three decades, especially Chinese capital stocks, the technology pool, and other physical resources. But political choices, especially the one-child policy, will prospectively result in a problematic contraction of the labor force, with real risks to China's ability to sustain its long-term future growth. The decision to control factor prices, even as China liberalized commodity prices as part of its marketization, has produced considerable wastefulness in utilizing natural resources, with painful environmental degradation as a result.

Rolland's chief conclusion, however, is that while China's quest for power thus far has produced incredible and arresting results both nationally and globally—not least because its impressive growth has yielded regionally disequilibrating military capabilities—Beijing's achievements could be at risk because of the contradictions in its state-society relations, the kernel of national performance. Referring to the current Chinese effort to sustain a market economy controlled by an authoritarian leadership, she concludes that "the nation's capacity to convert…resources into tangible forms of usable civilian and military power is hindered by a contradiction in terms between the essence of power in the 21st century—inspirational, technologically advanced, outward-looking, and innovative—and the intrinsic nature of the regime that is currently governing China." This leads to the unsettling possibility that intensified coercion within China and diversionary adventurism abroad could increasingly come to define Beijing's quest for national power in the future.

Unlike China, which is still a rising power in Asia, Japan is now a mature industrial economy that has suffered some eclipse because of Beijing's ascendency. Michael Auslin's study of Japan, however, is a reminder of the country's enduring importance and abiding strengths: high levels of development and wealth, social stability, and capacity for technological innovation. Japan, in fact, remains an extraordinary example of how a country can flourish despite possessing the most meager resource base—so long as it enjoys a capable state with reasonably effective infrastructural power, maximizes the benefits of international trade, and maintains a relatively efficient domestic market—though in Tokyo's case, the advantages of having the United States as a protector, as a guarantor of the safety of the global commons, and as an external consumer of Japanese products cannot be underestimated. Japan's success in accumulating national power remains a remarkable testament to the benefits of an effective state, productive state-society relations, and high levels of rationalization.

These virtues, Auslin emphasizes, will be tested in the years ahead as Japan copes with an increasingly dangerous regional environment produced by growing Chinese assertiveness at a time when Japanese society is graying, its economy is hobbled by both debt and inefficient capital allocation, and the country is reeling from natural disasters, energy crises, and long deflation. In such circumstances, Japan's extant strengths in national performance—its elite cohesion and highly regulated social relations—could end up being weaknesses if they entrench groupthink, prevent policy innovation, and reinforce the nation's propensity for risk aversion. These shortcomings could be intensified if the interest-group politics that made corporatism successful in an earlier era now impede the national restructuring that requires sacrificing some of these lobbies for the sake of greater economic efficiency and social transformation. At a time when Japan has to think more seriously about military threats, its leadership is undoubtedly challenged in ways that it has never been before. Auslin notes that Japan has the capacity to respond to these challenges, though whether it can do so adequately—because of its cultural conservatism—remains an open question.

Chung Min Lee's chapter on the Republic of Korea highlights the similarities between South Korea and Japan where the production of national power is concerned. Like Japan, South Korea was born out of the crucible of conflict and still copes daily with an ever-present security threat to its north. It is a geographically small nation with poor stocks of natural resources but has compensated remarkably for these deficiencies through building up its human capital. Thanks to its integration into the U.S.-led liberal international order, South Korea has used the mechanisms of international trade to spur its national development in ways that are the envy of many developing countries. As Lee summarizes, "South Korea has joined a relatively small group of states that possess an advanced economy, significant conventional military capabilities, a sizable population base, growing technological capacities, good governance, and a robust democracy."

Lee's analysis substantiates the expectation that, as in Japan, favorable state-society relations have been fundamental for South Korea's success. A highly effective and purposeful state "acted as the principal architect, financier, and monitor of an export-driven industrialization policy"; through competent social control, it "supported [the] *chaebols* (family-run conglomerates) that spearheaded an economic turnaround"; and, in an example of the productive regulation of social relations, it "most importantly, harnessed the sheer industriousness of the Korean people, who were determined not to let endemic poverty become their national destiny."

For all these successes, however, Lee flags the gray clouds now appearing on the horizon: South Korea's population is aging and will not be able to provide either the growth in the labor force or the effective demand of yesteryear, unless peaceful reunification with the North occurs (which is likely to bring its own unique problems). South Korea's export advantages are progressively diminishing, as newer low-cost competitors such as China eat into its market share, and its traditional markets could reach saturation at some point in the future. Most significantly, the controlling power of the South Korean state is declining in the face of new social forces, which at a time when the developmental state model has reached the limits of its success requires both "a 'new political consensus' that goes beyond the reforms that were implemented in 1987" and "a new developmental model that ensures a viable but limited role for the state reflecting the key changes in Korean society." In a situation where, as Lee notes, "virtually every facet of…[South Korea's]…ability to produce and maintain core national capabilities will require unparalleled political and social re-engineering," the tasks of regeneration are formidable indeed. Yet for a society that represents a genuine miracle of contemporary social transformation, the odds of success in the continued production of national power must be judged as better than even.

In contrast to Japan and South Korea, but akin to China, Russia is a vast country with substantial natural resources, especially minerals and energy assets. As a result of its wrenching modernization during the twentieth century, the Soviet Union—contemporary Russia's progenitor—created a bureaucratic state that was highly proficient technologically, with a major military-industrial complex that defined its existence as a superpower. The convulsions resulting from the Soviet collapse weakened not only Russia's industrial capabilities but also its social order. Today, over two decades after that denouement, Andrew Kuchins's chapter in this volume suggests that Russia is still struggling to overcome varying degrees of weakness in regard to technological change, capacity for innovation, human capital development, and even GDP growth. Although appearing to have survived the worst of the economic crises that had bedeviled it after the Soviet collapse, Russia still possesses an unbalanced economy that remains too dependent on energy exports, is saddled by poor demographic indicators, is susceptible to capital flight, and is constrained by unfavorable migration trends that promise a net loss in human capital as "the best and brightest professionals…[leave]…Russia in droves, only to be replaced by less-educated, less-skilled migrants."

While Russia still commands significant military prowess (though even this is a pale reflection of its Soviet incarnation), the country's failure to thrive—beyond the current crises precipitated by its aggressive actions in Ukraine—is rooted largely in problematic state-society relations. The Russian state is anchored in "charismatic" authoritarian politics with wide varieties of contentiousness pervasive in state-society relations, even though these societal protest movements do not pose an existential threat to the political status quo. Because state power is preoccupied with the preservation of the apex holder's domination, national performance, unfortunately, comes to be focused on the twin objectives of political legitimation, on the one hand—where strategies of economic rewards, co-optation, and the transformation of political resistance into officially sanctioned contention are all equally valuable— and the protection of access to resources, on the other. With regard to the latter objective, the assistance offered to old enterprises, companies with government stakes, and firms that preserve jobs is complemented by the favorable treatment extended to certain business magnates in exchange for their explicit support for and alignment with the true center of power in Moscow. Because these activities are oriented fundamentally toward expanding the leadership's personal power rather than strengthening the vitality of the state or country writ large, and have in recent times been ideologically buffered by a virulent form of Russian nationalism that, centered on the demonization of the West, has assumed a priority position as state ideology and in Russian society, Russia likely will continue to falter in the production of national power for some time to come.

Rajesh Rajagopalan's chapter on India finds a state possessed of great potential power. Like China and Russia, India is a subcontinental-sized state with significant natural resources (excepting energy and strategic materials). It also possesses a large population, which, unlike its major-power peers in Asia, is conspicuously young, thus assuring continued growth of the labor force for many decades. On other counts, however, India displays significant deficits where national resources are concerned: although its economy has been growing at a relatively high rate in recent years—from a low starting point over many decades—this success masks considerable weaknesses in its high-technology base, innovation ecosystem, and quality of human resources as well as in national savings and gross capital formation.

India's greatest shortcomings, however, reside not in the quality of its national resources but in the realm of national performance. As Rajagopalan succinctly concludes, India remains "encumbered by domestic politics and incompetent state management," reducing the country's power capacity. Although India continues to be challenged by both Pakistan and China, its limitations are scarcely external. In fact, New Delhi enjoys the advantages of a "broad elite consensus in major policy areas," yet finds it hard to translate this general agreement into elite cohesion, partly because of the pressures of democratic politics. Furthermore, the Indian state is highly autonomous relative to society, but neither penetrates that society nor extracts resources from it as efficiently as a state should. India's biggest weaknesses, however, lie in infrastructural power more broadly and in the ideational deficits embedded in its institutions: the bureaucracy is inadequate in capacity yet overbearing in reach; ossified governmental policies over the decades have stifled private initiative and choked the development of efficient markets; and while the country as a whole has expressed a consistent desire to maximize its national power, India has failed to demonstrate adequate instrumental rationality—if its public policies and institutional design constitute evidence—that enables it to get there. Thus, even India's otherwise impressive military capabilities in this context do not undermine Rajagopalan's sobering conclusion "that while India has considerable capabilities to generate national power, they rest on relatively narrow foundations."

Like India, Indonesia, another large and strategically located country, remains a sleeping giant. Its archipelagic character has constrained its national cohesion in some ways, but its tropical bounty has yielded, in Vikram Nehru's apt description, "a cornucopia of natural wealth, replete with oil, hydropower, geothermal power, various minerals, timber, rice, palm oil, cocoa, and coffee," which "has attracted traders in search of raw materials from time immemorial and foreign investors in more recent decades." Given these endowments, Indonesia is one of the world's largest commodity exporters, with an industrial base that is increasingly oriented toward natural resource processing and servicing the domestic market. Indonesia has demonstrated relatively rapid economic growth in recent times, with reasonably high rates of domestic savings and investment. But its most conspicuous weaknesses are manifested in innovation and technological capacity, which have had knock-on effects in all sectors of the economy. The poverty of Indonesia's human capital base has only further reduced its national capacity and, as Nehru concludes, "together with infrastructure deficiencies, persist as a binding constraint to future economic growth, technological development, and by implication the expansion of capabilities essential to Indonesia's national performance over the long term and projection of national power in coming decades."

Indonesia's relatively benign external environment in the past only muted pressures for the rapid accumulation of national power. And although managing internal challenges dominated Jakarta's security calculations for many years, state-society relations were shaped fundamentally by the authoritarian politics of charismatic strongmen, which in recent years have been replaced by the struggle to institutionalize democracy. This effort is ongoing—with the implication that the core task remains not maximizing national power to shape outcomes abroad but rather renegotiating the terms of rule and the control over resources at home. The democratization and decentralization that have become the hallmarks of Indonesian democracy today have done wonders for social stability. As Nehru notes, however, they have also produced "national coalition governments with little ability to reach consensus on new strategies" at a time when the "decentralization of political and fiscal power has weakened the center's ability to wield these important instruments of social control" and political leaders have failed "to craft a compelling vision of the national interest, unite the nation, and give credence and credibility to policy reforms and new development initiatives." For some time to come, therefore, Indonesia—despite its growing concerns about China—will continue to be engrossed by internal challenges that limit its ability to play a significant role beyond Southeast Asia.

The last chapter in this volume, authored by Dennis Blair, focuses on the United States and its capacity to sustain national power in ways that preserve its primacy in the international system—a policy goal that is perhaps just as important as the academic exercise of evaluating the robustness of U.S. power. Because the United States remains the most powerful country internationally, its standing automatically defines the extremity of the global production-possibility frontier, meaning the curve that depicts a nation's maximum output possibilities for "guns" and "butter," given the available inputs and the existing state of technology. Therefore, in this instance more than others, the study of U.S. national power is relevant because it also helps identify what gaps might exist relative to the country's closest competitors. Blair succinctly captures the extent of U.S. national resource advantages when he notes that "the U.S. economy is both advanced and balanced, not dependent on a single sector. The United States possesses a large internal market and domestic supplies of raw materials and is roughly half as dependent on foreign trade as the Organisation for Economic Co-operation and Development (OECD) average."

Because the United States remains a system-maker rather than a system-taker, it is able to overcome any resource deficits it may have through sturdy access to international trade, which occurs under the seigniorage of the dollar and under trade rules shaped by American power. A quick survey of U.S. national resources, in fact, suggests that the United States enjoys unparalleled advantages in technology creation, economic innovation, and natural resources; it has some weakness in human capital formation but compensating advantages in immigration; and its awkward dependence on foreign capital for financing both trade and budgetary deficits is ironically a function of prosperity at home and the stability of the U.S. economic system.

Changing the pattern of the U.S. consumption-investment mix is perhaps the biggest contemporary challenge, which bears importantly on the obsolescence of the national infrastructure that Blair highlights as a critical weakness. This challenge is linked intimately with the United States' only national weakness of significance: national performance. As Blair notes damningly,

> Despite increasing evidence of deep-seated national problems that require legislative solutions along with competent executive branch action—for

example, entitlement payments, healthcare, education, national infrastructure, immigration, and energy and disaster response—for the past fifteen years there has been scant government progress on the great majority of these issues. As the political parties have moved away from the center, propelled by the nature of their primary elections, unrestrained campaign contributions, gerrymandering, and the controversy-obsessed media, discussions of solutions to every major national problem degenerate relatively quickly into a stalemate. It has been impossible to fashion practical compromises that blend both public and private action. Beyond their failure to take on big problems, Congress and the executive branch have become less capable of carrying out even the routine functions of government—passing budgets on time and confirming appointees to key positions.

A more succinct summary of the challenges facing the United States could not have been articulated. Yet when the country's enormous strengths are placed in context—including its formidable military power that shows little sign of ebbing—the conclusion that many other nations would love to trade their problems for those of the United States is perhaps amply justified.

Conclusion

The chapters in this volume suggest that national performance matters more than any other variable for the production of national power. National performance is a specific manifestation of power as ability, and the diverse national analyses contained here indicate that the capacity to orchestrate successful social action makes all the difference to mobilizing the national resources that ultimately support the deployment of various military capabilities. Thus, even countries that are very well endowed with natural resources of different kinds, such as Russia, China, and Indonesia, risk being unable to sustain the levels of success that should otherwise accrue to them, given their natural endowments, because of weaknesses in their state-society relations. This same variable also accounts in different ways for whether countries like Japan and South Korea will be able to sustain continued success even as their early industrial advantages atrophy. And national performance again will determine whether India can finally grasp the great-power capabilities it has sought for many decades, even as the management of domestic politics also will determine the felicity with which the United States will be able to sustain its primacy in international politics in the decades to come.

EXECUTIVE SUMMARY

This chapter examines the foundations of China's national power: its national resources, national performance, and military capabilities.

MAIN ARGUMENT

In terms of resources, China looks like a colossal land of milk and honey. Its bureaucracy is robust and its political elites have a conscious plan to expand national power, a vision encapsulated in Xi Jinping's "China dream." But the nation's capacity to convert these resources into tangible forms of usable civilian and military power is hindered by a contradiction in terms between the essence of power in the 21st century—inspirational, technologically advanced, outward-looking, and innovating—and the intrinsic nature of the regime currently governing China. This contradiction will test the Chinese Communist Party's will and ability to implement necessary, and possibly politically costly, reforms.

POLICY IMPLICATIONS

- For the last two decades, the ascent of China appeared inexorable, but a careful study of its foundations of power yields a more sober conclusion. The U.S. and its allies need to start planning for alternative scenarios to China's linear development.

- As China's economic growth slows and the country enters a new phase in its development, marginal adaptation is no longer sufficient. The leadership is aware of the problems but is not necessarily responding with the right remedies. Outside actors have a strong interest in encouraging those who favor far-reaching market-oriented reforms to China's current economic model.

- As the prospect of material gain now looks less promising, nationalism and repression are the most likely instruments of choice for the party to maintain its monopoly on power. Shows of force or military adventurism are thus possible consequences of China's slowing growth.

China's National Power:
A Colossus with Iron or Clay Feet?

Nadège Rolland

Three decades after Deng Xiaoping chose to bring "socialism with Chinese characteristics" to his country, China is now a global economic powerhouse, its influence over Asia is growing stronger, and its military modernization is altering the regional balance of power. In addition to its distinctively huge geographic and demographic scale, China's rapid economic and social development seem so astonishing that many believe it is inevitably bound to overtake the United States as the largest economic power. And yet Chinese leaders still define their country as developing. Addressing the Boao Forum participants in April 2013, Xi Jinping expressed the leadership's "full confidence in China's future" but also its awareness that "China remains the world's largest developing country and it faces difficulties and challenges on its road to progress."[1]

This is but one of the many contradictions inherent in China's re-ascent as a global power. Studying the foundations of China's national power—a civilization pretending to be a nation-state, as sinologist Lucian Pye reminded us—inevitably elicits an abundance of superlatives but also reveals a nation torn between extremes.[2] Like the Song Dynasty poet gazing at Mount Lushan from different angles and getting a different impression each time, observers of China's national power find themselves conjecturing about the country's

Nadège Rolland is Senior Project Director for Political and Security Affairs at The National Bureau of Asian Research. She can be reached at <nrolland@nbr.org>.

---

[1] "Full Text of Xi Jinping's Speech at Opening Ceremony of Boao Forum," Xinhua, April 10 2013, http://www.china.org.cn/business/Boao_Forum_2013/2013-04/10/content_28501562.htm.

[2] See, for example, Lucian W. Pye, "China: Erratic State, Frustrated Society," *Foreign Affairs*, Fall 1990.

true face.[3] A Leninist state in form and structure, China abandoned its centrally planned economy for a market-oriented model. National unity is paramount to its political narrative, but diversity is what best defines the country's essence. Led by an atheist Communist party that extols Confucian values and intends to intervene in the Dalai Lama's reincarnation process, China is, by some estimates, on track to have the world's largest population of Christians by 2030. Home to 22% of the world's population and to 3.6 million millionaires (in U.S. dollars), China pulled 660 million people out of poverty in 30 years; but 250 million of its citizens (roughly Indonesia's total population) still live on less than $2 a day.[4] Nearly 650 million Internet and 450 million mobile device users operate in a commercially vibrant yet managed "gilded cage" that looks increasingly like a separate Chinese Intranet.[5] The People's Liberation Army (PLA), the largest military force in the world with 2.3 million active personnel, remains the party's (not the nation's) foremost guardian, and its modernization, which has included formidable offensive capacities, is still described by the leadership as entirely defensive in nature.

If navigating among these extremes and apparent contradictions to define the foundations of China's national power is not complex enough, one also must mention the difficulty in finding accurate statistics for a country that still struggles with transparency. Despite this important caveat, the Research Institute for Social Development affiliated with the National Development and Reform Commission (NDRC) proclaimed in 2013 that, based on the measurement of China's economic, social, and environmental conditions, China was 65.3% of the way to the fulfillment of its renaissance, a rise of 2.6 percentage points over 2010.[6] The road to achieving what Xi Jinping has described as the "Chinese dream of the great rejuvenation of the nation" includes completing the nation's two centenary goals—one by 2021, when the Chinese Communist Party (CCP) celebrates its hundredth anniversary, and the other by 2049, when the People's Republic of China (PRC) marks

---

[3] "It looks like a mountain ridge, when I see it from its facade. It becomes a mountain peak, when I look at it from its side face. It always has a different profile when I observe it from far away, near, high or low places. I cannot be sure of its true face, since I stand here in the midst of Lushan Mountains" (Su Dongpo, 1037–1101).

[4] Matthew DeBord, "The U.S. Has the Most Millionaires, but China Is Making Millionaires Faster," *Business Insider*, June 16, 2015; and Yin Pumin, "Rising Out of Poverty," *Beijing Review*, January 15, 2015, http://www.bjreview.com.cn/print/txt/2015-01/12/content_663433.htm.

[5] Bill Bishop, "China's Internet: Gilding the Cyber Cage," Sinocism China Newsletter, February 18, 2014, https://sinocism.com/?p=10672.

[6] Patrick Boehler, "Scholars Say China Has Regained 65.3% of Its Former Glory," *South China Morning Post*, November 22, 2013, http://www.scmp.com/news/china-insider/article/1362759/scholars-say-china-has-regained-653pc-its-former-glory.

its first century in power.[7] By 2021, Chinese leaders hope to double their country's 2010 GDP level to $13 trillion and build an "overall moderately well-off society" with per capita income of $7,000, 60% urbanization, and a life expectancy at birth of 76 years. By 2049, China aims to become a "modern socialist country that is prosperous, strong, democratic, culturally advanced and harmonious."[8] These centenary goals and their related benchmarks underline how much China's leaders are interested in the strategic assessment of power, especially in relation to other countries. "Comprehensive national power" (*zonghe guoli*), a concept that appeared in the 1980s, refers to an aggregate combination of measures in numerous areas in a given country that include territory, natural resources, economic capacity, military might, domestic government, foreign policy, and international influence. The concept is primarily meant to assess power through calculations and estimates of other states' strengths and weaknesses in comparison with China's own.[9]

Is national power a given? Do material assets automatically translate into power? A careful study of China's foundations for national power leads to the conclusion that the outcome of China's re-ascent is not preordained. China is immensely rich in many dimensions. But what matters are intangible and unquantifiable factors such as policy and sound political leadership. Samuel Huntington concluded his 1991 essay "Democracy's Third Wave" by stating that history "does not sail ahead in a straight line, but when skilled and determined leaders are at the helm, it does move forward."[10] So far, China's leaders have been determined and skilled, but their efforts have been focused mostly on keeping the Communist Party at the helm. For China to move forward and realize its dream of a national renaissance, its rulers will need to make a choice between the country's future power and the one-party system's grip on power.

This chapter will look at the same natural and manmade factors of both material (hard) and intangible (soft) power that Chinese thinkers deem essential to estimate a country's comprehensive national power. It will be organized around three main sections: the first will examine China's national resources (natural, economic, and human); the second will assess its national performance through a discussion of institutions, social cohesion,

---

[7] The two centenary goals first appeared in Jiang Zemin's report to the 15th National Congress of the Communist Party of China in September 1997. The leaders following Jiang have consistently reiterated these goals. For the full text, see "Jiang Zemin's Report at the 15th National Congress of the Communist Party of China," available at Federation of American Scientists, http://fas.org/news/china/1997/970912-prc.htm.

[8] Xi Jinping, *The Governance of China* (Beijing: Foreign Languages Press, 2014).

[9] Michael Pillsbury, *China Debates the Future Security Environment* (Washington, D.C.: National Defense University Press, 2000), 203–58.

[10] Samuel J. Huntington, "Democracy's Third Wave," *Journal of Democracy* 2, no. 2 (1991): 34.

and external constraints; and the third section will consider China's military capabilities (both in terms of capacity and aptitude).

China's National Resources: Size Matters

In the 1960s, South Korea, Taiwan, Singapore, and Hong Kong were considered as part of the "third world." In less than three decades, these four Asian "tigers" managed to transform into high-tech economies or major trading and financial hubs. But the impact of their success on the global balance of power is not on the same order of magnitude as China's. Size, space, and numbers matter—they are power-multiplying factors.

Natural Resources

China can first and foremost be defined by its sheer size, and most of its characteristics are measured in large numbers. China is the world's most populous country with 1.3 billion people (22% of the world's population) spreading across a large territory of 3.7 million square miles (ranking third-largest in the world). Distribution of the population is highly varied: 87% of the population lives on 39% of the country's landmass (in the coastal and central areas), while the remaining 13% lives on 61% of the territory. China's population is predominantly Han, but approximately 90 million PRC citizens belong to two hundred other ethnic groups that speak 55 different languages. In addition to Chinese people who live on the mainland, 50 million ethnic Chinese live overseas, half of them in the Asia-Pacific region. They were the main investors in China's economy back in 1979 when Deng opened the first special economic zones in Guangdong and Fujian, and they still stand out as a strong network for foreign investment in China.

China's demography is as much a blessing as a curse. Its large active workforce has constituted an asset for the country's economic dynamism. But, concerned by the potential pressure of a large population on economic development, the Chinese authorities decided to curb population growth. The one-child policy implemented in 1979 has two major consequences, which will not be reversed by the 2013 decision to relax some of its rules. First, starting in 2030 China's population will decline, and between 2010 and 2050 it will lose 180 million from its labor force, which comprised 940 million people in 2012. By then, 440 million Chinese will be over 60 years old (34% of the population, as opposed to 13% in 2013), meaning that China will most likely get old before it gets rich (see **Figure 1**). Today, one in three Chinese citizens under 30 has no siblings. This upcoming generation will have to bear the formidable weight of an aging population

FIGURE 1   China's population structure, 2010 and 2050

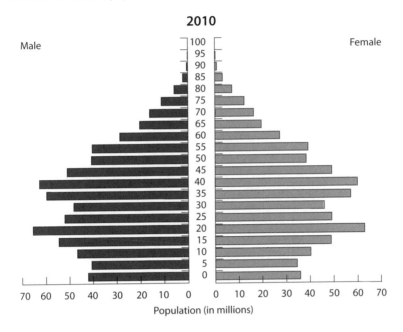

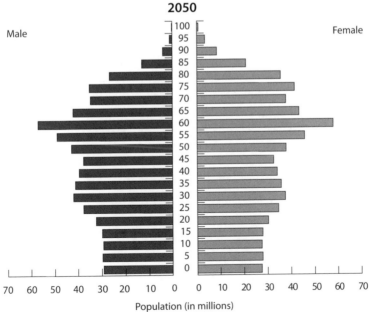

SOURCE: U.S. Census Bureau, International Programs database, http://www.census.gov/population/international/data/idb/region.php.

for which the government only provides a limited social security safety net. Second, China's one-child policy de facto translated into a "one boy" result, leading to a dramatic excess of young men in China today. The sex ratio at birth has kept widening, increasing from 108 males to every 100 females in the early 1980s to 116 to 100 in 2000 and 118 to 100 in 2010. The estimated cumulative deficit of women is about twelve million over the last twenty years. This is not only a population problem but also a serious social problem: by 2030, 20% of Chinese men of marriageable age will fail to find a wife on the mainland.[11]

To feed a quarter of the world's population, China relies on 106.5 million hectares of arable land (11.1% of its total territory).[12] In 2013, Chinese farms produced 601.1 million tons of grains (cereals and legumes), 35.2 million tons of oil-bearing crops, 250.9 million tons of fruit, and 128.2 million tons of sugar cane. The total gross output value of Chinese farmland was $838 billion. Combined, the total output value of China's farms, forests, animal husbandry activities, and fisheries was $1.58 trillion in 2013, up 63.7% over the decade. China also increasingly relies on imports of agricultural and basic food products and in 2013 imported $41.70 billion in food, up from $5.96 billion a decade before (see **Figure 2**).[13]

Although China ranks 5th in terms of total water resources (after Brazil, Russia, Canada, and the United States), it ranks 102nd in terms of per capita resources, with 2,072 cubic meters per person.[14] As the population and economy have rapidly grown, the country has experienced serious degradation of its water resources, including massive overuse and contamination. In 2013, China's first national census of water conceded that more than 28,000 rivers have disappeared in twenty years—equivalent to the United States losing the entire Mississippi River.[15] Chinese rivers are polluted, diverted, and dammed: China possesses the world's largest number of dams (46,758, which is about half the world's total) and generated 20% of the world's

---

[11] Isabelle Attané, "En Chine, des millions de femmes 'manquantes'" [In China, Millions of "Missing" Women], *Outre-Terre* 2, no. 15 (2006): 471–79.

[12] "Lands," Food and Agriculture Organization of the United Nations, Statistics Division, http://faostat3. fao.org/download/R/RL/E.

[13] "Foreign Trade and Economic Cooperation: Imports Value by Category of Goods," National Bureau of Statistics of China, http://www.stats.gov.cn/tjsj/ndsj/2014/zk/html/Z1104E.HTM.

[14] "Renewable Internal Freshwater Resources, Total (Billion Cubic Meters)," World Bank, World Development Indicators, http://data.worldbank.org/indicator/ER.H2O.INTR.K3. A small number of other major countries have less water per capita, notably Iran, Germany, Nigeria, India, South Africa, and Pakistan. The United States has 8,904 cubic meters per person, while Russia has 30,054 cubic meters.

[15] Angel Hsu and William Miao, "28,000 Rivers Disappeared in China: What Happened?" *Atlantic*, April 29, 2013, http://www.theatlantic.com/china/archive/2013/04/28-000-rivers-disappeared-in-china-what-happened/275365.

FIGURE 2   China's food and beverage trade

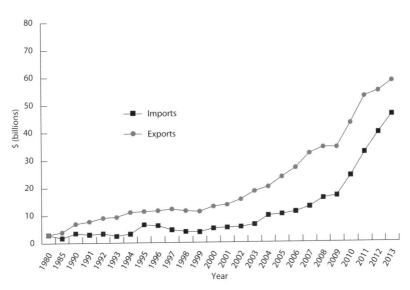

SOURCE: National Bureau of Statistics of China, *China Statistical Yearbook 2014* (Beijing: National Statistics Press, 2014), tables 11.3 and 11.4, http://www.stats.gov.cn/tjsj/ndsj/2014/zk/html/Z0902E.HTM.

total hydropower in 2012.[16] The government set a goal for non-fossil fuel to account for 15% of total energy consumption by 2020, with more than half coming from hydropower.[17] The target for installed hydropower capacity is 420 million kilowatts by 2020, a 70% increase from 2012.

China became the largest global energy consumer in 2011 and the second-largest net importer of crude oil and petroleum products in 2009. It surpassed the United States at the end of 2013 as the largest net importer of petroleum. In 2014 the PRC was the world's top coal producer (3.60 billion tons) at the same time as it was the world's top coal consumer (4.26 billion tons—half of the world's consumption) and importer (291.22 million tons). The country's proven coal reserves are

---

[16] Junguo Liu et al., "Water Conservancy Projects in China: Achievements, Challenges and Way Forward," *Global Environmental Change* 23, no. 3 (2013): 633–43, http://www.sciencedirect.com/science/article/pii/S0959378013000216; and Junguo Liu et al., "China's Rising Hydropower Demand Challenges Water Sector," *Scientific Reports* 5 (2015), http://www.nature.com/srep/2015/150709/srep11446/full/srep11446.html.

[17] Information Office of the State Council of the People's Republic of China (PRC), "China's Energy Policy 2012," October 2012, http://www.gov.cn/english/official/2012-10/24/content_2250497.htm.

the world's second-largest after the United States. Coal represents 77% of China's primary energy production, fueling 80% of its electricity. While China produced 211 million tons of oil, it consumed 519 million tons and imported 308 million tons. It also produced 127.9 billion cubic meters of natural gas and consumed 178.6 billion cubic meters while importing 57.8 billion cubic meters.[18]

In November 2014, the National Statistics Bureau announced that China's petroleum stockpile contained 12.4 million tons of petroleum—the equivalent of approximately nine days of oil supplies. China intends to increase this stockpile to a final volume that could meet about 48 days of petroleum consumption. In comparison, the U.S. strategic petroleum reserve holds about 137 days of supply.[19]

Chinese demand also accounts for very large proportions of world trade in critical minerals and metals. Overexploitation of soils and natural resources, depletion of water, rapid industrialization, extensive use of fertilizers, and excessive use of fossil fuel create massive irreversible degradation, environmental pollution, and health hazards. China is wealthy in resources and commodities but is also increasingly reliant on imports, which contradicts the government's desire for the security that comes from self-reliance. The long-term sustainability of China's economic growth will come at the cost of greater strategic risk. The government will need to relinquish its appetite for control and accept fluctuations in global commodities markets.

Economic Resources

Since initiating market reforms in 1978, China has shifted from a collectivist, centrally planned economy to a market-based economy and from autarchy to international integration. China's economic development is the result of the "socialism with Chinese characteristics" hybrid model, where the private sector's output is growing while the public sector's dominance is maintained in strategic sectors.[20] Under this model, China experienced rapid economic growth, averaging 10.12% per year between 1983 and 2013. In less than three decades, it pulled itself out of underdevelopment to become

---

[18] "2014 nian 12 yue tianranqi yunxing jiankuang" [December 2014 Natural Gas Toward a Simpler Situation], National Development and Reform Commission (China), January 27, 2015, http://www.sdpc.gov.cn/fzgggz/jjyx/gjyx/sh/201501/t20150127_661370.html; and Ministry of Land and Resources (China), 2014 zhongguo guotu ziyuan gongbao [2014 National Natural Resource Bulletin] (Beijing, April 2015), 10, http://www.mlr.gov.cn/zwgk/zytz/201504/P020150422317433127066.pdf.

[19] "SPR Quick Facts and FAQs," U.S. Department of Energy, Office of Fossil Energy, http://energy.gov/fe/services/petroleum-reserves/strategic-petroleum-reserve/spr-quick-facts-and-faqs.

[20] Nicholas R. Lardy, "Private Not State Firms Are China's Growth Engine," East Asia Forum, November 30, 2014, http://www.eastasiaforum.org/2014/11/30/private-not-state-firms-are-chinas-growth-engine.

the second-largest world economy—an achievement without historical precedent. Measured using purchasing power parity (PPP) exchange rates, the International Monetary Fund (IMF) estimates that China's GDP even surpassed U.S. GDP in 2014.[21] China accounted for 16.5% of the world's GDP in 2014 (up from 4% in 1990) and became the world's biggest exporter in 2009. China's accumulated foreign exchange reserves, which have been the world's largest since 2006, now amount to $3.69 trillion (compared to $140 billion in 1997), and the government is trying to convince the IMF to declare the renminbi a reserve currency alongside the dollar, the euro, and the yen.

Agriculture's share of the Chinese economy remains strong. Despite a constant decline over the years, the primary industry sector (the extraction and processing of natural resources) still accounted for 10% of the Chinese economy and employed 34% of the working population in 2013. Secondary industry (construction and manufacturing) represented 44% of the economy, while the tertiary sector (services) amounted to 46%.

After three decades of unabated growth delivered by massive investments in infrastructure and manufacturing as well as by exports, China now needs to transition into a healthy advanced industrialized economy and to undertake reforms toward a true market system with less state intervention and higher consumption rates. China's growth model created a number of imbalances, including excessive exports and investments given the country's low domestic consumption rate. The massive investment campaign initiated by the central government and executed by state-owned enterprises (SOE) to maintain growth during the 2008–9 financial crisis increased the debt burden, both in real terms and as a proportion of GDP. According to a McKinsey Global Institute study from 2015, the country's total debt-to-GDP ratio increased from 121% in 2000 to 158% in 2007 and 282% in 2014.[22]

Low-performing SOEs are a drag on growth. Corruption is endemic. In 2011 the People's Bank of China inadvertently published on its website a confidential study revealing that $126 billion had been siphoned overseas by more than 18,000 officials from the mid-1990s to 2008. Imbalances also show in the growing gap between those who benefit from growth and those who are likely to be left behind. In 2013, China's National Bureau of Statistics released a decade's worth of figures about the Gini index that showed a peak in

---

[21] International Monetary Fund, *World Economic Outlook: Legacies, Clouds, Uncertainties* (Washington, D.C.: International Monetary Fund, 2014), http://www.imf.org/external/pubs/ft/weo/2014/02.

[22] This figure includes central and local state government debt as well as corporate and household debt. For more information, see Richard Dobbs, Susan Lund, Jonathan Woetzel, and Mina Mutafchieva, "Debt and (Not Much) Deleveraging," McKinsey Global Institute, February 2015, http://www.mckinsey.com/insights/economic_studies/debt_and_not_much_deleveraging.

2008 (up to 0.491) followed by a constant but slow decline to 0.473 in 2013.[23] Finally, economic growth has slowed since 2008, and authorities have been struggling to meet the official growth target of around 7% for 2014.[24]

The Chinese government has long acknowledged that these problems must be tackled and that decisions must be made about how to deal with this new normal. In November 2013, Xi publicly spoke of "unbalanced, uncoordinated, and unsustainable" development and an increase in "social contradictions."[25] Envisaged reforms will not proceed smoothly unless the authorities can overcome deep resistance from SOEs, local governments, and other vested interest groups, including within the CCP itself. The prospects for reforms are also clouded by the very nature of the Chinese political system, especially its lack of accountability and an independent judiciary, which enables corruption on a massive scale, and the regime's continued reliance on controls, regulatory diktats, and massive government financing, which are contradictory to an open market. So far, there has been no indication that Xi intends to change the institutional structure of the state. Instead, he appears to favor the "rectification" of the people who make up the party-state rather than a substantial reduction of the CCP's role in the economy.

Human Resources

A large population does not necessarily equal a strong human resource base; a robust educational system with high standards of education and training is also required. In its 2010 National Plan for Medium and Long-Term Education Reform and Development, the Chinese government committed to expanding vocational education and increasing investment in secondary and university education and established a target of 90% secondary school enrollment by 2020. China now devotes 4% of its GDP to education. The Chinese Ministry of Education presently estimates that 99.8% of the population has achieved nine years of education and 200 million children are enrolled in primary and secondary education.[26]

---

[23] In the Gini index, zero represents absolute equality and one represents absolute inequality. See "Beida baogao: Zhongguo 1% jiating zhanyou quanguo sanfenzhiyi yishang caichan" [Beida Report: 1% of Chinese Households Own More Than One-Third of the Country's Wealth], *Renmin Wang*, July 26, 2014, http://news.163.com/14/0726/05/A22CNRP90001124J.html.

[24] Mark Magnier, "China Cuts 2014 Economic Growth Estimate to 7.3% from 7.4%," *Wall Street Journal*, September 7, 2015, http://www.wsj.com/articles/china-cuts-2014-economic-growth-to-7-3-from-7-4-1441593730.

[25] "The Party's New Blueprint," *Economist*, Analects, November 16, 2013, http://www.economist.com/blogs/analects/2013/11/reform-china.

[26] Ministry of Foreign Affairs (PRC), "China's Progress Towards the Millennium Development Goals: 2013 Report," 2013, 20, http://www.cn.undp.org/content/dam/china/docs/Publications/UNDP-CH-MDGs2013_english.pdf.

The proportion of Chinese workers with a secondary school diploma rose from roughly 50% in 1990 to about 60% in 2010. In June 2015, 9.42 million students took the national higher education examination (*gaokao*), which high-school seniors take to determine the university that they can attend. College-educated citizens account for 20% of the population (compared to 1.4% in 1978), and in 2014, 7.26 million students graduated with a master's, bachelor's, or technical college degree—more than seven times the number that did fifteen years earlier (see **Figure 3** for overall enrollment data).[27]

China has developed the quality of its human capital considerably. But there is still room for improvement. The government's resolute educational policy pressed programs to grow too quickly, mostly without properly preparing teachers, and the overall quality of graduates, still far from equal

FIGURE 3   Total number of students in China's higher education system

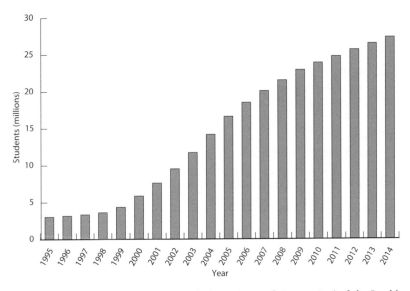

SOURCE: National Bureau of Statistics of China, *Statistical Communiqué of the People's Republic of China on National Economic and Social Development* (Beijing, 1996–2015).

---

[27] "China: Education," UNESCO Institute for Statistics, Data Centre, http://www.uis.unesco.org/ DataCentre/Pages/country-profile.aspx?code=CHN&regioncode=40515; and "Guojia zhongchangqi jiaoyu gaige he fazhan guihua gangyao (2010–2020 nian)" [National Mid-Long Term Education Reform and Development Plan (2010–2020)], Xinhua, September 29, 2010, http://www.gov.cn/ jrzg/2010-07/29/content_1667143.htm.

across the country, has declined with the expansion.[28] The Chinese system still emphasizes rote learning, memorization, and following orders instead of cultivating critical thinking, creative problem-solving, and personal judgment or initiative, qualities that are required for a skills-based economy in the 21st century.

According to a 2013 McKinsey report, at the lower end of the labor market in 2020 there will be 23 million more people with a primary school education or less than there will be jobs suited for their limited education. At the upper end, Chinese employers will demand 142 million more high-skilled workers—those with university degrees or vocational training—which is about 24 million more than the country will likely be able to supply.[29]

To sustain its economic growth, China now needs to increase its labor and productivity as well as its technological and innovation capacities. In 2014, the PRC ranked second in R&D spending—$216 billion, compared to the United States' $450 billion—representing 17.5% of global R&D spending (compared to 31.1% for the United States, 10.2% for Japan, and 21.7% for Europe).[30] But China's investments heavily favor research that directly translates into commercial opportunities, namely "experimental development," while it spends less on basic and applied research of the sort that leads to more fundamental innovations.[31] In 2013, China spent approximately $9 billion on basic research and $20.5 billion on applied research, representing 4.7% and 10.7%, respectively, of the country's gross R&D funding.[32] This funding mostly was provided by state investments that the government began to increase in 2014 in an attempt to foster innovation.

As in most other domains, China's approach to innovation is mainly top-down: the government has determined quantitative targets and has designed several programs, such as the National High Technology Research

---

[28] Henan Cheng, "Inequality in Basic Education in China: A Comprehensive Review," *International Journal of Educational Policies* 3, no. 2 (2009), http://ijep.icpres.org/2009/v3n2/hcheng.pdf; and Helen Gao, "China's Education Gap," *New York Times*, September 4, 2014, http://www.nytimes.com/2014/09/05/opinion/sunday/chinas-education-gap.html.

[29] Li-Kai Chen, Mona Mourshed, and Andrew Grant, "The $250 Billion Question: Can China Close the Skills Gap?" McKinsey & Company, May 2013, http://mckinseyonsociety.com/downloads/reports/Education/china-skills-gap.pdf.

[30] "2014 Global R&D Funding Forecast," *R&D Magazine*, December 2013, http://www.battelle.org/docs/tpp/2014_global_rd_funding_forecast.pdf.

[31] Yutao Sun and Cong Cao, "Demystifying Central Government R&D Spending in China," *Science*, August 29, 2014.

[32] By comparison, in 2011 the United States spent $75 billion on basic research and $82.4 billion on applied research, which represented 18% and 19%, respectively, of gross R&D spending for that year. See National Science Board, "Research and Development: National Trends and International Comparisons," *Science and Engineering Indicators 2014* (Arlington: National Science Foundation, 2014), chap. 4, http://www.nsf.gov/statistics/seind14/content/chapter-4/chapter-4.pdf.

and Development Program, or "863" program, initiated in March 1986; the National Basic Research Program, or "973" program, introduced in 1997; and the National Key Technologies R&D Program (in 1982) in order to steer research and innovation in high-tech fields deemed important to the country's long-term development. In addition to technological acquisition (legal and illegal) from foreign companies, China intends to attract the very best scientists and entrepreneurs from around the world. The Thousand Talents Program, also known as the Recruitment Program of Global Experts, was created in December 2008 to attract one to two thousand top-notch experts—both Chinese nationals and non-Chinese scientists and engineers—by 2020 in science and engineering.[33]

Despite some substantial efforts, however, no major Chinese innovation or technological breakthrough has been viewed globally. Yet, innovation is critical to the country's overall economic performance and key to military power, and China's leadership knows it. From Deng Xiaoping's "four modernizations" to the Chang'e lunar exploration program, China has proved its willingness to invest political will and vast sums of money in advancing the country's scientific and technological capacities, backed by a comprehensive set of national policies and high-quality education and research institutions. It has demonstrated an ability to learn and adapt—not merely copy—technologies to fill its needs by incrementally improving on the work of others. China does not seem ready to replace the United States at the pinnacle of technological achievement, however. There are limits to what the government can mandate. The freedom to pursue ideas wherever they may lead is a precondition for innovation and creativity.[34] China's one-party state can summon and mobilize the necessary material resources on a scale seemingly impossible elsewhere in the world, but the very nature and structure of its domestic system impose strict limits on the ability of its people to think and communicate freely in order to advance the frontiers of science and technology.

Nature blessed China with a massive territory, a large population, and an abundance of natural resources and economic wealth. These material factors offer solid foundations but are not sufficient for the country's overall power. Policy is the determining factor.

[33] "The Thousand Talents Plan," Recruitment Program of Global Experts, http://www.1000plan.org/en/plan.html.

[34] Regina M. Abrami, William C. Kirby, and F. Warren McFarlan, "Why China Can't Innovate," *Harvard Business Review*, March 2014, https://hbr.org/2014/03/why-china-cant-innovate.

National Performance: Strong Party Control Limits the Nation's Potential

In order to gather the resources necessary to build the instruments of power, a nation needs strong governing institutions and dedicated rulers capable of mobilizing society around common values and objectives. But an excessively powerful state can stifle long-term growth. China's party-state structure is solid, but its Achilles' heel is its desire to keep a monopoly on political power. The regime sees any internal or external challenge as a threat to its survival and will always act to maximize the party's power, though not necessarily the nation's as a whole.

Robust Institutions

Since its founding in 1921, the CCP has evolved from a revolutionary to a ruling party. It remains a mass organization with a membership estimated at more than 85 million in 2013, including educated urban middle-class members and private entrepreneurs.[35] After 40 years of Maoism that had led the country and the population through periods of devastating upheavals and to the verge of self-destruction, Deng Xiaoping initiated a new era of "peace and development" that still benefits China. Whereas the Soviet Union collapsed, China's political regime has demonstrated a striking resilience. It has survived, adapted, amalgamated, and finally, to some extent, consolidated its power.[36] The underpinnings of the political system and its Leninist structures remain the same as when the PRC was founded in 1949 on a triangular power structure comprising the party, the state, and the military. The party controls the state, the propaganda, the security apparatus, and the PLA. It also permeates civil society thanks to mass organizations such as the Communist Youth League and party committees and cells that directly oversee business and academic governance structures.

While the regime's structure has remained the same, it has mutated incrementally into a renewed neo-authoritarian construct that contains within itself both proponents of further reforms and beneficiaries of the status quo who are impervious to change. Meanwhile, China's integration with the world economy, along with rising living standards, higher education levels, and greater access to information, has created a new environment in which the party now must operate as Chinese society undergoes profound changes,

---

[35] "China's Communist Party Membership Exceeds 85 Million," Xinhua, June 30, 2013, http://english. cpc.people.com.cn/206972/206974/8305636.html.

[36] David Shambaugh, *China's Communist Party: Atrophy and Adaptation* (Oakland: University of California Press, 2008).

with long-term familial, societal, spiritual, and political consequences for the edifice's overall cohesion.[37]

China's national performance will thus be measured against the current regime's ability to manage the dialectic and relationship with an increasingly complex society while maintaining its monopoly on power. So far, this objective has been achieved in three ways: inspiration, suppression, and bribery. Dogma and fear were Mao Zedong's favorite instruments of control over Chinese society. Wealth and material benefits were later introduced by Deng's opening-up policy and represent a crucial part of the tacit social contract that appeared after the Tiananmen Square incident in 1989, under which the populace is expected not to challenge the party's monopoly on power in exchange for economic development and prosperity. These three elements—ideology, repression, and wealth—remain the same under Xi Jinping, but their substance and relative importance have evolved over time.

The Marxist revolutionary ideology used by Mao to mobilize the people has given way to a narrative in which nationalism now takes precedence and the party is portrayed as the paramount patriotic force. This nationalist narrative has two faces—one of shame, one of pride—both of which are essentially encapsulated in Xi's "dream of the great rejuvenation of the Chinese nation." The shameful face seeks to expunge the concessions forced on the Chinese government during the "century of humiliation" (1840–1949), demands respect from China's aggressors at the time (Europe, Japan, and the United States, or "the West"), highlights national unity and territorial sovereignty, and tilts toward a strong anti-foreign, anti-Japanese edge. The proud face promotes the party's achievements in bringing national wealth and military strength to the country, vaunts China's traditions and values in the form of a cultural exceptionalism or celebration of "Chinese-ness," boasts national aspirations for grandeur and a flourishing civilization, and fosters national champions to compete with foreign global brands.[38]

The "patriotic education campaign" launched after the Tiananmen incident continues to instill the nationalistic narrative into Chinese classrooms. Since January 2015, universities have been urged to strengthen ideological education and champion Marxism, traditional culture, core socialist values, and the Chinese dream. As part of this process, government

---

[37] Minxin Pei, "China's Precarious Balance: Cohesiveness and Stability in a Fast-Changing Society" (paper from the Asia-Pacific Symposium, Washington, D.C., March 7–8, 2000), http://www.isn.ethz.ch/Digital-Library/Publications/Detail/?ots591=0c54e3b3-1e9c-be1e-2c24-a6a8c7060233&lng=en&id=20938.

[38] Christopher R. Hughes, *Chinese Nationalism in the Global Era* (New York: Routledge, 2006); Jessica Chen Weiss, *Powerful Patriots: Nationalist Protest in China's Foreign Relations* (New York: Oxford University Press, 2014); and Zheng Wang, *Never Forget National Humiliation: Historical Memory in Chinese Politics and Foreign Relations* (New York: Columbia University Press, 2012).

officials are being called to give regular political lectures to students.[39] The media, literature, film, and the arts have also been assigned a key role in the dissemination of the patriotic message, herding popular opinion toward loyalty to the nation, which ultimately means loyalty to the CCP.[40] Thanks to the multiple tools at its disposal, the propaganda apparatus works to create an ideological filter through which Chinese society has access only to information and knowledge that the authorities deem correct.[41]

Conspiracy theories, reminiscent of Cold War ideological campaigns, have also been on the rise. Ill-defined "hostile foreign forces" are accused of plotting to undermine or overthrow the party in ways similar to the color revolutions in Eastern Europe, and foreigners are blamed for any major disturbance, whether ethnic violence in western China, pro-democracy demonstrations in Hong Kong, or a stock market crash.[42] In April 2013, "Document No. 9," which outlined seven dangers that threatened the party's control, was distributed within the CCP. The most menacing of these dangers was described as "Western forces hostile to China and dissidents within the country still constantly infiltrating the ideological sphere."[43] In May 2015, Xi emphasized that religion could be used by hostile external forces, especially separatists in Tibet and Xinjiang, to infiltrate and weaken Chinese society.[44]

Instruments of Control: Propaganda, Censorship, and Repression

A pervasive siege mentality permeates the nationalist narrative. While it glorifies the party's achievements, it also portrays them as being potentially threatened by challenging internal conditions and hostile external forces that the CCP must fight and suppress. In this sense, the threats the party

---

[39] "Officials Required to Lecture on Xi Jinping's Speeches, Socialism in Colleges Each Semester," *Global Times*, August 6, 2015, http://english.sina.com/china/2015/0805/836307.html.

[40] Marie Lall and Edward Vickers, eds., *Education as a Political Tool in Asia* (New York: Routledge, 2009); and Anne-Marie Brady, "Mass Persuasion as a Means of Legitimation and China's Popular Authoritarianism," *American Behavioral Scientist* 53, no. 3 (2009): 434–57.

[41] Chin-Fu Hung and Stuart Dingle, "Revisiting the Role of the Media in the Chinese Communist Party's Legitimation Strategy in Post-Tiananmen China: Case Study of News Corporation," *International Journal of China Studies* 5, no. 2 (2014): 371–98.

[42] Peter Ford, "China Targets 'Hostile Foreign Forces' in Crescendo of Accusations," *Christian Science Monitor*, November 9, 2014, http://www.csmonitor.com/World/Asia-Pacific/2014/1109/China-targets-hostile-foreign-forces-in-crescendo-of-accusations.

[43] The seven dangers were listed as (1) Western constitutional democracy, (2) universal values of freedom and human rights, (3) civic participation, (4) pro-market neoliberalism, (5) Western-inspired notions of media independence, (6) nihilist criticisms of the party's past, and (7) deviating from socialism with Chinese characteristics. For more information, see "Document 9: A ChinaFile Translation," ChinaFile, November 8, 2013, http://www.chinafile.com/document-9-chinafile-translation.

[44] "Warning over Religious Believers in Chinese Communist Party Ranks," Radio Free Asia, May 25, 2015, http://www.rfa.org/english/news/china/china-religion-05252015112309.html.

faces are many and take several forms. One of them is popular discontent. In response to rising unrest and the possibility of popular protests similar to the Arab Spring, in 2011 China started to spend more on internal security than on national defense.[45] Concepts of "social management" and "stability maintenance" were introduced, which called for tighter public security and for "containment and management" of "mass incidents."

Group protests in mainland China are not motivated by political demands but principally caused by social inequalities, corruption, environmental degradation, land grabs, abuse of power by local officials, or unpaid wages for which people wish to gain redress.[46] The central leadership gave responsibility to local governments to make sure that protests stay localized and to give individuals material compensation so that a spark does not start a fire. In some cases, local cadres are also reprimanded in order to placate the public.

Political dissent is also targeted by the Chinese regime. Human Rights Watch claimed in its 2015 report that under Xi the government has unleashed the harshest campaign of politically motivated investigations, detentions, and sentencing in the past decade, marking a sharp turn toward intolerance of criticism.[47] The regime has imposed tighter controls on the already-limited space for media, Internet, and academic expression and has cracked down on civil society, especially rights activists and lawyers, as well as ethnic minorities.

The subtle "authoritarian upgrading" of China's security apparatus is also palpable in the reinforcement of the country's legal body and in the cybersphere.[48] A new national security law is supposed to "safeguard national security, defend the people's democratic dictatorship and the socialist system

---

[45] There were 87,000 incidents nationwide in 2005, the year when official data stopped being published. Sun Liping, a professor at Tsinghua University, estimated that the number rose to 180,000 in 2010. See Feng Shu, "A National Conundrum," *People's Daily*, February 10, 2012, http://en.people. cn/90882/7725198.html. China spent $111 billion on domestic security, compared with $106 billion on defense. In 2013 the internal security budget rose to $124 billion, compared with $119 billion for the military. Full figures for 2014 (including spending by provincial and regional governments) were not available at the time of writing. See Ben Blanchard and John Ruwitch, "China Hikes Defense Budget, to Spend More on Internal Security," Reuters, March 5, 2013, http://www.reuters.com/ article/2013/03/05/us-china-parliament-defence-idUSBRE92403620130305.

[46] Since 1996, the number of environmental protests in China has been growing at a rate of 29% per year, according to an official at China's Ministry of Environmental Protection. See Peng Tian, "China's Next Leader Looks to Soothe Environmental Angst," *Chemistry World*, January 4, 2013, http://www. rsc.org/chemistryworld/2013/01/china-president-xi-jinping-environment-protests-pollution. See also "Growing Concerns in China about Inequality, Corruption," Pew Research Center, October 16, 2012, http://www.pewglobal.org/2012/10/16/growing-concerns-in-china-about-inequality-corruption; and Richard Wike, "What Chinese Are Worried About," Pew Research Center, March 13, 2013, http://www. pewglobal.org/2013/03/13/what-chinese-are-worried-about.

[47] "China: Political Repression at a High Mark," Human Rights Watch, January 29, 2015, https://www.hrw. org/news/2015/01/29/china-political-repression-high-mark; and "World Report 2015: China," Human Rights Watch, 2015, https://www.hrw.org/world-report/2015/country-chapters/china-and-tibet.

[48] Sebastian Heilmann, "Economic Governance: Authoritarian Upgrading and Innovative Potential," in *China Today, China Tomorrow: Domestic Politics, Economy and Society*, ed. Joseph Fewsmith (New York: Rowman & Littlefield Publishers, 2010): 109–26.

with Chinese characteristics."[49] China's National Security Commission has also drafted legislation to regulate foreign-based nonprofits. A proposed antiterrorism law requires technology firms to provide encryption keys and install backdoors to allow law enforcement to access information.[50] Meanwhile, cyberspace is subject to sophisticated filtering and control technology, and tens of thousands of human censors also monitor, identify, delete, and manipulate online content. Most of China's 650 million Internet users have only limited access to information other than that filtered through government control and censorship.

With regime survival as its core concern, the party-state devotes a significant proportion of resources to propaganda, control, and repression—resources that are diverted from the objective of maximizing the country's power.

Party Rectification

No authoritarian regime can depend solely on the use of repression and control to ensure its longevity. It also must develop a narrative and pursue the delivery of benefits to the population—what Samuel Huntington described as the need for "performance legitimacy."[51] Only in return for socioeconomic benefits would the population be ready to surrender its political liberties. The regime also gains the people's trust by showing evidence that it is competent in governing the country and that its policies make things better for the citizens.

After decades of sacrifice and deprivation, Deng's reform and open-up policy finally allowed Chinese citizens to feel glorious about getting rich. Economic development has enabled the population to enjoy a better material life. People can afford houses, raise children, and provide for their elders as long as they can continue to benefit from the fruits of the overall prosperity that is brought under the party's guidance. Nevertheless, economic performance in itself may be necessary but not sufficient for the party to sustain its popular support in the absence of other bases for legitimacy.

A 2011 Pew Research Center poll revealed that 87% of Chinese were satisfied with their country's direction and enthusiastic about its economic future. Two-thirds of Chinese judged their lives were better than

---

[49] "China Expands National Security Law to Cyber Threats, Space," *Bloomberg Business*, July 1, 2015.

[50] Elizabeth C. Economy, "China's Stock Market Crash Scapegoat: 'Hostile Foreign Forces,'" *National Interest*, July 9, 2015, http://nationalinterest.org/blog/the-buzz/chinas-stock-market-crash-scapegoat-hostile-foreign-forces"-13293.

[51] Samuel P. Huntington, *The Third Wave: Democratization in the Late Twentieth Century* (Norman: University of Oklahoma Press, 1991).

five years earlier.[52] Public fury against the government over the high-speed train crash in 2011 or the Sichuan earthquake in 2009 had nothing to do with the country's GDP growth figures. In the first case, popular indignation was sparked by the government's attempts to control coverage of the incidents, prompting allegations of a cover-up. In Sichuan, the schools where more than five thousand children had died were believed to have crumbled because of local officials' corruption and mismanagement of construction.

A higher GDP per capita does not necessarily equal a stronger popular satisfaction rate for the government. What matters most is trust in the ruling elite's capacity to govern and deliver the social goods that will improve individual lives and the country's overall success. To preserve cohesion between the society and its ruling elites, the CCP must address a growing popular sense of injustice and lack of government accountability. The rejuvenation of the nation projected by Xi must happen through the rejuvenation of the party. But how can China reform without suffering the Soviet Union's fate? The first step is to clean up the cadres' practices.

Following the Confucian precept of "rule by virtue," Xi launched a large-scale anti-graft campaign at all levels of the single-party state, including the military. According to the Central Commission for Discipline Inspection, the party body leading the campaign, since the end of 2012, 414,000 officials have been disciplined for corruption, roughly half of whom have been prosecuted in court.[53] This attempt to purify the party is meant to assuage public grievances against rampant corrupt practices, especially by low-level officials. Targeting corrupt high-ranking officials such as Zhou Yongkang and Xu Caihou might also reflect Xi's desire to purge some of his rivals, using the same tactics employed against Bo Xilai in 2012 prior to Xi's accession to the Politburo Standing Committee.[54] The investigations, which have been led by the Central Commission for Disciplinary Inspection since 2013, publicly reveal how deep and entrenched government-business ties have become as the party benefits from the country's economic development through a form of state capitalism that guarantees regime control over key sectors of

[52] "Upbeat Chinese Public May Not Be Primed for a Jasmine Revolution," Pew Research Center, March 31, 2011, http://www.pewglobal.org/2011/03/31/upbeat-chinese-public-may-not-be-primed-for-a-jasmine-revolution.

[53] "Qingfeng zhengqi, duoshao qian dou maibulai de hongli" [Honest Environment, All the Money Cannot Buy Bonus], Central Commission for Discipline Inspection, February 13, 2015, http://www.ccdi.gov.cn/yw/201502/t20150212_51324.html.

[54] In 2012, Bo Xilai was contending for a seat at the Politburo Standing Committee. He allegedly tried to prevent Xi Jinping's succession as secretary general and was ousted from the CCP and found guilty of corruption, embezzlement, and abuse of power. See John Garnaut, *The Rise and Fall of the House of Bo: How a Murder Exposed the Cracks in China's Leadership* (New York: Penguin, 2012).

the economy such as banks, energy, heavy industry, and armament.[55] The ability to allocate economic rents allows the CCP to operate a huge political patronage system through which it can reward loyalists with perks and desirable jobs, thereby reinforcing party cohesion.[56]

Cronyism, unchecked power, and the concentration of resources in the hands of a few, combined with fierce inner-party power struggles, do not bode well for elite or national cohesion. China's elites appear increasingly willing to put their own interests above those of the nation as a whole. In order to divert the public's attention by creating a sense of external threat and urgency, the party-state has ramped up a strong nationalistic discourse that may constrain its freedom of action while raising the risk of external conflict.

Regime Insecurity Creates Additional External Constraints

China's external constraints principally stem from the Chinese regime's insecurities. There exists a tight linkage between internal and external security because the party identifies itself as the vanguard of the Chinese people and the embodiment of the state.[57] If the party's rule is not secure, the nation is also not secure. China's external constraints, as considered by its leadership, therefore grow out in concentric circles.

At the core lies the imperative to protect the CCP's monopoly on power from its domestic and foreign enemies, as described earlier. China's continued development comes second, which includes safeguarding the country's sovereignty and territorial integrity—the East and South China Seas were added to Taiwan, Xinjiang, and Tibet as "core interests" in 2010 and 2013, respectively.[58] As its economic footprint has grown, China's national interests have also expanded. Geographically, the government has prioritized protecting overseas assets and Chinese citizens working and traveling abroad,[59] safeguarding energy and other natural resources, securing strategic sea lanes of communication, and promoting ethno-religious stability in China's western provinces and addressing security concerns along its western

---

[55] Marie-Claire Bergère, *Chine, le nouveau capitalisme d'état* [China, the New State Capitalism] (Paris: Fayard, 2013).

[56] Minxin Pei, "The Chinese Political Order: Resilience or Decay?" *Modern China Studies* 21, no. 1 (2014), http://www.modernchinastudies.org/us/issues/current-issue/1361-the-chinese-political-order-resilience-or-decay.html.

[57] David M. Lampton, "Xi Jinping's High-Risk Policy Needs a National Security Commission," *Yale Global*, May 5, 2015, http://yaleglobal.yale.edu/content/xi-jinping's-high-risk-policy-needs-national-security-commission.

[58] Caitlin Campbell, Ethan Meick, Kimberly Hsu, and Craig Murray, "China's 'Core Interests' and the East China Sea," U.S.-China Economic and Security Review Commission, May 10, 2013.

[59] Jonas Parello-Plesner and Mathieu Duchâtel, *China's Strong Arm: Protecting Citizens and Assets Abroad* (New York: Routledge, 2015).

borderlands. Spatially, China has evolved from a traditional land power into a blue water naval power, while also improving operations in air, space, and cyberspace. And thematically, China's global interests have expanded from "safeguarding stability" to "safeguarding rights"—that is, from strictly defending China's borders to participating in UN peacekeeping operations and facing nontraditional security challenges.[60]

These orientations were laid out to the PLA by Hu Jintao in December 2004 as its "new historic missions."[61] Xi Jinping further tightened the nexus between internal and external challenges by proposing a new "holistic security concept" (*zongti anquan guan*) during the first session of the newly appointed National Security Commission in January 2014.[62] Politics, economics, and military affairs are now interrelated and inseparable, as "China needs to safeguard its sovereignty, security, and international interests while maintaining its political security and social stability."[63]

So far, the party-state has managed to increase the power of the nation while strengthening its own grip on power. Yet as the economy matures, the CCP will have to choose between genuine, liberalizing reforms that may undermine its rule and measures that maintain tight central control at the cost of continuing improvements in national prosperity.

Military Capabilities: Strong Nation, Strong Army

Military modernization was one of the four modernizations Deng Xiaoping called for in 1978 and is one major domain in which the PRC's efforts have been consistent over the years. First motivated by a necessity to overcome equipment obsolescence and poor training, military modernization became a clearer priority after 1995–96, when the Chinese authorities realized that the PLA lacked true capacity to deter and ultimately prevent U.S. forces from intervening in the Taiwan Strait. Although China's military is shrouded in secrecy, various assessments of the PLA's transformation conducted over the

---

[60] Timothy Heath, "The 'Holistic Security Concept': The Securitization of Policy and Increasing Risk of Militarized Crisis," Jamestown Foundation, China Brief, June 19, 2015; and Murray Scot Tanner and Peter W. Mackenzie, *China's Emerging National Security Interests and Their Impact on the People's Liberation Army* (Arlington: Marine Corps University Press, 2015), http://www.mcu.usmc.mil/mcu_press/PublishingImages/Pub%20images/ChinaSecurityInterest_web.pdf.

[61] Daniel M. Hartnett, "The 'New Historic Missions': Reflections on Hu Jintao's Military Legacy," in *Assessing the People's Liberation Army in the Hu Jintao Era*, ed. Roy Kamphausen, David Lai, and Travis Tanner (Carlisle: U.S. Army War College Press, 2014), 31–80; and James Mulvenon, "Chairman Hu and the PLA's 'New Historic Missions,'" Hoover Institution, China Leadership Monitor, no. 27, 2009.

[62] Heath, "The 'Holistic Security Concept.'"

[63] Liu Jianfei, "An Evaluation of China's Overall National Security Environment," China Institute of International Studies, November 14, 2014, http://www.ciis.org.cn/english/2014-11/14/content_7369467.htm.

years and across several countries show that, through political determination and financial perseverance, the gap between where the Chinese military is now and where it aspires to be is narrowing.[64] Nevertheless, as is true in other domains, material resources do not automatically translate into power. Building a modern and strong military is an extremely costly long-term endeavor that requires a sustained commitment from the leadership, which the current Chinese ruling elite appears willing to give. Network-centric warfare, for which advanced armed forces prepare today, requires complex systems that are integrated and interoperable. Logistics, training, strategy, and the existence of a reliable indigenous industrial base are also factors that must be taken into account. Finally, the professionalization and level of training of the people in the PLA is a crucial factor, as a military force "is only as effective as the people who constitute it."[65]

China's military modernization is comprehensive, but it does not aim to equal the United States' forces in every respect. Instead, it follows a core strategic principle of "active defense" [66] that focuses primarily on deterrence and seeking asymmetric advantage when positioned as the weaker protagonist, but that also calls for "winning informationized local wars."[67] While a Taiwan contingency remains at the center of its development, the PLA is also now charged with safeguarding the national interests in the expanding concentric circles described earlier and has enhanced its preparations for contingencies beyond both China's immediate periphery and the traditional military realm (e.g., humanitarian assistance/disaster relief, peacekeeping operations, and counterpiracy). Over the last few years, the PLA has demonstrated its ability to conduct a wide range of operations. These include small-scale, long-distance naval operations for extended durations despite a lack of overseas military bases (e.g., antipiracy operations in the Gulf of Aden since 2009); long-range air strikes and air-ground operations (e.g., the 2010 Shanghai Cooperation Organisation Peace Mission drills); the rapid mobilization of civilian assets for military operations (e.g., the evacuation of

---

[64] China's military modernization has been the object of careful scrutiny, especially in the United States. This section does not attempt to equal the quality of detailed accounts that can be found in the Department of Defense's indispensable and authoritative *Annual Report to Congress*, the Office of Naval Intelligence's *The PLA Navy: New Capabilities and Missions for the 21st Century*, or the various volumes from the National Bureau of Asian Research (NBR) and the Strategic Studies Institute's annual PLA conferences; rather, the section aims to give readers a broad sense of China's military capabilities in relation to its national power.

[65] Roy Kamphausen, Andrew Scobell, and Travis Tanner, "Introduction," in *The 'People' in the PLA: Recruitment, Training, and Education in China's Military,* ed. Roy Kamphausen, Andrew Scobell, and Travis Tanner (Carlisle: Strategic Studies Institute, 2008), 1.

[66] Information Office of the State Council (PRC), *China's Military Strategy* (Beijing, May 2015), http://eng.mod.gov.cn/Database/WhitePapers/.

[67] M. Taylor Fravel, "China's New Military Strategy: 'Winning Informationized Local Wars,'" Jamestown Foundation, China Brief, June 23, 2015.

Chinese citizens in Libya in 2011 and Yemen in 2015); and combat readiness patrols (e.g., patrols in the Indian Ocean in 2014).[68] But more financial resources and advanced weapons will be needed to conduct high-intensity combat operations further away from China's borders (including air projection, extended maritime depth, and long-distance mobility) and to build a robust strategic nuclear deterrent.

Military Resources

Defense budget. Although China publishes its defense budget every March as part of its annual state budget, the exact amount of its defense expenditure is not publicly known. The official figure does not include additional large categories such as strategic forces, foreign acquisitions, military-related R&D, pensions, and paramilitary forces. The Stockholm International Peace Research Institute (SIPRI) estimates that total military spending is 55% higher than the official figure.[69] For 2015, China announced a budget of $144.2 billion, a 10.1% increase from 2014, making it the second-largest military spender in the world.

Although China's military expenditure has been constantly on the rise for the last twenty years (see **Figure 4**), it does not constitute a growing burden, given that the military's share of GDP has not increased significantly. China continues to spend only between 2.0% and 2.5% of its total output on defense.

Manpower. The 2006 edition of China's national defense white paper announced that the PLA active duty force totaled 2.3 million. The 2013 defense white paper for the first time announced numbers for the PLA Army's "mobile operational units" (850,000), the PLA Navy (235,000), and the PLA Air Force (398,000).[70] This total of 1,483,000 personnel does not include the Second Artillery, border and coastal defense units, or the personnel assigned to the four general departments in Beijing, the seven military region headquarters, military academies, and universities.[71]

---

[68] Campbell et al., "China's 'Core Interests,'" 282–346.

[69] Sam Perlo-Freeman, "Mar. 2014: Deciphering China's Latest Defence Budget Figures," Stockholm International Peace Research Institute (SIPRI), http://www.sipri.org/media/newsletter/essay/perlo-freeman-mar-2013.

[70] Information Office of the State Council (PRC), *The Diversified Employment of China's Armed Forces* (Beijing, April 2013), available from Xinhua, http://news.xinhuanet.com/english/china/2013-04/16/c_132312681.htm. For previous Chinese defense white papers, see Information Office of the State Council (PRC), http://eng.mod.gov.cn/Database/WhitePapers/.

[71] Jane Perlez and Chris Buckley, "China's Leader, Seeking to Build Its Muscle, Pushes Overhaul of the Military," *New York Times*, May 24, 2014, http://www.nytimes.com/2014/05/25/world/asia/chinas-leader-seeking-to-build-its-muscle-pushes-overhaul-of-the-military.html?_r=0; and Dennis J. Blasko, "The 2013 Defense White Paper in Perspective," Jamestown Foundation, China Brief, April 25, 2013.

FIGURE 4 China's official defense budget

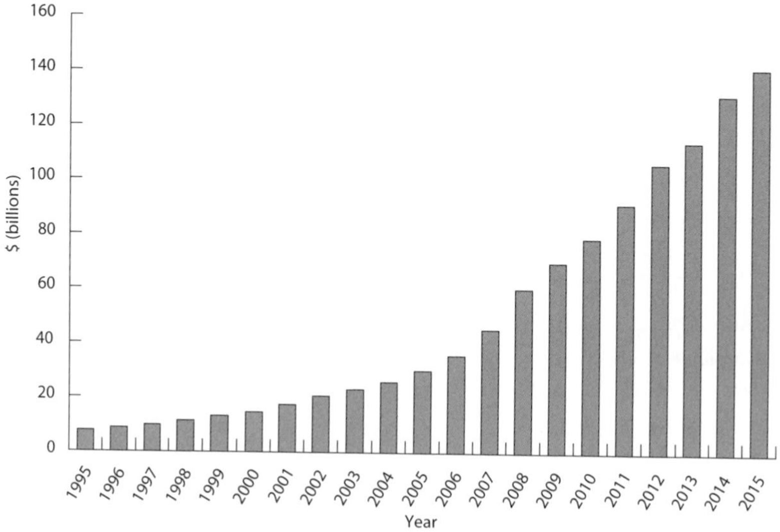

SOURCE: Ministry of National Defense (PRC), Defense White Papers (Beijing, various years); "China's Defense Budget to Grow 12.7 pct in 2011: Spokesman," Xinhua, March 4, 2011; "China's Defense Budget to Grow 11.2 pct in 2012: Spokesman," Xinhua, March 4, 2012; Zhou Erjie, "China Defense Budget to Grow 10.7 pct in 2013: Report," Xinhua, March 5, 2013; Lu Hui, "China Defense Budget to Increase 12.2 pct in 2014," Xinhua, March 5, 2014; and Xiang Bo, "China 2015 Defense Budget to Grow 10.1 pct, Lowest in 5 Years," Xinhua, March 5, 2015.

NOTE: Currency conversion based on exchange rates.

Xi has repeatedly insisted on the need for a strong professional force fully capable of fighting and winning wars. Yet, the military apparatus suffers from long-standing institutional and structural problems that could limit the PLA's ability to sustain combat operations despite its growing capabilities.[72] The leadership has vowed to engage in "thoroughgoing reform of leadership and command systems, force structure and policy institutions" that would include recasting the seven regional commands, streamlining the ground forces, shifting personnel and resources to the navy and air force, and reducing noncombat positions. Xi announced a 300,000 personnel cut during the September 2015 military parade commemorating the 70th anniversary of

---

[72] Michael S. Chase et al., *China's Incomplete Military Transformation: Assessing the Weaknesses of the People's Liberation Army* (Santa Monica: RAND Corporation, 2015), 43.

the end of World War II, but overhauling the military will require overcoming the legacy of the ground force's domination of the military and finding jobs for former soldiers.[73]

The quality of the Chinese military's human capital is also a challenge. As the PLA evolves toward an increasingly modern force, officers and soldiers must operate ever more sophisticated weapon platforms. Many recruits, however, are still drawn from rural areas and possess limited education and insufficient exposure to advanced technologies.[74] The PLA is making efforts to recruit civilian technical experts and increase technological training in the military education system, but it will take time before the overall quality of the recruits matches the PLA's needs.

Industrial base. China's military industrial complex went through a thorough reorganization and streamlining in the late 1990s. But according to some estimates, more than two million employees still work in one thousand SOEs organized under ten large state holding companies that are each dedicated to a particular sector.[75]

Military R&D, with a budget equivalent to $6 billion according to some estimates, is coordinated by the Central Special Committee, which brings together civilian and military leaders and top technical experts who direct high-priority programs.[76] The objective of "combining the military and civilian sector," proclaimed in 1978, remains the guiding principle for China's military industrial development. Military R&D has incrementally evolved into an integrated dual-use system, in which civilian industry contributes to the nation's defense and the defense industry increasingly aids civilian industries in developing dual technologies.[77] It also benefits from intimate cooperation between the military sector and universities specializing in high-technology, including 60 "key laboratories for national defense" directly financed by the PLA's General Armament Department.[78]

The aviation industry is engaged simultaneously in the development and production of more than half a dozen combat and transport aircraft, and China has become one of the world's leading producers of unmanned aerial

---

[73] Perlez and Buckley, "China's Leader"; and Timothy Heath, "Restructuring the Military: Drivers and Prospects for Xi's Top-Down Reforms," Jamestown Foundation, China Brief, February 7, 2014.

[74] Chase et al., *China's Incomplete Military Transformation*, 58–68.

[75] Emmanuel Puig, "L'industrie de défense Chinoise, forces et faiblesses du gigantisme" [The Chinese Defense Industry, Strengths and Weaknesses of Gigantism], *Géoéconomie* 2, no. 57 (2011).

[76] Tai Ming Cheung, ed., *Forging China's Military Might: A New Framework for Assessing Innovation* (Baltimore: Johns Hopkins University Press, 2014), 203; and Tai Ming Cheung, ed., *China's Emergence as a Defense Technological Power* (New York: Routledge, 2013).

[77] Tai Ming Cheung, *Fortifying China: The Struggle to Build a Modern Defense Economy* (Ithaca: Cornell University Press, 2009).

[78] Puig, "L'industrie de défense Chinoise."

vehicles (UAV). The shipbuilding industry has at least four active nuclear and conventional submarine programs along with the design and construction of an aircraft carrier, destroyers, and other surface combatants.[79] The space industry also is highly ambitious across the board and includes manned, lunar, antisatellite, and satellite programs. According to one observer, the colossal scale and intensity of China's military technological and industrial undertaking "has not been seen since the Cold War days of intense U.S.-Soviet technological and military rivalry."[80]

Quantity does not equal quality, however. While the space and missile industries have made impressive progress up the innovation ladder, other sectors continue to engage in a mixture of imitation and marginal improvements (including the aviation, shipbuilding, and ordnance sectors).[81] China still relies on imported technology, especially from Russia, as well as on espionage to gain access to sensitive or export-restricted equipment with military applications.[82]

SIPRI estimates that China has now surpassed Germany as the world's third-largest arms trader. Its military exports have risen by 143% over the past five years and now constitute a 5% share of international arms exports (comparable to France and Germany, but far behind the United States and Russia). Chinese military equipment and weapons are mostly shipped to China's Asian neighbors, with Pakistan, Bangladesh, and Myanmar accounting for almost two-thirds of its market share, but also to African countries.[83]

Weapons. China's arsenal is a hybrid mix of obsolete and high-tech equipment, but it is making progress toward a more modern arsenal across the board. Lingering older equipment creates challenges for logistics, maintenance, and training.

China's military modernization is aimed at improving warfighting capacity in every dimension. But for the last two decades, the PLA has been investing particularly heavily in anti-access/area-denial capacities in order to conduct "active strategic counterattacks on exterior lines."[84] The land-based reconnaissance strike complex is anchored in an extensive intelligence, surveillance, and reconnaissance system that includes terrestrial

---

[79] Gabe Collins, "China Has Become a Top Global Warship Builder," Institute on Global Conflict and Cooperation, SITC Research Briefs, January 2013, https://escholarship.org/uc/item/8635t00n.

[80] Cheung, *Forging China's Military Might.*

[81] Ibid.

[82] William C. Hannas, James Mulvenon, and Anna B. Puglisi, *Chinese Industrial Espionage: Technology Acquisition and Military Modernization* (New York: Routledge, 2013).

[83] Pieter D. Wezeman and Siemon T. Wezeman, "Trends in International Arms Transfers, 2014," SIPRI, SIPRI Fact Sheet, March 2015, http://books.sipri.org/files/FS/SIPRIFS1503.pdf.

[84] Anton Lee Wishik II, "An Anti-Access Approximation: The PLA's Active Strategic Counterattacks on Exterior Lines," *China Security*, no. 19 (2011): 37–48.

and space-based sensors to detect, track, and target hostile forces operating offshore.[85] China's precision-strike arsenal is also a key component and a cornerstone of its warfighting capacity. Drawing on a long history of missile developments, the Second Artillery possesses at least 1,330 and potentially more than 1,895 ballistic and cruise missiles and is developing and testing several new classes of offensive missiles, including hypersonic glide vehicles, even as it upgrades older systems.[86] The PRC maintains the largest short-range ballistic-missile force in the world and developed the world's first operational anti-ship ballistic-missile system in 2014. China's nuclear modernization program is also ongoing, resulting in the deployment of new mobile intercontinental-range land-launched ballistic missiles and submarine-launched ballistic missiles. Newer missiles have been upgraded to carry multiple independently targetable reentry vehicle technology (MIRV).[87] The Second Artillery is also developing methods to counter ballistic-missile defenses.[88] The PLA Navy now possesses the largest number of vessels in Asia, with more than three hundred surface ships, submarines, amphibious ships, and patrol craft, supplemented by civilian "maritime militias."[89] Most Chinese naval vessels carry anti-ship cruise missiles of varying range. The PLA Air Force is the largest air force in Asia and the third-largest in the world, possessing more than 2,800 total aircraft and 2,100 combat aircraft. Of those, approximately 600 are modern aircraft.[90]

Command, control, communications, computers, intelligence, surveillance, and reconnaissance (C4ISR). China also devotes much attention and resources to the less tangible realms of space, cyberspace, and electronic warfare.[91] The country already possesses many of the systems necessary for an efficient C4ISR capability. To increase its situational awareness,

---

[85] Ashley J. Tellis and Travis Tanner, eds., *Strategic Asia 2012–13: China's Military Challenge* (Seattle: National Bureau of Asian Research, 2012); and Roger Cliff et al., *Entering the Dragon's Lair: Chinese Antiaccess Strategies and Their Implications for the United States* (Santa Monica: RAND Corporation, 2007), http://www.rand.org/content/dam/rand/pubs/monographs/2007/RAND_MG524.pdf.

[86] Campbell et al., "China's 'Core Interests,'" 15.

[87] U.S. Department of Defense, *Annual Report to Congress: Military and Security Developments Involving the People's Republic of China 2015* (Washington, D.C., 2015); and David Sanger and William J. Broad, "China Making Some Missiles More Powerful," *New York Times*, May 16, 2015, http://www.nytimes.com/2015/05/17/world/asia/china-making-some-missiles-more-powerful.html.

[88] U.S. Department of Defense, *Annual Report to Congress*.

[89] Ibid.; Ronald O'Rourke, "China's Naval Modernization: Implications for U.S. Navy Capabilities—Background and Issues for Congress," CRS Report for Congress, RL33153, July 28, 2015; and Andrew S. Erickson and Conor M. Kennedy, "Meet the Chinese Maritime Militia Waging a 'People's War at Sea,'" *Wall Street Journal*, China Real Time, March 31, 2015, http://blogs.wsj.com/chinarealtime/2015/03/31/meet-the-chinese-maritime-militia-waging-a-peoples-war-at-sea.

[90] U.S. Department of Defense, *Annual Report to Congress*; and Andrew S. Erickson and Lyle J. Goldstein, eds., *Chinese Aerospace Power: Evolving Maritime Roles* (Annapolis: Naval Institute Press, 2011).

[91] U.S. Department of Defense, *Annual Report to Congress*.

China has developed the KJ-2000 airborne early warning command and control aircraft, along with a dozen specialized C4ISR aircraft that are capable of detecting, locating, and tracking targets and coordinating attacks against them.[92] UAVs are also being steadily incorporated into the force, enhancing over-the-horizon targeting for long-range missiles. Finally, the integrated civil-military Beidou-2 space program has achieved full regional coverage and aims for global coverage by 2020.

Civil-Military Relations

In November 2014, Xi Jinping restated the conclusions of the Gutian Conference, which 85 years earlier had established the inviolable principle of the party's authority over the military. In a speech full of both exhortation and warning, the Chinese leader rejected the concept of *guojiahua* (the idea that the PLA should serve the country instead of the party), demanded that the ideological commitment to party leadership and political work among the military be strengthened, and highlighted General Xu Caihou's corruption case as a cautionary tale.[93]

In any Leninist system, the armed forces are a politicized institution.[94] The PLA is no exception. The party "commands the gun" and penetrates the armed forces at every level to guarantee its political control. The PLA's influence over civilian leaders, however, has been reduced over the years as the political succession process became institutionalized and fewer senior officers are represented in core CCP decision-making bodies. Aside from the personal (*guanxi*) and patronage networks, Xi appears to rely on a group of "princeling generals" to advise him on certain topics.[95] The most important institutionalized channels for PLA influence on military or foreign policy issues are the Central Military Commission; the Foreign Affairs, Military Affairs, and Taiwan Affairs Leading Small Groups; and the new National

---

[92] Campbell et al., "China's 'Core Interests,'" 313.

[93] Roy Kamphausen, "China's New Military Leadership and the Challenges It Faces," interview by Greg Chaffin, NBR, January 18, 2013, http://www.nbr.org/research/activity.aspx?id=303; and James Mulvenon, "Hotel Gutian: We Haven't Had That Spirit Here Since 1929," Hoover Institution, China Leadership Monitor, no. 46, 2015, http://www.hoover.org/sites/default/files/research/docs/clm46jm.pdf.

[94] Amos Perlmutter and William M. LeoGrande, "The Party in Uniform: Toward a Theory of Civil-Military Relations in Communist Political Systems," *American Political Science Review* 76, no. 4 (1982): 778–89.

[95] Willy Lam, "White Paper Expounds Civil-Military Relations in Xi Era," Jamestown Foundation, China Brief, June 19, 2015.

Security Commission.[96] The National Defense Education Program, jointly established in 2013 by the CCP's Organization Department and the PLA's General Political Department, specifically trains central and local officials on state security, border, and coastal defense issues.[97]

The military is subservient to the party, and its influence on political decisions has narrowed into institutional mechanisms that are primarily focused on security issues.[98] The CCP leadership has final authority on war, the armed forces, and national defense building, and there are no openly available examples of PLA officers disobeying orders from CCP leaders.[99] Even if the exact dynamics are difficult for outsiders to evaluate, there seems to be no evidence of a dominant military role in major strategic decisions. At the same time, "all signs point to the existence of a broad consensus on national objectives, strategy and tactics" between civilian and military leaders on the most important questions of foreign and defense policy.[100]

Combat Proficiency

The Chinese military's actual combat proficiency is hard to gauge. Some key questions remain about a series of shortcomings that render its transformation incomplete—in particular its enduring problems in coordinating joint operations.[101] The PLA has reached a certain level of coordination among the services but is not yet capable of performing integrated operations where assets from units of multiple services operate in unison.[102] Jointness has been hampered by a stove-pipe structure still overwhelmingly dominated by the army, the absence of a genuine joint command (with the exception of the Central Military Commission), and technological barriers, including incompatible models and different

---

[96] Michael D. Swaine, "China's Assertive Behavior—Part Three: The Role of the Military in Foreign Policy," Hoover Institution, China Leadership Monitor, no. 36, 2012, http://carnegieendowment. org/files/CLM36MS.pdf; James Mulvenon, "The New Central Military Commission," Hoover Institution, China Leadership Monitor, no. 40, 2013; and Willy Lam, "The Generals' Growing Clout in Diplomacy," Jamestown Foundation, China Brief, April 3, 2015.

[97] Lam, "White Paper Expounds Civil-Military Relations in Xi Era."

[98] Alice Miller, "The PLA in the Party Leadership Decision Making System," in *PLA Influence on China's National Security Policymaking*, ed. Philip C. Saunders and Andrew Scobell (Stanford: Stanford University Press, 2015).

[99] Saunders and Scobell, *PLA Influence on China's National Security Policymaking*.

[100] Aaron L. Friedberg, "The Sources of Chinese Conduct: Explaining Beijing's Assertiveness," *Washington Quarterly* 37, no. 4 (2015): 133–50.

[101] Chase et al., *China's Incomplete Military Transformation*.

[102] Kevin Pollpeter, "Informationization and Joint Operations" (presentation at the Jamestown Foundation's China Defense and Security Conference, Washington, D.C., February 2012).

generations of equipment that diminish the military's overall effectiveness.[103] PLA leaders are aware of the necessity of overcoming this critical issue. Reforms aim at establishing a theater joint command system. Military-wide training is emphasized, with a focus on joint command and control utilizing integrated command platforms during joint operations.[104]

Xi has made clear on several occasions that national defense and army-building are central to the realization of the "China dream." Strengthening the military, he insisted in March 2013, requires "building a military force that obeys the party's command, is able to fight victorious battles, and has a good style" (i.e., character and quality).[105] In a relatively short time, the PLA has made impressive progress in its ability to execute assigned missions, and it is still attempting to optimize its structure and command system, intensify training, and continue its hardware modernization program. Not all of the PLA's capabilities are state of the art—it lacks actual combat experience and is not yet fully prepared for joint, informationized warfare—but the PLA is still formidable compared to other Asian armed forces. General Liu Yuan allegedly declared in 2012: "No country can defeat China. Only our own corruption can destroy us and cause our armed forces to be defeated without fighting."[106]

Conclusion

China stands out as a colossus whose characteristics and national resources are measured almost exclusively in large numbers. And size does matter—it is essentially the magnitude and breadth of China's all-encompassing development over the last two decades that have led many observers to conclude that China's re-ascent is inexorable and inevitable. But it would be a mistake to draw conclusions about the trajectory of national power based solely on projections of material capabilities. In the long run, a country's fate is determined not primarily by its coal reserves, demographics, or number of nuclear warheads but rather by intangible, unquantifiable, and yet crucial factors—namely policy and sound political leadership.

---

[103] Andrew Scobell, "Discourse in 3-D: The PLA's Evolving Doctrine, Circa 2009," in *The PLA at Home and Abroad: Assessing the Operational Capabilities of China's Military*, ed. Roy Kamphausen, David Lai, and Andrew Scobell (Carlisle: Strategic Studies Institute, 2010).

[104] U.S. Department of Defense, *Annual Report to Congress*.

[105] James Mulvenon, "Military Themes from the 2013 National People's Congress," Hoover Institution, China Leadership Monitor, no. 41, 2013, http://www.hoover.org/sites/default/files/uploads/documents/CLM41JM.pdf.

[106] John Garnaut, "Rotting from Within: Investigating the Massive Corruption of the Chinese Military," *Foreign Policy*, April 16, 2012, http://foreignpolicy.com/2012/04/16/rotting-from-within.

China's leadership has a conscious plan to expand national power, a vision encapsulated in Xi's China dream, and has proved its determination to invest political will and considerable money in developing the country's overall comprehensive national power. But the nation's capacity to convert these resources into tangible forms of usable civilian and military power is hindered by a contradiction in terms between the essence of power in the 21st century—inspirational, technologically advanced, outward-looking, and innovative—and the intrinsic nature of the regime that is currently governing China. Openness, outwardness, philanthropy, and the free flow of goods and ideas are anathema to a distrustful party-state that is not willing to relinquish control. Paradoxically, the very same party that has raised China up to where it is today may ultimately prevent the country's ascension to the pinnacle of power.

Mao Zedong said contradictions are present in every single thing. Seemingly incompatible realities, one precluding the existence of the other, such as socialism and a market economy, do coexist in China, at least for now. But how much longer will the political system be able to deal with these contradictions and, more importantly, with the intricacies of what Friedrich Hayek called the "spontaneous order" of the market—an unplanned order that evolves as the result of innumerable individual human actions, not top-down state control?[107]

For the last three decades, the Chinese leadership has managed to increase the power of the nation while at the same time strengthening the party's own power. This has been possible thanks to unprecedented economic growth. Massive financial resources have been invested in the country's infrastructure, state-owned enterprises, education system, research laboratories, internal security apparatus, and national defense forces. But tight government control has also imposed limitations on China's overall performance, notably in the innovation and high-tech domains. Collusion between government and business, combined with a lack of public accountability, has created rampant, pervasive corruption. China has now entered a period of slower growth, and the party-state faces increasingly difficult choices. As growth slows, what are the leadership's options? The fundamental challenge is squaring the circle between the CCP's desire to maintain its monopoly on power and the necessity of achieving a sustainable growth model. Genuine economic reforms would mean relinquishing state control, relying more on the market, and expanding the private sector. Instead, the party seems determined to rule the markets as

---

[107] W.W. Bartley III, ed., *The Collected Works of F.A. Hayek* (London: Routledge, 1988).

well as the people and to blame problems on foreign interference.[108] Absent meaningful reforms, the regime will face increasingly tough trade-offs among its various goals.

Xi Jinping's China dream has set ambitious goals for the nation, but also ultimately for the CCP itself. The party will suffer a serious loss of credibility if it cannot deliver on its promises. Faced with challenges to its legitimacy, a real danger exists that the regime will fight for its own future and opt for internal repression, external aggression, or both.

---

[108] Robert Zoellick, "China Will Stumble If Xi Stalls on Reform," *Financial Times*, September 7, 2015.

EXECUTIVE SUMMARY

This chapter argues that Japan has the economic strength, political cohesiveness, and state infrastructure to develop and deploy comparatively significant military capabilities in Asia.

MAIN ARGUMENT

As the first non-Western country to modernize its society, government, and economy, Japan has been one of the most powerful Asian states since the late nineteenth century. Despite over two decades of economic stagnation, it remains highly developed, and its economy is slowly adjusting to a postindustrial era. The government is competent and organizationally complex, while elites in both the public and private sectors are highly educated and capable. Japan's natural resources are limited, but its other national resources are well-developed. Though hampered by groupthink and risk aversion, Japan's political, corporate, and intellectual leaders achieve high levels of national performance, despite ongoing internal rivalry, group interests, and the lack of individual leadership. These strengths translate into military capabilities that are unmatched by most states in the Asia-Pacific region. However, Japan's self-imposed restrictions on overseas military operations and an unwillingness to build a military force commensurate with its economic size have resulted in a smaller and less operationally experienced military than would otherwise be expected.

POLICY IMPLICATIONS

- Japan's greatest need is to embrace radical structural reform in its economy, thereby revitalizing innovation and competitiveness and sparking sustainable postindustrial growth.

- Japan should embrace Prime Minister Shinzo Abe's plans for a more regionally and internationally engaged foreign policy that offers unstinting liberal support for an open, rules-based order in the Asia-Pacific.

- Japan should expand and modernize its military, even beyond Abe's current plans, and free itself from restraints that prevent it from playing a central role with liberal allies in maintaining regional stability.

Japan's National Power in a Shifting Global Balance

Michael Auslin

Despite two decades of economic difficulty and political evolution, Japan remains one of Asia's great powers. Its position as one of the oldest democracies in Asia, combined with its level of development and wealth as the world's fourth-largest economy (by purchasing power parity valuation), gives it a leadership role in Asia's geopolitical hierarchy. Social stability, a skilled workforce, and an ethnically and linguistically united citizenry add to Japan's overall strength.

Yet Japan faces significant uncertainties in both its foreign and domestic politics. Adequately responding to these uncertainties will tax both Japan's policymakers and its population and make clear whether the country's national power remains sufficient to deal with the challenges it faces. Over the past several decades, a number of external threats and problems have emerged. China has grown to become Japan's primary geopolitical competitor in East Asia and seeks political, economic, and military supremacy in the region. Japan's security environment is threatened by North Korea's nuclear and missile programs as well as by ongoing uncertainty about the intentions of the Kim Jong-un regime. Japan's relations with South Korea present another problem, as historical grievances and territorial disputes continue to hamstring relations between Tokyo and Seoul.

On the domestic front, Japan continues attempting to revitalize its economy, a quarter-century after the popping of its asset and real estate bubbles. Regaining competitiveness and innovation remains a challenge for

Michael Auslin is a Resident Scholar and the Director of Japan Studies at the American Enterprise Institute. He can be reached at <michael.auslin@aei.org>.

The author thanks Eddie Linczer for research assistance with this chapter.

businesses. While socially stable, the country faces a significant demographic decline and must create policies to deal with labor shortages, an aging population, and a decline in the viability of rural areas.[1] A lack of immigration and a drop in the number of Japanese studying or living abroad also contribute to potential insularity. While seemingly politically paralyzed, Japan in fact has gone through a twenty-year political realignment in which the long-ruling Liberal Democratic Party (LDP) lost power to the opposition Democratic Party of Japan (DPJ), only to return to power after three years with a larger majority than before. Nonetheless, voter participation levels have steadily declined, and doubts about the LDP's ability to revive economic growth foster continuing pessimism among Japanese voters.[2]

In some ways, Japan is at a crossroads. It must plan for a future with a reduced population and ongoing economic lassitude. At the same time, it struggles to respond to the shift in the balance of power in the Asia-Pacific toward China. Long-held taboos on security cooperation abroad and military operations overseas are beginning to weaken as a result of both the change in Asia's security environment and Prime Minister Shinzo Abe's activist foreign policy. Nonetheless, political culture and a postwar sensibility continue to hold Japan back from passing the full range of economic and security reforms that are needed in order to respond to the challenges at home and abroad. While deficient in natural resources, Japan has every other significant element of national power and remains one of Asia's richest nations. Yet it could do more to tear down the barriers to increasing national power so as to not only retain but also expand its leadership role in Asia. This, in turn, requires the national will for reforming itself.

This chapter begins with a review of the inherent strengths that Japan derives from its national resources. These include its diverse yet challenging geography, significant human resources, and long-developed capital and financial resources. The chapter then assesses how these inputs are expressed in national performance, or more precisely, Japan's capacity to mobilize resources to exercise national power. This assessment begins with an overview of Japan's threat environment and then examines the role of its government structure and corporate institutions. It then considers how cohesion among elites both helps and hinders national performance, along with the question of how much political reform is needed to optimize the system. The final section of this chapter turns to the ultimate output of national resources and performance: military capability. A review of Japan's defense budget and force

---

[1] Statistics Bureau, Ministry of Internal Affairs and Communication (Japan), *Statistical Handbook of Japan 2014* (Tokyo, 2014), http://www.stat.go.jp/english/data/handbook/pdf/2014all.pdf#page=4.

[2] "Voter Turnout Data for Japan," International Institute for Democracy and Electoral Assistance, http://www.idea.int/vt/countryview.cfm?id=114.

structure leads into an examination of the nation's particular constitutional limitations on the use of force. The changes in Japan's security environment are then analyzed in a discussion of Tokyo's "new internationalism" and its security component. The chapter concludes by highlighting the key takeaways of this analysis, stressing the limitations on Japan's ability to generate and employ its military capability in a challenging regional environment.

Japan's National Resources

Geography

Japan is strategically located at the extreme eastern end of the Eurasian landmass and stretches some 3,300 kilometers from Siberia in the north to Taiwan in the south. It thus forms a potential barrier between continental Asia and the northern Pacific Ocean. As an archipelagic nation with no land borders, Japan comprises four main islands and 2,456 claimed smaller islands, with no part of the country more than 150 kilometers from the ocean. Its total area is just under 378,000 square kilometers, making it approximately the size of Norway.[3]

Japan's location is strategic as well, given that its neighbors include China, Russia, Taiwan, and the two Koreas. Its relations with each of these nations has political, economic, and security implications for Asia and the globe. Despite its economic importance and strategic position, however, Japan has struggled to develop relations of trust or cooperation with its neighbors. With China, it is increasingly locked into a competition for leadership in Asia, while ties with South Korea are strained by unresolved historical issues relating to Japan's 35-year colonization of the Korean Peninsula and war crimes during World War II. Further, Japan has found itself involved in a complex triangle with Russia and China over energy resources, control of vital sea lanes, and regional politics. Looking for geopolitical maneuvering room, Tokyo often has viewed Moscow as a potential partner to help balance China.

Japan is embroiled in territorial disputes with each of its main neighbors, further straining its geopolitical position in Asia. Russia has controlled four of the Kuril Islands (known as the Northern Territories in Japan) north of Hokkaido since 1945 and has announced plans to upgrade the islands' defenses in the coming years, thus complicating Tokyo's desire for closer

---

[3] Statistics Bureau, Ministry of Internal Affairs and Communication (Japan), *Statistical Handbook of Japan 2014*.

relations.[4] South Korea and Japan are locked in a diplomatic and legal dispute over the status of the Liancourt Rocks (known as Takeshima in Japan and Dokdo in South Korea) in the Sea of Japan, raising tensions between local activist groups in both countries. Most seriously, China actively challenges Japan's administrative control and claim of sovereignty over the Senkaku Islands (known as Diaoyu in China and Diaoyutai in Taiwan), which are located just northeast of Taiwan and are thus strategic for controlling access from the East China Sea to the western Pacific Ocean. The Senkakus also lie on rich reserves of undersea gas and oil, coveted by both nations.

Natural Resources

Japan's history has been shaped by its lack of natural resources. It has almost none of the resources needed for a modern, industrialized economy. The country must import 96% of its primary energy resources, primarily natural gas and oil, along with coal, making it one of the world's largest importers of fossil fuels.[5] Until the 2011 Tohoku earthquake, nuclear energy accounted for approximately 30% of Japan's energy supply, but almost all of the country's nuclear power plants have been shut down since then, increasing reliance on imported fossil fuels.[6] In recent years, Japanese government agencies have sponsored exploration of the seabed around Japan's home islands and have discovered potentially massive amounts of methane hydrates. If these hydrates were exploited, they could provide much of Japan's natural gas for the next century.[7]

In April 2015, the Ministry of Economy, Trade and Industry released a draft report on the country's energy mix looking ahead to 2030. The plan calls for nuclear energy to provide 20%–22% of the country's energy needs, while liquefied natural gas (LNG) would shrink to 27% from the current level of 43%. Oil, meanwhile, would drop from 15% to just 3% of energy consumed.[8] At the same time, Prime Minister Abe has pledged to cut Japan's greenhouse gas emissions by 26% by the same year, though his plans call for just a 4%

---

[4] Gabriela Baczynska, "Russia Orders Quicker Build-Up of Military Facilities in Kurile Islands," Reuters, June 8, 2015, http://www.reuters.com/article/2015/06/08/us-russia-japan-islands-idUSKBN0OO23E20150608.

[5] "Japan's Energy Supply Situation and Basic Policy," Federation of Electric Power Companies (Japan), http://www.fepc.or.jp/english/energy_electricity/supply_situation.

[6] U.S. Energy Information Agency, "Japan: International Energy Data and Analysis," January 30, 2015, http://www.eia.gov/beta/international/analysis.cfm?iso=JPN.

[7] Ministry of Economy, Trade and Industry (Japan), "Reference Materials: Present State of Development of Methane Hydrate," February 2009, 12, http://www.meti.go.jp/english/report/downloadfiles/lowcarbon2009_02.pdf.

[8] "Japan's New Energy Mix," Ministry of Economy, Trade and Industry (Japan), http://www.pl.emb-japan.go.jp/keizai/documents/2030%20Energy%20mix%20of%20Japan_ENG.pdf.

drop in the use of coal.[9] The bulk of the change in the energy mix over the next fifteen years will come from restarting Japan's nuclear reactors, thus providing an element of energy security by reducing reliance on the global market to supply the country's needs.

In addition, Japan imports the vast majority of its minerals and precious metals, including rare earths, many of which come from China. The only natural resources it has in abundance are timber, with just under 70% of its landmass being forested, and rich fisheries in the Pacific Ocean.[10] The country produces only approximately 40% of its annual food supply, importing the rest.[11] Although Japan's geographic position as an island state would naturally push it toward becoming a trading nation, this lack of natural resources mandates that it be fully integrated into maritime and aerial trading networks to support its national existence.

Human Resources

Japan has always made up for its lack of natural resources with its human resources. Its 127 million people are ethnically homogenous, sharing the same language, writing system, culture, and main religions. Japan achieved nearly 100% literacy in the twentieth century, as well as universal secondary education, and has one of the world's most developed tertiary educational systems, which includes major research universities in the country's main urban areas.[12] According to the Organisation for Economic Co-operation and Development's 2012 Programme for International Student Assessment, Japanese students ranked second globally in mathematics and first in both reading and science performance.[13]

In other social rankings, Japan also scores high globally. It has the world's third-longest life expectancy, universal healthcare, advanced sanitation throughout the country, and one of the world's lowest crime rates.[14]

---

[9] "Prime Minister's Statement on the Draft Version of 'Japan's Promise,'" Prime Minister of Japan and His Cabinet website, July 17, 2015, http://japan.kantei.go.jp/97_abe/actions/201507/17article1.html.

[10] *The World Factbook* (Washington, D.C.: Central Intelligence Agency, 2015), https://www.cia.gov/library/publications/the-world-factbook/geos/ja.html.

[11] "Japan: Trade," U.S. Department of Agriculture, http://www.ers.usda.gov/topics/international-markets-trade/countries-regions/japan/trade.aspx.

[12] UNESCO Institute for Lifelong Learning, "Country Profile: Japan," 2015, http://www.unesco.org/uil/litbase/?menu=14&programme=131.

[13] Organisation for Economic Co-operation and Development (OECD), "Japan," Programme for International Student Assessment, Country Note, 2012, http://www.oecd.org/pisa/keyfindings/PISA-2012-results-japan.pdf.

[14] *The World Factbook*; and UN Office on Drugs and Crime, "Global Study on Homicide," 2013, https://www.unodc.org/documents/data-and-analysis/statistics/GSH2013/2014_GLOBAL_HOMICIDE_BOOK_web.pdf.

Teen pregnancy has traditionally been among the world's lowest, with approximately five births per one thousand women ages 15–19, according to the World Bank, and Japan thus has avoided many of the socioeconomic problems associated with young, one-parent families.[15]

Yet not all social and economic indicators are positive. While Japan's educational achievements have ensured the type of skilled workforce needed for maintaining an advanced industrial and postindustrial economy, critics have long questioned whether Japanese students are taught the critical thinking skills required to sustain innovation and deal with complex crisis situations.[16] Further, with only 49% of women in the workforce, despite high educational levels, Japan lags behind other developed nations in employing the full talents of its citizenry.[17] This is one reason for Abe's so-called womenomics policy, introduced in 2014, which is designed to increase the number of women in the workforce.[18] These weaknesses serve to hinder national economic performance over the long run, particularly in an increasingly competitive global economy where innovation and flexibility are especially important.

As is well known, Japan's overall demographic picture is negative. Fertility rates dropped below replacement level in the 1970s, leading to a loss in population beginning in 2007. The number of children in Japan aged 15 or under has been declining annually since 1981, and currently those aged 65 or older make up a full quarter of the population.[19] It is estimated that the elderly will constitute 40% of Japan's population by 2060 and that the total population could fall under 100 million by 2050, and as low as 86 million by 2060.[20] Historically, Japan has severely restricted legal immigration, although illegal day laborers from Southeast Asia and the Middle East are common

---

[15] "Adolescent Fertility Rate (Births per 1,000 Women Ages 15–19)," World Bank, World Development Indicators, http://data.worldbank.org/indicator/SP.ADO.TFRT.

[16] For a comparative study, see Hyunjoon Park, *Re-Evaluating Education in Japan and Korea: Demystifying Stereotypes* (London: Routledge, 2013); for an earlier study, see Kaori Okano and Motonori Tsuchiya, *Education in Contemporary Japan: Inequality and Diversity* (Cambridge: Cambridge University Press, 1999), chap. 6.

[17] "Labor Force Participation Rate, Female (% of Female Population Ages 15+) (Modeled ILO Estimate)," World Bank, World Development Indicators, http://data.worldbank.org/indicator/SL.TLF.CACT.FE.ZS.

[18] For a public statement of the policy, see Shinzo Abe, "Unleashing the Power of 'Womenomics,'" *Wall Street Journal*, September 25, 2013, http://www.wsj.com/articles/SB10001424052702303759604579 091680931293404.

[19] Statistics Bureau, Ministry of Internal Affairs and Communication (Japan), *Statistical Handbook of Japan 2014*.

[20] National Institute of Population and Social Science Research, "Population Projections for Japan: 2011–2060," January 2012, http://www.ipss.go.jp/site-ad/index_english/esuikei/h1_1.html.

in the construction and services industries.[21] However, the country does not incorporate highly skilled international talent into society, thus retarding innovation and skill transfer in Japanese companies.

Japan's citizens benefit from its liberal sociopolitical system. Japan is perhaps Asia's most stable democracy, with universal suffrage and free and fair elections at the national, prefectural, and local levels. Political parties are plentiful and free from government interference. Civilian control over the military, the Japan Self-Defense Forces (JSDF), is absolute. The rule of law, which is upheld through a largely transparent legal system, underpins individual freedom as expressed in the postwar constitution. Questions about the latitude given to the national police in detaining suspects and the secrecy of capital punishment cases mar an otherwise open legal system. Freedom of the press is guaranteed in Japan, and the country boasts one of the most free-wheeling environments in both print and broadcast media.[22] However, recent concerns about the Abe administration's pressure on media companies over stories critical of government policies have increased wariness among journalists.

Capital and Financial Resources

Relying on its human capital, Japan has become one of the world's most developed nations. Its GDP is estimated at $4.8 trillion (in both purchasing power parity and at official exchange rates), with a per capita GDP of $37,800, making Japan one of the world's wealthiest societies.[23] Agriculture accounts for just 2.9% of the labor force and only 1.2% of GDP, while 70% of workers are in the service sector, which accounts for 73% of GDP.[24] Japan became a world leader in advanced manufacturing during the post–World War II era and maintains a developed industrial base, especially in automotive, machinery, textiles, and electronics production.[25] While no longer the leading producer of steel, computer chips, or consumer electronics, Japan has become central to the global value-added supply chain by producing electronic components for automobiles, smartphones, personal computers, and machinery. It has one of the world's highest concentrations of Internet

---

[21] Chikako Kashiwazaki and Tsuneo Akaha, "Japanese Immigration Policy: Responding to Conflicting Pressures," Migration Policy Institute, November 1, 2006, http://www.migrationpolicy.org/article/japanese-immigration-policy-responding-conflicting-pressures.

[22] "Freedom of the Press: Japan," Freedom House, 2012, https://freedomhouse.org/report/freedom-press/2012/japan#.VaBFPU3JDoo?.

[23] *The World Factbook.*

[24] Ibid.

[25] Ibid.

users, and computers are used widely in educational and business settings.[26] Research universities and corporations invest heavily in R&D, and Japan has the world's third-largest concentration of R&D investment at 10% of the global total, trailing only the United States and China, although the annual growth in R&D is comparatively slow at just 3.5%.[27]

Japan's technological development has been expressed through its largely open economy and advanced corporate community. Japan has a free-market economy, though one that through the postwar period experienced a significant level of government intervention. Domestic consumption accounts for 60% of GDP (less than the United States at 68%), and export of goods and services accounts for just over 17%.[28] Japan is thus relatively less dependent on the global market than other developed Asian states, such as South Korea, whose export of goods and services accounts for fully 50% of GDP.[29] Nonetheless, exports totaled over $700 billion in 2014, and numerous Japanese firms are global leaders in their market sectors, such as Toyota or Honda in motor vehicle manufacturing and Panasonic or Sony in consumer electronics.[30] Conversely, the country has run current account surpluses for many years, yet the cost of energy imports has resulted in a trade deficit that shrank the country's surplus to just $22 billion in 2014, the lowest since 1985.[31] By some estimates, the cost of importing energy increased by $100 billion from 2011 to 2013, driven in large part by Japanese companies using a weak yen to purchase LNG, due to the loss of nuclear power generation after the 2011 earthquake.[32]

Japan's corporations have modern governance structures but often remain encased in informal vertical relationships with banks, distributors, lower-level suppliers, and the like that serve to hinder broader competition in the economy. Over more than the past decade, these companies have

---

[26] According to the World Bank, Japan has the sixteenth-highest concentration of Internet users globally. See "Internet Users (per 100 People)," World Bank, World Development Indicators, http://data.worldbank.org/indicator/IT.NET.USER.P2?order=wbapi_data_value_2014+wbapi_data_value+wbapi_data_value-last&sort=desc.

[27] National Science Foundation, "Science and Engineering Indicators 2014," 2014, chap. 4, http://www.nsf.gov/statistics/seind14/index.cfm/chapter-4/c4s2.htm.

[28] "Household Final Consumption Expenditure, etc. (% of GDP)," World Bank, World Development Indicators, http://data.worldbank.org/indicator/NE.CON.PETC.ZS; and *The World Factbook*.

[29] *The World Factbook.*

[30] Ibid.

[31] "Balance of Payments Statistics, 2014 CY (Preliminary)," Ministry of Finance (Japan), February 9, 2015, https://www.mof.go.jp/international_policy/reference/balance_of_payments/preliminary/bpcy2014.pdf.

[32] Ministry of Economy, Trade and Industry (Japan), "FY2013 Annual Report on Energy (Energy White Paper 2014) Outline," June 2014, 8, http://www.meti.go.jp/english/report/downloadfiles/2014_outline.pdf.

become less competitive relative to South Korean, Taiwanese, and Chinese manufacturers, and innovation has similarly suffered. Japan likewise lags in FDI, with just over $2 billion in 2013, accounting for only 3.5% of GDP.[33] Yet the country still ranks third globally for patents filed, behind only China and the United States, with over 328,000 in 2013.[34]

The lack of foreign capital and ideas in Japan's economy has meant a sluggish response to lower growth and the maturing of the manufacturing sector. Start-ups and entrepreneurship occupy a smaller space in the economy than in comparably developed nations, particularly the United States. For example, in 2012, direct public R&D funding in Japan stood at less than 0.1% of GDP and was primarily directed at large companies, to the disadvantage of start-ups. In comparison, direct public R&D funding levels in the United States were 0.2% of GDP in 2012, while South Korea's hovered just below 0.2% of GDP.[35] This low level of public R&D is mirrored in Japan's relatively underdeveloped venture capital market, which accounts for just 0.02% of GDP, far behind the United States and even South Korea.[36]

Trade and an open economy have given Japan significant capital and financial resources. It has the fourth-highest stock of broad money (currency in circulation plus all deposits) at $8 trillion and the second-largest holding of foreign reserves and gold, with over $1.25 trillion, along with almost $5 trillion of wealth in publicly traded shares on Japanese stock markets.[37] Postal system savings alone represent almost $3 trillion in liquid assets, while Japanese firms hold $2.1 trillion in cash.[38] Although these resources give Japan an enormous amount of capital that can be used for investment, many of these assets are inefficiently allocated, as companies hoard cash and an aging population refrains from saving.[39] Worse, despite its huge capital resources, Japan has the world's highest debt-to-GDP ratio at an enormous 227%.[40] Interest rates in Japan have been kept low and credit ratings relatively high only because over 90% of that debt is held domestically.

---

[33] OECD, "Japan: Advancing the Third Arrow for a Resilient Economy and Inclusive Growth," Better Policies Series, April 2014, 18, http://www.oecd.org/japan/2014.04_JAPAN_EN.pdf.

[34] World Intellectual Property Organization (WIPO), *World Intellectual Property Indicators* (Geneva: WIPO, 2014), http://www.wipo.int/edocs/pubdocs/en/wipo_pub_941_2014.pdf.

[35] OECD, *OECD Economic Surveys: Japan 2015* (Paris: OECD Publishing, 2015), 86–87.

[36] Ibid., 28.

[37] *The World Factbook.*

[38] "Corporate Saving in Asia: A $2.5 Trillion Problem," *Economist*, September 27, 2014, http://www.economist.com/news/leaders/21620203-japanese-and-south-korean-firms-are-worlds-biggest-cash-hoarders-hurts-their.

[39] Ibid.

[40] *The World Factbook.*

The broader macroeconomic picture in Japan reflects both strengths and weaknesses. Since the collapse of the real estate and asset price bubble in 1990, Japan's growth has slowed dramatically and the country has drifted in and out of recession and deflation. Falling from 10% annual growth in the 1960s, Japan has averaged under 2% annual growth since the 1990s.[41] Its export-oriented model has made the country particularly sensitive to global trade trends, even if less so than other Asian countries. The economy was severely affected by the 2008 global financial crisis and concomitant recession, with overall exports dropping by nearly half during the 2008–9 timeframe.[42] Japan's inefficient agricultural sector and traditional hostility to FDI, which harm its overall economic competitiveness, are slowly and unevenly being challenged by new free trade agreements, such as the unfinished Trans-Pacific Partnership (TPP), and moderate reforms initiated by Abe. With one of the world's oldest populations, Japan also has an extremely expensive entitlements and social-spending system, costing approximately $300 billion per year.[43]

On top of these macro problems, the country suffered an almost unprecedented natural disaster on March 11, 2011, when a powerful earthquake struck Japan's northeastern Tohoku region. The earthquake caused a massive tsunami that destroyed hundreds of miles of coastline and killed an estimated 16,000 people.[44] The tsunami also swamped the Fukushima nuclear power plant, causing a partial meltdown and the release of radiation into both the air and Pacific Ocean. Thousands of residents were evacuated from the afflicted radiation zones, while over four million homes in the region lost electricity for extended periods of time.[45] The World Bank estimated that the total cost of the disaster would reach $235 billion, placing an enormous strain on Japan's public finances due to disaster relief and reconstruction efforts over the succeeding decade.[46]

As a mature economy, Japan thus faces structural and sociopolitical limitations that have been long in the making. Demographic decline is perhaps the most serious threat to continued national power, as this trend

---

[41] World Bank, World Development Indicators Databank, http://databank.worldbank.org/data//reports.aspx?source=2&country=JPN&series=&period.

[42] Statistics Bureau, Ministry of Internal Affairs and Communication (Japan), *Statistical Handbook of Japan 2014*.

[43] "Abe Shies Away from Entitlement Cutbacks," *Nikkei Asian Review*, January 14, 2015, http://asia.nikkei.com/Politics-Economy/Policy-Politics/Abe-shies-away-from-entitlement-cutbacks.

[44] "Great East Japan Earthquake (Details)," Ministry of Foreign Affairs (Japan), September 11, 2012, http://www.mofa.go.jp/j_info/visit/incidents/index2.html.

[45] "Overview of Damage Situation and METI Measures," Ministry of Economy, Trade and Industry (Japan), March 23, 2011, http://www.meti.go.jp/english/electricity_supply/pdf/20110323_1200overview.pdf.

[46] Victoria Kim, "Japan Damage Could Reach $235 Billion, World Bank Estimates," *Los Angeles Times*, March 21, 2011, http://www.latimes.com/business/la-fgw-japan-quake-world-bank-20110322-story.html.

will reduce national economic performance. A modern yet rigid educational system also hampers the country's ability to produce the skills needed to compete in an increasingly globalized economy. While Japan is still a rich nation, the lack of investment, venture capital, and start-ups further reduce its economic power. Exogenous shocks such as the 2008 global recession and the 2011 earthquake and tsunami add to the drags on national resources. Yet Japan at least partly makes up for these deficiencies and weaknesses through its well-developed political, bureaucratic, and corporate systems, as well as through ethnic and social cohesion. The next section will analyze how these inputs interact to shape national performance so as to further illuminate the country's ability to generate national power.

Japan's Capacity to Mobilize Resources to Exercise National Power

Japan's Threat Environment

Japan faces an international environment of increasing external constraints that demand the application of national power. Chief among these are its geographic isolation in Northeast Asia, rising geopolitical competition with China, nuclear and missile threats from North Korea, poor political relations with South Korea, and dependence on vulnerable sea lanes for critical energy and other natural resources. These constraints are partly offset by Japan's growing relationships with India, Australia, and Southeast Asian nations, as well as its long-standing alliance with the United States.

In particular, Japan has two immediate security concerns. The first is the threat posed by North Korea, which has been ongoing since at least the launch in 1998 of a Taepodong ballistic missile over Japanese territory.[47] Tokyo's response included deepening security cooperation with the United States and investing heavily in ballistic missile defense (BMD) capabilities, all of which were undertaken in an environment of continuing economic stagnation.[48] Japan struggled to maintain defense spending during these years and chose to invest in asymmetric capabilities in order to ensure protection of the homeland. With no end in sight to the North Korean threat, and with Pyongyang possibly achieving the ability to put nuclear weapons on missiles, Japanese policymakers will face increased demands to invest in BMD

[47] Sheryl WuDunn, "North Korea Fires Missile over Japanese Territory," *New York Times*, September 1, 1998, http://www.nytimes.com/1998/09/01/world/north-korea-fires-missile-over-japanese-territory.html.

[48] Richard Dean Burns, *The Missile Defense Systems of George W. Bush: A Critical Assessment* (Santa Barbara: Praeger, 2010), 102.

systems and intelligence, surveillance, and reconnaissance (ISR) activities.[49] Eventually, an aerial or missile strike capability may also be deemed necessary for national security.

The second immediate security constraint is the dispute with China over the Senkaku Islands, located just northeast of Taiwan at the end of the Ryukyu island chain. The islands have been under Tokyo's administrative control since the reversion of Okinawa to Japan in 1972. Since 2010, Tokyo and Beijing have been locked in an increasingly bitter struggle over asserting administrative control over the surrounding waters and skies, often related to illegal fishing by Chinese boats within the islands' exclusive economic zone. Tokyo's decision to nationalize several of the islands in 2012 resulted in a dramatically enhanced Chinese military presence around the Senkakus, particularly through the regular deployment of maritime patrol vessels to harass Japanese fishing ships and confront the Japanese Coast Guard.[50] Chinese air force jets regularly fly into contested airspace to test Japan's resolve to defend its claims. This dispute has been the focus of security planning for close to half a decade and imposes continuous operational costs on the JSDF.

Yet the Senkaku dispute is but one manifestation of a much larger and longer-term external constraint on Japan, namely, the rise of China. While Japan, like other Asian nations, has reaped economic benefits from China's integration into the global trading system, it has also increasingly felt political pressure and concerns over its long-term security. Politically, China's attempts to be recognized as Asia's dominant political power have challenged Japan's position, and Beijing has sometimes sought to marginalize Tokyo's role in major international organizations such as the United Nations or in regional ones, such as the East Asia Summit or summits of the Association of Southeast Asian Nations (ASEAN). More specifically, China's announced intent to become a nation that can project maritime power globally raises concerns in Japan about freedom of navigation and the potential for intimidation and harassment in contested waters. More generally, the growth of China's naval and air power, along with its space and cyber capabilities, poses a potential threat to the security of the Japanese homeland as well as to Japan's access to the global commons. The latter threat could imperil the country's ability to provide basic resources for its people, including food and energy.

A third constraint that Japan faces is its strained relationship with South Korea, its closest neighbor and one of Asia's leading liberal states, due to lingering issues related to World War II, including recognition of the comfort

[49] Ministry of Defense (Japan), "Defense Programs and Budget of Japan: Overview of FY2015 Budget Request," August 2014, 1, http://www.mod.go.jp/e/d_budget/pdf/261003.pdf.

[50] Yuzo Hisatsune, "Chinese Boats Harass Japanese Fishing Vessels Near Senkakus," *Asahi Shimbun*, February 28, 2013, http://ajw.asahi.com/article/asia/china/AJ201302280058.

women and the portrayal of Japanese colonialism in contemporary textbooks. The relative isolation that Japan suffers, given its tense relations with both China and South Korea, constrains its ability to act more broadly in Asia. In particular, the lack of a close working relationship with Seoul leaves Tokyo fewer options for containing North Korea, as well as for challenging China's attempts to increase its military and political influence in Asia.

In contrast with the threats outlined above, Japan faces a relatively supportive environment in both South and Southeast Asia. Since the 1970s, beginning with Prime Minister Takeo Fukuda, Tokyo has emphasized outreach to Southeast Asia and the creation of political and economic bonds.[51] Given current tensions between China and some Southeast Asian nations, including Vietnam, the Philippines, and Malaysia, over maritime territorial disputes in the South China Sea, Tokyo has found an opportunity to increase its political influence. Prime Minister Abe recently has reached out to those nations in particular and offered Japanese assistance, such as by providing or selling maritime patrol vessels to build up their capabilities and working on coast guard training, counterterrorism, and the like.[52]

Similarly, Tokyo has developed what some are calling a "quasi-alliance" with Australia that includes the deepening of military exchanges, the sharing of military-related intelligence, and an agreement to co-develop advanced submarine technology.[53] In South Asia, Abe has forged a close personal relationship with the new Indian prime minister Narendra Modi, which has enhanced political and military dialogues and spurred discussions of the larger geopolitical equation in Asia.[54] Both Tokyo and New Delhi, concerned about the rise of China, see their relationship as a strategic partnership linking together Asia's two great democratic powers, although the specifics of just how the two might act together to shape Asia's security and political environment remain vague and undecided. Nonetheless, Japan's relationships with countries outside Northeast Asia have helped reduce its regional isolation and provided a set of potential partners to mitigate the threat environment that it faces.

---

[51] William W. Haddad, "Japan, the Fukuda Doctrine, and ASEAN," *Contemporary Southeast Asia* 2, no. 1 (1980): 10.

[52] Toko Sekiguchi, "Japan to Provide Patrol Vessels to Philippines," *Wall Street Journal*, June 4, 2015, http://www.wsj.com/articles/japan-to-provide-patrol-vessels-to-philippines-1433424771; and Tim Kelly and Nobuhiro Kubo, "Insight—Testing Beijing, Japan Eyes Growing Role in South China Sea Security," Reuters, March 11, 2015, http://uk.reuters.com/article/2015/03/11/uk-japan-southchinasea-insight-idUKKBN0M62BN20150311.

[53] John Garnaut, "Australia-Japan Military Ties Are a 'Quasi-alliance' Says Officials," *Sydney Morning Herald*, October 26, 2014, http://www.smh.com.au/national/australiajapan-military-ties-are-a-quasialliance-say-officials-20141026-11c4bi.html.

[54] Masaaki Kameda, "Abe, India's Modi Agree to Boost Security, Economic Ties amid China's Increasing Territorial Ambitions," *Japan Times*, September 1, 2014, http://www.japantimes.co.jp/news/2014/09/01/national/politics-diplomacy/abe-indias-modi-agree-boost-security-economic-ties-abe-amid-chinas-increasing-territorial-ambitions/#.VZ7F_19Vikp.

Government Structure

Despite these domestic and regional constraints, which are growing in intensity over time, Japan is a highly developed state, possessing the infrastructural capacity to quickly mobilize its national resources. Its democratic form of government has unquestioned legitimacy, and Japanese society is culturally unified. The government can rely on a citizenry that is overwhelmingly law-abiding and fully participates in the legal economy, rather than diverting national assets into unregulated markets or criminal activities. The state possesses a full apparatus of bureaucratic departments that can translate political preferences into policy and is endowed with the means of raising and disbursing revenue to enable its activities.

Traditionally, Japan's ministries, run by professional bureaucrats, were the source of most policy planning, drafting, and implementation. Particularly powerful in this regard were the Ministry of Finance, which is often considered the most elite civil service position and which held de facto veto power over budgetary proposals; the Ministry of Economy, Trade and Industry, which earned a mixed record in selecting and promoting, often through protectionist policies, market sectors and individual companies to develop a high-tech export-driven economy; and the Ministry of Foreign Affairs, which had nearly sole charge over foreign relations and a powerful influence over security planning.[55]

The human capital populating these institutions constitutes Japan's professional civil service. These lifetime bureaucrats are widely considered among the elite and are regularly drawn from the country's most prestigious institutions of higher learning. In particular, the Faculty of Law at Tokyo University has been the traditional producer of the country's top bureaucrats, particularly for the Ministries of Finance and Foreign Affairs. At one point in the early 1990s, over 90% of the executive-track positions in the Ministry of Finance were held by Tokyo University graduates, while fifteen of Japan's postwar prime ministers graduated from the same institution.[56] Japanese bureaucrats form a cohesive group with lifelong intra-ministry ties and a seniority system in which meritocratic competition takes place within class cohorts.

Ties among bureaucrats are replicated more broadly, if somewhat more loosely, by the elite as a whole. Politicians, corporate executives,

---

[55] For more on Japan's past industrial policies, see Chalmers Johnson, *MITI and the Japanese Miracle: The Growth of Industrial Policy, 1925–1975* (Stanford: Stanford University Press, 1982); and Tomohito Shinoda, *Koizumi Diplomacy: Japan's Kantei Approach to Foreign and Defense Affairs* (Seattle: University of Washington Press, 2007).

[56] Peter Hartcher, *The Ministry: How Japan's Most Powerful Institution Endangers World Markets* (Cambridge: Harvard Business School Press, 1998), chap. 1, https://www.nytimes.com/books/first/h/hartcher-ministry.html.

and bureaucrats form a tightly integrated community, often having been classmates at Japan's most prestigious universities and encountering each other regularly throughout their careers. The advantage of such cohesion and familiarity is that it creates effective bonds that can be leveraged for intra- and intergroup policymaking and implementation. This adds to the state's ideational resources across a broad spectrum ranging from economic to foreign policy and from conceptualization of preferences to policy formation.

A powerful example of this was the influence of the precursor to the Ministry of Economy, Trade and Industry, known as the Ministry of International Trade and Industry, which was credited with helping formulate Japan's successful export-driven industrial strategy in the 1960s and 1970s. One of the key institutional arrangements that maintained smooth relations between politicians and bureaucrats was the long-standing practice of having the administrative vice-ministers meet weekly to screen all policies that were being sent to the cabinet for approval.[57] This, combined with regular input from corporate organizations such as the Japan Business Federation, ensured a tight alignment among government, civil service, and industry.

Corporate Institutions

Japan's elite bureaucracy was mirrored by the personnel of its leading corporations, whose abilities helped these companies become global leaders in their sectors. Japan's prewar *zaibatsu* (business conglomerate) system, though formally abolished by the U.S. occupation after World War II, nonetheless continued to provide the basic organizational structure and communal links among newly autonomous corporate entities.[58] The ability to draw on long-established financial, supply, and trade networks has made Japanese corporations remarkably effective and focused, yet it has also led to an insularity of thinking and an aversion to structural change.

Japan's large industrial manufacturers were the first to make their mark on the global stage. Steelmaking and shipbuilding capabilities made Japan central to the burst of postwar global industrialization, but it was the ability of Japanese producers to flexibly respond to changing consumer demand in advanced Western economies that ignited the Japanese export machine. By the 1980s, manufacturers such as Toyota and Honda or Sony and Panasonic either dominated or were highly competitive in their respective sectors.[59]

---

[57] Masami Ito, "DPJ's Promise to Change the System Failed," *Japan Times*, December 1, 2012, http://www.japantimes.co.jp/news/2012/12/01/national/dpjs-promise-to-change-the-system-failed.

[58] For more on zaibatsu and their postwar incarnations, see John G. Roberts, *Mitsui: Three Centuries of Japanese Business*, 2nd edition (New York: Weatherhill, 1989), chap. 25.

[59] David Halberstam, *The Reckoning* (New York: William Morrow & Co, 1986).

In addition, Japan's trading companies played a major role in ensuring that overseas economic activity benefited the accrual of state power, if indirectly. Companies such as Mitsubishi and Mitsui carved out major positions in the global resources trade and established operations on nearly every continent. This strategy of minimizing the risk involved in massive importation helped ensure that Japan never suffered from a lack of access to critical resources, ranging from energy to food.

Elite Cohesion and National Performance

In both the public and private sectors, Japan's cultural cohesion both adds to and detracts from national performance. On the positive side, policy decisions are preceded by gaining consensus among all major stakeholders. This means that any finalized policy has a far greater chance of being implemented, with little ambiguity about goals. Yet the decision-making process also is often extremely slow so as to ensure consensus. Neither the government nor the corporate sector is particularly nimble, and Japan often takes far longer to make decisions than other countries do or misses opportunities while doing so. In addition, the painstaking process of gaining consensus (*nemawashi*) limits the ability to quickly reform policies that are not working.[60] Instead of a quick decision to move in a different direction, both the government and business often are trapped by the inertia of a cultural process that privileges group cohesion. Muddling through is often seen as the least risky option. Like other sociopolitical systems, Japan's network of elites is also naturally riven by tribal politics in which each group or subgroup tries to ensure its own success in setting national goals. Further, although elites are highly educated, they are bound by sociocultural norms that discourage innovative and individual approaches to problem solving.

This leads to the prevalence of groupthink, which often stifles innovation and can lead to policy stagnation. Japan's long flirtation with stimulus spending during the 1990s, despite its lack of success, is one example of the tendency to hew to familiar policies. Stakeholders in Japan are often extremely risk averse, preferring suboptimal results to high-risk, high-reward bets, whether in the political or economic sphere.[61] This is one reason Japanese firms have steadily fallen behind regional competitors from South Korea,

---

[60] For more on consensus-gaining issues, see Karel van Wolferen, *The Enigma of Japanese Power: People and Politics in a Stateless Nation* (New York: Vintage, 1990), 338.

[61] Michael A. Witt, *Changing Japanese Capitalism: Societal Coordination and Institutional Adjustment* (Cambridge: Cambridge University Press, 2006), 53.

Taiwan, and China over the past two decades and have also seen a precipitous drop in new product innovation.[62]

Another negative result of elite cohesion is interest group pressure that results in suboptimal policy decisions. The vested interests that form a tight bond between bureaucrats and the economic elite have often resulted in misallocation of resources and malinvestment. Public spending on unnecessary no-bid construction projects, for example, resulted in a major waste of financial resources during the 1990s and 2000s.[63] Fiscal decisions are not the only ones thus affected. Japan's powerful corporations have long resisted calls to liberalize their executive management structure, leading to insularity among the top business entities. This has made a political impact, as corporate interests have prevented the drafting of rules and regulations that could force companies to be more transparent, end the practice of "poison pill" defenses against foreign takeovers, and more generally open up their ranks to women and foreign skilled workers.

The agricultural industry provides perhaps the best example of interest group pressure on state actors and a consequent negative impact on national performance. In order to ensure votes from overweighted agricultural districts, the LDP acquiesced to high tariffs and wasteful subsidies that have kept Japanese agriculture the most inefficient among developed nations.[64] Resources that could have been spent on R&D or a reduction in the tax burden were instead lavished on the unproductive agricultural sector—a practice that largely continues.

Corruption, too, has played a part in reducing national performance, as the construction, financial, and agricultural sectors liberally bribed politicians, who then voted for wasteful spending, lax oversight, and the like. Top bureaucrats, meanwhile, received expensive dinners and other entertainment throughout their careers and "golden parachutes" into industry after having looked out for corporate interests. Major bribery and corruption scandals have been a fixture of Japan's postwar era. These usually snare politicians, but during the 1990s illegal activities by bureaucrats from the Ministry of Finance resulted in attempts to curb their ties to outside interests.[65]

---

[62] Heang Chhor, "A 20-year Road Map for the Future," McKinsey & Company, http://www.mckinsey.com/features/reimagining_japan/20_year_road_map.

[63] Benjamin Powell, "Explaining Japan's Recession," Mises Institute, November 19, 2002, https://mises.org/library/explaining-japans-recession.

[64] "Assessing the Power of Japan's Agricultural Lobby," Stratfor Global Intelligence, May 4, 2015, https://www.stratfor.com/analysis/assessing-power-japans-agricultural-lobby.

[65] Tamotsu Hasegawa, "Investigation of Corruption in Japan," UN Asia and Far East Institute for the Prevention of Crime and the Treatment of Offenders, Resource Materials Series, no. 56, http://www.unafei.or.jp/english/pdf/PDF_rms/no56/56-36.pdf.

Political Reform

Over the past decade and a half, the nature of elite interconnections and their influence on policy has undergone certain changes. To begin with, under popular former prime minister Junichiro Koizumi (2001–6), the role and structure of the Cabinet Office grew dramatically. Koizumi and his successor Abe (during his first administration in 2006–7) expanded the policymaking and centralizing aspect of the Cabinet Office. Both prime ministers drew heavily on elite bureaucrats as staff, thereby temporarily breaking their direct connection with their home ministries.[66] Koizumi and Abe sought in particular to increase the strength of the Cabinet Office in national security decision-making, and Abe proposed the establishment of a formal national security council (NSC) and centralized intelligence agency based on U.S. models. What had been up to then a largely ad hoc process of responding to crises or emergencies was slowly regularized, beginning with the seconding of leading experts to the Cabinet Office. This trend continued when Abe returned to the premiership in 2012 and formally established an NSC, headed by a veteran diplomat and directed by experts from the Ministries of Foreign Affairs and Defense.[67]

A more jarring interruption of the traditional bureaucrat-politician relationship occurred when the DPJ took power in 2009. After more than a half-century of rule by the LDP, the DPJ entered office with a reformist agenda and an activist approach to policymaking. Under Prime Minister Yukio Hatoyama, the party took direct control of policymaking, often failing to even consult with leading bureaucrats and instead simply sending passed legislation for implementation. Even more sensationally, a series of public hearings (known as *shiwake*) on ways to cut the bloated budget led to bureaucrats being forced to testify before hostile politicians and citizens in what often became a show-trial environment.

With the return of the LDP to power in 2012, the traditional system of interaction among politicians, bureaucrats, and business largely resumed. Yet Abe's ambitious plans to expand Japan's global role pose both opportunities and challenges for national performance. Abe has articulated a coherent vision of Japan's national interests and the actions it should be taking on the regional and global stage to fulfill his goals. In doing so, he has provided new ideational resources for the country's bureaucrats, business elite, and academics, among others. His economic reform plan, known colloquially as "Abenomics," is the most comprehensive plan for economic revitalization

---

[66] Sebastian Moffett, "Koizumi's Success Charts the Path to Japan's Future," *Wall Street Journal*, August 28, 2006, http://www.wsj.com/articles/SB115672233528846881.

[67] Alexander Martin, "Japan to Form Own National Security Council," *Wall Street Journal*, November 21, 2013, http://www.wsj.com/articles/SB10001424052702303653004579210881381219784.

offered by a recent Japanese leader. Soon after entering office in December 2012, Abe successfully implemented two of his three so-called arrows: fiscal stimulus and monetary easing.[68] Both were designed to end Japan's flirtation with deflation and jump-start growth. However, the third arrow, meaningful structural reform, has been a far more difficult policy to craft and implement.[69] Similarly, while controversial to many, Abe's foreign and security policies, which include plans for the exercise of collective self-defense and the creation of new security partnerships in Asia, offer a clear path forward for expanding Japan's security activities and relationships abroad.

This ideational program also presents challenges to Japan's stakeholders. Abe's economic goals require reforms that will reduce the power of corporations and business collectives to operate in traditional ways.[70] Abe has proposed numerous small steps, such as a new corporate governance code, increases in the number of women and foreigners on boards of directors, and greater overall transparency in regulation. Opposition to labor and agricultural reform, not to mention objections from anti–free trade groups, has already caused Abe to backtrack or slow down on many of his initial reform policies.[71] In 2015, he finally pushed through reforms intended to ease restrictions on the selling of land as well as reduce the power of the national agricultural cooperative over individual farms and local cooperatives, though neither of these promise to quickly improve the efficiency of Japanese agriculture. Similarly, liberal opposition to his foreign and security policies, along with significant public doubt, raises the possibility that the LDP could suffer at the polls if Abe's plans to reinterpret the constitution are pushed through.[72] In some ways, Abe is forcing through an ideational revolution designed to orient Japan for the next generation. As such, the opposition of numerous stakeholders increases the friction in Japanese domestic politics.

Yet there is a widely shared sense in Japan that business as usual cannot continue and that the external environment is turning against the country's

---

[68] International Monetary Fund, "Japan: Staff Report for the 2013 Article IV Consultation," July 12, 2013, http://www.imf.org/external/pubs/ft/scr/2013/cr13253.pdf.

[69] See Naoyuki Yoshino, "Three Arrows of 'Abenomics' and the Structural Reform of Japan: Inflation Targeting Policy of the Central Bank, Fiscal Consolidation, and Growth Strategy," Asian Development Bank, August 2014, http://www.adb.org/publications/three-arrows-abenomics-and-structural-reform-japan-inflation-targeting-policy-central-0.

[70] James McBride, "Abenomics and the Japanese Economy," Council on Foreign Relations (CFR), CFR Backgrounder, March 10, 2015, http://www.cfr.org/japan/abenomics-japanese-economy/p30383.

[71] Tetsushi Kajimoto and Izumi Nakagawa, "Ahead of Election Win, Japan's Abe Pivots Away from Painful Reforms," Reuters, December 12, 2014, http://www.reuters.com/article/2014/12/12/us-japan-election-economy-idUSKBN0JQ0GE20141212.

[72] Robin Harding, "Shinzo Abe's Approval Ratings Fall to New Low," Financial Times, June 15, 2015, http://www.ft.com/intl/cms/s/0/67689c7c-131d-11e5-bd3c-00144feabdc0.html#axzz3i8yGE4i8.

interests. This social concern has provided Abe with sufficient electoral and popular support to pursue his policies since returning to office in 2012. This is an established pattern in Japan. When a national need is identified, steady adherence to paradigm-changing policies is almost guaranteed; such was the response to the North Korean Taepodong missile launch over Japan in 1998, from which evolved a more forward-leaning security strategy in the 2000s. With no other leading politician offering an alternative economic reform program, it is likely that many of Abe's reforms will survive his administration. There will be an ongoing struggle, however, to protect vested interests. For example, unions will likely try to roll back labor reforms that make it easier to fire workers, while corporate boards will resist becoming more open. However, the biggest danger facing Japan is that Abe's plans ultimately will not go far enough to ensure that the economy breaks out of its post-bubble stagnation and competes successfully in a more globalized environment.

Although Japan has maintained a position near the top of the developing world throughout the 1990s and 2000s, its returns in producing national power have steadily shrunk. Traditional ways of doing business have become increasingly inefficient, yet vested interests prevent fundamental change. The country has drawn on the inertia of a fixed system of producing and exercising national power, while simultaneously struggling with the challenge of implementing meaningful reforms that enhance national performance without causing instability. Perhaps nowhere is this tension more evident than in the generation of military capability, which is subject to both natural and political friction because of Japan's unique strategic resources and conversion capability. The next section will discuss how Japan can ensure that its deep national resources are translated into the military capability required to deal with its foreign challenges.

Harnessing National Power for Sufficient Military Capability

Although Japan's military capacity is comparatively small, outstripped by China and both Koreas, the country boasts a modern, well-equipped, and well-trained military. The JSDF is a fully rounded force, comprising sea, land, and air elements along with BMD, communications, and ISR capabilities. Traditionally restricted from overseas deployment, the JSDF has participated in antiterrorism operations since 2001 and is undertaking a decades-long modernization that makes it one of Asia's most capable military forces.

Defense Budget

Japan has traditionally spent only 1% of GDP on its military, although there has never been a constitutional ceiling on defense spending.[73] Instead, the nation's adherence to the country's postwar pacifist constitution has created cultural opposition to a larger or offensively based force. Nonetheless, given the size of Japan's economy, the country has been spending nearly $40 billion per year on defense over the past several decades.[74]

Today, after a decade-long leveling off, the country still appropriates approximately $42 billion per year for the JSDF, and Abe has increased the defense budget three years in a row, although the increases are modest. The requested 2.8% increase for 2015, amounting to just over a billion dollars, will nonetheless give Japan its largest-ever defense budget.[75] By comparison, China has been increasing its defense spending by double-digits for the past quarter-century and spends an estimated $100–$300 billion on modernizing its military.[76]

Military Capability

In terms of quality, if not quantity, the JSDF is among the best military forces in Asia. A total of 240,000 personnel belong to the Ground, Air, and Maritime Self-Defense Forces.[77] Japan is attempting to move to a higher tier of capabilities with stealth, cyber, space, and potentially special operations forces.[78] Modernization of the overall force is required, especially in the Japan Air Self-Defense Force (JASDF). In addition, Japan is beginning to implement joint commands and unified areas of responsibility, especially in its southwest island chain, reflecting a new national security strategy.[79]

Its coast guard is perhaps the best in Asia and comprises approximately four hundred ships.[80] Japan's navy, the Japan Maritime Self-Defense

---

[73] *The World Factbook.*

[74] Stockholm International Peace Research Institute (SIPRI), SIPRI Military Expenditure Database, http://www.sipri.org/research/armaments/milex/milex_database.

[75] Ankit Panda, "Japan Approves Largest-Ever Defense Budget," *Diplomat*, January 14, 2015, http://thediplomat.com/2015/01/japan-approves-largest-ever-defense-budget.

[76] International Institute for Strategic Studies (IISS), *The Military Balance 2015* (London: Routledge, 2015), 216.

[77] Ibid., 257.

[78] Ministry of Defense (Japan), "Defense Programs and Budget of Japan: FY2015 Overview," January 2015, http://www.mod.go.jp/e/d_budget/pdf/270414.pdf.

[79] "Organizations Responsible for Japan's Security and Defense: Organization of the Ministry of Defense and the Self-Defense Forces," in Ministry of Defense (Japan), *Defense of Japan 2014* (Tokyo, 2014), 130–31, http://www.mod.go.jp/e/publ/w_paper/pdf/2014/DOJ2014_2-2-2_web_1031.pdf.

[80] IISS, *The Military Balance 2015*, 260.

Force (JMSDF), has 40 guided-missile destroyers, 4 of which possess the advanced Aegis system and SM-3 missiles that are increasingly effective in BMD.[81] Since the end of the Cold War, Japan's antisubmarine warfare (ASW) capability has been of secondary importance, but the country still maintains significant ASW assets, including 80 P-3C patrol planes and ASW-capable submarines and surface vessels.[82] Having a credible antisubmarine force once again is becoming increasingly important to Japan's defense doctrine, given the buildup of the Chinese navy. In addition, Tokyo is in the process of delaying the retirement of its older submarines, thus effectively increasing its modern diesel fleet from 18 to 22 in coming years.[83]

The acquisition of two 27,000-ton Izumo-class helicopter carriers, with the first one being commissioned in March 2015, also provides the capability of aerial power projection far from the home islands. Given the size of the Izumo-class, it is conceivable that they could be retrofitted to carry F-35B vertical takeoff and landing fighters.[84] This would give Japan the potential to compete directly with China in aircraft carrier operations in remote areas.

Equally important is the protection of Japan's airspace, which is necessary to control the vital shipping routes through the region's seas and into the oceans. Both Chinese and Russian fighters and bombers repeatedly cross into Japan's air defense identification zone or into the airspace around contested isles like the Senkakus. Each year, Japan scrambles its air defenses hundreds of times in response to such provocations.[85] Japan's fighter fleet comprises almost three hundred aging 40-year-old F-4s, 25-year-old F-15s, and newer indigenous F-2s.[86] In 2012, Tokyo selected the stealthy F-35 as the next-generation fighter to replace these older platforms.[87] Japan is also currently receiving four aerial tankers, which will allow for inflight refueling, and thus potentially long-range strike missions, especially against foreign ballistic missile sites.[88]

---

[81] "JMSDF Ships," Global Security, http://www.globalsecurity.org/military/world/japan/ship.htm.

[82] IISS, *The Military Balance 2015*, 259.

[83] Kyle Mizokami, "Japan Increasing Size of Submarine Fleet," New Pacific Institute, Japan Security Watch, July 27, 2010, http://jsw.newpacificinstitute.org/?p=2031.

[84] Sam LaGrone, "Japan Commissions Largest Warship Since World War II," U.S. Naval Institute News, March 25, 2015, http://news.usni.org/2015/03/25/japan-commissions-largest-ship-since-world-war-ii.

[85] "Japan Jet Scrambles 'Near Cold War Record,'" BBC, April 16, 2015, http://www.bbc.com/news/world-asia-32330096.

[86] IISS, *The Military Balance 2015*, 260.

[87] Terje Langeland et al., "Lockheed Martin Wins Japan Order for 42 F-35 Fighter Planes," Bloomberg Business, December 20, 2011, http://www.bloomberg.com/news/articles/2011-12-20/lockheed-martin-wins-japan-jet-fighter-contract-over-boeing-eurofighter.

[88] "Boeing Delivers 4th KC-767 Tanker to Japan Ministry of Defense," Boeing, January 12, 2010, http://boeing.mediaroom.com/2010-01-12-Boeing-Delivers-4th-KC-767-Tanker-to-Japan-Ministry-of-Defense.

Japan has one of the world's best BMD capabilities. Spurred by the 1998 Taepodong launch from North Korea, Tokyo invested heavily in BMD, often working in close cooperation with the U.S. military. It continues to upgrade its Aegis BMD-capable destroyers, and plans to add two more for a total of six ships. The JASDF also operates six PAC-3 anti-missile batteries and is upgrading those systems as well, working with two U.S. X-band radar installations in Japan.[89]

Given the country's constitutional restrictions on the use of force, which will be discussed below, the JSDF has, for all intents and purposes, not been tested in battle since 1945. The actual warfighting capability of the JSDF is therefore unknown. The military has no combat experiences that would indicate the degree to which it can adapt and respond to adversity while maintaining battle-readiness. Of particular concern are Japan's ability to project power over extended periods of time, conduct operations on multiple fronts, and undertake joint operations. While the JSDF is gaining experience in basic power projection and jointness, it would be unrealistic to expect that the military could operate with the sophistication or at the tempo that it recognizes as needed in responding to Chinese or North Korean contingencies. Nonetheless, despite long-standing restraints on its use, the JSDF has gained significant noncombat operational experience both at home and abroad, indicating the degree to which national performance is improving in the military sphere.

Constitutional Limitations on the Use of Force

Japan's postwar constitution, written by U.S. occupation forces, is famous for its prohibition against the use of force, spelled out in Article 9.[90] While Tokyo has ignored the prohibition against having military forces, also in Article 9, it has hewn far more closely to the restrictions on overseas military activity. A later interpretation by the government instituted a ban on the exercise of collective self-defense, thereby isolating Japan from larger coalitions and partnerships that could have reintroduced Japanese military forces to cooperative action with other nations. For nearly 50 years after World War II, no Japanese troops were deployed outside Japan until the passage of the International Peace Cooperation Law in 1992, followed by the dispatch of limited numbers of Japanese forces on UN peacekeeping missions

---

[89] Paul Kallender-Umezu, "Japan to Focus on Atago, PAC-3 Upgrades," *Defense News*, November 18, 2014, http://archive.defensenews.com/article/20141118/DEFREG/311180044/Japan-Focus-Atago-PAC-3-Upgrades.

[90] "The Constitution of Japan," Prime Minister of Japan and His Cabinet website, http://japan.kantei.go.jp/constitution_and_government_of_japan/constitution_e.html.

to Cambodia, Rwanda, Mozambique, and the Golan Heights.[91] Not until 2003 was the JSDF deployed into an actual combat zone (in Iraq). But since the resumption of overseas military deployments in 1992, no Japanese combat troops have taken part in any military action.

Despite these restrictions, the JSDF has gained close to fifteen years of operational experience since 2001, due mainly to participation in the U.S.-led war on terrorism. The Japan Ground Self-Defense Force (JGSDF) sent reconstruction teams to Iraq and designated the Japan-Iraq Reconstruction and Support Group. From 2001 to 2008, the JMSDF conducted allied refueling operations in the Indian Ocean under the designated Operation Enduring Freedom–Maritime Interdiction Operation.[92] While none of the deployed military forces undertook a combat role, they gained invaluable experience from operating at distance from the Japanese homeland and in conjunction with the militaries of other nations.

Another milestone, both operationally and culturally, for the JSDF was the response to the March 2011 earthquake and tsunami. Within 48 hours of the catastrophe, 100,000 JGSDF troops—over 40% of the country's total military force—had been mobilized and deployed to the stricken region.[93] For the next weeks, they engaged in disaster-relief and rescue operations, often working side by side with U.S. troops. Operationally, the rapid and effective deployment of so many military personnel highlighted the professional nature and capabilities of the JSDF. From a cultural perspective, a military that for decades had been shunted to the side was instantly perceived as a powerful force for good and an integral part of society.[94]

Tokyo's New Realism

The changes in Japan's security environment over the past two decades—in particular, North Korea's improving missile capabilities and China's military modernization—have occasioned a generational shift in Japanese force planning and strategy. The threat of being held at risk by a rogue and aggressive totalitarian regime in Pyongyang spurred Tokyo to begin developing BMD systems and seek to deepen the alliance with

---

[91] "Participation by Japan in United Nations Peace-keeping Operations," Ministry of Foreign Affairs (Japan), 1995, http://www.mofa.go.jp/policy/economy/apec/1995/issue/info9.html.

[92] David Fouse, "Japan's Dispatch of the Ground Self-Defense Force to Iraq: Lessons Learned," Asia-Pacific Center for Security Studies, July 2007, http://www.apcss.org/Publications/Japan's%20Dispatch%20of%20the%20GSDF%20to%20Iraq.Fouse.doc.pdf.

[93] Kyle Mizokami, "Great Tohoku Earthquake: Military Movements," New Pacific Institute, Japan Security Watch, March 11, 2011, http://jsw.newpacificinstitute.org/?p=5267.

[94] Yuki Tatsumi, "Great Eastern Japan Earthquake: 'Lessons Learned' for Japanese Defense Policy," November 2012, 38, http://www.stimson.org/images/uploads/research-pdfs/Yuki_1.pdf.

Washington to incorporate "situations in areas surrounding Japan."[95] More worrisome from the long-term perspective is China's modernization of its military forces. As it became clear that Beijing was developing power-projection capabilities, Tokyo began to worry about both the potential threat to its outlying islands and the broader shift in the regional balance of power that could lead to China dominating crucial sea lanes of communication and access to the global commons.

These trends sparked debate in Japan over the appropriate future security strategy. Prime Minister Koizumi began the process of centralizing foreign policy decision-making inside the cabinet during his time in office in 2001–6, thereby removing this responsibility from the Foreign Ministry.[96] Under Koizumi, the goal of defending the homeland did not change, but the idea that Japan might need to become more involved in actively shaping the regional environment slowly entered the national discussion.

Koizumi's ideas were broadened and given fuller articulation during Abe's first stint as prime minister in 2006–7. Abe came up with an ideological argument that linked Japan's future security to closer cooperation with Asia's key democracies, including Australia and India.[97] During his year in office, Abe broached ideas about revising the country's ban on collective self-defense and drew up plans for a more integrated security strategy, including the formation of a U.S.-style NSC and centralized intelligence agency. Abe's sudden resignation in mid-2007 left these proposals in limbo, and they were all but ignored by his two LDP successors through 2009.

The recognition that Japan's security strategy was outdated crossed party lines. After the long-ruling LDP was ousted from power by the DPJ in 2009, early DPJ moves to reconsider certain alliance agreements with the United States led to significant strains on the alliance. However, the third DPJ premier, Yoshihiko Noda, made important changes in Japan's defense strategy, including the codification of a gradual shift away from a focus on defending the northeast to greater emphasis on the growing threat to Japan's southwestern islands.[98] Noda also indicated the direction that Japan would take to modernize its military by purchasing fifth-generation F-35 fighters from the United States and continuing to expand missile defense capabilities.

---

[95] "The Guidelines for Japan-U.S. Defense Cooperation," Ministry of Foreign Affairs (Japan), http://www.mofa.go.jp/region/n-america/us/security/guideline2.html.

[96] Daniel Kliman, *Japan's Security Strategy in the Post-9/11 World: Embracing a New Realpolitik* (Santa Barbara: Greenwood, 2006), 82.

[97] In 2007, Abe proposed the Quadrilateral Security Dialogue as a forum to develop security ties between Australia, India, Japan, and the United States.

[98] Chico Harlan, "With China's Rise, Japan Shifts to the Right," *Washington Post*, September 20, 2012, http://www.washingtonpost.com/world/asia_pacific/with-chinas-rise-japan-shifts-to-the-right/2012/09/20/2d5db3fe-ffe9-11e1-b257-e1c2b3548a4a_story.html.

Much of this agenda derived from new fears about China's intentions regarding the Senkaku Islands, which became the focal point of renewed tensions when Noda's government decided to nationalize several of the privately owned islands.

By the time Abe returned to power at the end of 2012, the stage was set for a revolution in Japan's security strategy. The conceptual framework was underpinned by what he called Japan's "proactive contribution to peace," or "proactive diplomacy."[99] Abe began by dusting off his plans for an NSC and a revision on the ban on security cooperation abroad. He also modestly increased Japan's defense budget, reversing a decade-long trend of declining spending on the military. Within one year of taking office, he established the NSC and published Japan's first national security strategy in December 2013.[100] The goal of the new strategy is to increase cooperation with the United States and seek to shape the security environment instead of simply responding to it. In addition, Tokyo formally shifted its defense focus away from the Kuril Islands and the northeast, where Russia has long been the major focus, and instead toward the southwest and the Ryukyu Island chain in the East China Sea, as part of a response to China's dramatic military modernization and increased assertiveness.

For the first time, Japan has attempted to rationalize its national security decision-making. The national security strategy now guides the National Defense Program Guidelines (NDPG), which in turn is translated into actual military procurement through the midterm defense plan. With the national security strategy prioritizing proactive defense and the necessity to "improve the international security environment," the 2014 NDPG calls for building a "comprehensive defense architecture," which not least of all will be aimed at defending Japan's outlying islands.[101] This includes maintaining sufficient surface-to-air and surface-to-ship missile capabilities "to prevent invasion of Japan's remote islands while still at sea, as far as possible," thereby requiring significant airborne warning and control and other ISR assets, along with targeting and tracking capabilities.[102] In addition, the NDPG stresses the capability to respond to so-called gray-zone contingencies that are not clear-cut cases of aggression against Japanese interests but that affect the

---

[99] Ministry of Foreign Affairs (Japan), "Overview: International Situation and Japan's Diplomacy in 2013," in *Diplomatic Bluebook 2014 Summary* (Tokyo, 2014), chap. 1, http://www.mofa.go.jp/policy/other/bluebook/2014/html/chapter1/japansdiplomacy.html.

[100] Ministry of Foreign Affairs (Japan), "National Security Strategy," December 17, 2013, http://japan.kantei.go.jp/96_abe/documents/2013/__icsFiles/afieldfile/2013/12/17/NSS.pdf.

[101] Prime Minister's Cabinet and National Security Council (Japan), "National Defense Program Guidelines for FY 2014 and Beyond," December 17, 2013, 5, 8, http://www.mod.go.jp/j/approach/agenda/guideline/2014/pdf/20131217_e2.pdf.

[102] Ibid., 22.

country's security.[103] These are scenarios that include actions short of war but where national power is used by aggressor states to intimidate other nations. Recognizing the demands this will put on the military, the NDPG calls for increasing the mission-capable rate of equipment and improving training and exercises.

The government has pursued these goals by investing in defense procurement programs for, among other items, new communications systems, satellites, and airborne ISR platforms, along with maintaining its commitment to upgrading BMD systems, purchasing F-35s, and procuring JMSDF destroyers and Aegis systems.[104] A particular focus in the national security strategy is on cybersecurity, given the dangers posed by the increasing number of cyberattacks, many undoubtedly coming from China and North Korea.[105] However, the NDPG's guidance on cyber issues remains vague as to how Japan would develop its capabilities. Overall, Japan's defense programs are ambitious and reflect the national resources of Asia's second-wealthiest nation. However, they still operate on the assumption that Japan's military forces will remain relatively middle-sized instead of expanding to a level more commensurate with the country's economic power. The ambitious plans also mean that capabilities are slowly, if steadily, being added and implemented, underscoring the long-term nature of Japan's military modernization.

Following through on Abe's controversial proposal to reinterpret the ban on collective self-defense, his cabinet in 2014 approved a plan for allowing the country to exercise its right to collective self-defense.[106] This was an important decision that will enable the JSDF to work more closely on security issues with allies and partners in Asia. However, in order to actualize expanded security activities abroad, the Diet must pass a complex set of enabling legislation. Abe submitted the first package of proposed laws in May 2015. Yet tight restrictions remain on when collective self-defense can be invoked, and limitations on other types of combat roles are still in force. Significant public opposition is slowing the passage of the required legislation and may indeed cause Abe to scale back some of his plans. Nonetheless, the ending of decades of blanket restrictions is propelling Japan into a new era in security activities.

---

[103] Prime Minister's Cabinet and National Security Council (Japan), "National Defense Program Guidelines for FY 2014 and Beyond," 7.

[104] Ministry of Defense (Japan), "Defense Programs and Budget of Japan: FY2015 Overview."

[105] Franz-Stefan Gady, "Japan Hit by Cyberattacks at an Unprecedented Level," *Diplomat*, February 20, 2015, http://thediplomat.com/2015/02/japan-hit-by-cyberattacks-at-an-unprecedented-level.

[106] Justin McCurry, "Japan PM to Overturn Pacifist Defense Policy," *Guardian*, June 30, 2014, http://www.theguardian.com/world/2014/jun/30/japan-pm-overturn-pacifist-defence-policy-shinzo-abe.

This reorientation of Japanese defense doctrine has been accompanied by a new realism. Abe has removed a decades-old ban on Japanese weapons exports, which will allow Japan to jointly produce and sell weapons with foreign partners and participate far more widely in the global defense market, thereby introducing new efficiencies into defense production.[107] Abe has moved quickly to take advantage of this new policy. He agreed to jointly develop submarine technologies with Australia in 2014, signed defense agreements with several Southeast Asian nations, approved the transfer of maritime patrol vessels to Vietnam and the Philippines, and revitalized security discussions with India, especially once Indian prime minster Narendra Modi took office.

Much of Japan's current and contemplated security activity takes place within the context of the U.S.-Japan alliance. First signed in 1960, the Mutual Security Treaty pledges U.S. support to Japan in case of armed attack.[108] As East Asia's security environment has evolved, however, the alliance has slowly adapted. Revisions to the alliance in 1997 incorporated security concerns over North Korea, and a second revision in 2015 focused on challenges emerging from China's rise, though without naming China as a threat.

The 2015 "Revised Guidelines" reflected the Abe administration's new security activism. The document included new cooperation on areas such as space and cybersecurity, reflected the spread of asymmetric methods of warfare, and emphasized the importance of increased ISR.[109] It also broadened the potential scope of the alliance by explicitly discussing the ways in which Japan might provide aid to a third party under attack, as well as in gray-zone situations.[110] The structure of the alliance mechanism was also upgraded in 2015, with the establishment of an alliance coordination mechanism and a commitment to increased cooperation in researching, developing, producing, and testing defense equipment and technology.[111] Increasing the colocation of commands means more information-sharing, similar situational awareness, and more integrated decision-making.

By any accounting, Japan maintains one of the premier militaries in Asia. Only China's military force combines greater size and capabilities, although Chinese forces are not as well trained. In terms of advanced capabilities,

---

[107] Martin Fackler, "Japan Ends Decades-Long Ban on Export of Weapons," *New York Times*, April 1, 2014, http://www.nytimes.com/2014/04/02/world/asia/japan-ends-half-century-ban-on-weapons-exports.html.

[108] For the full treaty, see "Japan-U.S. Security Treaty," Ministry of Foreign Affairs (Japan), http://www.mofa.go.jp/region/n-america/us/q&a/ref/1.html.

[109] "The Guidelines for Japan-U.S. Defense Cooperation," U.S. Department of Defense, April 27, 2015.

[110] Ibid.

[111] Ibid.

Japan is steadily moving up the value chain, putting it ahead of almost every other Asian military. While it remains defensively oriented, the JSDF is slowly pursuing power-projection capabilities that will allow it to play a larger role in Asia. Japan's ability to project power is slowly developing, and it is also exploring greater cyber and space activities. Although political restrictions have limited opportunities to gain operational experience, especially in the combat arena, as the JSDF modernizes it will become an increasingly important tool of national power. The greatest limitation on Japan's military will perhaps be its capacity, given the range of missions that Abe envisions. As a product of the cyclical interaction of national resources and national performance, the JSDF faces continual pressure to ensure the reservoir of funding, skills, and base capabilities in a tense regional environment. Yet it remains constrained by sociopolitical barriers to fuller expansion, implementation, and conceptualization of the role of military power in harnessing and protecting overall national power.

Conclusion

Since first embarking on a modernizing path in the last quarter of the nineteenth century, Japan has transformed itself into one of the world's most advanced nations. It became a major colonial power in the late nineteenth and early twentieth centuries and then rebuilt itself after World War II into the world's second-largest economy. Ethnic and linguistic unity helped mold a united, well-educated populace, and by focusing in the postwar years on its export economy, the country improved its standard of living to become one of the highest in Asia. As perhaps the United States' most important Asian ally, Japan assumed a role at the center of U.S. strategy in the region.

Japan's modern history shows how a relatively small nation with limited natural resources can nonetheless develop and deploy national power for various ends. From the late 1800s through 1945, Japanese policymakers focused largely, though not exclusively, on military expressions of national power. Since 1945, they have concentrated almost exclusively on the economic facet of national power. Now, however, the rise of China and a nuclear North Korea, among other concerns, are forcing yet another debate in Japan over the type of national power to pursue and how to attain it.

This third era of modern Japanese history will likely see a balanced approach to developing both postindustrial economic and military power. Recognizing that imbalanced investment is no longer possible in a middle-class society, Japanese policymakers will seek to revitalize the country's moribund economy so as to provide the opportunity for greater military power and political influence in Asia and beyond. Japan's strengths make such a policy feasible, though difficult. Its economy, while still struggling to recover from the popping of the asset bubble of the 1980s, remains the world's fourth-largest by purchasing power parity. Japan maintains an advanced high-tech sector and modern corporations that can compete globally. Its skilled labor force also means that industrial production is at the upper end of the value-added chain.

Yet Japanese leaders face significant challenges to ensuring a strong economy that can translate national resources into national power. Lack of competitiveness and innovation at home and a powerful regulatory state remain drags on economic activity. Energy production continues to be a major problem more than four years after the Fukushima nuclear disaster resulted in the government taking all of Japan's nuclear plants offline. Prime Minister Abe's economic policies offer the most coherent plan for economic revitalization but must be bolder in order to release entrepreneurial activities.

On the security front, political culture and public pacifism make it difficult for Japanese leaders to reform defense policy. Nonetheless, the steady modernization of the JSDF over the past two decades has made advances in responding to Asia's changing security environment. Japan has yet to fully divest itself of its postwar shackles, both constitutional and cultural, but it has moved toward far greater integration with the U.S. military and is now expanding its security partnerships abroad.

Japan's current capability, its future potential, and its hesitant evolution away from postwar restrictions are an increasingly important part of the Asia-Pacific security equation. For the United States, a Japan that is able to increase its national power so as to develop greater military capability will be an even greater asset in coming decades. No other Asian military can boast the diverse capabilities that Japan has or is in the process of procuring. Its ability to provide ISR and logistics to forces engaged in operations, to undertake maritime and aerial patrols over critical waterways or in tense areas, and to help train and even provision smaller Asian militaries would add tremendously to stability in Asia. As the United States' focus on the South China Sea grows, Washington may well ask Tokyo to fill any potential gaps in Northeast Asia in steady-state operations. As U.S. forces shrink in comparison to China's and as North Korea's nuclear capability grows, Japan's role as a military partner for the United States will become both more necessary and better understood. The question of Japan's ability to generate military capability and maximize its national performance will thus become one of greater importance.

Given the growth of tension between China and its neighbors, it appears that the security environment in Asia will continue to degrade in the short and medium term. Japan will feel more at risk from the uncertainty arising from an assertive China and will keenly watch for any signs that the United States is reconsidering its security presence in the Pacific. Given these uncertainties, Tokyo must consider whether its modest increases in defense budgeting are sufficient and contemplate the degree to which it can expand its power-projection capabilities. Doing so requires a melding of political will with economic performance. While concerns over Japan's security environment have moved the country far from its traditional postwar defense posture, whether the Abe administration will be willing to risk domestic political opposition by planning even more radical reforms remains an open question.

While Abe has become one of Japan's most controversial prime ministers, many of his policies reflect a long-term evolution in the country's security strategy. This evolution has been spurred by a combination of changes in the external environment and an inability to revitalize the economy to generate greater national power. Future Japanese governments may alter specific policies, but in the absence of fundamental change in China's actions or in the North Korean regime, it is likely that Abe's broad security reform program will remain intact. Public opinion that is wary of Abe's proposals is equally concerned about the growth of Chinese military power and the threat from North Korea. Ensuring a robust set of security relationships, a more comprehensive alliance with the United States, and updated security legislation to allow for overseas collective self-defense is the best way to guarantee that Japan is able to respond to a changing security environment in the coming decades. While that program will likely increase friction with China, and possibly South Korea, Abe has already taken advantage of Southeast Asia's growing concern over China and desire for new security partners. A Japan that is increasingly active in supporting Asia's open, rules-based order will find increasing regional support for its expanded role, though smaller nations will also be careful to avoid entrapment in a broader alliance with Tokyo.

On the economic side, there remains no credible alternative to Abe's economic reform platform, even though the liberalization he has promoted so far will likely take time to transform the system. A successful conclusion of the TPP will force further restructuring but will also tie Japan into a global trade agreement that will help reshape Pacific economic relations. Voices calling for a return to business as usual are increasingly isolated, given the challenge Japan faces in maintaining its economic position vis-à-vis competitors like South Korea and China. With the country's demographic decline already having commenced, planning for a potentially weaker Japan in another generation takes on even greater importance. The security reforms that Abe is proposing will require a strong economy and a mature industrial base, both of which can only come from greater economic liberalization and increased innovation and entrepreneurship.

Both of these long-term Japanese goals to increase national power enhance U.S. interests and policies in Asia. A vibrant, democratic Japan that can play a larger security role will be a more important ally. The ability to work in concert to maintain stability and uphold norms of conduct will allow Tokyo and Washington to have a greater influence on the shaping of Asia's security and political relationships. Similarly, with both the United States and Japan in the TPP, economic liberalization throughout the region will be given impetus. Tokyo and Washington will not agree completely on every issue; however, the community of interests that has bound the two countries together for the past 60 years serves as a bedrock for liberal values in Asia and will be strengthened by enhanced cooperation on economic and security issues. Washington should therefore not merely welcome Japan's attempts to increase its national power but do what it can through economic, political, and security cooperation to encourage Tokyo to hew to the path of greater reform, liberalization, and regional engagement.

What is little in doubt is that Japan has the greatest potential national power in Asia outside of China. While its national resources will remain taxed, Japan nonetheless can maximize those resources to advance goals that few other Asian nations can hope to achieve. Military capability is but one element of national performance, though an increasingly important one. Japan's desire to play a pivotal role in Asian security, not least due to its dependence on an open, rules-based trading order, calls for an expansion of its military capabilities and an embrace of a more proactive military stance abroad.

The logic of Japan's slow security reform over the past decade will likely lead it to take on ever-broader missions and add new capabilities. Isolationist voices may well try to hark back to a less complicated time when Japan could supposedly seal itself off from the world, but the reality of China's hegemonic intentions and North Korea's nuclear aspirations will prevent any revived isolationism from taking hold. Enhanced partnerships with the United States and Asian nations will further encourage Japan to play a larger role in the Asia-Pacific. Whether Japan lives up to its interests and potential will be a test of its ability to remain a powerful actor in the region and the world.

EXECUTIVE SUMMARY

This chapter provides a comprehensive analysis of the national capabilities of the Republic of Korea (ROK), assesses the outlook for its future development, and draws implications for the region and the U.S.

MAIN ARGUMENT

Commensurate with its rapid economic growth since the late 1960s, South Korea has made enormous strides in virtually all categories of hard power. The ROK has also been joined in a critical alliance with the U.S. since the end of the Korean War. Despite these achievements, however, South Korea faces core challenges heading into the late 2010s and beyond, such as a growing North Korean nuclear arsenal, a rapidly aging society with falling birthrates, rising social welfare costs, and a developmental state model that can no longer sustain higher rates of growth. Moreover, while the ROK remains focused on meeting a range of threats from North Korea, it must also take into consideration other major drivers such as China's increasingly robust and sophisticated power-projection and access-denial capabilities.

POLICY IMPLICATIONS

- Given both the country's rapidly changing demographic profile and the limitations of the developmental state model that was used to engineer its dramatic growth, South Korea needs to consider revising the so-called 1987 constitution and formulating a new "developmental consensus."

- To ensure that South Korea remains competitive economically, it should continue to strengthen the global trade regime through the implementation of existing free trade agreements and should support trade diversification, greater deregulation, and both defense and nondefense R&D.

- The ROK should shift the focus of its military reform strategy from structural changes to operational and managerial changes in order to enhance the military's ability to modernize its force, including through greater investments in command, control, communications, computers, intelligence, surveillance, and reconnaissance (C4ISR) capabilities and advanced precision-guided munitions.

Challenges to South Korean Power in the Early 21st Century

Chung Min Lee

Over the past half century, the Republic of Korea (ROK) has engineered a remarkable transformation that has enabled it to become Asia's fourth-largest economy and one of the world's most dynamic markets.[1] In 2014, South Korea's total trade volume was $1.17 trillion, and the nation ranked as the world's seventh-largest trading country.[2] By these and other indicators, South Korea has joined a relatively small group of states that possess an advanced economy, significant conventional military capabilities, a sizable population base, growing technological capacities, good governance, and a robust democracy. In essence, the ROK's membership in the G-20—the grouping of the world's top twenty industrialized powers—encapsulates the country's postwar journey.

Although numerous theories have accounted for South Korea's accelerated economic drive since the late 1960s, what stands out is the successful amalgamation of a government-led "developmental troika." Through this

Chung Min Lee is a Professor of International Relations in the Graduate School of International Studies at Yonsei University and a Nonresident Senior Associate at the Carnegie Endowment for International Peace. He can be reached at <chungminlee@runbox.com>.

[1] "Gross Domestic Product, PPP Based," World Bank, World Development Indicators, July 1, 2015, http://data.worldbank.org/data-catalog/GDP-PPP-based-table.

[2] Korea International Trade Association (KITA), "Suchul-ib chong-gwal" [General Management of Imports and Exports], K-Stat database, http://stat.kita.net/stat/kts/sum/SumImpExpTotalList. screen. According to WTO data based on 2013 figures, South Korea's total trade volume was $1.07 billion ($560 billion exports and $516 billion imports), which placed it as the world's seventh-largest exporter and ninth-largest importer. For more details, see *International Trade Statistics 2014* (Geneva: World Trade Organization, 2014), 28.

framework, the government acted as the principal architect, financier, and monitor of an export-driven industrialization policy; supported *chaebols* (family-run conglomerates) that spearheaded an economic turnaround; and, most importantly, harnessed the sheer industriousness of the Korean people, who were determined not to let endemic poverty become their national destiny.[3] Equally significant was the fact that South Korea succeeded despite five major obstacles: (1) a war-torn economy with only limited natural resources, (2) constant military threats, provocations, and challenges from North Korea, (3) a regional geopolitical environment characterized by historically dominant and, during various intervals, aggressive major powers, (4) weak political institutions and fractured administrative capabilities, and (5) virtually nonexistent scientific and technological know-how.

Nevertheless, South Korea's ability to retain strategic competitiveness and produce the requisite amount of national power over the next two to three decades will hinge on a range of political and strategic choices that the country must make. Foremost among them is whether the two dominant political parties—the conservative and currently ruling Saenuri (New Frontier) Party and the progressive New Politics Alliance for Democracy (NPAD)—can forge a new national development strategy. Specifically, the parties must move beyond the so-called 1987 framework, which was crafted to ensure basic democratic rule and firm civilian control over the armed forces rather than to make optimal public policy choices.[4]

Consonant with the central theme of this volume, this chapter provides a bird's-eye view of South Korea's national capabilities and traces the outlook for future development through four main sections: (1) a comprehensive assessment of South Korea's hard- and soft-power attributes, such as economic, technological, and educational assets, as well as related challenges, (2) an analysis of South Korea's national performance and global competitiveness, (3) a measurement of the ROK's military capabilities, including the role of U.S. forces in supporting and augmenting its deterrence and defense capabilities, and (4) a summary of key findings and policy implications for South Korea, the broader region, and the United States.

---

[3] Chaebols have come to dominate the South Korean economy since the 1960s, with Samsung, Hyundai, and LG being the best-known examples. While they have made major contributions to South Korea's economic development, greater corporate transparency and accountability to shareholders remain as core issues.

[4] Under the revised 1987 constitution, the president has considerable powers but is limited to a single five-year term in order to fundamentally block long-term presidencies. A strength of this system is that South Korea's democracy is vibrant and institutionalized with the military's firm acceptance of civilian control. A weakness is that every single president who has entered office since 1987 has wielded enormous power for the first two to three years but then rapidly become a lame duck. Thus, a major drawback of the five-year term is that even good policies have been shunted aside primarily for political reasons.

Evaluating South Korea's National Capabilities

Economics and Trade

In 1960, South Korea's nominal GNP was $2.97 billion with a per capita GNP of $155, which meant that it was one of the poorest countries in the world, on par with sub-Saharan African economies. By 2014, its nominal GDP had increased to $1.4 trillion ($1.77 trillion in purchasing power parity, or PPP, terms), with a per capita income—adjusted for PPP—of $35,400.[5] South Korea opted to export itself out of poverty: from the mid-1960s, its economic growth has depended critically on export earnings. The government targeted specific industries, and over time South Korea emerged as a global player in the production of electronics, automobiles, chemicals, and ships.[6] Based on decades of intensified exports, it has become one of the world's leading export powers, with a total trade volume in 2014 of $1.17 trillion ($628.0 billion in exports and $542.9 billion in imports).[7] The largest share of exports goes to China (including Hong Kong), and with the exception of the United States and Mexico, all the other top ten destinations for South Korean exports are in Asia (see **Figure 1**). Since 2000, South Korea has run a trade surplus in every year but 2008, when it registered a $13 billion trade deficit due to the outbreak of the global financial crisis.[8]

As it looks ahead, one key "blue ocean" opportunity that the government is targeting is defense exports. Beginning from a low base of only $144 million in arms exports in 2002, South Korea's defense exports rose to $3.6 billion in 2014.[9] According to the Defense Acquisition Program Administration, the main exporting arm of the defense ministry, South Korea hopes to increase defense exports to $10 billion by 2020. However, Japan lifted its self-imposed ban on arms exports in April 2015.

---

[5] Charles R. Frank Jr., Kwang Suk Lim, and Larry E. Westphal, "Economic Growth in South Korea Since World War II," in *Foreign Trade Regimes and Economic Development: South Korea*, ed. Charles R. Frank Jr., Kwang Suk Lim, and Larry E. Westphal (Washington, D.C.: National Bureau of Economic Research, 1975), 15; "Korea, South," in *The World Factbook* (Washington, D.C.: Central Intelligence Agency, 2015), https://www.cia.gov/library/publications/the-world-factbook/geos/ks.html; and "Korea: GDP per Capita," IndexMundi, http://www.indexmundi.com/facts/korea/gdp-per-capita.

[6] While these industries are still the backbone of the South Korean economy, the government has shifted attention to four emerging sectors for future growth: biotechnology, software development, high-tech communications, and comprehensive health services. See "Economic Overview," ANZ Business, http://www.anzbusiness.com/content/anz-superregional/countries/south-korea.html#overview.

[7] KITA, "Suchul-ib chong-gwal."

[8] Ibid.

[9] Joyce Lee and Tony Munroe, "South Korea Wants to Turn Its Arms Industry into an Export Powerhouse," *Business Insider*, April 22, 2015, http://www.businessinsider.com/r-south-korea-seeks-bigger-role-in-global-arms-bazaar-2015-4.

FIGURE 1   South Korea's top ten export destinations and percentage of total trade, 2014

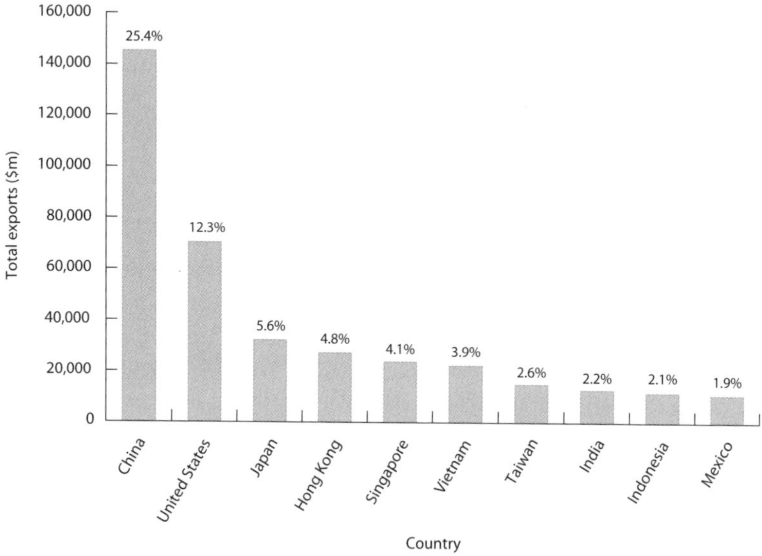

SOURCE: Korea International Trade Association, K-Stat database, 2015, http://stat.kita.net/stat/cstat/peri/ctr/CtrTotalList.screen.

Although Tokyo still bans arms exports to conflict-plagued countries, analysts expect Japanese defense firms to be very competitive in markets targeted by South Korea, such as Southeast Asia.[10]

For the past half century, the ROK has seldom veered off course from its relentless trajectory of export-driven growth, but this strategy has also increased vulnerabilities such as overreliance on the Chinese market. Moreover, ever since the Asian financial crisis of 1997–98 and the global recession of 2008, "transnational investors or the stock market, not the state bureaucracy, now seem to have attained the place of 'commanding heights' in the whole economy, turning the age of globalization into that of the post-developmental state in South Korea"[11] and coinciding with rising spending on social welfare.

---

[10] "Japan Lifts Own Blanket Arms Export Ban," *Defense News*, April 1, 2014, http://archive.defensenews.com/article/20140401/DEFREG03/304010013/Japan-Lifts-Own-Blanket-Arms-Export-Ban.

[11] Kyusook Um, Hyun-Chin Lim, and Suk-Man Hwang, "South Korea's Developmental State at a Crossroads: Disintegration or Re-emergence," *Korea Observer* 45, no. 2 (2014): 240–41.

South Korea's total budget in 2015 is $345 billion, with $106 billion earmarked for social welfare spending. As indicated in **Table 1**, social welfare spending accounted for 30.8% of the total budget, far higher than education ($48.7 billion, or 14.1% of the budget) and defense ($34.5 billion, or 10.0% of the budget).[12] In just five years, from 2005 to 2010, welfare spending rose from $14.2 billion (7.9% of the budget) to $74.5 billion (27.8% of the budget).[13] Nearly one-half of South Korea's annual budget, or 44.9%, is now spent on social welfare and education, compared with just 11.2% for defense, foreign relations, and unification affairs.

Because of South Korea's rapidly aging society, healthcare and social welfare, including retirement benefits, are projected to account for 55% of the central government's budget in 2020. South Korea will most likely be able to afford higher spending on social welfare over the next decade, but it will face growing financial pressures. For now, South Korea's national debt of $524 billion (35.7% of GDP) is considerably lower than Japan's, but if economic growth slows to 3% or less over the next ten to fifteen years, as most economists predict, South Korea will need to increase deficit spending.[14]

TABLE 1   Breakdown of South Korea's budget, 2005–15

Items	2005		2010		2015	
	$b (2014)	%	$b (2014)	%	$b (2014)	%
Welfare	14.2	7.9	74.5	27.8	106.2	30.8
Education	23.5	13.1	34.7	12.9	48.7	14.1
Culture	1.1	0.6	3.4	1.3	5.5	1.6
Environment	3.0	1.7	4.9	1.8	6.1	1.8
R&D	61.6	34.4	12.5	4.7	17.2	5.0
Defense	19.1	10.7	27.2	10.1	34.5	10.0
Foreign affairs	1.0	0.6	3.1	1.2	4.1	1.2

SOURCE: Ministry of Strategy and Finance (South Korea), Open Fiscal Data, 2015, available at http://www.openfiscaldata.go.kr/portal/service/openInfPage.do.

---

[12] Ministry of Strategy and Finance (South Korea), "2005–2015 Daehan Minguk joongang jeongbueui jopoyo yaesan hangmok-kwa yaesan-ek bijung" [Major Items in the Republic of Korea's Central Government Budget and Share of Total Budget], Open Fiscal Data, 2015, available at http://www.openfiscaldata.go.kr/portal/service/openInfPage.do.

[13] Ibid.

[14] Ministry of Strategy and Finance (South Korea), "Government Debt 2005–2015," http://www.index.go.kr/portal/main.EachDtlPageDetail.do?idx_cd=1106.

Although the country has taken a number of measures since the 1997–98 Asian financial crisis, such as boosting its foreign currency reserves to $362 billion (the sixth-largest in the world) as of April 2015, the government also continues to issue bonds to make up for incrementally declining tax revenues.

Science and Technology, R&D, and Higher Education

Over the past two decades, the South Korean government has invested heavily in information and communications technologies (ICT) as a key area for future growth. According to *The Global Information Technology Report 2014*, South Korea now ranks tenth in the world on the Networked Readiness Index, which measures each country's network regulatory environment, infrastructure and digital content, public and private sector usage, and socioeconomic impacts.[15] While data on Internet use changes constantly, 91.5% of South Korea's 50 million people have access to the Internet,[16] and in 2013 the ROK ranked fifth in broadband subscribers (37.5%) and first on the E-Government Readiness Index.[17] South Korea ranked 43rd in mobile telephone subscribers in 2012, with 1,094 mobile phones per 1,000 persons;[18] according to the Ministry of Science, ICT and Future Planning, the country registered 3.8 million new mobile phone subscribers in 2014.[19] In 2009, there were 810,000 smartphone users, but the number jumped to 36 million in 2014 (72% of the population).[20]

One of the most significant developments in the field of science and technology has been in intellectual property (IP). In 1999, South Korea filed 200,378 IP applications (80,642 patents, 87,332 trademarks, and 32,404 industrial designs), whereas in 2013 it filed 419,196 applications (204,589 patents, 147,667 trademarks, and 66,940 industrial designs), which was the fourth-highest total in the world (see **Table 2**).[21] South Korea also now has the fourth-highest number of patents in force, having increased

---

[15] Beñat Bilbao-Osorio, Soumitra Dutta, and Bruno Lanvin, eds., *The Global Information Technology Report 2014* (Zurich: World Economic Forum and INSEAD, 2014), 169.

[16] "Internet Users by Country (2014)," Internet Live Stats, http://www.internetlivestats.com/internet-users-by-country.

[17] Institute of International Trade (South Korea), "2014 segyesokeeui Daehan Minguk" [The Republic of Korea in the World in 2014], 59–60.

[18] Ibid., 61.

[19] Korea Internet Security Agency, *Korea Internet Statistics 2014: Trends in Smartphone Subscribers* (Seoul, 2014), 56.

[20] Kim Kuk-be, "Kukga jeonbohwa 20nyeon ICTga bakun ilsandeul" [Daily Life Changes Twenty Years after the Beginning of the National Informatization Drive], iNews 24, December 4, 2014.

[21] World Intellectual Property Organization (WIPO), "Statistical Country Profiles, Republic of Korea," http://www.wipo.int/ipstats/en/statistics/country_profile/profile.jsp?code=KR.

sharply from 331,437 in 2004 to 812,595 in 2013.[22] Unsurprisingly, the fields of technology with the most patent applications correspond closely with South Korea's leading industries, such as semiconductors, audio-visual technology, electrical machinery, telecommunications, digital communication, and civil engineering (see **Figure 2**).

TABLE 2   Filed IP applications and economic growth, 1999–2013

Year	Patents	Trademarks	Industrial designs	GDP ($b)
1999	80,642	87,332	32,404	896
2004	140,115	108,464	41,184	1,183
2009	170,233	134,531	68,903	1,412
2013	204,589	147,667	66,940	1,642

SOURCE: Korea Intellectual Property Office, "2014 Annual Report," September 24, 2014, http://www.kipo.go.kr/kpo/user.tdf?a=user.html.HtmlApp&c=3041&catmenu=m02_05_01.

FIGURE 2   South Korea's patent applications by technologies, 1999–2013

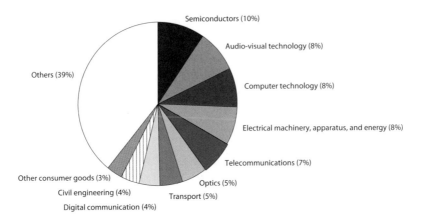

SOURCE: World Intellectual Property Organization, "Statistical Country Profiles: Republic of Korea," 2015, http://www.wipo.int/ipstats/en/statistics/country_profile/profile.jsp?code=KR.

---

[22] WIPO, "Statistical Country Profiles, Republic of Korea."

Another critical ingredient in South Korea's rapid economic development was its unprecedented and overriding commitment to education at all levels. In 2014, 96.4% of eligible students were enrolled in primary school, 97.7% in middle school, 93.7% in high school, and 68.2% in colleges or universities.[23] A 2012 report on education investments from the Organisation for Economic Co-operation and Development (OECD) estimated the average total spending on education by OECD countries at 6.7% of GDP in 2009, whereas South Korea spent 7.9%.[24] One of the major differences in South Korea's educational policy is the critical role of private funding. For example, in 2012 the total share of private sources of early childhood education was 48% in South Korea, whereas the OECD average was only 18%.[25] However, a pervasive side effect of this trend is the proliferation of private academies that focus nearly exclusively on preparing students for intensive college exams. These private institutions have proliferated to the extent that the quality of public sector schools has suffered, widening the "educational opportunity gap." Overall, South Korea's total public expenditure on education as a percentage of GDP rose from 6.1% in 2000 to 7.6% in 2010, while the percentage of total public expenditure remained relatively consistent at 16.6% in 2000 and 16.2% in 2010.[26] Moreover, according to the OECD, South Korea's R&D spending as a percentage of GDP was the second-highest in the OECD at 4.1%, or $64.70 billion ($48.94 billion in the private sector and $14.76 billion in the public sector).[27]

Natural Resources

South Korea is the world's seventh-highest consumer of energy, with total energy consumption of 277 million tons of oil equivalent in 2014. The country imports 95.7% of its oil and liquefied natural gas (LNG) from abroad, with 86% coming from the Middle East and Persian Gulf states, including Saudi Arabia, Kuwait, Qatar, Iraq, and the United Arab Emirates.[28]

---

[23] Statistics Korea, "Bumunbyeoljipyo: Chwihaglyul mich jinhaglyul" [School Enrollment and Entrance Rate], http://www.index.go.kr/potal/main/EachDtlPageDetail.do?idx_cd=1520.

[24] Organisation for Economic Co-operation and Development (OECD), "What Share of National Wealth Is Spent on Education?" in Education at a Glance 2012: Highlights (Paris: OECD Publishing, 2012), http://dx.doi.org/10.1787/eag_highlights-2012-18-en.

[25] OECD, "Education at a Glance 2013, Country Note: Korea," 2013, http://www.oecd.org/edu/Korea_EAG2013%20Country%20Note.pdf.

[26] Ibid.

[27] OECD, "Gross Domestic Expenditure on R&D by Sector of Performance and Source of Funds," OECD.Stat, http://stats.oecd.org/Index.aspx?DataSetCode=GERD_FUNDS.

[28] "Global Energy Statistical Yearbook 2015, Total Energy Consumption 2014," Enerdata, https://yearbook.enerdata.net; and Daehan Minguk enoejee pyulram 2014 [2014 Korea Energy Handbook] (Seoul: Korea Energy Agency, 2014), 3.

Oil constitutes the largest share of South Korea's energy supply (38.1%), followed by bituminous coal (27.0%), LNG (18.0%), nuclear energy (11.4%), and other energy sources (5.5%). Although South Korea is a net importer of energy, refined oil products have emerged as a growing source of exports.[29] Commensurate with Asia's rapid economic development, the world's top five oil importers after the United States are all in Asia. This means that South Korea has to compete with Japan and China not only on key exports such as automobiles, ships, and consumer electronics but also for critical energy imports such as oil and natural gas. Although concerns increased after the Fukushima Daiichi nuclear disaster in March 2011, South Korea remains firmly committed to nuclear energy, and its 24 reactors provide about one-third of its electricity needs, or 21.6 gigawatt electric (GWe). Plans are underway to increase capacity by 70% to 37 GWe by 2029.[30]

With very limited natural resources, South Korea is also heavily dependent on imports of major strategic minerals such as bituminous coal, iron ore, copper, uranium, nickel, and rare earth minerals. In particular, South Korea needs rare metals for its heavy machinery, chemical, and electronics industries, with China supplying 19% of South Korea's rare metals, followed by Japan (14%), South Africa (9%), the United States (9%), Germany (5%), and Australia (5%).[31]

South Korea's critical reliance on imported energy and key strategic minerals is a source of vulnerability. The country has no choice, however, but to continue working to mitigate such risks. In addition to adroit energy diplomacy, South Korea will need to sustain its advanced nuclear energy grid with higher safety mechanisms and expand the service sector to reduce its dependence on imported energy sources and strategic minerals to the extent possible.

Assessing National Performance

Winning the Inter-Korean Contest

As the South Korean economy grew at an average rate of 11% per annum in the 1980s and 1990s, the economic gap between South and North Korea

---

[29] *Daehan Minguk enoejee pyulram 2014*, 6.

[30] "Nuclear Power in South Korea," World Nuclear Association, July 22, 2015, http://www.world-nuclear.org/info/Country-Profiles/Countries-O-S/South-Korea/.

[31] Kim Yu Jeong and Lee Hwa Suk, "Gukne heeyu gemsok soogeup kujo bunseok yeongu" [Analysis of Structure in the Domestic Supply and Demand of Raw Materials and Rare Metals], *Journal of Korean Institute of Resources Recycling* 23, no. 3 (2014): 59.

became irreversible.[32] The notable exception where North Korea has surpassed South Korea is in military capabilities, in particular with respect to asymmetric warfare, including nuclear weapons. Nevertheless, if one compares South and North Korea in terms of aggregate power, there is no doubt that the South had won the economic competition by the mid-1970s. Since then, the economic and technological gap between the Koreas has grown to the point where it is virtually impossible to foresee a scenario where North Korea could catch up with the South. As can be seen in **Table 3**, the biggest difference in the overall power balance between the two Koreas is South Korea's extensive linkages with the global economy and a very advanced manufacturing base that has enabled it to become one of the world's top trading powers. This situation contrasts with North Korea's nearly total dependence on limited trade with China. Moreover, South Korea leads North Korea in every category of human development. Despite North Korea's incessant propaganda that the South

TABLE 3 The national capabilities of the two Koreas

	South Korea	North Korea
Population	50 million	24.8 million
GDP (PPP)	$1.7 trillion (2014)	$40 billion (2012 estimate)
Human Development Index	0.891 (15th in the world)	N/A
GDP per capita (PPP)	$33,000 (2014)	$1,800 (2011 estimate)
Exports	$628 billion	$3.9 billion
Imports	$542 billion	$4.8 billion
Internet penetration rate/ wireless access	81%/100%	N/A
Mobile phone subscribers	57 million (2014)	4–5 million (2013 estimate)
Armed forces	667,000	1.1 million
Defense budget	$36 billion	$8.2 billion

SOURCE: "Korea, South," in *The World Factbook* (Washington, D.C.: Central Intelligence Agency, 2015); "Korea, North," *The World Factbook*; Stockholm International Peace Research Institute (SIPRI), SIPRI Military Expenditure Database, 2015, http://www.sipri.org/research/armaments/milex/milex_database; and Ministry of Science, ICT and Future Planning (South Korea), *2014 Nyun inteonet eeyong shiltae josa yoyak bogoseo* [2014 Summary Report on Internet Usage] (Seoul, 2014), 2.

---

[32] Jaymin Lee, "A Half Century of Korean Economic Development," *Korean Economic Review* 18 (2002): 396–406, 425; and Marcus Noland, "Six Markets to Watch: South Korea," *Foreign Affairs*, January/February 2014, 17–22.

continues to live in poverty, a growing percentage of North Koreans are aware of South Korea's advanced economy through watching pirated movies and dramas and surreptitiously listening to South Korean radio.

After the end of the Cold War, North Korea's only real economic patron was China. This trend has continued, particularly in the aftermath of the imposition of UN and other multilateral sanctions owing to North Korea's nuclear and WMD programs. According to data compiled by the Korea Trade-Investment Promotion Agency, Sino–North Korean trade accounted for 89% of North Korea's total trade volume of $7.3 billion in 2013.[33] North Korea continues to face a trade deficit given its reliance on energy imports, while its top exports are natural resources, which constituted 58.8% of total trade in 2013.[34]

As a result of this widening economic gap, even though South Korea continues to perceive North Korea as a critical security threat, it no longer sees the need to compete with North Korea in the international arena. This in turn has enabled the ROK to expand its international role, including by increasing its overseas development assistance contributions, supporting UN peacekeeping operations, and becoming a conduit for green growth (such as the decision to host the Green Climate Fund in South Korea).

South Korea's Global Competitiveness

South Korea has become incrementally more competitive both regionally and internationally over several decades. According to the *IMD World Competitiveness Yearbook 2014*, it ranked 26th in global competitiveness in 2014, slightly down from 22nd the previous year. With respect to economic competitiveness, however, South Korea ranked 8th overall in 2014, ahead of both Japan (17th) and China (20th), and 12th in terms of maintaining an environment that encouraged business development.[35]

In terms of technology and innovation, South Korea was ranked first in the 2014 Bloomberg Global Innovation Index, based on a composite score of R&D capability, productivity, technology intensity, and patent activity. *Forbes* reported in February 2014 that five factors accounted for South Korea's rise as a new start-up powerhouse: (1) leadership in patent activity, with a particular edge in ICT, (2) broadband penetration and speed, (3) success in manufacturing and exporting cutting-edge electronics products, (4) growing

---

[33] Korea Trade-Investment Promotion Agency, "2013 Bukhan daewae muyeok dongyang" [North Korea's Foreign Trade Trends in 2013], Report, no. 14-07, July 2014, 1, http://openknowledge.kotra. or.kr/handle/2014.oak/3917.

[34] Ibid.

[35] *IMD World Competitiveness Yearbook 2014* (Lausanne: IMD, 2014), http://www.imd.org/news/2014-World-Competitiveness.cfm.

entrepreneurship by young technologists who are willing to assume risks to expand regionally and globally, and (5) increasing interest from overseas venture capitalists in the South Korean venture ecosystem.[36] Likewise, South Korea ranked seventh, behind only the United States, Switzerland, Japan, Germany, Sweden, and the Netherlands, in the 2014 Composite Science and Technology Innovation Index comparing 30 OECD countries.[37]

In relative terms, a report by the Ministry of Science, ICT and Future Planning and the Korea Institute of Science and Technology Evaluation and Planning noted that South Korea's level of science and technology was 78.8% that of the United States. Seen from the perspective of ten major fields, South Korea's level was estimated at 84.3% in industrial manufacturing and 83.2% in ICT, whereas it was 68.8% in aviation and aerospace—significantly lower than China's 81.9%.[38] At the same time, the report noted that in contrast with the United States, where 29.3% of science and technological capabilities were deemed to be based on resources (for example, human capital, patents, and leading global firms), South Korea's resource potential stood at 14.4%.[39]

What comes out very clearly in reviewing South Korea's remarkable economic and technological progress over the past three to four decades is the success of the developmental state strategy and the premium that the government placed on enhancing South Korea's hard-power capabilities. According to one recent measurement of national power developed by the Hansun Foundation for Happiness and Freedom, South Korea in 2014 ranked ninth among the G-20 countries in terms of cumulative power. What makes the Hansun Total National Power Index unique is that it defines "total national power" as "a country's ability to transform specific national goals and visions into policies and strategies and *if necessary, the ability also to cooperate with or to receive support from other countries*" (emphasis

---

[36] Alan McGlade, "Why South Korea Will Be the Next Global Hub for Tech Startups," *Forbes*, February 6, 2014, http://www.forbes.com/sites/alanmcglade/2014/02/06/why-south-korea-will-be-the-next-global-hub-for-tech-startups.

[37] Ministry of Science, ICT and Future Planning (South Korea) and Korea Institute of Science and Technology Evaluation and Planning (KISTEP), "2014 nyeon guk-ga kwahak kisul hyukshin yeokryang pyung-ka" [2014 Composite Science and Technology Innovation Index], March 2015, 20.

[38] Ibid., 17.

[39] Ibid., 4.

added).⁴⁰ **Table 4** presents the 2014 rankings for the United States, China, the United Kingdom, Germany, France, Japan, South Korea, India, Russia, Mexico, and Indonesia.

To be sure, as much as these and similar rankings attempt to provide an accurate measurement of a country's national capabilities, many variables are at play with widely divergent assumptions. Thus, these rankings should be taken as "relative snapshots."⁴¹ The 2014 data showed that South Korea's

TABLE 4   The Hansun Total National Power Index, 2014

Country	Cumulative power		Hard power		Soft power	
	Score	Rank	Score	Rank	Score	Rank
United States	68.3	1	43.9	1	24.5	1
China	55.9	2	35.3	2	20.7	7
United Kingdom	53.6	3	30.7	5	22.8	2
Germany	53.2	4	30.9	4	22.3	3
France	52.0	7	30.4	6	21.7	6
Japan	51.5	8	31.7	3	19.8	8
South Korea	48.4	9	29.4	10	19.0	11
India	48.0	11	28.6	13	19.5	9
Russia	46.5	13	30.1	8	16.4	19
Mexico	45.8	14	29.4	10	19.0	11
Indonesia	44.1	18	26.6	17	17.4	17

SOURCE: Hansun Foundation for Happiness and Freedom, "2014 Hansun jonghap gukryeok jisu bunseok kyulkwa" [Assessment of Findings, the 2014 Hansun Total National Power Index], 2014.

---

⁴⁰ The Hansun Total National Power Index is based on a cumulative assessment of six hard-power variables with corresponding relative weights in percentages (defense, 10%; economic, 20%; education, 5%; science and technology, 10%; information, 5%; and environmental management, 5%) and six soft-power variables (state management, 5%; political, 10%; diplomatic, 10%; cultural, 5%; social infrastructure, 5%; change management, 5%), along with "foundations of national power," such as territory, natural resources and food supplies, and population, that together constitute 5%. The first index was released in 2008 and the second was published five years later in February 2014. For the full index, see Hansun Foundation for Happiness and Freedom, "2014 Hansun jonghap gukryeok jisu bunseok kyulkwa" [Assessment of Findings, the 2014 Hansun Total National Power Index], 2014, 18.

⁴¹ According to the 2014 Hansun Total National Power Index, South Korea made the greatest improvements in the area of change management (10th to 6th), environmental management (15th to 11th), defense (8th to 5th), information (11th to 9th), economics (11th to 10th), education (11th to 10th), and state management (10th to 9th). The areas where it registered a downturn were political (14th to 15th) and foundations of national power (13th to 14th).

hard power continued to be more significant than its soft power, evinced by the fact that it moved up to ninth from fourteenth in 2008 on the basis of improved scores on defense, change management, and science and technology. Importantly, however, political, social infrastructure, foundations of national power, cultural, and diplomatic capabilities declined slightly from the 2008 assessments.[42] IHS's 2014 country report for South Korea provided a fairly similar assessment. The report estimated that South Korea's average economic growth from 2015 to 2019 will likely be 3.2% and that its nominal GDP of $1.41 trillion in 2015 will increase to $1.83 trillion in 2019, with per capita income rising from $28,536 in 2015 to $36,209 in 2019.[43] However, the IHS report noted several weaknesses: "South Korea is politically stable, but party politics continue to be volatile despite the maturation of the country's democracy. The lack of transparency among the country's main conglomerates (chaebols) is exacerbated by a business culture in which decisions are at times guided by personal ties rather than commercial considerations."[44]

Looking ahead, a key factor that will affect South Korea's longer-term economic well-being and international competitiveness is the country's changing demographics. As one of Asia's most rapidly aging societies, and with one of the lowest birth rates, South Korea is expected to experience a net population decline from the 2020s onward that will affect its ability to produce and maintain core national capabilities. Although the full effect of these negative demographic drivers will not be known until the 2030s and 2040s, South Korea's continued economic success will depend critically on its ability to mitigate and ameliorate the worst consequences of progressively worsening demographic trends.

South Korea's Demographic Future: Population Projections into 2050–60

Despite having achieved one of the world's most impressive postwar economic transformations, South Korea's—or even a unified Korea's—future competitiveness and ability to remain a major Asian economic powerhouse will depend heavily on overcoming negative demographic trends (see **Figure 3**). South Korea's population is expected to reach a peak of 52 million in 2030 before rapidly dropping to 43 million in 2060 based on medium population growth projections. Using lower growth projections,

---

[42] Hansun Foundation for Happiness and Freedom, "2014 Hansun jonghap gukryeok jisu bunseok kyulkwa," 20–21.

[43] IHS, "Country Reports—Republic of Korea," Economics and Country Risk, April 30, 2015, 2.

[44] Ibid., 15.

FIGURE 3   South Korea's population projections, 2010–60

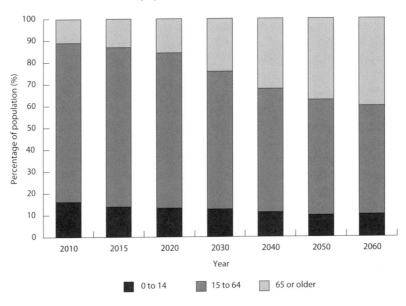

SOURCE: Statistics Korea, 2015, https://www.index.go.kr/potal/enaraIdx/idxField/userPageCh.do.

the population declines even more sharply to 34 million in 2060.[45] In 2010, South Korea's population growth rate was only 0.46%, and it is expected to fall to 0.28% in 2020. The growth rate will be negative from 2031 onward, and by 2060 it will be -1.0%.[46] South Korea's economically active labor force will decline from 2016 after reaching a height of 37 million (or 72.9% of the total population), and those in the 15–64 age bracket will fall to 21 million by 2060 (just 49.7% of the total population).[47]

Equally worrisome is the fact that the total number of the aged population (65 years and older) will surpass the population of infants and children in 2017 and is projected to increase twofold in 2030 and fourfold in 2060. In such a scenario, every ten economically active persons will be responsible

[45] Tong-gye Cheong, "Jangrae inguchoogye mit koryungwha inkoo, 2010–2060" [Statistics Korea, Longer-Term Population Projections and Aging Population, 2010–2060], December 7, 2011, 1–2.

[46] Ibid.

[47] Ibid.

for taking care of ten other persons (eight elderly and two children).[48] To be sure, key preventive steps could be taken to ameliorate this trend, including immigration, mandatory regulations for providing childcare facilities in the workplace, more favorable tax rebates, and educational benefits for parents who have two or more children. Moreover, while the population growth rate is slated to fall to zero over the next fifteen years, the labor force is currently growing twice as fast as the general population at approximately 1% per year, enabling South Korea to remain economically competitive for the foreseeable future. An April 2015 IHS report noted that "even after the population peaks, the labor force will continue to grow for another ten years. This means that GDP growth will not be constrained by a lack of workers for the next two decades. Only in the very long term, after 2030, will growth rates move toward the 1% level."[49]

Nevertheless, even though the government may be able to implement stop-gap measures, these policies are unlikely to fundamentally alter South Korea's very low fertility rate. This trend is being driven by, among other factors, ballooning household debt from mortgage payments (up to 25% of household income) and child education (on average 10% of income). The latter, in particular, has emerged as a major deterrent against having more children.[50] For example, South Korean parents spent $18 billion in 2013—the highest per capita amount in the world—to send their children to various private institutions (known as "cram schools" in South Korea) in order to ensure entrance into top universities.[51]

Coping with Declining Military Manpower

South Korea's accelerated aging and falling birthrates are not just a social issue, however. These demographic trends are also emerging as a national security threat and have already begun to affect how much manpower the military can count on into the 2020s and 2030s. According to the Korean Social Welfare Institute, South Korea will face a military manpower shortage of 8,000 in 2020, 84,000 in 2030, and 120,000 in 2050.[52] The ROK military

---

[48] Cheong, "Jangrae inguchoogye mit koryungwha inkoo, 2010–2060."

[49] IHS, "Country Reports—Republic of Korea," 5.

[50] Danny Leipziger, "South Korea's Japanese Mirror," *Diplomat*, February 6, 2014, http://thediplomat.com/2014/02/south-koreas-japanese-mirror.

[51] Jeyup S. Kwaak, "South Korea's $18 Billion Education Problem," *Wall Street Journal*, Korea Real Time, August 28, 2014, http://blogs.wsj.com/korearealtime/2014/08/28/south-koreas-18-billion-education-problem.

[52] Kim Seung Seon, "2030nyeon byeonglyeogjawon 8manmyeong bujog…jeonmunga jagjeongyehoeg bakkwoya" [Military Manpower Faces 80,000 Shortfall in 2030…Officials Must Alter Operational Plan], News1, January 16, 2015.

must contend with two parallel issues: a sharp decline in available conscripts and the need to downsize its armed forces without hindering key military objectives in the case of a major crisis on the Korean Peninsula that may require intensive stabilization operations.

The basic pool of young men eligible for the 21-month military duty has been declining since the early 2000s. From 1977 to 2002, some 400,000 young men were annually eligible for conscription. This enabled the ROK military to maintain a force structure of some 690,000 troops.[53] When the Roh Moo-hyun administration introduced the Defense Reform Plan 2020 in 2005, the goal was to set comprehensive defense reforms that would enable the ROK armed forces to achieve four key goals: (1) transition from a troop-intensive force to one driven by a revolution in military affairs (RMA), (2) streamline the 690,000-strong forces down to approximately 520,000 by 2020 (from 47 active and reserve army divisions to 28 divisions), (3) significantly upgrade, modernize, or replace outdated weapons systems, including aging combat aircraft and ground forces through an annual 10% increase in the defense budget, and (4) allow the ROK to assume the leading role in peninsular defense by transferring wartime operational control (OPCON) to the ROK forces from the U.S.-ROK Combined Forces Command.[54]

Since the late 1980s, each incoming administration has announced major military reforms, but none has left office with major achievements. The obstacles to implementing such reforms include a combination of entrenched bureaucratic resistance by the armed forces and the Ministry of Defense (MND), contrasting priorities by incoming administrations that often have diluted or replaced previous reform programs, perceived political costs by the civilian leadership in the event of overemphasizing military reforms, and a lack of time and political capital to oversee comprehensive reforms in a single five-year presidential term. Although the Park Geun-hye administration had pledged to increase defense spending over the next several years, annual increases have fallen below the 8.8% mark that has been considered a key budgetary baseline since the early 2000s. Owing to rising social welfare costs, the military budget only constitutes 10% of the central government's budget and is unlikely to increase significantly in the years ahead.

---

[53] Bruce W. Bennett, "The Korean Defense Reform 307 Plan," Asan Institute for Policy Studies, Issue Brief, no. 8, April 18, 2011, http://en.asaninst.org/contents/issue-brief-no-8-the-korean-defense-reform-307-plan-by-bruce-w-bennett-the-rand-corporation1.

[54] Kim Dong Hwan, "Yeokdae jeongbu-eui kunkujo kaepyun kyehwek-kwa jeongchek-jeok jameui" [Previous Governments' Military Structure Reforms Plans and Policy Implications], *Kukka Jeolryak* 17, no. 1 (2001): 72–74.

South Korea's Transformational Capacity

South Korea's ability to undertake key reforms needed to produce and maintain requisite national capabilities well into the mid-21st century depends mostly on political will rather than lack of early warning, as evinced by the clear challenges posed by rapidly shifting demographic dynamics. Ever since South Korea adopted an export-driven growth strategy in the mid to late 1960s, the key to accelerated economic growth, military modernization, and growing linkages with the international community has been a persistent developmental state strategy that was, for the most part, embraced by both the private sector and the public. South Korea's ability to focus like a laser on accelerated economic growth and make a more self-reliant military was premised on two national goals that superseded all others: extricating the country from generations of poverty and strengthening its military capabilities to meet a growing spectrum of threats from North Korea. Virtually every facet of South Korean society, including educational institutions, chaebols, small- and medium-sized enterprises (SME), civic groups and organizations, and national and local media, was pressed to offer direct and indirect assistance to South Korea's exporting endeavors. The desire to outperform its enemy, North Korea, at all levels of national development was a critical incentive, along with a yearning to catch up with Japan—Korea's former colonial ruler and Asia's most advanced and powerful economy at the time.

As South Korea looks toward the 2020s and beyond, however, maintaining its success will require a new social contract with matching political reforms to balance economic growth and expanding social welfare needs and a much more bipartisan foreign policy to meet an array of unparalleled geopolitical challenges. In addition, South Korea must build the foundations of a truly multicultural society owing to the following developments. First, as a rapidly maturing, advanced economy, its growth rates are likely to remain between 2% and 3% over the next ten to fifteen years, which means that state-driven growth is no longer possible. Instead, South Korea must further deregulate its economy—not only to attract more FDI but also to streamline tax codes to enable SMEs to develop new technologies, expand the service sector and service-related exports, and maintain a qualitative edge over rapidly growing emerging economies. Second, the range of new geopolitical and economic challenges that South Korea is likely to face in the next 20–30 years will call for much more intensive and open collaboration networks between the government, private sector, and academia. This will require a major shift in South Korea's education system that balances core foundational skills with creativity, innovation, and out-of-the-box thinking. Third, South Korea needs to continue to stress the critical importance of foreign languages and multicultural interactions, not only to enhance its international competitiveness but also to enable Korean society to become much more welcoming and amenable to wider immigration, given the expected decline in the population base.

South Korea's Current Military Capabilities

Over the past half century, the South Korean armed forces have grown into one of Asia's, if not the world's, most capable militaries, with a very high degree of interoperability with U.S. forces. Since the early 1990s, the ROK military has also adapted its own version of RMA upgrades. Over the years, South Korea has invested significantly in augmenting its command, control, communications, computers, intelligence, surveillance, and reconnaissance (C4ISR) capabilities, including airborne warning and control systems, asymmetrical counterattack assets such as advanced precision-guided munitions, the incremental replacement of aged combat aircraft with F-15s and F-35s, and stronger naval capabilities such as the setting up of a separate submarine command. Nonetheless, as one analyst has noted, "the compelling and relatively ambitious character of Korean RMA-oriented defense plans have been in sharp contrast to the prevailing structural and political realities coupled with historical legacies that have sustained the relevance of traditional security concepts and operational conduct."[55] As the ROK military looks toward the horizon, however, it faces three principal challenges.

First, the most urgent challenge lies in coping with the asymmetric threat posed by North Korea, particularly its nuclear weapons capabilities. Efforts to combat this threat must include measures to enhance extended-deterrence capabilities on the part of the United States, improve South Korea's missile defense capabilities in conjunction with more advanced counter-ballistic missile assets, and upgrade the ROK armed forces' C4ISR capabilities. Second, the ROK must improve its ability to cope with a range of potential nonlinear developments in North Korea such as regime collapse, prolonged political-military instability, and a variety of low-intensity conflict scenarios. While the U.S. Forces Korea (USFK) and the U.S. military overall have prepared for major war contingencies on the Korean Peninsula since the end of the Korean War, tactics and strategies related to military operations other than war on the peninsula have only been refined since the late 1990s. Third, although the ROK military is focused heavily on peninsular operations, it also needs to prepare for very different regional strategic dynamics, the foremost being

---

[55] Michael Raska, "RMA Diffusion Paths and Patterns in South Korea's Military Modernization," *Korean Journal of Defense Analysis* 23, no. 3 (2011): 374.

the People's Liberation Army's rapidly accelerating power-projection as well as anti-access/area-denial capabilities in Northeast Asia. At the same time, two major domestic obstacles discussed in the preceding sections will complicate efforts to address these security challenges: the progressive decline in military manpower and the growing budgetary competition created by the accelerated rise in South Korea's social welfare budget.

Meeting North Korea's Asymmetric Threats

South Korea's principal deterrence and defense mission continues to be heavily focused on meeting an array of asymmetric threats from North Korea. In contrast with its formerly static approach, the ROK military is transitioning to a "proactive deterrence" posture. As one senior ROK defense analyst noted, the "military is working hard to identify the best mix of all available options it has at its disposal." These include "attack operations when there is a sign of provocation, active defense on their routes, enhancing the passive defense capacity, and making revenge attacks proportionate to the damage caused by the provocation."[56] In tandem with such thinking, the current defense plan (2013–17) from South Korea's MND has been focused on strengthening ballistic missile capabilities against North Korea, including the Hyunmu-2 and the Hyunmu-3 cruise missiles, the F-X combat aircraft modernization program (focusing on the acquisition of U.S. F-35s), fourth-generation diesel submarines (the Son Won-il class), next-generation frigates, and an additional Dokdo-class helicopter carrier.[57]

Given the enormous economic gap between the two Koreas and South Korea's ability to outspend the North in the military arena, North Korea has opted for strengthening its asymmetric capabilities, including by developing nuclear weapons. Beginning with the country's first nuclear test in 2006, open sources have provided various estimates that North Korea possesses 6–8 nuclear warheads at the lower end and 10–12 at the higher end.[58] In addition, a 2015 study made three baseline projections for the size of North Korea's nuclear arsenal by 2020: a low-end estimate of up to 20, a medium estimate of up to 50, and a high-end estimate of up to 100.[59] But most worrisome is the high likelihood that North Korea is on the cusp of or

---

[56] Bang Hyo-bok, "Security Issues and Challenges for South Korea 2014: Domestic and Regional," *Korean Journal of Defense Analyses* 26, no. 1 (2014): 5.

[57] International Institute for Strategic Studies, *The Military Balance 2014* (London: Routledge, 2014), 202.

[58] "Nuclear Weapons: Who Has What at a Glance," Arms Control Association, April 2015, http://www.armscontrol.org/factsheets/Nuclearweaponswhohaswhat; and "Nuclear Notebook: Nuclear Arsenals of the World," *Bulletin of Atomic Scientists*, http://thebulletin.org/nuclear-notebook-multimedia.

[59] Joel S. Wit and Sun Young Ahn, "North Korea's Nuclear Futures: Technology and Strategy," U.S.-Korea Institute, Johns Hopkins School of Advanced International Studies, 2015, 17–21.

has already successfully developed warhead miniaturization technologies. The ROK government noted for the first time in 2014 that "North Korea's capability to miniaturize nuclear warheads has proceeded to a formidable level." Moreover, ever since the long-range missile tests in 2009 and 2012, "it is estimated that North Korea has the ability to threaten the continental United States with its long-range ballistic missiles."[60]

More recently, North Korea announced in May 2015 that it had successfully test-fired a submarine-launched ballistic missile (SLBM). While this claim has not been independently verified, "a fully-developed SLBM capability would take the North Korean nuclear threat to a new level, allowing deployment far beyond the Korean peninsula and the potential to retaliate in the event of a nuclear attack."[61] The MND has stated that North Korea actually conducted a successful SLBM test, whereas U.S. officials have been more circumspect. For example, U.S. admiral James Winnefeld in a presentation at the Center for Strategic and International Studies in May 2015 stated that North Korea was "many years" away from developing SLBMs. European defense specialists also noted that the pictures released by the Korean Central News Agency of the SLBM test were "strongly modified" and, furthermore, that "considering the track record of North Korean deceptions, it seems sensible to assume that any North Korean SLBM capability is still a very long time in the future, if it will ever surface."[62] Of key concern, however, is that if North Korea ultimately succeeds in developing SLBMs, this technology would provide a second-strike capability and complicate South Korea's current "kill chain" counter-missile strategy of taking out North Korea's land-based ballistic missiles before launch. SLBMs would limit South Korean air and missile defense assets, thereby "possibly rendering 'Kill Chain' obsolete even before it starts properly."[63]

Although the United States and the ROK are confident that North Korea would ultimately be defeated in another Korean conflict, such a victory would come at tremendous costs to South Korea. According to South Korea's *2014 Defense White Paper*, the Korean People's Army (KPA) continues to upgrade its forces—with approximately 70% of those forces now deployed south of the

[60] Ministry of National Defense (South Korea), *2014 kukbang baekseo* [2014 Defense White Paper] (Seoul, December 31, 2014), 28–9.

[61] "N. Korea Test-Fires Submarine-Launched Ballistic Missile," *Defense News*, May 10, 2015, http://www.defensenews.com/story/defense/international/asia-pacific/2015/05/10/north-korea-submarine-launched-ballistic-missile-test-fired/27083023.

[62] "North Korea Submarine Launch Photos May Be Fake, Say Experts," *Guardian*, May 20, 2015, http://www.theguardian.com/world/2015/may/20/north-korea-submarine-missile-launch-photos-may-be-fake-say-experts.

[63] James Hardy, "North Korean SLBM Test Leaves More Questions Than Answers," *IHS Jane's 360*, May 12, 2015, http://www.janes.com/article/51356/north-korean-slbm-test-leaves-more-questions-than-answers.

Pyongyang-Wonsan line—in order to implement a blitzkrieg attack on the South should the need arise. North Korea is thought to have 200,000 special forces with an array of options for rear penetration into South Korea in case of war. (See **Table 5** for a comparison of South and North Korean military forces.) The U.S. Department of Defense thus continues to perceive North Korea as a major threat in and around the Korean Peninsula and has provided the following assessment of the situation:

> North Korea's large, forward-positioned military can initiate an attack against the ROK with little or no warning, even though it suffers from resource shortages and aging equipment…. Although North Korea is unlikely to attack on a scale it assesses would risk its survival by inviting overwhelming counterattacks by the ROK and the United States, North Korea's calculus of the threshold for smaller, asymmetric attacks and provocations is unclear…. The KPA is a large ground force–centric military, supported by a large ballistic missile arsenal, extensive SOF, and smaller air and naval forces. With approximately 70 percent of its ground forces and 50 percent of its air and naval forces deployed within 100 kilometers of the DMZ, which has served as the de facto shared border since 1953, the KPA poses a continuous threat to the ROK and deployed U.S. forces.[64]

Military Reforms and Postponing Wartime OPCON

Since the mid-1990s, the South Korean military has understood that key structural reforms need to be implemented in order to ensure that it transitions into a more technology-intensive force structure that can meet emerging and growing challenges. Yet the MND has insisted that so long as the ROK faces pronounced threats from the North, there is not much leeway to implement these structural reforms. Given that the ROK military has always faced a significant threat from the North, the more likely reason it has postponed the implementation of critical reforms—such as transitioning to a more RMA-intensive force structure—lies in bureaucratic resistance throughout all three services, but overwhelmingly within the army, which bears the lion's share of downsizing forces. Ever since military reforms were introduced in the late 1980s, the military has strongly resisted structural reforms, including more recent attempts such as the Defense Reform Plan 2020 and the Defense Reform Plan 307. The Park Geun-hye administration announced its own reforms in March 2014 with a time frame of 2030, including a force reduction of 110,000 soldiers. This change and the acquisition of new weapons systems and equipment signal a shift to a more corps-centered army structure, but analysts have stated that many of

---

[64] Office of the Secretary of Defense, *Annual Report to Congress: Military and Security Developments Involving the People's Republic of China 2013* (Washington, D.C., 2013), 8, 11.

TABLE 5   South Korean and North Korean military forces

	Total forces	Main battle tanks/ artillery	Ships	Aircraft	Missiles	Nuclear weapons
South Korea	655,000	2,414	• Principal surface combatants: 22 • Patrol/coastal: 110 • Submarines: 35	• 3 sqn F-4EII • 11 sqn F-5E/F • 3 sqn F-15K • 10 sqn F-16C/D	• 206 SAMs • 48 Patriot PAC-2	None
North Korea	1,190,000	3,500/21,100	• Principal surface combatants: 6 • Patrol/coastal: 383 • Submarines: 72	• 3 regt H-5 • 1 regt F-7 • 6 regt J-5 • 4 regt J-6 • 5 regt J-7 • 1 regt MiG-23 • 1 regt MiG-29	• 24 FROG-3/5/7 • Some Musadan • Est. 10 Nodong (90+ missiles) • 30 Scud-B/C (200+ missiles)	A small number of nuclear devices, including possible miniaturization of warheads

SOURCE: International Institute of Strategic Studies, *Military Balance 2014* (London: Routledge, 2014).

NOTE: According to various open sources such as the *Bulletin of the Atomic Scientists*, North Korea is believed to have ten to twelve nuclear warheads.

these components stem from the earlier Defense Reform Plan 2020 that was introduced by the Roh Moo-hyun administration.[65]

As a case in point, since the early 2000s, the ROK and the United States have worked toward modernizing OPCON arrangements. The two allies agreed in 2006 to full OPCON transfer to the ROK by April 2012, provided that the security environment at the time of the transfer was appropriate. However, given North Korea's first nuclear test in 2006, Seoul and Washington decided to postpone the transfer until December 2015. In February 2013, the incoming Park Geun-hye administration reviewed the planned timetable and argued that it was still unrealistic, owing to the prevailing security environment. Subsequently, Seoul and Washington agreed to undertake the OPCON transfer when the ROK was ready following a comprehensive assessment in 2018.[66] During the annual U.S.-ROK Security Consultative Meeting that was held in Washington, D.C., in October 2014, the two sides agreed on a "conditions-based" approach rather than a fixed timeline for the OPCON transfer.[67]

Defense Spending and Advanced Defense Technologies

One of the key reasons the Park administration decided to postpone the OPCON transfer was to allow more time for the ROK military to put into place requisite force and C4ISR upgrades. In July 2015 the South Korean MND announced that it was seeking $8.03 billion in additional defense funding in the 2015–2020 Mid-Term Defense Plan—a 7% increase from the previous plan—in order to address North Korea's growing nuclear and missile capabilities.[68] The MND also stressed that the 7% annual increase should be maintained throughout the current midterm defense plan cycle and that, if possible, the defense budget's share of GDP should increase from the current level of 2.38% to 2.5%–2.8% over the next decade. This figure is

---

[65] Hwee Rhak Park, "South Korea's Failure to Implement 'Defense Reform 2020,'" *Korean Journal of International Studies* 12, no. 2 (2014): 380.

[66] Jeong Yong-Soo and Kim Bong-Moon, "Terms of Wartime OPCON Discussed," *Joongang Daily*, September 20, 2014, http://koreajoongangdaily.joins.com/news/article/Article.aspx?aid=2995120; and Choe Sang-Hun, "U.S. and South Korea Agree to Delay Shift in Wartime Command," *New York Times*, October 24, 2014, http://www.nytimes.com/2014/10/25/international-home/us-and-south-korea-agree-to-delay-shift-in-wartime-command.html.

[67] "Joint Communiqué: The 46th ROK-U.S. Security Consultative Meeting," U.S. Department of Defense, October 23, 2014.

[68] Oh Seok-min, "S. Korea to Raise Defense Spending by 2020," Yonhap News, July 12, 2015, http://english.yonhapnews.co.kr/search1/2603000000.html?cid=AEN20150417009700315. The proposed increase is slated for strengthening South Korea's so-called kill chain, including additional funding for the Korea Air and Missile Defense System, such as additional Patriot battery M-SAMs. However, the final amount will be decided after deliberations with the ROK Ministry of Strategy and Finance and hearings in the National Assembly.

still considerably lower than the 3.69% average of countries like Israel that also face critical military threats.[69] Defense spending currently constitutes 10% of the central government's budget, and while the MND's request for an average 7% increase into 2020 may be sustainable, it remains doubtful whether the South Korean defense budget as a percentage of GDP will increase significantly over the next decade. This owes to the fact that, as already noted, the ROK government spends nearly 45% of its budget on social welfare and education. As can be seen in **Table 6**, China leads defense spending among Asian countries by a significant margin, followed by Japan, India, and South Korea.

For South Korea, the political question is whether current and future governments are willing to provide the requisite funds for the ROK military to transform itself to address security challenges, given increased spending on social welfare. One key way for the military to overcome negative demographic drivers is to invest upfront in emerging technologies and to move toward a much more RMA-driven force structure. According to an August 2014 report from the MND, South Korea's defense R&D as a

TABLE 6   Defense spending trends in key Asian states, 1990–2013 ($m)

Country	1990	2000	2010	2013
China	10,244	22,190	123,333	191,228
India	10,537	14,288	46,090	47,403
Indonesia	1,614	1,130	4,663	8,364
Japan	24,973	45,976	53,796	48,728
Pakistan	2,810	2,973	5,975	7,645
Singapore	1,802	4,331	8,109	9,600
South Korea	10,111	13,801	27,573	33,940
Taiwan	8,701	8,801	9,092	10,530
Thailand	2,214	1,881	4,962	5,901
Vietnam	512	705	2,672	3,727

SOURCE: SIPRI, SIPRI Military Expenditure Database, 2015.

---

[69] "2016 kukbang yaesan yoguan, 40 jo 1,395 won" [2016 Ministry of National Defense Budgetary Request of 40,139 Trillion Won], Ministry of National Defense (South Korea), Press Release, June 17, 2015, 1–2.

percentage of total government R&D funding has declined from 20.5% in 2000 to 16.3% in 2011.[70] The MND's mid- to long-term defense R&D policy seeks to increase the share of R&D in the defense budget from the current level of 6.4% to 8.5% in 2018 and 15% by 2028. Defense R&D would focus on three key areas: network-centric operational environment capabilities, C4ISR, and precision-guided munitions assets.[71] The MND has also targeted eight strategic areas for emerging defense science and technology: (1) C4ISR, (2) early warning and surveillance, (3) unmanned technologies, (4) surface combatants and submarines, (5) unmanned aerial vehicles and combat aircraft, (6) artillery, (7) air defense, ballistic, and cruise missiles, and (8) operational management.[72] Closely related to these R&D efforts, South Korea plans to boost defense exports to $5 billion by 2020 and up to $10 billion by 2030 (from the current level of $3.6 billion).[73]

The Centrality of the U.S.-ROK Alliance

Since the end of the Korean War in 1953, the United States and South Korea have been joined in one of the most unique military alliances. While the alliance has faced significant challenges—such as the withdrawal of the U.S. 7th Infantry Division in 1971 and the Carter administration's initial inclination to withdraw the 2nd Infantry Division by the late 1970s—it has been indispensable in keeping the peace on the Korean Peninsula and helping sustain strategic stability in Northeast Asia. Commensurate with its accelerated economic development since the 1970s and the ROK military's significant force modernization efforts over the past four decades, South Korea has evolved into a major regional military partner of the United States. But the single biggest achievement of the alliance is the depth and level of strategic jointness between the forces in the face of a growing North Korean military threat.

During a press conference in October 2014, General Curtis Scaparrotti, commander of the USFK, reaffirmed the magnitude of the threat faced by the ROK and the United States:

> North Korea has focused on development of asymmetric capabilities. These capabilities include several hundred ballistic missiles, one of the world's largest

[70] Ministry of National Defense (South Korea), *2014–2018 kukbang kwahak kisul jinheung jeongchek-seo* [2014–2028 Defense S&T Promotion Policy] (Seoul, August 2014), 12–13.

[71] Ibid., 40–41.

[72] Ibid., 65–67.

[73] "Military R&D Share to Be Raised to 8.4% in Total Defense Budget," *Korea Economic Daily*, April 21, 2015, http://english.hankyung.com/news/apps/news.view?c1=01&nkey=201504211220231.

chemical weapons stockpiles, a biological weapons research program, and the world's largest special operations force, as well as an active cyber-warfare capability.[74]

The joint communiqué from the U.S.-ROK Security Consultative Meeting in October 2014 included the following statement:

> The secretary and the minister reaffirmed the continued U.S. commitment to provide and strengthen extended deterrence for the ROK using the full range of military capabilities, including the U.S. nuclear umbrella, conventional strike, and missile defense capabilities…[and that] the United States and the ROK are committed to maintaining close consultation on deterrence matters to achieve tailored deterrence against key North Korean threats and to maximize its deterrent effects.[75]

Looking ahead, the U.S.-ROK military alliance must reconfigure itself to be better positioned to deal effectively with a range of possible nonlinear contingencies in North Korea, including regime collapse. Coordinated planning is thus critical.[76] Multiple forces will influence the pace and direction of regime collapse, including the political and military resilience of the KPA, the ability of a successor regime in the event of a military coup to effectively manage the armed forces, and responses from other key security and intelligence organizations in a highly uncertain and volatile process. In this respect, although Korean-Japanese security cooperation is constrained by highly charged political sensitivities, trilateral coordination and cooperation between the United States, South Korea, and Japan is an important element in coping with the range of threats from North Korea. In December 2014, the South Korean MND announced that the three countries had signed a trilateral intelligence-sharing agreement. Although the agreement limits the sharing of intelligence to North Korea's nuclear weapons and ballistic missiles, the MND emphasized that the "intelligence-sharing agreement has the strategic effect of preventing, to the extent possible, North Korea's provocative designs" and that "in the event of a North Korean provocation, more rapid and accurate coordination of response between the three countries is possible."[77]

In sum, even though the United States and South Korea have forged one of the most unique military alliances in the post–World War II era and

---

[74] "Press Conference by Commander, U.S. Forces Korea, General Curtis Scaparrotti," U.S. Department of Defense, October 24, 2014, http://www.defense.gov/Transcripts/Transcript.aspx?TranscriptID=5525.

[75] "Joint Communiqué: The 46th ROK-U.S. Security Consultative Meeting."

[76] Bruce W. Bennett and Jennifer Lind, "The Collapse of North Korea: Military Missions and Requirements," *International Security* 36, no. 2 (2011): 89.

[77] "Bukhan hek-misail weehyeop-eh kwanhan hanmiil jeongbogongyu yakjeong chaekyul balhyo" [South Korea-U.S.-Japan Intelligence-Sharing Agreement Relating to North Korea's Nuclear and Missile Threats Comes into Force], *Chosun Ilbo*, December 29, 2014, http://news.chosun.com/site/data/html_dir/2014/12/29/2014122901057.html.

continue to play a key role in fostering a favorable strategic balance, the alliance faces new strategic realities. These include the acceleration of Chinese military power and the need to enhance defense cost-sharing while forming a bipartisan consensus on the mutual strategic benefit of sustaining the alliance into the 2020s and beyond. Although public support in South Korea for the alliance is at a record level of 80%, this hardly means that the alliance will not be affected by partisan politics, particularly after the next South Korean presidential election in December 2017.[78]

Recalibrating South Korean Power for the 21st Century

Despite the fact that South Korea has been one of Asia's most vibrant democracies, successive governments since the late 1980s have been unable to formulate, implement, and improve on critical long-term policies to ameliorate the country's coming demographic decline and institute meaningful military reforms. In short, South Korea needs to construct a developmental state model for the 21st century. Priorities include providing affordable social welfare programs, developing critical capacity-building policies for unification, and enabling South Korea to retain its economic and military competitiveness in the shadows of a preponderant China. Thus, Seoul faces a range of challenges going into the mid to late 2010s that are likely to accelerate in the 2020s and 2030s. Three developments, in particular, threaten the country's future prosperity.

First, as discussed earlier, a confluence of domestic and external drivers—such as a rapidly aging population and a progressively lower birth rate—are challenging the foundations of South Korea's economic competitiveness. These two changes alone will have significant repercussions for prospects of economic growth and the ability to satisfy military manpower demands. In addition, the country confronts exponentially increasing social welfare costs compounded by a maturing, low-growth economy and a declining tax base. South Korea also faces stiff competition from China in virtually all the areas where South Korea currently has an edge, such as consumer electronics, shipbuilding, heavy chemicals, automobiles, and ICT.

Second, although the issue is beyond the scope of this chapter, the prospects for the peaceful unification of the Korean Peninsula following a North Korean collapse will depend heavily on organizational flexibility, crisis management capabilities, the availability of financial resources, the ability to conduct adroit diplomacy under compressed time frames, and political

---

[78] "South Koreans and Their Neighbors: 2015," Asan Institute for Policy Studies, Asan Poll, May 2015, 11, available at http://en.asaninst.org/contents/south-koreans-and-their-neighbors.

acumen at all levels of national leadership.[79] At the same time, the ROK has only just begun to pay more attention to out-of-area operations, and it has been careful to not overtly criticize China's growing military capabilities, given the importance of securing Chinese support on the Korean Peninsula. However, as the People's Liberation Army assumes more assertive and even aggressive stances in the East and South China Seas—not to mention China's unconcealed opposition to the possible stationing of a Terminal High Altitude Area Defense system in South Korea—the ROK has needed to respond. For example, in November 2013 the Chinese Ministry of National Defense unilaterally announced a new air defense identification zone, which spurred South Korea to revise its own air defense identification zone in December 2014.[80]

Third, despite the continuing role of the state in steering economic policies and its near monopoly in implementing national security policies, South Korea can no longer be managed and governed primarily on the basis of the developmental state model. The state remains powerful but not nearly as preponderant as it once was. South Korea today can be described as a "hybrid state" that retains key aspects of a developmental, neoliberal, and welfare state.[81] Civil society has also expanded significantly, owing to the twin forces of globalization and democratization. Despite these changes, according to Jennifer Oh, "participation in groups that could potentially impact policies, such as professional or issue-focused groups—what we conventionally view as interest groups—is still fairly low."[82] In the same vein, David Hundt has observed that "the Korean government retains the capacity to intervene in the economy and orchestrate industrial policies for economic and social development as a developmental state…[and] is not likely to forgo this capacity to intervene in the near future."[83] Hundt's assertion is correct inasmuch as South Korea continues

---

[79] South Korea's ability to transition into a unified Korea is highly dependent on a range of unknowns such as the pace and direction of regime collapse in North Korea, the depth and breadth of military fallout, and potential third-country military intervention, including by China. But assuming for the moment that South Korea takes the lead, it must cope with a range of transitions including, but certainly not limited to, the dissolution of the KPA, the destruction of North Korea's nuclear and WMD assets, configuration of a new military force with requisite doctrinal and force compositions, coordination with the United States on constituting the appropriate U.S. military footprint in a unified Korea, and the recalibration of the roles and missions of the U.S.-ROK military alliance in the post-unification era.

[80] "Gun, jubyeonguggwa Hangugbang-gongsigbyeolguyeog ubalchungdol bangji hyeob-uijung" [Military Is Undertaking Consultations to Prevent Accidents in the Korean Air Defense Identification Zone with Neighboring Countries], Yonhap News, August 25, 2013, http://www.yonhapnews.co.kr/politics/2014/08/25/0505000000AKR20140825088200043.HTML.

[81] Chung-Sok Suh and Seung-Ho Kwon, "Whither the Developmental State in South Korea? Balancing Welfare and Neoliberalism," Asian Studies Review 38, no. 4 (2014): 680–81.

[82] Jennifer S. Oh, "Strong State and Strong Civil Society in Contemporary South Korea: Challenges to Democratic Governance," Asian Survey 52, no. 3 (2012): 530, 534.

[83] Suh and Kwon, "Whither the Developmental State in South Korea?" 680.

to depend on the developmental state model. The more appropriate question, however, is whether state-driven economic growth is still possible when key building blocks of the old structure—such as overwhelming reliance on the chaebols—are no longer viable, or even beneficial.

Policy Implications for South Korea

As noted at the onset of this chapter, South Korea's success in developing, strengthening, and expanding its national capabilities by no means guarantees that it will continue to do so over the next two to three decades. In order for the ROK to remain prosperous in the 21st century, a new developmental contract must be forged between the country's political leadership and political institutions, the chaebols and SMEs, and civil society. To the extent that South Korea is well aware of its most pressing and important challenges, it can put into place key policies that will enable the modernization and refinement of core national capabilities. To this end, South Korea should consider the following policy options.

Revise the 1987 constitution and forge a new political consensus. Both the ruling and opposition political parties need to work toward a "new political consensus" that goes beyond the reforms that were implemented in 1987. As noted above, under the 1987 constitution the president serves a single, five-year term. There is a broad consensus across the political spectrum that the time has come to revise the constitution to limit presidential powers while also enabling the president to serve up to two four-year terms (as in the current U.S. presidential system). Alternatively, South Korea could adopt a fully parliamentarian system like the established European democracies.

South Korea must also find a pathway to a new developmental model that ensures a viable but limited role for the state reflecting the key changes in Korean society, such as institutionalized democratization, accelerated globalization, political liberalization, and the emergence of a vibrant civil society. One of the key areas that needs to be addressed by all stakeholders is reforming South Korea's pension funds and controlling the escalating cost of social welfare programs. What South Korea should avoid is an increasingly likely debate about social security versus national security. As long as the ROK faces critical military threats from North Korea, in addition to growing Chinese military capabilities, maintaining credible deterrence and defense capabilities makes strategic sense for South Korea.

Provide political and financial support for industrial competitiveness and innovation. One of the perennial concerns of South Korean companies is growing competition from China, India, and other emerging economies. Within the next decade, South Korea's advantages in core industries are likely to be overtaken by Chinese firms, given the wage gap between China and South Korea and the sheer scale of Chinese manufacturing capabilities. As a result, South Korea needs to embrace innovation and liberalization through sustained investments in R&D, branding, and design and marketing so that over time it can become a truly advanced, innovative economy.[84] As the *Economist* notes,

> the South Korean model of 1960–2010 remains an example for developing countries; but Korea itself now needs something new. The Korean model had four distinctive features: a Stakhanovite workforce; powerful conglomerates; relatively weak smaller firms; and high social cohesion. All these are either coming under strain, or in need of reassessment, or both.[85]

The Park administration has stressed the importance of developing a "creative economy action plan," including "eliminating financial and regulatory barriers to entrepreneurs and SMEs" and fostering a "Silicon Valley–like venture funding ecosystem by improving the environment for financing and increasing the investment capital available to entrepreneurs."[86] As the country that has signed the most free trade agreements, South Korea should move toward full implementation of the Korea-U.S. Free Trade Agreement. Likewise, policymakers and businesses should prepare for entry into the Trans-Pacific Partnership (TPP) by considering "how provisions likely to be included in [the] TPP could augment and advance the creative economy agenda."[87]

Switch from structural to operational and management military reform. The ROK military's resistance to structural reforms has actually been aided by South Korea's single five-year presidential term. Every incoming president has announced major military reforms at the beginning of the administration, with an emphasis on fundamental structural changes; however, progressively weaker presidential authority after the midterm mark, the military's exploitation of contending interests within various political factions, budgetary shortfalls, decisions on major acquisition programs, and the outbreak of military crises have all combined to stall structural reforms. Thus, the government must emphasize cost-effective measures, including the legislation of budgetary sequestrations if the MND does not follow through with cutting wasteful and redundant force-improvement programs.

---

[84] Michael Schuman, "Why South Korea Matters," *Time*, March 24, 2010, http://business.time.com/2010/03/24/why-south-korea-matters.

[85] "What Do You Do When You Reach the Top?" *Economist*, November 12, 2011, http://www.economist.com/node/21538104.

[86] Sean P. Connell, "Creating Korea's Future Economy: Innovation, Growth, and Korea-U.S. Economic Relations," *Asia Pacific Issues*, no. 111 (2014): 4.

[87] Ibid., 6.

Much more stringent auditing reviews should be taken by not only the Office of Defense Reform in the MND but also the National Assembly.[88]

U.S. and Regional Implications

One of the most remarkable developments in the post–World War II era is the web of bilateral alliances that were formed in the aftermath of the Korean War. This conflict drew Japan, South Korea, Australia, Thailand, and the Philippines under the U.S. security umbrella. Japan and South Korea have often been characterized as the linchpins or cornerstones of U.S. security policy in East Asia, and all three countries have gained key dividends for more than six decades. From the perspective of the United States, the net value of the U.S.-ROK alliance rests in having a major Asian power as a key strategic partner at the epicenter of continental and maritime Asia during a time of accelerating Chinese economic and military power. South Korea is a critical middle power that has all the requisite capabilities, including shared values, key military assets, decades of institutionalized jointness, and extensive linkages across Asia that can serve as a major anchor of U.S. policy in East Asia. The ROK is also the only U.S. treaty ally that has maintained centuries of historical ties with China—a strategic asset for the United States as it prepares for a long-term contest with China.

While the U.S.-Japan alliance will play a central role in fostering U.S. strategic interests in East Asia, the U.S.-ROK alliance is no less important given that South Korea is the only country in continental Asia that houses U.S. forces. South Korea also has one of the most able, modern, and powerful armed forces in Asia, with the highest degree of interoperability with U.S. forces. The single biggest challenge for the United States and South Korea lies in managing future transitions on the Korean Peninsula in a way that would enable the alliance to survive well into the post-unification era, albeit with key adjustments in the roles and missions of the USFK and a qualitatively different force presence.

For South Korea, the value of its alliance with the United States will become even more pronounced owing to the alliance's importance for achieving two critical objectives: first, overcoming the challenges associated with transitions on the Korean Peninsula; and second, providing maximum strategic leverage for South Korea—and especially a unified Korea—as China continues to grow in power and influence and develop the requisite capabilities to much more effectively pressure neighboring states when it chooses to do so. Given the pronounced asymmetry between South Korea (or a unified Korea) and China, it is in South Korea's interest to sustain its

---

[88] Park, "South Korea's Failure," 396–97.

alliance with the United States. The key weak link lies in outstanding historical issues in the Korean-Japanese relationship. As two key democracies, advanced economies, and critical U.S. allies with shared security interests, South Korea and Japan have more common interests than both are willing to admit, even if they have profoundly different historical memories. Compartmentalizing core and emerging security interests while coping with a deep historical divide remains essential if South Korea, the United States, and Japan are to work together to foster a regional balance conducive to their national and collective security interests.

The biggest challenge confronting South Korea as it looks out over the next two to three decades is that virtually every facet of its ability to produce and maintain core national capabilities will require unparalleled political and social re-engineering. The bad news is that the magnitude of the domestic and external challenges is likely to be extremely daunting. In particular, the country will no longer be able to depend on relatively high levels of economic growth and is likely to be increasingly sandwiched by the growing demand for more social welfare spending, even as it must satisfy critical national defense imperatives. The geopolitical tasks are no less daunting given the accelerating need to not only balance but also accommodate China's growing capabilities, even as South Korea maintains its most important source of leverage (i.e., the military alliance with the United States). The silver lining is that the ROK is among very few countries to transform itself from one of the world's poorest countries to one of the richest in some four decades. South Korea has already successfully undergone multiple political and economic transitions. In more ways than one, responding to rapid change has been an indelible feature of the country's postwar story. While it will face many challenges in the decades ahead, South Korea is also likely to demonstrate its ability to survive and prosper in the world's most geopolitically complicated and potentially dangerous region.

EXECUTIVE SUMMARY

This chapter assesses the foundations and trajectory of Russia's national power, including its resources, national performance, and military capabilities.

MAIN ARGUMENT

Although no longer a superpower, Russia remains formidable and capable of projecting military power west to Europe, south to the greater Middle East, and, to a lesser extent, east to Asia. Russia additionally possesses many other highly developed tools of power, including its energy resources, economic links, intelligence services, and diplomacy, which the Kremlin actively deploys in ways that often challenge U.S. interests. In a highly authoritarian, centralized, and nontransparent political system, Vladimir Putin has consolidated political dominance, which assists in mobilizing human and natural resources for state purposes. In the near term, his actions have enhanced state power and increased the central government's capacity for decisive and rapid action. Simultaneously, however, Putin has weakened the social, economic, and political institutions that are crucial for promoting economic growth and the development of new commercial technologies.

POLICY IMPLICATIONS

- As anti-Americanism and nationalism are central pillars of Putin's political legitimacy strategy, Washington should expect many challenges to its interests from Moscow as long as Putin remains in power.

- The U.S. should take a more active role in trying to resolve the Ukraine crisis and quietly take a more flexible approach to encouraging Russia's rapprochement with Europe.

- Although increased energy exports to China, Japan, and other Asian states are raising Russia's influence, the Russian Far East remains comparatively underdeveloped, and Moscow has only tentatively engaged in emerging regional forums. The U.S. should encourage Russia to diversify its turn to the East so that it does not become overly dependent on China.

Russian Power Rising and Falling Simultaneously

Andrew C. Kuchins
with Allen Maggard and Narek Sevacheryan

Russia is an unusual case among the countries under consideration in this volume of *Strategic Asia*. Despite its much vaunted "turn to Asia" since hosting the annual summit of the Asia-Pacific Economic Cooperation (APEC) in Vladivostok in 2012, Russia's first priorities in foreign and security policy are toward the West, with Asia remaining a secondary or even tertiary theater. However, because of the war in Ukraine and the resulting economic sanctions by the United States, the European Union, and a few other states (including only Japan in Asia), the significance of Asia, and especially ties with China, has increased for Russia. Even without its recent alienation from the West, the rapidly growing economic and political power of Asian states would naturally attract more attention from the world's largest state straddling much of northern Eurasia. In February 2007, in his famous speech to the Munich Security Conference, Russian president Vladimir Putin's main message was that the economic, and thus eventually political, balance of power in the world was shifting from the West to Asia.[1] Putin suggested that the United States' unipolar moment was over and that Washington needed to recognize this situation and act accordingly.

Andrew C. Kuchins is a Senior Fellow in the Edmund A. Walsh School of Foreign Service at Georgetown University and can be reached at <ack5@georgetown.edu>.

Allen Maggard and **Narek Sevacheryan** assisted with researching and drafting this chapter. Allen Maggard is an intern with the Center for Strategic and International Studies (CSIS) Russia and Eurasia Program. Narek Sevacheryan is an intern with the CSIS Russia and Eurasia Program.

[1] See Thom Shanker and Mark Landler, "Putin Says U.S. Is Undermining Global Security," *New York Times*, February 11, 2007, http://www.nytimes.com/2007/02/11/world/europe/11munich.html.

The task of attempting to measure Russian national power is particularly timely given the role of Russian military forces and intelligence structures in assisting, if not instigating, an insurgency in eastern Ukraine since spring 2014. Russian military aircraft and naval incursions into NATO members' airspace and territorial waters have reached levels not experienced since the Cold War ended a quarter century ago. Yet despite an ambitious military modernization program, much of Russia's current weaponry remains part of the Soviet legacy dating back decades, and currently the Russian economy is experiencing its deepest recession since the 2008–9 financial crisis. The old adage that "Russia is never as weak nor as strong as it appears" seems as true today as anytime in the country's long history.

Indeed, measuring Russian power has never been an easy task. During the Cold War, the U.S. government allocated more intellectual resources to this problem than any other, yet could not reach a consensus as Soviet power was peaking in the 1970s and 1980s. Fortunately, our task is not as daunting as that of previous generations of Sovietologists. Putin's Russia is much more transparent than the Soviet Union was, and while there is excessive state intervention, the Russian economy is still based on market principles and pricing structures similar to other market economies. One can thus assess national power with greater confidence using data and statistical measurements.

There is no doubt that Russian power has been on quite a roller coaster ride over the past three decades, from superpower to supplicant of humanitarian aid to rising regional power once again. Major questions about the sustainability of economic growth have underpinned the country's resurgence over the past fifteen years, and a significant part of the following analysis will address the potential for growth and the key factors behind it. The chapter first assesses Russia's national resources, including its economy, natural resources and logistics, human capital, and capacity for innovation and technology. The chapter then considers the state's national performance in terms of how Russia defines and pursues national power at home and abroad and manages state-society relations. The third section examines in some detail an important product of these resources and performance: the capacity, modernization, and economics of Russia's military and armaments industry. The chapter concludes with a discussion of the implications of Russia's baseline position in Asia for the United States.

Russia's National Resources

Economic Resources

The status of the Russian economy is the most important foundation for Russian national power. Russian macroeconomic performance has experienced great volatility over the past three decades. Essentially the country went bankrupt twice in the 1990s, with the first instance contributing to the collapse of the Soviet Union. Revenue from oil and gas sales, which is linked to the price of oil, is the most important factor influencing economic growth or decline. As in most economies highly dependent on revenues derived from hydrocarbons, a high oil price environment both discourages good governance and inflates the currency, thus making other manufactured domestic products less competitive—the so-called Dutch disease. Conversely, lower oil prices depress macroeconomic growth but promote economic diversification and generally better economic policymaking.

The vicissitudes of Russian national power are illustrated by **Figure 1**, which charts Russian GDP as measured in nominal dollar terms from 1999 to 2014. The Russian economy hit its relative low point in the post-Soviet period in 1998–99 following the Asian financial crisis. Shortly thereafter, the oil price

FIGURE 1   Russia's GDP, 1999–2014

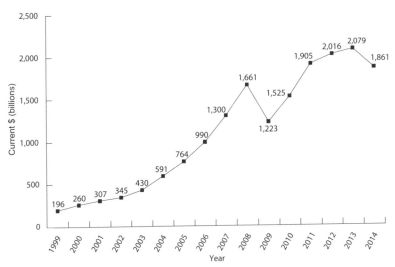

SOURCE: World Bank, World Development Indicators Databank, http://databank.worldbank. org/data/reports.aspx?source=2&country=RUS&series=&period=.

began to rise from a low of less than $10 per barrel in 1998. And thus began the "golden decade" during which Russian economic growth averaged 7% at fixed exchange rates and over 25% at nominal dollar rates that factor in the appreciation of the Russian ruble.[2]

The oil price remains the most important macroeconomic factor for Russia. Revenue from the oil and gas sector constitutes approximately 25% of Russian GDP and 70% of export earnings. Hydrocarbons also account for approximately 50% of revenue for the Russian federal budget, with oil to gas revenue running at a rate of about 4 to 1.[3] The key takeaway here is that oil production and sales are most important for Russian macroeconomic stability, while gas production and sales play a relatively more important role for management of Russia's domestic political economy.

Russia's extraordinary economic recovery, which has been largely driven by high revenues from the energy sector, is the principal explanation for Putin's popularity.[4] But the economic foundation for Russia's political stability has eroded. Economic growth was still approximately 4.0% when Putin returned to the presidency in May 2012 but fell sharply in 2013 to 1.3%.[5] On the eve of the annexation of Crimea, the Russian economy was hardly growing at all, despite the fact that the oil price was above $100 per barrel and the West had not yet imposed economic sanctions.

Capital outflows are a significant indicator of a lack of faith by the Russian financial community in the prospects for the Russian economy. Along with structural inefficiencies and stagnant growth, the combination of the war in Ukraine, Western sanctions, and the collapse of oil prices beginning in June 2014 contributed to a record $153 billion in capital outflows, more than 8% of GDP (see **Figure 2**). But from a financial standpoint, it was the fall of oil prices that contributed most fundamentally to the deep depreciation of the ruble in 2014 (see **Figure 3**).

Although the Russian economy is not declining in 2015 as steeply as it did in 2009 during the global financial crisis, it appears that the oil price is more likely to remain closer to $50 per barrel than $100 per barrel in the next few years. Given this poor outlook for a rapid economic recovery, the Russian

---

[2] Anders Åslund and Andrew Kuchins, *The Russia Balance Sheet* (Washington, D.C.: Peterson Institute for International Economics, 2009).

[3] Ibid.

[4] Daniel Triesman, "Russian Politics in a Time of Economic Turmoil," in *Russia after the Global Economic Crisis*, ed. Anders Aslund, Sergei Guriev, and Andrew Kuchins (Washington, D.C.: Peterson Institute for International Economics, 2010).

[5] "Rosstat: Rost VVP RF za devyat' mesyatsev sostavil 3,9%" [Rosstat: Russian GDP Growth in the First Nine Months Amounted to 3.9%], RIA Novosti, November 20, 2012, http://ria.ru/economy/20121120/911471421.html; and "Russian Economic Growth Slows More Than Estimated in 2013," Bloomberg Business, January 31, 2014, http://www.bloomberg.com/news/articles/2014-01-31/russian-economic-growth-slows-more-than-estimated-in-2013.

FIGURE 2   Net capital inflow/outflow in the private sector, 2004–14

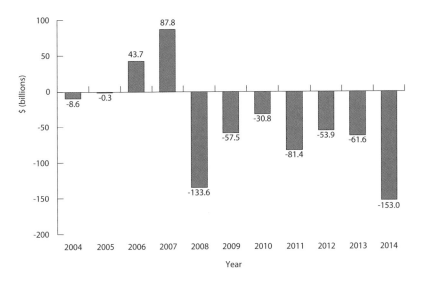

SOURCE: Central Bank of Russia, "Net Inflows/Outflows of Capital by Private Sector for 2000–2014 and in the First and the Second Quarters of 2015," August 2015, http://www.cbr.ru/eng/statistics/credit_statistics/bop/outflow_e.xlsx.

FIGURE 3   Oil prices and the ruble exchange rate, January 2014–August 2015

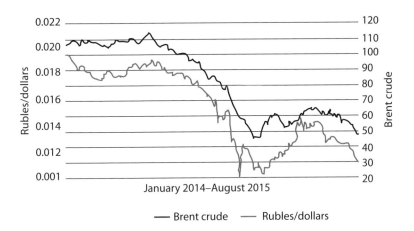

SOURCE: U.S. Energy Information Agency; and International Monetary Fund.

Central Bank projects a stagnant Russian economy for the next several years based on an average $60 oil price.[6]

Natural Resources

Energy. The combination of Western energy sanctions and a dip in global oil prices has given Moscow additional impetus to reorient its oil and natural gas exports to Asia. Russia's 2030 Energy Strategy stipulated that exports of oil and natural gas to the Asia-Pacific region should grow to around 25% and 20%, respectively, over the next decade.[7] According to BP, Russia possesses 103.2 thousand million barrels and 32.6 trillion cubic meters worth of proven oil and natural gas reserves, respectively, and as such would seem to have more than enough supply to slake the thirst of eastern energy markets.[8] The major obstacles, however, are the commercial feasibility of developing new oil and gas resources in eastern Russia and the cost of transiting these resources to customers. Even before the collapse of oil prices, Russian expansion into Asian markets was hampered by a problematic investment environment for new oil and gas fields in Eastern Siberia and the Russian Far East as well as the Arctic. The recent halving of the oil price, coupled with decreased demand from China, places considerably more doubt on the capacity of Russia to reach its ambitious goal of Asian market penetration by 2030.

Russia's quest to diversify its fossil fuel export profile makes sense from the perspective of the domestic economy, since the country uses these resources to great effect already in powering its own electrical grid. BP ranks Russia as the fourth-largest global producer of electricity, with 1,064,100 gigawatt hours (GWh) produced in 2014 alone (compared with China's and India's 23,536,500 GWh and 1,208,400 GWh, respectively).[9] Much of this production comes from fossil fuel sources: according to the International Energy Agency, between 2000 and 2012 Russia derived 66.3% of its electricity from fossil fuels, of which natural gas accounted for roughly 70% on average.[10]

---

[6] "Russia Sees GDP Shrinking at Least 4.5% in 2015 with $60 Oil," *Bloomberg Business*, December 15, 2014, http://www.bloomberg.com/news/articles/2014-12-15/russia-sees-economy-shrinking-at-least-4-5-in-2015-with-60-oil.

[7] Eric Yep, "Russia to Pump Up Oil Exports to Asia," *Wall Street Journal*, December 4, 2014, http://www.wsj.com/articles/russia-to-pump-up-oil-exports-to-asia-1417676709.

[8] BP plc, "BP Statistical Review of World Energy June 2015," June 2015, http://www.bp.com/content/dam/bp/excel/Energy-Economics/statistical-review-2015/bp-statistical-review-of-world-energy-2015-workbook.xlsx.

[9] Ibid.

[10] "Russian Federation: Electricity and Heat for 2012," International Energy Agency, http://www.iea.org/statistics/statisticssearch/report/?country=RUSSIA&product=ElectricityandHeat&year=2012.

Russia also currently operates 34 nuclear reactors with a combined generative capacity of approximately 25,200 megawatts electrical (MWe). The state-owned nuclear utility Rosatom has successfully extended the operational lifetime of several reactors and plans to construct up to 30 new reactors with a combined installed capacity of more than 30,000 MWe by the end of 2030.[11] Russia has extended technical assistance to China, India, and several other international partners interested in developing their own civilian nuclear sectors. Rosatom currently manages over twenty such projects across ten countries and hopes to generate $150 billion in additional foreign tenders from reactor exports by 2020.[12] Some experts, however, doubt that Rosatom by itself can afford to deliver on every one of these contracts.[13]

The Russian government is also working to develop the hydropower sector, which is thought to operate at only 20% of its total generative potential.[14] In recent years, Russia has sought out various international partners to invest in the construction of new hydroelectric plants in Siberia and the Russian Far East. China in particular has demonstrated interest in a number of such projects, which it sees as opportunities to develop a more sustainable means of energizing economic growth. RusHydro and China's Three Gorges Corporation signed a joint contract to construct a 320-megawatt plant on the Bureya River in the Russian Far East. Russia has also invested in joint hydroelectric projects with the Indian government, which like China has set its sights on tapping into the Himalayan headwaters in order to underwrite its own economic development.

Mining. In contrast with the energy sector, Russia's metallurgical industries have weathered the current crisis without radical contortions to their commercial posture. The Ministry of Industry has even begun to contemplate introducing tariffs on exports of ferrous and nonferrous metals to stimulate domestic consumption.[15] According to the World Steel Association, Russia manufactured around 71 million tons of crude steel

---

[11] "Nuclear Power in Russia," World Nuclear Association, http://www.world-nuclear.org/info/Country-Profiles/Countries-O-S/Russia--Nuclear-Power.

[12] "Key Figures," Rosatom, http://www.rosatom.ru/en/about/key_figures; and "Russia's Rosatom Plans to Boost Orders Portfolio to $150 Bln by 2020," TASS, June 1, 2015, http://tass.ru/en/economy/797897.

[13] Kendra Ulrich, "Fukushima Impact: Accelerating the Nuclear Industry's Decline," Greenpeace Japan, February 2015, http://www.greenpeace.org/japan/Global/japan/pdf/Briefing_Fukushima_Impact.pdf.

[14] UN Economic Commission for Europe, "Summary on Reports from the National Experts on Development of Renewable Energy in the Russian Federation and CIS Countries," December 2011, http://www.unece.org/fileadmin/DAM/energy/se/pdfs/eneff/RES_RF_CIS/SummaryNationalReports.pdf.

[15] Vitalij Petlevoiy, "Rost eksporta chernykh metallov zamedlyaetsya" [Growth of Ferrous Metal Exports Slowed Down], *Vedomosti*, August 9, 2015, http://www.vedomosti.ru/business/articles/2015/08/10/604102-rost-eksporta-chernih-metallov-zamedlyaetsya.

in 2014 (up 1.2% from 2013), thus making it the sixth-largest producer of crude steel in the world.[16]

Russia produced 42,000 metric tons of titanium in 2014, down from 44,000 tons in 2013.[17] Despite already being the world's largest titanium producer, Russia's VSMPO-AVISMA hopes to raise its production capacity by a third within the next five years.[18] The success of this target program may well prove critical, as some industry insiders believe that China will begin to challenge Russia's virtual monopoly on the manufacture and export of aviation-grade titanium over the coming decade.[19]

Rosatom's mining arm, ARMZ Uranium Holding Co., extracted 3,000 tons of uranium in 2014, down from 8,300 tons in 2013.[20] Despite Rosatom's claim to possess enough uranium on hand to supply its domestic and foreign nuclear power plants for another century, CEO Sergei Kiriyenko has pledged to triple his company's operations to extract natural uranium by 2017.[21] Experts maintain that concerns over Russia's strategy of acquiring foreign uranium mining enterprises are overblown, given that these international assets only bring the country's share of global uranium production and reserves to 14% and 12%, respectively.[22]

Agriculture. Russia seeks to attain agricultural self-sufficiency in the long term so that it can, in the words of Prime Minister Dmitri Medvedev, "not only feed itself but supply other countries."[23] However, the country's shrinking agrarian workforce poses a significant challenge; indeed, according to the World Bank, Russia's rural population dropped from 39,067,982 in

---

[16] "World Crude Steel Output Increases by 1.2% in 2014," World Steel Association, Press Release, January 22, 2015, https://www.worldsteel.org/media-centre/press-releases/2015/World-crude-steel-output-increases-by-1.2--in-2014.html.

[17] U.S. Geological Survey, *Mineral Commodity Summaries 2015* (Reston: U.S. Geological Survey, 2015), http://minerals.usgs.gov/minerals/pubs/mcs/2015/mcs2015.pdf.

[18] "Russia's VSMPO Seeks to Boost Global Lead in Titanium Production," *Moscow Times*, July 29, 2015, http://www.themoscowtimes.com/news/business/article/russia-s-vsmpo-seeks-to-boost-global-lead-in-titanium-production/526442.html.

[19] Andrey Lemeshko, "Boeing Titanium Supplier Sees China as Risk for Market," Bloomberg Business, April 6, 2015, http://www.bloomberg.com/news/articles/2015-04-07/boeing-titanium-supplier-sees-chinese-output-as-risk-for-market.

[20] "Key Figures," Rosatom.

[21] "Russia Has Enough Uranium for Domestic, Foreign NPPs for 100 Years—Rosatom," TASS, August 9, 2014, http://tass.ru/en/economy/744215; and "Russia to Triple Uranium Production in Next 2 Years—Rosatom," Sputnik, January 9, 2014, http://sputniknews.com/russia/20140109/186378565/Russia-to-Triple-Uranium-Production-in-Next-2-Years--Rosatom.html.

[22] Steve Fetter and Erich Schneider, "The New York Times Was Wrong; Russian Uranium Deals Don't Threaten World Supply Security," *Bulletin of the Atomic Scientists*, May 19, 2015, http://thebulletin.org/new-york-times-was-wrong-russian-uranium-deals-dont-threaten-world-supply-security8329.

[23] "Medvedev: Rossiya mozhet i dolzhna kormit' sebya sama" [Medvedev: Russia Can and Must Feed Itself], BBC Russian Service, August 13, 2014, http://www.bbc.com/russian/russia/2014/08/140813_medvedev_food_reform.

2000 to 37,502,391 in 2014.[24] Although a 4% contraction may sound trivial, it is consistent with a broader trend of socioeconomic disintegration in the countryside. The Russian government has responded by attempting to entice foreign investors with offers of cheap and bountiful land. With its surplus agrarian workforce, China in particular has shown a keen interest in expanding its agricultural sector into parts of Siberia and the Russian Far East, where arable land exists in abundance yet lies fallow due to the region's remoteness from population centers. Moscow recently entered an equal partnership with Beijing to establish a joint agricultural investment fund to the tune of $2 billion.[25]

Most observers, however, are pessimistic in their assessment of this investment scheme, which appears to benefit Beijing at Moscow's expense. Although some Russian officials have been only too happy to accommodate Chinese agricultural interests, some have bristled at the thought of ceding land to China given its environmental record, while still others object on patriotic grounds. In a 2015 Rosbalt poll conducted shortly after the Zabaikalsky Krai government had signed a preliminary agreement with a Chinese company to lease out 115,000 hectares of fallow land for a term of 49 years, roughly half of respondents indicated that the deal would open the door to Chinese colonization, thereby leading to a future war with China.[26]

Transportation logistics. As the world's largest country, Russia is blessed with a natural resource abundance second to none. But its curse for centuries has been efficiently transiting this natural resource wealth to global markets. The massive distances add tremendous costs to Russian goods and place a huge burden on developing and maintaining modern transit infrastructure for supplying foreign as well as domestic markets. With more than 80,000 kilometers (km) of railway track and 1,283,387 km of roadways, Russia maintains one of the world's largest land transportation networks. New road and railway construction has traditionally been driven by the oil and natural gas industry. Nevertheless, the country's transportation networks remain quite limited—for example, high-capacity federal highways only constitute approximately 4% of the

---

[24] "Rural Population," World Bank, World Development Indicators, http://data.worldbank.org/indicator/SP.RUR.TOTL.

[25] Chuin-Wei Yap, "China, Russia Prepare $2 Billion Agricultural Investment Fund," *Wall Street Journal*, May 8, 2015, http://www.wsj.com/articles/china-russia-prepare-2-billion-agricultural-investment-fund-1431080535#livefyre-comment.

[26] "Opros: Peredacha na 49 let v arendu Kitajskoij kompanii 115 tys. ga sel'khhozzemel' v Zabajkal'e…" [Survey: Transfer of Lease of 115 Thousand Hectares of Agricultural Land in Transbaikal to Chinese Company…], Rosbalt, June 25, 2015, http://www.rosbalt.ru/main/poll/957/results.

total road network.[27] Prior to the Ukraine crisis, Russia's Ministry of Transport had planned to invest around 500 billion rubles in new rail and road construction; however, present economic constraints will probably dampen these plans due to Moscow's prioritization of spending on military modernization.[28]

Confronted with this dilemma, the Kremlin has increasingly looked to Beijing as a source of financial and material support for several transportation projects. In May 2015 the Chinese government agreed to help fund more than 30 Russian infrastructure projects, ranging from a 410 km railway between Tuva and southern Siberia to a 770 km high-speed rail corridor that would link Moscow and Kazan to China proper.[29] This latter effort, however, could provide jobs to more Chinese than Russian workers, as tenders for the actual construction of the route will likely go to Chinese contractors.[30] Moreover, many of these projects appear to complement existing transport links and as such do not penetrate into some of Russia's more remote regions. What transport links to these regions do already exist—the Trans-Siberian railway, for instance—are beset with so many bottlenecks that shipping freight and cargo is impractical.[31] Indeed, the World Bank ranks Russia just 155th worldwide in terms of ease of conducting cross-border trade.[32] Russia hopes to benefit from increased Chinese investment in its transit sector via the Silk Road Economic Belt fund and Asian Infrastructure Investment Bank, although it remains wary of becoming overly dependent on Chinese investment.

Human Resources: Demography, Healthcare, Education, and Migration

Demography and healthcare. While most Northern Hemisphere states in Europe and Asia are experiencing demographic decline, it is no exaggeration to describe the Russian case as an ongoing crisis. The crisis is rooted in a death rate that for much of the post-Soviet period has dramatically outpaced

---

[27] EY, "The Road to 2030: A Survey of Infrastructure Development in Russia," 2014, http://www.ey.com/Publication/vwLUAssets/EY-russia-infrastructure-survey-2014-eng/$FILE/EY-russia-infrastructure-survey-2014-eng.pdf.

[28] Jason Bush, "Putin's Defence Fixation Deepens Russian Budget Problems," Reuters, January 15, 2015, http://www.reuters.com/article/2015/01/15/russia-crisis-budget-idUSL6N0US25520150115.

[29] "China Throws Russia Financial Lifeline," DW, May 8, 2015, http://www.dw.com/en/china-throws-russia-financial-lifeline/a-18439666.

[30] Paul Sonne, "China to Design New Russian High-Speed Railway," *Wall Street Journal*, June 19, 2015, http://www.wsj.com/articles/china-to-design-new-russian-high-speed-railway-1434729400.

[31] Oleg Barabanov, "Problems of Siberia and the Russian Far East," Valdai Discussion Club, September 4, 2012, http://valdaiclub.com/economy/48480.html.

[32] "Dealing with Construction Permits," World Bank, Doing Business 2015, http://www.doingbusiness.org/data/exploreeconomies/russia#dealing-with-construction-permits.

the birth rate. The crisis is most acute among working-age men whose life expectancy is in the mid-60s, nearly ten years shorter than that for Russian women and far below the life expectancy for a country of Russia's relative per capita wealth. Following the Soviet Union's collapse, the population of the new Russian Federation was close to 150 million. Today it is 141 million, despite the influx of millions of migrants from Central Asia, the South Caucasus, and other post-Soviet states over the last two decades. Although there has been a recent uptick in the birthrate, by 2050 the population is expected to decline to a level in the range of 100 to 130 million.[33] The overall health of the Russian population is likewise significantly worse than that of countries with comparable per capita GDP. These major demographic constraints have significant implications for labor productivity, the quality of military personnel, and other key indices of Russian power.

Russia's healthcare infrastructure faces significant deficiencies that limit the ability of the state to protect its human resources. Fundamental issues within the healthcare sector itself include declining numbers of hospitals and other medical facilities, outdated equipment, low wages over long hours, and the government's general inability to implement effective sector-wide reforms.[34] Russia has a low average life expectancy at birth (69 years), with 74% of men and 40% of women likely to die before the age of 70.[35] Access to potable water pales in comparison with other developed economies, with Russia placing 99th among 178 states.[36] A 2014 survey by the Levada Center pointed to widespread dissatisfaction with domestic medical services, with only 17% of respondents voicing contentment with the quality of healthcare and over 60% indicating strong dissatisfaction.[37]

Education. The Russian Federation pays considerable attention to maintaining high educations rates for the population, with 94% of the 24–64 age group holding at least upper-secondary education degrees,

---

[33] Nicholas Eberstadt, "The Dying Bear: Russia's Demographic Disaster," *Foreign Affairs*, November/December 2011, https://www.foreignaffairs.com/articles/russia-fsu/2011-11-01/dying-bear.

[34] Tatiana Stanovaya, "Health Care Reform as a Catalyst for Progress," Institute for Modern Russia, November 21, 2014, http://imrussia.org/en/analysis/nation/2089-health-care-reform-as-a-catalyst-for-progress.

[35] See "Russian Federation: WHO Statistical Profile," World Health Organization, January 2015, http://www.who.int/gho/countries/rus.pdf?ua=1. Over 50% of all deaths are thought to stem from cardiovascular disease.

[36] "Improved Sanitation Facilities (% of Population with Access)," World Bank, World Development Indicators, http://data.worldbank.org/indicator/SH.STA.ACSN; and "Issue Ranking: Water and Sanitation," Environmental Performance Index, Yale University, http://epi.yale.edu/epi/issue-ranking/water-and-sanitation.

[37] "Healthcare System in Russia," Levada Center, Press Release, September 19, 2014, http://www.levada.ru/eng/healthcare-system-russia.

compared with the G-20 average of 60%.[38] Russia ranks relatively high in terms of intergenerational educational upward mobility, although its spending on education is lower than the Organisation for Economic Co-operation and Development (OECD) average.[39] Russia spends around 5% of its budget ($50 billion) on formal education, with approximately 20% of the total education budget allocated to institutions of higher learning.[40] No less notable is that Russia produces more graduates in engineering, manufacturing, and construction than any other country in the world. Although academic publishing in the humanities remains a weak point, Russian scholars tend to be well-represented in global mathematics and the hard sciences.

Migration. A March 2015 survey by the Levada Center paints an interesting portrait of the attitude of Russian society toward emigration: an overwhelming 81% of respondents claimed to have not even thought about leaving Russia, whereas 8% claimed to think about it only from time to time and just 5% wanted to leave the country permanently.[41] Those aspiring émigrés who were either thinking about leaving the country or already in the process of doing so cited dissatisfaction with their economic condition as the principal rationale. However, experts believe that educated, financially secure, and urban-dwelling Russians are more likely to emigrate than are other segments of the population, as they are better positioned to find work abroad.[42]

Yet Russia is also the world's second-most attractive country in terms of numbers of immigrants. In 2014, for example, 270,036 people migrated to Russia, of whom over 96% came from the Commonwealth of Independent States, which comprises countries that belonged to the former Soviet Union. This is largely a result of cultural and linguistic similarities, geographic proximity, and facilitated visa regimes. Many of these migrants are seasonal workers performing unskilled labor in the construction and

---

[38] Organisation for Economic Co-operation and Development (OECD), "Education at a Glance 2013: Russian Federation," Country Note, http://www.oecd.org/edu/Russian%20Federation_EAG2013%20 Country%20Note.pdf.

[39] OECD, "Education at a Glance 2013: Russian Federation," 24; and OECD, *Education at a Glance: 2014: Highlights* (Paris: OECD, 2014), 51, http://www.oecd-ilibrary.org/docserver/download/9614031e. pdf?expires=1437144559&id=id&accname=guest&checksum=AC86A57180C47DFE0C0DB6B6 BA248196.

[40] "Raskhodi konsolidirovannogo byudzheta Rossiyskoy Federatsii po razdelu obrazovaniye v 2014 godu, mlrd. rub." [Education-related Expenditures under the Consolidated Budget of the Russian Federation for 2014, in Billions of Rubles], Ministry of Education and Sciences (Russia), http://fin. edu.ru/InfoPanel/min_obr1.html#page0_target.

[41] "Chemodannye nastroeniya" [Suitcase Moods], Levada Center, March 20, 2015, http://www.levada. ru/20-03-2015/chemodannye-nastroeniya.

[42] "Uezhat' ili ostat'sya?" [To Leave or To Stay?], Radio Svoboda, June 17, 2015, http://www.svoboda. org/content/transcript/27077566.html.

manufacturing sectors. Of this same cohort, only 14% had higher education.[43] The net result of these migration trends is a loss in human capital: the best and brightest professionals are leaving Russia in droves, only to be replaced by less-educated, less-skilled migrants.

Innovation and High Technology

Cornell University ranked the Russian Federation 49th in its 2014 Global Innovation Index, thus qualifying Russia as a moderately efficient innovator.[44] The country's innovation environment, however, still suffers from the prevailing bureaucratic, regulatory, and judiciary frameworks; inadequate intellectual property protection; and an uncompetitive business environment.[45] Although the government has introduced several changes into the regulatory system, in 2015 Russia fell to 65th place in the World Bank's Doing Business sub-index "resolving insolvency."[46] Most importantly, Russia's private sector does not have sufficient access to the modern technologies essential for competitive innovation, not to mention that many Russian businesses tend to be risk-averse and are thus disinclined to adopt new technologies.[47]

High-tech products accounted for only 7.5% of total imports (less re-imports) and 1.5% of net exports in 2012.[48] Russia spends only 1.2% of its GDP (private and public) on applied R&D—far less than the leading European countries, as well as China, Korea, or Japan.[49] The gross expenditure on R&D by businesses was 58.3%, indicating significant lag behind China and the United States (76% and 69%, respectively). On the other hand, Russia is

---

[43] "Chislennost' i migratsiya naseleniya Rossijskoj Federatsii v 2014 godu" [Population and Migration of the Russian Federation in 2014], Federal State Statistics Service (Russia), http://www.gks.ru/bgd/regl/b15_107/main.htm.

[44] "Data Analysis: 2014 Country Rankings," Global Innovation Index, Cornell University, INSEAD, and World Intellectual Property Organization (WIPO), https://www.globalinnovationindex.org/content.aspx?page=data-analysis.

[45] "Global Information Technology Report 2015 (Country/Economy Profiles): Russian Federation," World Economic Forum, http://reports.weforum.org/global-information-technology-report-2015/economies/#economy=RUS.

[46] World Bank, Doing Business 2015: Going Beyond Efficiency, Russian Federation (Washington, D.C.: World Bank, 2014), 98–102, http://www.doingbusiness.org/~/media/giawb/doing%20business/documents/profiles/country/RUS.pdf.

[47] Susanne Dirks and Mary Keeling, "Russia's Productivity Imperative: Leveraging Technology and Innovation to Drive Growth," IBM Institute for Business Value, 6–8, http://www.ibm.com/smarterplanet/global/files/us__en_us__government__gbe03244usen.pdf.

[48] Soumitra Dutta, Bruno Lanvin, and Sacha Wunsch-Vincent, eds., The Global Innovation Index 2014: The Human Factor in Innovation (Ithaca, Fontainebleau, and Geneva: Cornell University, INSEAD, and WIPO, 2015), 340, 354.

[49] "Research and Development Expenditure (% of GDP)," World Bank, World Development Indicators, http://data.worldbank.org/indicator/GB.XPD.RSDV.GD.ZS?order=wbapi_data_value_2012+wbapi_data_value+wbapi_data_value-last&sort=desc.

ranked 30th in the performance of R&D by businesses (at 0.7% of GDP), which lags behind the leading economies but is still competitive worldwide.[50]

The main issue that Russia faces in the high-tech sector is its extreme reliance on imported components, especially in light industrial production. The government's program of import substitution is designed to address this issue and seeks to decrease the average industrial dependence to around 50%–60% by 2020.[51] To support this policy, Russia's defense sector started to increase orders from domestic producers in 2010, which is intended to help domestic production in heavy industry, particularly those branches supporting the high-tech sector.[52]

Information and communication technologies (ICT). Russia's ICT sector has experienced impressive growth over the past several years amid relatively competitive market conditions. The World Economic Forum ranked Russia 41st in its 2015 Network Readiness Index, up nine rungs from its position the previous year.[53] Although Russia still lags behind the OECD average, the Kremlin has begun to embrace ICT-supported tools as a means of streamlining various bureaucratic and governance-related functions.[54]

This rise in ICT usage comports with the government's "Information Society (2011–2020)" development strategy, which aims to develop infrastructure for equal access to and increased utility of ICT among public and private users, albeit while maintaining strict state oversight.[55] Yet although ICT connectivity is increasing in Russia, the basic infrastructure is still not fully developed: network coverage, for example, remains unevenly distributed between urban and rural markets such that some populations remain outside mobile signal range. Likewise, although average Internet speeds in Russia surpass those of France and Italy, only 56.5% of rural and 72.0% of urban populations enjoy Internet access.[56]

---

[50] Dutta et al., *The Global Innovation Index 2014*, 247.

[51] "Zavisimost' promyshlennosti Rossii ot importa k 2020 gody snizitsya v 1,5 raza" [Russian Industry's Dependence on Imports Decreased by 1.5 times], Ministry of Industry and Trade (Russia), July 10, 2014, http://minpromtorg.gov.ru/press-centre/all/#!8750.

[52] Ivan Safronov, "Tech-Challenged Russia Ready to Import Foreign Arms for the First Time," World Crunch, January 19, 2012.

[53] "Global Information Technology Report 2015 (Country/Economy Profiles): Russian Federation."

[54] Dutta et al., *The Global Innovation Index 2014*, 247.

[55] "Gosudarstvennaya programma 'informatsionnoe obshchestvo' (2011–2020)" [State Program "Information Society" for 2011–2020], Ministry of Communications and Mass Media (Russia), August 27, 2014, http://minsvyaz.ru/ru/activity/programs/1.

[56] "Skorost' interneta v Rossii vyshe, chem vo Frantsii i Italii" [The Speed of the Internet in Russia Is Higher Than in France or Italy], Ministry of Communications and Mass Media (Russia), June 22, 2015, http://minsvyaz.ru/ru/events/33516; and Broadcasting Board of Governors and Gallup, "Contemporary Media Use in Russia," http://www.bbg.gov/wp-content/media/2014/02/Russia-research-brief.pdf.

Cultivating a nationwide network through ICT platforms is especially important for the state as it seeks to expand its control over the flow of information in order to cultivate societal consensus around specific state-sponsored policies. In this context, greater state involvement in the ICT sector through public financing augers even greater state influence over public attitudes and perceptions.

Information technology (IT). Closely linked to the ICT sector is the development of the IT field, which despite improving projections still possesses only a small share of the international market. Human capital in the software development field has seen%–11% annual growth, with around 130,000 professional specialists working in software companies and around 430,000 software developers in the entire industry. Nevertheless, over 70% of IT companies in Russia experience shortages of qualified human capital. In order to meet demand, the government has increased federal financing to fill quotas for students specializing in the information sciences. By 2018, Russian universities will produce 150,000 IT graduates, although this still falls well short of projected demand.[57]

Despite these weaknesses, the IT sector has managed some growth and is one of the few sectors of the Russian economy other than the energy and arms industries to experience increased penetration of foreign markets.[58] Sales of Russian software products abroad accounted for a little over 1% of total exports in 2013, up from 0.88% in 2012 and 0.80% in 2011.

National Performance and State-Societal Relations

Russian Views of National Power

Russia's status as the world's largest country has been a point of pride for Russians for centuries. Not surprisingly, then, Moscow measures national power to a considerable extent by its capacity to control territory and exercise influence on its periphery. Culturally, the Russian sense of security is likewise deeply grounded in territorial control. Stalin's personification of the traditional Russian leader with an inclination to control and coerce rather than to attract, convince, or shape coalitions was at the heart of the Cold

[57] "Russian Universities to Offer More Government-Funded Places for IT Students," TASS, February 17, 2014, http://tass.ru/en/russia/719507; and "Eksport Rossijskoj industrii razrabotki programmnogo obespecheniya: 11-e ezhegodnoe issledovanie" [Export of the Russian Software Development Industry: 11th Annual Survey], Russoft, 125–131, http://www.russoft.ru/upload/RUSSOFT_Survey_11_ru.pdf.

[58] F. Joseph Dresen, "The Growth of Russia's IT Outsourcing Industry: The Beginning of Russian Economic Diversification?" Woodrow Wilson International Center for Scholars, Kennan Institute, http://www.wilsoncenter.org/publication/the-growth-russias-it-outsourcing-industry-the-beginning-russian-economic.

War conflict that emerged in the late 1940s.[59] Putin shares these core traits, as is most evident in his policy toward what the Russians colloquially refer to as the *blizhnii zarubezh* (near abroad), which is constituted by the states that were formerly part of the Soviet Union. Russia's slightly covert war in eastern Ukraine since 2014 and its five-day war against Georgia in 2008 mark the most violent expressions of its exercise of power. Under both Yeltsin in the 1990s and Putin for the past fifteen years, Moscow has manipulated an extensive set of tools to influence and constrain the sovereignty of its nearest neighbors to the West, in the South Caucasus, and in Central Asia, particularly through the control of oil and gas supplies to many of these states. Russia's territorial sense of security is less relevant for Asia perhaps, with the exception of its dispute with Japan over the Northern Territories/Kuril Islands and its deep-seated insecurity that China wants to retake the territory in the Russian Far East and Eastern Siberia that became part of the Russian empire in the mid-nineteenth century.

Due to its vast territorial holdings, lack of defensible land boundaries, and complex geopolitical relationships, Russia faces significant military threats in all strategic directions. To the east, China remains the primary potential adversary, although this is never stated explicitly in official security and military documents. In the center and the south, Russia faces various threats, including insurgency, separatism, Islamic extremism, and regime instability among allies. To the west, it faces challenges both from former Soviet states seeking greater independence and from NATO itself, which seeks to contain Russia's latent neoimperialist ambitions. Of all these threats, Russia clearly views NATO as the most serious and urgent challenge.[60]

To meet this complex threat environment, Russia has adopted an equally complex set of strategies. In the east, it maintains large conventional forces backed by nonstrategic nuclear weapons to engage in a potentially large-scale combined arms conflict with China.[61] In the center and south, it relies primarily on rapid reaction forces backed by traditional military forces to conduct counterinsurgency, counterterrorism, and stability operations. In the west, Russia relies on a strategy of limited intervention to maintain influence over post-Soviet states, such as Georgia and Ukraine, and asymmetric strategies, such as hybrid warfare and the threat of limited nuclear strikes, to counter technologically superior NATO conventional forces. Russia remains

---

[59] John Lewis Gaddis, *We Now Know: Rethinking Cold War History* (London: Oxford University Press, 1997).

[60] "Vojennaya doktrina Rossijkoj Federatsii" [Military Doctrine of the Russian Federation], President of the Russian Federation, http://static.kremlin.ru/media/events/files/41d527556bec8deb3530.pdf.

[61] Märta Carlsson, Johan Norberg, and Fredrik Westerlund, "The Military Capability of Russia's Armed Forces in 2013," in *Russian Military Capability in a Ten-Year Perspective*, ed. Jakob Hedenskog and Carolina Vendil Pallin (Stockholm: FOI [Swedish Defence Research Agency], 2013), 52.

dissatisfied with its limited options against NATO, however, and is seeking to rebuild its conventional forces in response.

Given that the present government maintains a nearly complete monopoly on political power, it should be no surprise that it also maintains effective control over the military. The ability of the government to impose significant and unpopular reforms on the military following the war with Georgia is ample evidence of its authority.

Russia has also more recently begun to emphasize the importance of soft power, though not perhaps precisely in the manner first laid out by Joseph Nye more than twenty years ago.[62] Moscow has been influenced in this regard by its interpretation of the role of U.S. support for regime change in countries on Russia's periphery, especially in Ukraine in 2004–5 and again in 2014, as well as in the Middle East during the Arab Spring. Many of the tools deployed by Moscow, such as media penetration and support for political parties and NGOs, are not particularly new, but the deployment of these tools is far more deft and effective today than it was in the Soviet Union. An excellent example is RT (formerly Russia Today), the Russian state's global television network founded ten years ago that competes effectively for viewers with CNN International, the BBC, Al Jazeera, CCTV, and the Voice of America. However, with the notable exception of the Central Asian states on its southern periphery, most of these newly rediscovered instruments of soft power are far less relevant for Asia than they are in Europe, the South Caucasus, and the greater Middle East.

Until the annexation of Crimea in March 2014 and their support for the insurgents in the Donbass, Russian leaders and officials emphasized that Russian power was essential to constrain the alleged U.S. predilection for the illegal use of military force. On this account, Russia was seen as a more status quo power, whereas the United States was viewed as the irresponsible revisionist. In the past couple of years, the Russian argument has increasingly emphasized that U.S. military intervention and policies have not been so much illegal as incompetent, increasing rather than decreasing instability, especially in the Middle East. The cases of Iraq and Libya are often brought to bear and cited not only as violating state sovereignty but also as worsening regional security and not even serving U.S. interests.[63] The two most commonly cited tools for checking the United States—the first rhetorical (at this point) and

---

[62] For the first time in 2014, Russia's official foreign policy doctrine included a discussion of the importance of soft power with special emphasis on foreign support for nongovernmental organizations, influencing the media narrative in foreign countries, and other measures.

[63] Vladimir Putin's discussion with the Valdai Discussion Club in October 2014 laid this argument out in particularly stark and derisive terms. For the full transcript, see "Meeting of the Valdai International Discussion Club," President of Russia, October 24, 2014, http://en.kremlin.ru/events/president/news/46860.

the second used on multiple occasions—are Russia's nuclear arsenal and its veto on the UN Security Council.

These Russian arguments about Washington's misuse of power and illegal violations of sovereignty appeal to many large emerging powers, including the BRICS countries (Brazil, Russia, India, China, and South Africa), as well as to smaller states. Russia's willingness to stand up to the United States on a variety of issues earns credibility and support from many Asian states, especially China and India, but the growing concerns of much of Asia about rising Chinese power makes this proclivity to counter Washington less appealing. Indeed, as discussed above, Russia itself has very mixed feelings about the rapid growth of Chinese power on its periphery.

Russian Diplomacy and Intelligence Services as Tools of National Power

Any effort to measure and qualify Russian national power must include some discussion of diplomacy and intelligence services because of their long and storied traditions during the tsarist and Soviet periods, as well as their contemporary relevance during Putin's long tenure as Russian leader. Foreign Minister Sergei Lavrov is fond of reminding his colleagues and the world that no major global foreign or security challenge can be resolved without the participation of Russia. Indeed, Russia's self-perception is so deeply steeped in its status as a great power that Russian leaders and diplomats rarely shy away from vocalizing the country's interests as virtually unimpeachable. In many instances, especially in the post-Soviet period, Russia has seemingly "punched above its weight" in the arena of international relations. Its possession of veto power on the UN Security Council is an especially important diplomatic arrow in its quill that has deeply frustrated the Obama administration.

But only focusing on Russia's readiness to obstruct diplomatic negotiations and block policies would be an inaccurate caricature. Russian diplomacy may be noted for its dogged persistence, but it can also take measures with impressive speed, adeptness, and creativity. For example, where the new BRICS institution will go is not entirely clear, but it is safe to say that efforts under Putin to catalyze this grouping have been critical for its existence. One of the most unexpected lightning strikes of Russian diplomacy was Putin's proposal in September 2013 for the United States and Russia to work together to dispose of Syria's declared chemical weapons arsenal. More recently, Obama was nearly effusive in his praise of Putin for Russia's indispensable role in the multilateral negotiated deal on Iran's nuclear program.

It is well known that Putin is a trained Soviet intelligence officer, and many of his ruling circle also were recruited and trained in the KGB during 1967–82.

Historically the ethos of Russian intelligence services has been to recruit the "best and the brightest" to perform a special mission to save Russia from its internal and external enemies. Intelligence and security forces in general (such as the Ministry of the Interior) have enjoyed a major prioritization in the allocation of human and financial resources since Putin came to power in 2000. Yet their comeback from the bitter loss of power with the Soviet collapse predated Putin's arrival on the national scene and was perhaps best exemplified by the appointment of intelligence veteran Yevgeny Primakov as foreign minister and later prime minister in the second half of the 1990s. With a trained intelligence officer at the helm, intelligence and security personnel have reclaimed immense authority and wealth. U.S. and Western intelligence and security authorities routinely claim that intelligence activity in contemporary Russia is at as high a level as it ever was during the Cold War.[64]

This phenomenon of intelligence services wielding immense power is perfectly suited to the ideational narrative of a Russia surrounded by U.S.-led Western enemies that seek to weaken and destabilize it. This narrative has slowly gained currency in Putin's Russia and drowned out other narratives. If one is to judge by Putin's record-high popularity ratings, it has apparently been widely accepted by the Russian people. Of course, this narrative is not new, but it is an essential feature of contemporary Russia that must be acknowledged in any consideration of current national power and Putin's hold on political power.

State Capacity for Societal Mobilization and Power Conversion

Comparing Putin's Russia today with Yeltsin's Russia of the 1990s, there is no question that the state capacity for mobilizing national resources for statist goals has increased. Indeed, Putin saw restoration of effective state power in a market democratic context as his principal mission when he assumed power on December 31, 1999. The critical relationship between state and society has dramatically shifted twice in the last three decades. The Soviet Union was an authoritarian, at times totalitarian, state that completely dominated society. With the collapse of the Soviet state in 1991, the balance of power between state and society shifted almost 180 degrees, which explains Putin's obsession with restoring state power now. To this end, independent economic, social, and political institutions outside the state have been systematically weakened over the course of the last fifteen years.

---

[64] Richard Norton-Taylor, "Russian Spies in UK 'at Cold War Levels,' Says MI5," *Guardian*, June 29, 2010, http://www.theguardian.com/world/2010/jun/29/russian-spies-cold-war-levels; and Stephen Collinson, "Why the Alleged Russian Spy Ring Matters," CNN, January 28, 2015, http://www.cnn.com/2015/01/27/politics/us-russia-spies-analysis.

Several watershed events in the years following Putin's assumption of power enhanced the Kremlin's capacity to control the flow of key national resources, communicate effectively its narrative to the Russian people, and eventually control the outcome of key national elections. Control of Russian power after the collapse of the Soviet Union diffused to Russian society in the 1990s. Step by step, however, the Russian state has re-established its control over key national resources, although not to the extent of its Soviet predecessor. Putin's Russia might be described as the "Soviet Union lite" in this regard.

In his capacity as president, Putin reasserted state control over national television networks, as they are the key medium, even today in the Internet age, for the majority of the Russian population to get information about what is happening in their country and the world. Next the Kremlin took on the "commanding heights" of the economy, starting with the oil sector, by renationalizing many private companies and intimidating business leaders not to cross the Kremlin. The arrest and jailing of Mikhail Khodorkovsky in 2003 and the destruction of his company, Yukos, marked the key moment for the Kremlin. This development coincided with increased control over the electoral process and destruction of independent political actors and parties during the 2003–4 electoral cycle of parliamentary and presidential elections. With these and other acts, over time the balance of power between the Russian state and society shifted dramatically in favor of the state and its capacity to mobilize national resources. Over the past ten years, NGOs have been seriously hamstrung by legislation that has placed onerous reporting demands on their activities and virtually made it impossible to receive foreign funding. The Putin government sees foreign-funded NGOs as potentially organizing institutions for the opposition that could even work to overthrow the government. And while the Internet is far less restricted in Russia than in China, the state nonetheless monitors it closely and develops strategies for mobilizing society for state purposes through various Internet initiatives. Occasional strategic arrests and legal hassling of opposition figures, such as the house arrest of the anticorruption lawyer Alexei Navalny, and new restrictive legislation have virtually decimated the opposition that emerged in December 2011 with large protests in Moscow and other Russian cities in response to violations of electoral procedures in the Duma elections.

As power has shifted so much to the state authorities from Russian society in the past fifteen years, there is not much negotiation that occurs in a regular fashion between state and society over key national goals. With state control over electoral processes, national television, and civil society, independent institutions that represent society's interests have been deeply stifled. Consequently, society remains for the most part apathetic or apolitical. And without legal structures to promote its interests, occasionally these interests emerge in the form of demonstrations and protests, as happened following allegations of fraud in the December 2011 Duma elections. The government's legitimacy for most of Putin's rule has been founded on robust economic growth, and this is reflected in high popularity ratings for Putin the political leader, if less so for his government.

The core question for this study is the degree to which Russian national power has increased as a result of this centralization and consolidation of political power, and one must conclude that it has increased quite significantly over the past fifteen years. Russia does have considerably greater economic resources that can be mobilized to serve state or national purposes. The Russian military has also significantly increased its capacity to mobilize resources to pursue state goals. We saw this trend in Georgia in 2008; we are seeing it in Ukraine; and most recently we have seen this trend with Russian military transfers to Syria. As an unambiguously authoritarian state, Russia can often act far more quickly and nimbly than its democratic Western competitors. Such speedy mobilization can be an advantage unless the action taken fails. The longer any authoritarian leader is entrenched in power, the less likely it is that another person, let alone an institution, questions the leader's mistakes or seeks to prevent his or her actions.

The question becomes more complicated when assessing Russian power in comparative terms, as well as most importantly when making judgments about the sustainability of these trends. As discussed above, Russia's capabilities in innovation and high technology rank globally in the 40s and 50s rather than in the top 10. Health and demographic trends are also not promising over the next 30 years. The Russian economy overall is hampered by endemic corruption and overly bureaucratized procedures that stunt the private sector. A still underdeveloped and arbitrary legal system hampers domestic and foreign investment. And finally, macroeconomic performance remains very closely tied to the whims of the oil price. The failure of the state to provide for improving social health and welfare services, as well as to address corruption in state institutions, may be a vulnerable point in the state's capacity to control society. Precisely these issues brought tens of thousands of Russians into the streets in Moscow and other large cities in winter 2011–12. The tacit social contact for most of the Putin years, based on increasing prosperity and personal freedoms at the expense of political freedoms and independent political institutions, may be called into question if the current economic decline becomes protracted for more than two years.

There is no question that Russian national power is significantly greater than fifteen years ago when Putin first became president of Russia. There is also no question that Russian national power is significantly weaker in both overall and relative terms than 30 years ago when Mikhail Gorbachev assumed the leadership of the larger Soviet Union. And as we saw with the 2008–9 financial crisis and the current deep recession, Russia remains just as vulnerable to the vicissitudes of the oil price as it was before the Soviet collapse. The current Russian economy is actually less diversified than its Soviet predecessor, but it is more efficient with the adaption of market principles at its foundation. Yet the current trend toward increasing state intervention in the economy does not bode well for either increasing productivity or developing new, innovative high-tech sectors, despite strong foundations of human capital.

Although greater state control over Russian society has increased state power in the short term, many of Moscow's policies are deeply weakening core societal institutions that are the foundation for promoting the longer-term growth of Russian national power. Looking five to ten years into the future, it is hard to be optimistic about Russian power because too many fundamental economic, demographic, and geopolitical trend lines are negative or performing mediocrely at best. The state is more powerful, but also corrupt and inefficient, and without major political change, it will undermine Russia's long-term status as a great power.

Russian Military Power

Russia's military is currently in the midst of a major, multiyear reform process, which, despite a number of setbacks, has already generated real improvements in military capability. To this end, the Kremlin has focused on rationalizing the structure of the armed forces, achieving higher readiness levels through a program of intensified training and military exercises, and pursuing an ambitious rearmament program that aims to modernize no less than 70% of the armed forces' military equipment by 2020.[65] While the final outcome of these reforms remains uncertain, the sophistication exhibited by Russia's military in Ukraine represents a significant leap forward from its relatively poor performance during the 2008 war with Georgia. Even so, the present reform effort still faces a number of significant financial, technological, and demographic constraints that threaten to compromise its desired effects.

---

[65] Yurij Fedorov, "Gosydarstvennaya programma vooruzhenij-2020: Vlast i promyshlennost" [State Armaments Program for 2020: Power and Industry], *Security Index* 19, no. 4 (2013): 41–59, http://www.pircenter.org/media/content/files/12/13880454280.pdf.

Strategic and Human Resources

Increased defense spending has been a key factor in the improvement of Russia's military capabilities. According to the Stockholm International Peace Research Institute's Military Expenditure Database, Russia's defense budget grew 16% per year from $9.2 billion in 2000 to $84.5 billion in 2014. During this same period, expenditures on the armed forces on average constituted 3.8% of Russia's GDP (see **Figure 4**). Moscow's willingness to sustain such high levels of defense spending over a long time period confirms its commitment to the military reform program.

Despite that commitment, Russia's recent economic problems as a result of Western sanctions and low oil prices may soon compel the Kremlin to scale back its ambitions. Although Putin has pledged publicly not to reduce military expenditures, the country increasingly appears to be facing a stark choice between "guns and butter."

Personnel challenges. The Kremlin regards the reorganization of the armed forces as a top concern. This initiative originally included several targets, of which rationalization of the officer corps was one of the most important. Prior to 2008, there was one headquarters-level staff member for

FIGURE 4   Russian military spending, 2000–2014

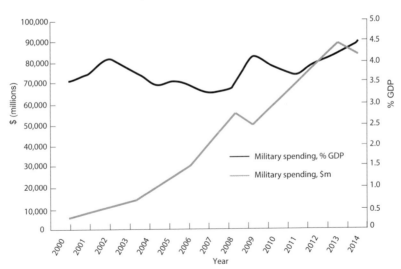

SOURCE: "SIPRI Milex Data 1988–2014," Stockholm International Peace Research Institute (SIPRI), SIPRI Military Expenditure Database, http://www.sipri.org/research/armaments/milex/milex_database/milex-data-1988-2014; and "Military Expenditure (% of GDP)," World Bank, World Development Indicators, http://data.worldbank.org/indicator/MS.MIL.XPND.GD.ZS.

every combat-ready soldier and officer.[66] The Ministry of Defense addressed this lopsided distribution by slashing the number of staff from 335,000 to 150,000 while increasing the number of junior officers from 50,000 to 60,000. At the same time, 60,000 warrant officers were forcibly retired, with their responsibilities redistributed to other servicemen.[67] While the Ministry of Defense did meet this target more or less on schedule, it did so in part by transferring 70,000 of the original 335,000 posts over to the new Aerospace Defense Forces.[68]

The Russian armed forces have long suffered from a shortage of adequate personnel. For starters, roughly half of all potential draftees are believed to dodge conscription. During the first quarter of 2014 alone, Rosstat documented 1,409 instances of draft evasion, up 15% from 1,224 cases during the first quarter of 2013.[69] (The autumn 2014 draft, however, apparently did show a 20% reduction in the number of such cases.)[70] Yet while the Russian government has attempted to rein in draft-dodging through various legal measures, the problem neither begins nor ends with draft evasion alone. Poor service conditions also contribute. It is well known, for example, that many of those who seek to escape military service do so because of endemic hazing of new enlistees.

Despite a recent uptick in population growth, the population pool from which the Russian military pulls its conscripts and contractors remains far from ideal. One recent government study found that more than 40% of potential recruits fail to meet standard health and fitness criteria.[71] Moreover, the substandard level of education among potential recruits hinders their ability to handle complex weapons systems. For these and other reasons, some experts believe that Russian military capability is more

---

[66] Mikhail Barabanov, Konstantin Makienko, and Ruslan Pukhov, "Military Reform: Toward the New Look of the Russian Army," Valdai Discussion Club, Analytical Report, July 2012, 5, http://vid-1.rian.ru/ig/valdai/Military_reform_eng.pdf.

[67] Aleksey Gayday, "Reform of the Russian Army," in *Russia's New Army*, ed. Mikhail Barabanov (Moscow: Centre for Analysis of Strategies and Technologies, 2011), 23, http://www.cast.ru/files/book/NewArmy_sm.pdf; and Clifford J. Levy, "Russian Military Cuts Leave Soldiers Adrift," *New York Times*, June 11, 2009, http://www.nytimes.com/2009/06/12/world/europe/12russia.html?pagewanted=all&_r=0.

[68] Andrzej Wilk, "Toward a Professional Army: Changes to the Structure of the Officer Cadre and the Manning System of the Russian Armed Forces," Centre for Eastern Studies, OSW Commentary, no. 73, March 28, 2013, 2, http://aei.pitt.edu/58361/1/commentary_73.pdf.

[69] "Voiny-pobegonostsy" [Warriors-Escapees], *Kommerstant*, February 17, 2015, http://www.kommersant.ru/doc/2668258.

[70] International Institute for Strategic Studies, *The Military Balance 2015* (London: Routledge, 2015), 163.

[71] "Senator: Bolye 40% Rossijskikh prizyvnikov ne sootvetstvuyut trebovaniyam po zdorov'yu" [Senator: More Than 40% of Russian Recruits Do Not Meet Health Criterion], TASS, April 24, 2015, http://tass.ru/obschestvo/1927963.

likely to be constrained by specific demographic and institutional factors than by broader financial limitations.[72]

Defense industry and R&D challenges. Problems in Russia's defense industry have also adversely affected the military reform program. Lack of career opportunities and poor working conditions have encouraged a massive brain drain, with the number of research professionals in Russia dropping from more than one million in 1999 to just 376,000 in 2008.[73] Worse still, declining standards in postsecondary technical education have left those researchers and engineers entering the military-industrial complex substantially less prepared to meet the demands of the rearmament program. Although the Ministry of Defense has begun to reverse this trend as a result of new state orders and higher salaries, the shortage of interested and qualified workers remains a serious problem for the Kremlin.

While Russia's defense industry is technologically competitive in certain sectors such as anti-access/area-denial (A2/AD), military aircraft, and cyber, the rearmament program continues to be technologically backward in many other sectors of the defense industry. The Russian government has stressed the need for major innovations in several key defense-related technology clusters. Putin himself has called for the creation of cutting-edge weapons systems "based on new physical principles," while officials in the defense establishment have advocated for greater research into the various military applications of exotic bio-, nano-, and cognitive technologies.[74] Deputy Prime Minister Dmitry Rogozin meanwhile has urged the defense industry not to "fall behind" the West in the development of new aerospace defense complexes, precision-guided munitions, and unmanned systems, among other areas.[75]

Despite a lack of detailed open source data on military spending after 2006, experts believe that the Ministry of Defense allocates a significant portion of funding for applied research, development, test, and evaluation (RDT&E) efforts.[76] According to some estimates, military RDT&E expenditures grew 11%–22% on an annualized basis between 2008 and 2013, although the share

---

[72] Barabanov, Makienko, and Pukhov, "Military Reform," 12.

[73] Julian Cooper, "The Innovative Potential of the Russian Economy," *Russia Analytical Digest*, no. 88, November 29, 2010, 9, http://www.css.ethz.ch/publications/pdfs/RAD-88.pdf.

[74] Vladimir Putin, "Byt' sil'niymi: Garantii natsional'noij bezopasnosti dlya Rossii" [Being Strong: Guarantees of National Security for Russia], *Rossijskaya Gazeta*, February 20, 2012, http://www.rg.ru/2012/02/20/putin-armiya.html; and Vasilij Buryenok, "Vooruzheniya XXI veka budut imet' intuitsiyu i nastroenie" [Weapons of the 21st Century Will Have Intuition and Mood], *Independent Military Review*, February 12, 2011, http://nvo.ng.ru/concepts/2011-12-02/6_nanobioinfo.html.

[75] Sergej Ptichkin, "Sil'niykh ne b'yut" [They Do Not Beat the Strong], *Rossijskaia Gazeta*, July 3, 2013, http://www.rg.ru/2013/07/03/kompleks.html.

[76] Julian Cooper, "Russian Military Expenditure: Data, Analysis and Issues," FOI, September 2013, 22.

of the overall defense budget decreased by approximately 8%–10% during that same period (see **Figure 5**).[77] Other analysts calculate that 35%–40% of overall government RDT&E spending goes toward defense-related projects.[78]

Nevertheless, RDT&E activities puzzlingly account for just 10% of the budget allocated for 2020 under the State Rearmament Program. Depending on whom ones asks, this meager allotment is either a tacit admission of a weak technical base or a sign that the Ministry of Defense believes that the military-industrial base is riddled with graft—or both.[79] Regarding the first scenario, few would disagree that the Russian defense industry has not yet fully regained the innovative potential of the late Soviet era.[80] Part of the problem

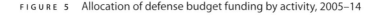

FIGURE 5   Allocation of defense budget funding by activity, 2005–14

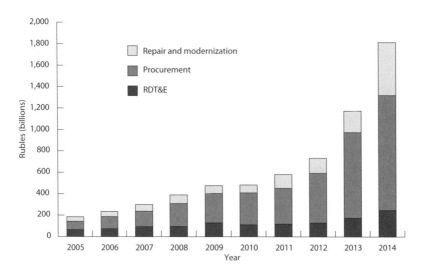

SOURCE: For 2005–13 data, see Julian Cooper, "Russian Military Expenditure: Data, Analysis and Issues," FOI, September 2013. For 2014 data, see "Poleznye tsifry" [Useful Figures], Centre for Analysis of Strategies and Technologies, July 2015, http://www.cast.ru/files/book/2015_rus.pdf.

---

[77] Cooper, "Russian Military Expenditure"; and "Voennij byudzhet i gosudarstvennij oboronnij zakaz" [The Military Budget and the State Defense Order], Centre for Analysis of Strategies and Technologies, November 2014.

[78] Cooper, "The Innovative Potential of the Russian Economy," 9.

[79] Barabanov, Makienko, and Pukhov, "Military Reform," 31.

[80] Iu. V. Erygin and A.M. Saakian, "Russia's Defense-Industrial Complex: Development Trends," *Problems of Economic Transition* 54, no. 4 (2011): 9, http://www.tandfonline.com/doi/abs/10.2753/PET1061-1991540401#.VfROrGTBzGc.

stems from the defense sector's lack of modern means of production, as some analysts estimate that up to 75% of its manufacturing assets are technologically obsolete and thus ill-suited to the production of advanced armaments and equipment.[81] This manufacturing deficit has forced Russia's defense industry to procure many of its most advanced components from foreign suppliers.

Arms sales. Prior to the recent large increases in government defense spending that followed the oil and natural gas boom of the 2000s, the Russian defense industry often had to rely on revenues from arms transfers and foreign military-technical cooperation in order to sustain itself and fund its own modernization.[82] Russia made $13.2 billion from foreign arms transfers in 2014 and now stands as the world's second-largest exporter of arms after the United States.[83]

Russian arms transfers have generally risen over the past decade as sales to key Asian markets weathered an annualized drop in global sales of weapons and equipment. According to data compiled by the Stockholm International Peace Research Institute, Asia accounted for more than two-thirds of all Russian arms transfers between 2004 and 2014 (see **Figure 6**). On average, India accounted for 31.8% of Russia's total arms transfers between 2004 and 2014, while China accounted for 23.3%. Meanwhile, as arms exports to India increased, with annualized growth of 3.7%, exports to China declined by almost 10%. Russia supplied 70% of India's arms imports over this period.[84]

Combat Proficiency

Russia deployed its combined arms capabilities to mixed effect during the 2008 Russo-Georgian war, as failures of command and control and interoperability resulted in joint operations "on only the most

---

[81] Natalia Kalinina and Vadim Kozyulin, "Russia's Defense Industry: Feet of Clay," *Security Index: A Russian Journal on International Security* 16, no. 1 (2010): 41, http://www.tandfonline.com/doi/pdf/10.1080/19934270903570661.

[82] Stephen J. Blank, *Rosoboroneksport: Arms Sales and the Structure of Russian Defense Industry* (Carlisle: Strategic Studies Institute, 2007), 11, http://www.strategicstudiesinstitute.army.mil/pdffiles/PUB749.pdf; and Sam Jones, "Russia Has Little to Lose from Arms Embargo," *Financial Times*, July 22, 2014, http://www.ft.com/intl/cms/s/0/ae366600-11ae-11e4-b356-00144feabdc0.html - axzz3fhOXTQVd.

[83] "Russian Arms Exports Hit $13 Billion in 2014—Rosoboronexport," *Moscow Times*, March 17, 2015, http://www.themoscowtimes.com/business/article/russian-arms-exports-hit-13-billion-in-2014--rosoboronexport/517554.html; and "SIPRI Yearbook 2015: Armaments, Disarmament and International Security," Stockholm International Peace Research Institute (SIPRI), 2015, 17, http://www.sipri.org/yearbook/2015/downloadable-files/sipri-yearbook-2015-summary-pdf.

[84] Pieter D. Wezeman and Siemon T. Wezeman, "Trends in International Arms Transfers: 2014," SIPRI, SIPRI Fact Sheet, March 2015, 6, http://books.sipri.org/files/FS/SIPRIFS1503.pdf.

FIGURE 6   Allocation of Russian arms transfers by region

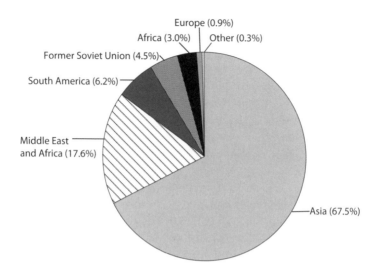

SOURCE: Pieter D. Wezeman and Siemon T. Wezeman, "Trends in International Arms Transfers: 2014," Stockholm International Peace Research Institute, SIPRI Fact Sheet, March 2015, 6, http://books.sipri.org/files/FS/SIPRIFS1503.pdf.

superficial level."[85] With the potential for interservice cooperation thus undermined by an "absence of unified command," the General Staff set out after 2008 to facilitate cross-service collaboration by creating new command-and-control structures at the district and federal levels.[86]

The Kremlin has evidently used the war in Ukraine as a proving ground for this new framework. According to the Royal United Services Institute, Russia's high command has drawn personnel from dozens of units across all four joint strategic commands in creating ad hoc combat tactical groups for deployment to Ukraine.[87] Yet while Russia has demonstrated an increased ability to mobilize forces for operations in Ukraine, the quality of assigned personnel has occasionally fallen short of tactical expectations.

---

[85] Paul B. Rich, *Crisis in the Caucasus: Russia, Georgia and the West* (London: Routledge, 2010), 160; and Ariel Cohen and Robert E. Hamilton, *The Russian Military and the Georgia War: Lessons and Implications* (Carlisle: Strategic Studies Institute, 2011), 35–36, http://www.strategicstudiesinstitute. army.mil/pdffiles/PUB1069.pdf.

[86] Barabanov, Makienko, and Pukhov, "Military Reform," 18–20.

[87] Igor Sutyagin, "Briefing Paper: Russian Forces in Ukraine," Royal United Services Institute, Briefing Paper, March 2015, https://www.rusi.org/downloads/assets/201503_BP_Russian_Forces_in_ Ukraine_FINAL.pdf.

At the same time, the effectiveness of Russia's military operations in Crimea and the Donbass points to an improved grasp of network-centric warfare and tactics. Unlike the 2008 Georgia war, which saw regular breakdowns in Russian command and control,[88] Moscow has generally conducted operations in Ukraine with much greater precision and coordination. In particular, Russia has demonstrated its ability to adjust the pitch of combat operations to match the evolving geopolitical situation. Moreover, the Kremlin has used this increased self-control in tandem with an elaborate information campaign to influence the operational environment in its favor.

Russia has also made considerable progress in developing some of the most robust cyber capabilities in the world. This was already apparent during the war with Georgia, when Russian hackers allegedly destroyed a section of the Baku-Tbilisi-Ceyhan pipeline and crashed Georgian bank and government websites through a flood of distributed denial-of-service attacks.[89] Russian cyberactivity has likewise featured prominently in the Ukraine crisis, as pro-Kremlin hackers reportedly targeted the Poroshenko government, NATO, and various European business entities with malware and spear-phishing attacks aimed at gathering sensitive information.[90]

Conventional and nuclear force modernization. More troublingly, since the onset of the Ukrainian crisis, the Russian leadership has engaged in nuclear saber-rattling of a kind not seen since the Cold War. Such belligerence neatly complements increased investment in the modernization of Russia's tactical and strategic nuclear forces, which are seen by the Kremlin to offer a vital means of offsetting NATO's relative conventional superiority. During the Cold War, the situation was reversed: the United States and NATO depended more on nuclear forces to contest Soviet conventional military advantages. The shape of the current procurement program dates back to February 2012, when Putin pledged to supply more than four hundred new intercontinental ballistic missiles (ICBM) to the military within the next decade.[91] Russian finance minister Anton Siluanov, however, has gone on record to state that

---

[88] Roger N. McDermott, "Russia's Conventional Armed Forces and the Georgian War," *Parameters* 39, no. 1 (2009): 69–71, http://strategicstudiesinstitute.army.mil/pubs/parameters/Articles/09spring/mcdermott.pdf.

[89] Jordan Robertson and Michael Riley, "Mysterious '08 Turkey Pipeline Blast Opened New Cyberwar," *Bloomberg Business*, December 10, 2014, http://www.bloomberg.com/news/articles/2014-12-10/mysterious-08-turkey-pipeline-blast-opened-new-cyberwar.

[90] "Operation Armageddon: Cyber Espionage as a Strategic Component of Russian Modern Warfare," Looking Glass, April 28, 2015, https://lgscout.com/operation-armageddon-cyber-espionage-as-a-strategic-component-of-russian-modern-warfare.

[91] Putin, "Byt' sil'niymi: garantii natsional'noij bezopasnosti dlya Rossii"; and Hans M. Kristensen and Robert S. Norris, "Nuclear Notebook: Russian Nuclear Forces, 2015," *Bulletin of the Atomic Scientists* 71, no. 3 (2015): 1–14, http://bos.sagepub.com/content/early/2015/04/13/0096340215581363.full.pdf.

the government lacks the necessary funds to meet all of its original 2020 targets.[92] In light of the strategic importance assigned to nuclear weapons under the current military doctrine, some experts believe that the Kremlin will continue to prioritize nuclear modernization efforts and compensate by increasing the share of ICBMs capable of carrying multiple independently targetable reentry vehicles (MIRV).[93]

The State Armament Program for 2020 looks to allocate more than 4 trillion rubles (or roughly $130 billion) to air force modernization—around 21% of the total 2020 procurement target. Under this scheme, Russia is to acquire more than 600 new aircraft and 1,000–1,100 helicopters by decade's end.[94] However, most of these products amount to modernized versions of Soviet-era aerial systems rather than new models. The major exception to this trend, the T-50 stealth fighter, was originally slated to enter into serial production by 2016.[95] However, in March 2015 the air force announced that it intended to reduce its 2020 procurement targets for the T-50 from 52 to just 12 aircraft and would instead focus on "squeezing everything possible" from its existing fighter fleet.[96] The outlook is even bleaker for Russia's next-generation bomber program, which appears to have been delayed past 2023 due to the government's prioritizing the modernization of the nuclear-capable Tu-160 Blackjack strategic bomber fleet.[97]

Russia's new 2015 naval doctrine foresees force deployment across all the world's oceans, including the Arctic Ocean.[98] In order to realize this objective, however, the navy must first restore its blue water capabilities. This will be no easy feat, given that it has lost more than 300 surface vessels since 1990.[99] To help bridge this gap, the Russian government in recent years

---

[92] Lidia Kelly, "Finance Minister Warns Russia Can't Afford Military Spending Plan," Reuters, October 7, 2014, http://www.reuters.com/article/2014/10/07/us-russia-economy-spending-defence-idUSKCN0HW1H420141007.

[93] Kirestensen and Norris, "Nuclear Notebook: Russian Nuclear Forces, 2015."

[94] Fedorov, "Gosudarstvennaya programma vooruzhenij-2020."

[95] "Russia to Begin Serial Production of 5th Generation T-50 Fighters in 2016," Sputnik, March 23, 2015, http://sputniknews.com/military/20150323/1019885476.html.

[96] Ivan Safronov, "Pyatoe s minusom pokolenie" [Fifth with a Minus Generation], Businessman (Russia), March 24, 2015, http://www.kommersant.ru/doc/2693130.

[97] Nikolaj Novichkov, "Russia's Future PAK DA Bomber to Be Delayed by Tu-160M2 Production," IHS Jane's 360, July 20, 2015, http://www.janes.com/article/53102/russia-s-future-pak-da-bomber-to-be-delayed-by-tu-160m2-production.

[98] "Morskaya doktrina Rossijskoj Federatsii" [Naval Doctrine of the Russian Federation], President of the Russian Federation, http://static.kremlin.ru/media/events/files/ru/uAFi5nvux2twaqjftS5yrIZUVTJan77L.pdf.

[99] Natalya Orlova, "Nalogi, kredity, kachestvo izdelij" [Taxes, Credit, Product Quality], Military-Industrial Courier (Russia), March 30, 2005, http://www.vpk-news.ru/articles/903.

has committed itself to the purchase of 50–54 new surface vessels by 2020.[100] Some analysts contend, however, that the navy cannot hope to deliver on this goal due to the already dire state of the Russian shipbuilding industry, which has seen its access to essential foreign components disrupted by sanctions related to the conflict in Ukraine.[101] For this reason, other experts suggest that while the Kremlin will push forward with naval modernization, it will likely defer recouping its blue water fleet for another decade.

Implications for Asia. The implications of Russian military capabilities are relatively limited for Asia, with the exception of Central Asia, where Russia already has forces deployed in Tajikistan and coordinates with regional militaries through the Collective Security Treaty Organization. Although some important military production facilities, particularly aviation, are located in the Russian Far East, and Moscow does maintain military deployments in the region, it is difficult to imagine the circumstances in which those forces might actually engage in conflict.

Foreign military relations play a smaller role in Russia's military conversion activities, primarily because Russia, as a former superpower, has less to gain from interacting with military partners than they do from Russia. Moscow has increasingly turned its attention to partnering with Beijing, New Delhi, and Central Asian members of the Collective Security Treaty Organization. Some outside observers contend that these sorts of exercises are intended to challenge Western narratives of Russia's international isolation.[102] These exercises are more valuable for their political symbolism than for the development of actual joint operational capabilities that might be utilized.

Arms sales to Asian partners, especially China, are now Russia's most significant tool of military power and its second most important tool of commercial power (behind oil and gas sales). There is no question that Russian sales of aircraft, naval vessels, and probably most importantly A2/AD systems have significantly contributed to accelerating China's military buildup, particularly its capacity to resist U.S. naval power in the region.

---

[100] "VMF Rossii poluchit v 2015 godu okolo 50 korablej" [The Russian Navy Will Receive around 50 Boats in 2015], *Lenta*, March 2, 2015, http://lenta.ru/news/2015/03/02/50newships; and "Russian Navy to Receive 24 Subs, 54 Warships by 2020," Sputnik, March 11, 2013, http://sputniknews.com/military/20130311/179945052/Russian-Navy-to-Receive-24-Subs-54-Warships-by-2020.html.

[101] Dmitry Gorenburg, "Russian Naval Capabilities and Procurement Plans," Russian Military Reform, January 14, 2015, https://russiamil.wordpress.com/2015/01/14/russian-naval-capabilities-and-procurement-plans.

[102] Damien Sharkov, "Russia Plans Joint Military Drills with North Korea and Cuba," *Newsweek*, February 2, 2015, http://europe.newsweek.com/russia-plans-joint-military-drills-north-korea-and-cuba-303836.

Implications of Russian Power for U.S. Policy and Asia

Analysts feared that the international humiliation and domestic deprivation that Russia experienced in the 1990s, akin to that of Weimar Germany after World War I, could lead to the resurgence of an aggressive, nationalist country. This Russia would be focused on revising international relations and vindicating itself after a period during which it perceived the U.S.-led West as taking advantage of Russian weakness. While no longer a superpower, as this chapter documents, Russia still has a powerful inventory of tools to advance its interests in multiple regions—from military assets to intelligence and diplomacy to economic, energy, and other resources. Moscow has evinced little reluctance to use these tools in traditional and nontraditional ways that undercut U.S. interests, whether in Ukraine, Georgia, Syria, or elsewhere. From the standpoint of Washington, much of U.S. diplomacy with Russia over the past two-plus decades has sought to prevent Russia from playing a spoiler role on core U.S. national security interests, such as the Iranian nuclear issue. The situation is tenser and possibly more dangerous today because Putin has wrapped himself in anti-Americanism for domestic political purposes as the Russian economy staggers in recession. Already Russian activities in Ukraine and elsewhere in Europe have led NATO to increase vigilance about a potential Russian threat to its member states.

Another significant area of concern now is how Russia conducts its antiterrorist policies in its own North Caucasus and how this strategy relates to its broader Middle East policy. With reports in 2015 that Russian intelligence forces have facilitated the migration of jihadists from the North Caucasus to Iraq and Syria to take up arms with the Islamic State of Iraq and Syria (ISIS), it appears that Moscow is increasingly dealing with its homegrown terrorist problem by exporting it.[103] If these reports are accurate, this amounts to an ingenious ploy to reduce dangers to the Russian homeland while increasing justification for Moscow's support of the Bashar al-Assad regime as a bulwark against international terrorism.

By far the most worrisome issue concerning Russian power in Asia is the future of the China-Russia relationship. In 1997, I wrote the following:

> If China and Russia continue to perceive U.S.-led alliance systems in Asia and Europe as exclusionary, this can only lead to the Sino-Russian relationship taking on more of a traditionally strategic rather than politically symbolic character. This could also lead to strengthening their ties with other states contiguous

---

[103] The author warned of this possibility in testimony before the Congressional Committee on Homeland Security in April 2014. See Andrew C. Kuchins, "Terrorism in the Caucasus," statement before the House Homeland Security Subcommittee on Counterterrorism and Intelligence, April 3, 2014, http://docs.house.gov/meetings/HM/HM05/20140403/102041/HHRG-113-HM05-Wstate-KuchinsA-20140403.pdf.

with Eurasia—potentially Indonesia, India, Pakistan, Iran, and others—which feel marginalized in a unipolar world. The worst-case scenario would be the emergence of a Eurasian security alliance led by Russia and China that is directed against the United States. Clearly this is unlikely, and it would require a series of major foreign and security policy blunders by the United States and its allies. Still, stranger things have happened in history.[104]

Eighteen years later, a genuine Sino-Russian alliance has not emerged, but the relationship has become perhaps too close for the United States and its Asian allies to take much comfort. As noted above, two decades of extensive Russian arms sales have significantly increased Chinese capabilities in a number of critical weapon systems. And while Moscow remains wary of Chinese economic leverage, as this chapter indicates, Chinese economic power, and thus political influence, has grown dramatically. China may not need to take over formerly Chinese territories in eastern Russia; Beijing can simply buy what it wants. Especially when the Russian economy is in deep recession and sanctioned by the West, these assets can be acquired by China for bargain prices. Unless current trends change, Russia will not be able to say no to China essentially conducting a leveraged buyout of the Russian Far East and Eastern Siberia.

Chinese experts on Russia consistently point to the three principles in Beijing's approach: (1) no alliance, (2) no conflict, and (3) a peaceful border. But there need not be a formal military alliance for this relationship to be a large problem for U.S. interests. I would argue that their relationship already is problematic for the United States. If the trends noted in the above paragraph continue, it is not hard to imagine that Beijing may demand some political *quid pro quo* from Moscow. This could involve Russia taking a less neutral stance on China's multiple border conflicts with neighbors or perhaps reaching a tacit agreement to support China's territorial goals in Asia in exchange for China not opposing Russian actions toward the West. We may already be witnessing such a nascent agreement. Beijing and Moscow could also occasionally join forces in cyberattacks of mutual interest or act in a more unified manner to seek greater control of access to Arctic resources. The point is clear: a further tightening of the China-Russia relationship to contest U.S. interests could cause the United States and its Asian allies and partners many problems.

A long-standing challenge is that the U.S. policy community responsible for Russia is overly Eurocentric. U.S.-Russia relations have been at an all-time low these past two years because of disputes over Ukraine and, more generally,

---

104 Andrew Kuchins, "The Emerging Sino-Russian Strategic Partnership and Eurasian Security," Stanford University, PONARS Policy Memo, no. 11, October 1997, http://www.ponarseurasia.org/sites/default/files/policy-memos-pdf/pm_0011.pdf.

Russian policy toward Eastern Europe. Has the United States adequately considered how this affects U.S. interests in Asia? Obama was basically correct when he characterized Russia in March 2014 as just a "regional power," and the region where it is most influential is Europe. China may be mainly a regional military power, but factoring in its rapidly expanding economic influence, it is quickly becoming a global power. Washington needs to assume a more flexible posture regarding Russia that can allow for a more rapid Russian-European rapprochement. Moscow certainly desires this outcome, as do most European countries. Second, Washington should encourage Moscow to diversify its Asian pivot so it is less dependent on China. The first step is to not obstruct the Abe government in Japan from strengthening its ties with Russia. The essence of strategy is first being able to view and understand complex phenomena in a broad and comprehensive way, and second to then prioritize very clearly one's interests in ways that are feasible. The United States' overall policy toward Russia, and particularly its impact on Russian power in Asia, is failing on both counts.

In conclusion, the challenge of Russian power today and in the years ahead is complex and multifaceted. Although Russian power is slowly waning in many respects, it would be a big policy mistake to dismiss or underestimate Russia, as Washington did before being surprised by the seizure of Crimea in 2014 or the attack on Georgia in 2008. The leadership in Moscow is determined to ensure that Russian interests are respected and has shown considerable tactical dexterity in manipulating very comprehensive instruments of power in its eternal quest to advance Russian influence in the world.

EXECUTIVE SUMMARY

This chapter assesses the foundations of India's power by examining the country's national resources, capacity for extracting these resources to enhance national power, and finally the scope of that power.

MAIN ARGUMENT

India has considerable strengths that have enabled the country to assume a fairly robust international role. In addition to a rapidly growing economy, it possesses significant national resources and a state elite that shares a broad consensus and stands above society. India, however, has failed to realize the full power potential of its human and natural resources because of bureaucratic inefficiency, coupled with political dysfunction resulting from the lack of elite cohesion. Therefore, though India is growing stronger, its power position relative to other countries such as China has not improved and indeed might have worsened. Unless its bureaucratic apparatus becomes more efficient or less dominant—or both—the country's capacity to generate power will continue to suffer.

POLICY IMPLICATIONS

- India's continued growth will further skew the regional balance of power in South Asia and make Pakistan even more anxious.

- Although India's growth will only marginally affect its relative power position vis-à-vis China, it is still likely to increase China's balancing efforts and strengthen Sino-Pakistan strategic ties.

- Stronger Sino-Pakistan ties could lead to greater cooperation between India and the U.S., even though India's domestic politics will continue to limit open acknowledgement of the strategic partnership.

India's Unrealized Power

Rajesh Rajagopalan

India's rapid economic growth since the early 1990s, nuclear weapons test in 1998, technological prowess, and new partnerships with the United States and various countries in Asia have heightened expectations about the country's rise as a great power, not least among Indians. But India has been in a similar situation before: in the 1950s, the newly independent country was seen as a future great power, courted by both sides in the Cold War; it took a leadership position in framing the concerns of many other states in the global arena on issues ranging from war and peace to decolonization and economic development. But India's attractiveness then was based on power potential rather than realized power, and it diminished with India's military defeat by China in 1962. Do the perceptions of India as a rising power rest on stronger foundations today, or are they as ephemeral as they were in the 1950s?

This chapter provides a comprehensive assessment of the foundations of India's national power by looking beyond economic growth rates and data on military equipment to consider variables such as India's technological strength, its human and natural resource base, and the Indian state's capacity to extract resources from society and convert them into usable national power.[1] It argues that India's power potential is still unrealized primarily because of administrative inefficiency coupled in many cases with political dysfunction resulting from the lack of elite cohesion. India is considerably

Rajesh Rajagopalan is a Professor in the Centre for International Politics, Organization and Disarmament at Jawaharlal Nehru University in New Delhi. He can be reached at <rajesh622@gmail.com>.

The author thanks Deep Pal for research assistance and anonymous reviewers for comments on earlier drafts of this chapter, while accepting responsibility for any remaining errors and inadequacies.

[1] For an earlier study that measures national power using these variables, see Ashley J. Tellis, Janice Bially, Christopher Layne, Melissa McPherson, and Jerry M. Sollinger, *Measuring National Power in the Post-Industrial Age: Analyst's Handbook* (Santa Monica: RAND, 2000).

stronger today than it was in the 1950s, and this power rests on stronger foundations than ever. However, because this accumulation of power over the last several decades has been slower than for other key players such as China, India's relative power position has not improved much and might actually have worsened. The first section outlines India's resource base, while the second section examines the country's capacity to convert that resource base into usable national power. The third section then examines the implications for India's military capabilities. The chapter concludes with an assessment of the implications of Indian power capacity for South Asia, for Asia more broadly, and for U.S. interests.

National Resources

Measuring national resources goes beyond an analysis of gross data on resources or growth. They also must be measured in terms of technological capacity, capacity for innovation (i.e., enterprise), the quality of human resources, financial and capital resources, and natural resources. Measured thus, India demonstrates strength in some pockets of technology and economic growth, potential strength in human resources, weakness in enterprise, and mixed prospects with respect to financial and natural resources. On the whole, the picture of India that emerges suggests the potential for continued growth but also exposes some important weaknesses that prevent the development of national resources, particularly the inefficiency of the state's administrative apparatus and dysfunctional domestic politics. These weaknesses need to be addressed if India's national resources are expected to support an ambitious international role.

Technology

The importance of technological capacity for national power is well recognized in India, with investment in technological development enjoying broad support among the elite. Since independence, India has invested in key areas of high technology, particularly in nuclear energy, aeronautics, space, and defense, and has also benefited from international cooperation and assistance, such as through the Atoms for Peace program.[2] As a result, India has made headway in some of these areas: for example, it is now a leading power in space launch, satellite fabrication, and outer space exploration. India has also developed self-sufficiency in many aspects of nuclear technology, though it lags in nuclear power plant design. But these are the

---

[2] Atoms for Peace was a U.S. program, begun by the Eisenhower administration, under which the United States shared civilian nuclear technology with other countries.

exceptions: despite considerable investment, India has struggled to reach even self-sufficiency in all the other areas of high technology. A key reason for this lack of progress is inefficient management by the Indian bureaucracy.[3] It is noteworthy that scientists rather than bureaucrats manage both the space and nuclear programs.[4]

Nevertheless, over the last two decades, India's image has shifted from a country of teeming poverty to an information technology (IT) superpower. This development is ironic not only because India is far from being an IT superpower but also because this new image is the consequence of private sector initiative rather than deliberate government policy.[5] Although the growth of India's IT sector has indeed been spectacular, contributing today to more than 9% of GDP and employing over 3.5 million people, it contributes little to India's technological strength.[6] The IT sector is concentrated in outsourcing markets, and Indian firms have not yet shown the innovation in their business models necessary to move up the value chain. In fact, India has had difficulty maintaining its position even in areas where it previously was relatively strong. Indian supercomputers, for example, were once among the fastest in the world, but the country has since been surpassed by China: in 2010, China possessed 41 supercomputers in the top 500, while India had just 4.[7] In 2011, India responded with the National Supercomputing Mission, which reportedly has a budget of $1 billion.[8] Yet this project did not advance very much and was relaunched in 2015.[9] India's overall technological capacity is thus still weak, save for space and nuclear technologies.

---

[3] Mathai Joseph and Andrew Robinson, "Policy: Free Indian Science," *Nature*, April 2, 2014, 36–38, http://www.nature.com/news/policy-free-indian-science-1.14956?referral=true.

[4] Ashok Parthasarathi, "A Different Model for DRDO," *Hindu*, January 10, 2014; and Gopal Raj, *Reach for the Stars: The Evolution of India's Rocket Programme* (New Delhi: Viking, 2000).

[5] On the complexity of assessing India's (and China's) technological capacity, see Andrew B. Kennedy, "Powerhouses or Pretenders? Debating China's and India's Emergence as Technological Powers," *Pacific Review* 28, no. 2 (2015): 281–302.

[6] "IT-BPM Industry: Unparalleled Contribution to India," National Association of Software and Services Companies, http://www.nasscom.in/impact-indias-growth.

[7] Vijay Bhatkar, "Launching of SAC Initiated Mission to Develop Exascale Supercomputing Capability, Capacity and ICT Infrastructure on Integrated National Knowledge Network," in Scientific Advisory Council to the Prime Minister (India), *Bi-Annual Report 2011* (New Delhi, 2011), 99, http://sactopm.gov.in/SAC_PM_AR2011.pdf.

[8] "Minutes of the 27th Meeting of the Scientific Advisory Council to the Prime Minister (SAC to PM)," Scientific Advisory Council to the Prime Minister (India), November 9, 2013, http://sactopm.gov.in/SAC%20to%20PM%20Minutes/Minutes-27the%20Meeting.pdf; and Dinesh C. Sharma, "Making Up Lost Ground: India Pitches for $1bn Leap in Supercomputers," *Daily Mail* (India), January 23, 2012, http://www.dailymail.co.uk/indiahome/indianews/article-2090309/Supercomputers-India-pitches-1bn-leap-make-lost-ground.html.

[9] "'National Supercomputing Mission (NSM): Building Capacity and Capability' to Be Jointly Implemented by the Department of Science and Technology and Department of Electronics and Information Technology," Press Information Bureau (India), Cabinet Committee on Economic Affairs, Press Release, March 25, 2015.

Enterprise

Technological development is dependent on investment in R&D and the resulting innovation and invention, which are often measured through the growth of patenting. Such activity is collectively referred to in this chapter as "enterprise." By these metrics, India's level of capacity for enterprise remains low.

While India's capacity for innovation is difficult to measure, it is clear that the country's innovation ecosystem—the public policy context within which innovation can prosper—is poor. A recent government report, noting that Indians working abroad were well known for innovation, argued that "what India lacks is not the innovative spirit, but an effective innovation eco-system."[10] Another report called India's innovation ecosystem "unstructured."[11] There is some recognition of the need for improvement, with the government declaring in 2009 that the coming decade would be the "decade of innovation."[12] India established the National Innovation Council, along with a large number of state-level innovation councils. A new science, technology, and innovation policy was also announced.[13] The policy document suggested a target of 2% of GDP for gross domestic expenditure on research and development (GERD)—a metric used to compare R&D spending across countries—which indicates confusion between innovation and R&D spending. The status of these bodies and policies, however, is unclear after the change of government in New Delhi in 2014. There are other reasons as well to be skeptical that these ambitions will be fulfilled: similar targets were set in 2003 to increase GERD funding to 2% of GDP, but the figure has barely moved from the baseline of 0.8% in 2003.[14]

India's level of R&D spending is low even among the BRICS countries (Brazil, Russia, India, China, and South Africa). Over 75% comes from the public sector, while private sector R&D efforts largely consist in offshore spending, with foreign companies setting up approximately six hundred R&D facilities in India.[15] One policy plan called for raising the private sector R&D expenditure from the current one-to-three ratio to at least match public

---

[10] Science Advisory Council to the Prime Minister (India), *Science in India (2004–2013): Decade of Achievements and Rising Aspirations* (New Delhi, 2013), 22, http://sactopm.gov.in/Science%20in%20India%20-%20Book.pdf.

[11] TAFTIE, "'Innovation Hotspots' in India," July 27, 2011, 6, http://www.vinnova.se/PageFiles/115782718/Innovation%20Hot%20Spots%20in%20India%20TAFTIE%20-%20Report.pdf.

[12] Pratibha Devisingh Patil, "Address by the Hon'ble President of India, Shrimati Pratibha Devi Singh Patil, to Parliament" (New Delhi, June 4, 2009), http://pratibhapatil.nic.in/sp040609.html .

[13] Ministry of Science and Technology (India), "Science, Technology and Innovation Policy 2013," 2013, http://dst.gov.in/sti-policy-eng.pdf.

[14] Sunil Mani, "India," in *UNESCO Science Report 2010: The Current Status of Science around the World* (Paris: UNESCO Publishing, 2010), 365.

[15] TAFTIE, "'Innovation Hotspots' in India," 19–20.

sector funding.[16] Other reports, however, have suggested that it is public sector R&D that is stagnant, whereas private sector R&D is increasing, even if not by a significant amount.[17]

Another measure of a country's capacity for invention is the number of patents filed. Although this number has almost quadrupled in India over the last decade, increasing from approximately 12,000 in 2003–4 to 42,951 in 2013–14, 32,010 of these patents, or almost 75%, were filed by nonresidents.[18] One report stated that "9 out of [the] top 10 entities receiving Indian patents are foreign."[19] Patent applications also appear to come more often from India's state-funded research bodies and universities than from the private sector, which leads to the concentration of innovation hubs in a few parts of the country.[20]

The key problem remains unrecognized: the assumption that state direction and bureaucratic management are necessary for innovation. To the contrary, they are more likely to be an obstacle because innovation is more likely to emerge in an environment that rewards achievement than in rule-based, government-funded institutions that emphasize seniority. If unaddressed, India's low level of capacity for enterprise will have negative cascading effects on the country's technological development and could be a significant constraint on the potential growth of Indian power.

Human Resources

Human resources are an important dimension of national power, especially in developing technological capacity. India's large and relatively young population, set to soon overtake China, should be a significant asset if it is developed effectively. Measuring a country's human resources requires examining both gross education levels and the quality of education and informal educational resources. In quantitative terms, there is no doubt that India's education sector is expanding dramatically. Yet the quality of education is low at all levels, which means that the general quality of India's human resources is also low.

Since the 1960s, the Indian government has aimed to reach 6% of GDP spending for education. However, the country has remained stuck at

---

[16] Ministry of Science and Technology (India), "Science, Technology and Innovation Policy 2013," 5.

[17] Mani, "India," 363.

[18] Office of the Controller General of Patents, Designs, Trademarks and Geographical Indicators (India), *Annual Report 2013–14* (New Delhi, 2014), 17, http://ipindia.gov.in/cgpdtm/AnnualReport_English_2013_2014.pdf.

[19] Science Advisory Council to the Prime Minister (India), *Science in India*, 24.

[20] TAFTIE, "'Innovation Hotspots' in India," 6.

around 3.5% of GDP for the last two decades. As a share of government expenditure, spending has stagnated at approximately 12%. But overall expenditure on education by the central and state governments increased from 1.5 trillion rupees (approximately $25 billion) in 2007–8 to 2.3 trillion rupees (almost $40 billion) in 2009–10. Consequently, India's educational institutions have expanded dramatically, with the number of elementary schools rising from 845,007 to 1,448,712 and secondary and higher secondary schools rising from 126,047 to 237,111 between 2000–2001 and 2013–14.[21] Yet, though comprehensive national assessments are not available, the quality of Indian education is generally poor because of multiple regulatory authorities, quantitative and qualitative inadequacies in teacher training, and school curriculum that emphasizes rote learning rather than thinking skills.

Just as in primary and secondary education, there has been a massive expansion of Indian higher education, with the number of universities almost doubling from 361 in 2007 to 712 in 2014.[22] But this is a system in crisis, whose dysfunction can be traced to the tight centralization of higher education in the hands of the Indian bureaucracy. As one analysis points out, state control creates a whole host of problems, including regulatory bottlenecks that distort private and philanthropic investment; allow political interference for ideological, pecuniary, and electoral purposes; and produce an ideological commitment to equality over distinction.[23] There is no relief in sight from political and ideological interference or tight administrative and bureaucratic controls, which means that the university sector will continue to remain in crisis. Because human resources are such a critical aspect of national power, the generally poor quality of Indian education at all levels limits India's power potential.

Financial and Capital Resources

Financial and capital resources are key to expanding the Indian economy and hence national power. These resources are measured by the extent of savings and economic growth rates as well as by sectoral growth. The savings rate is an important element of economic growth because a high savings rate could translate into higher investment in the economy

---

[21] Ministry of Human Resource Development (India), *Education for All, Towards Quality with Equity: India* (New Delhi, August 2014), 22–99, http://mhrd.gov.in/sites/upload_files/mhrd/files/upload_document/EFA-Review-Report-final.pdf.

[22] The current figure is from the Ministry of Human Resource Development (India), *Education Statistics at a Glance* (New Delhi, 2014), 3. The 2007 figure is from Devesh Kapur and Pratap Bhanu Mehta, "Mortgaging the Future? Indian Higher Education" (presentation at the Brookings-NCAER India Policy Forum, New Delhi, December 26, 2007), 3, https://casi.sas.upenn.edu/sites/casi.sas.upenn.edu/files/bio/uploads/Mortgaging%20the%20Future.pdf.

[23] Kapur and Mehta, "Mortgaging the Future? Indian Higher Education."

and generate greater growth. India's savings rate increased substantially over the last two decades—from 22.8% of GDP in 1990 to a peak of 36.9% in 2007—before declining.[24] But the ratio of savings to gross national disposable income declined from approximately 33% in 2011–12 to 30% in 2012–13.[25] This declining savings rate is reflected in the stagnation in gross capital formation, which stayed at 36 trillion rupees ($565 billion) for the last two years.[26] If India is to grow at a faster rate, a higher savings rate (35%, according to some estimates) is required.[27]

In addition to domestic savings, levels of access to external resources are also important. India has received significant amounts of international aid since it became independent. According to one estimate, by the early 1990s, India had received more aid than any other developing country (approximately $55 billion).[28] Though foreign aid has declined over the last two decades, it is still substantial. According to the World Bank, in 2013 India was the fourteenth-largest recipient of aid at almost $2.5 billion.[29]

Another external source of capital is foreign investment. This, however, requires a hospitable investment climate, which is difficult for India to foster because Indian political leaders on both the Left and the Right remain suspicious of foreign capital and resist pragmatic policies to promote it. Data from the Reserve Bank of India shows foreign investment exceeding $24 billion in 2011–12 but slowing to $16 billion in 2013–14.[30] For comparison, India receives only roughly a tenth of the FDI inflows that China receives. But FDI has jumped dramatically since the Narendra Modi government took office in 2014, reaching over $34.9 billion in 2014–15.[31] This appears to be the result of a number of policy changes on foreign investment,

---

[24] Reserve Bank of India, "Report of the Working Group on Savings during the Twelfth Five-Year Plan (2012–13 to 2016–17)," *Reserve Bank of India Bulletin*, June 2012, 1157–1208, https://rbidocs.rbi.org.in/rdocs/Bulletin/PDFs/0BLT080612_FULL.pdf.

[25] "New Series Estimates of National Income, Consumption Expenditure, Savings and Capital Formation (Base Year 2011–12)," Press Information Bureau (India), Ministry of Statistics and Programme Implementation, January 30, 2015, http://pib.nic.in/newsite/PrintRelease.aspx?relid=115084.

[26] Gross capital formation is defined as gross savings plus capital inflows.

[27] "India Needs to Up Savings Rate for 7 Per Cent GDP Growth: HSBC," NDTV Profit, November 6, 2014, http://profit.ndtv.com/news/economy/article-india-needs-to-up-savings-rate-for-7-per-cent-gdp-growth-hsbc-689713.

[28] Shyam J. Kamath, "Foreign Aid and India: Financing the Leviathan State," Cato Institute, Policy Analysis, no. 170, 1992, http://object.cato.org/sites/cato.org/files/pubs/pdf/pa170.pdf.

[29] "Net Official Development Assistance and Official Aid Received (Current US$)," World Bank, World Development Indicators, http://data.worldbank.org/indicator/DT.ODA.ALLD.CD?order=wbapi_data_value_2013+wbapi_data_value+wbapi_data_value-last&sort=desc.

[30] Unless otherwise indicated, data in this section is from the Reserve Bank of India, *Annual Report 2013–14* (New Delhi, 2014), 41–42.

[31] "In Boost for PM Modi, FDI Flows Hit Record High in FY 15," NDTV Profit, May 26, 2015, http://profit.ndtv.com/news/market/article-in-boost-for-pm-modi-fdi-flows-hit-record-high-in-fy15-766118.

including liberalization of norms for foreign investment in railways and defense. Although there is domestic political opposition to these policies, the Modi government is better placed to handle it because the Bharatiya Janata Party (BJP) enjoys a majority in the parliament. The overall picture of India's access to capital is thus mixed: access to external capital resources has grown over the last year as a consequence of policy changes, but the environment for FDI remains challenging.

Perhaps the best indicator of a country's capital resources is the size of its economy. India's economic growth rate has been dramatic since liberalization in the early 1990s, rising from the traditional rate of approximately 3.5% to a high of 10.3% in 2010, and it is set to overtake China in 2015. The World Bank puts India's GDP in 2014 at over $2 trillion and per capita GDP at $1,630, with both figures having quadrupled since 2000. Maintaining these high levels of growth over the long term would require increasing the share of the manufacturing sector in the economy, which has stagnated at around 16% (compared with over 20% for Brazil, China, and Indonesia).[32] Yet even though there remain questions about the sustainability of India's growth rate, the country's capital resources are expanding, and this expansion is likely to continue.

Natural Resources

In examining India's resource base, the last set of variables to be considered is natural resources, which include food and energy stocks and strategic materials. The country's food stocks are plentiful. Though India continues to be a poor and malnourished nation, this is no longer the consequence of inadequate domestic production of food but rather a symptom of the political quandaries that prevent India from rationalizing its agricultural policies. Food stocks of the country's two staple items, rice and wheat, are currently twice as much as the stated norms, and India is increasingly facing the problem of plenty. In 2013, it was the world's largest rice exporter, and wheat exports jumped fivefold from the previous year to over eight million tons.[33] Agricultural policy, in particular subsidies, poses a serious political challenge, but this issue does not represent a serious security vulnerability.

Unfortunately, the same cannot be said of India's energy situation because the country simply does not have sufficient domestic sources to supply its own

---

[32] "India Needs to Improve Manufacturing Sector Performance to Return to High-Growth Path, Says World Bank," World Bank, Press Release, October 27, 2014, http://www.worldbank.org/en/news/press-release/2014/10/27/india-needs-improve-manufacturing-performance-high-growth-path.

[33] Mayank Bhardwaj, Manoj Kumar, and Krishna N. Das, "Factbox: India's Food Stockpiling and WTO Stand-off," Reuters, July 29, 2014.

energy needs.[34] India possesses proven reserves of approximately 5.7 billion barrels of oil, 47 trillion cubic feet (tcf) of natural gas reserves, between 9 and 92 tcf of coal-based methane gas, 96 tcf of shale gas, and 66.8 billion short tons of coal. While these reserves are substantial, India remains energy deficient and a net importer of oil, natural gas, and even coal (though its coal reserves are the fifth-largest in the world and it is the third-largest coal producer). India is particularly dependent on imported oil: it is the fourth-largest consumer and the fourth-largest importer of oil products. The gap between India's oil production and consumption is approximately 3 million barrels a day, and this shortfall is projected to continue to rise as India's demand increases and its production stagnates. To deal with this vulnerability, India is in the process of setting up a strategic petroleum reserve, which by 2020 will store the equivalent of up to three months of the country's oil consumption.

For long-term energy security, India has been attempting to develop its nuclear energy sector, but nuclear energy still contributes only around 2% of the country's total installed energy capacity of 245,258 megawatts (MW).[35] India currently has 21 atomic reactors, generating 5,780 megawatts electric (MWe), and 5 more reactors are under construction, which would add 3,000 MWe of capacity.[36] India has also made strides in renewable energy, with wind, solar, bioenergy, and small hydro projects contributing 13% of installed capacity for electricity.[37] This translates to almost 34,000 MW of installed electricity capacity, with wind power accounting for roughly 22,000 MW, solar providing 3,000 MW, and bioenergy and small hydro projects each contributing around 4,000 MW. Moreover, India's installed capacity in wind power is increasing by over 2 gigawatts each year.[38] Yet despite the development of new sources of nuclear and alternative energy, India's energy situation represents a clear national security concern.

India is also substantially dependent on foreign suppliers for strategic materials.[39] Although the country is not entirely lacking in strategic materials,

---

[34] Data in this section is from U.S. Department of Energy, Energy Information Administration, "India: International Energy Data and Analysis," http://www.eia.gov/beta/international/country.cfm?iso=IND.

[35] Ministry of Power (India), Central Electricity Authority, "All India Installed Capacity (in MW) of Power Stations Located in the Regions of Main Land and Islands," March 31, 2015, http://www.cea.nic.in/reports/monthly/inst_capacity/mar15.pdf.

[36] "Plants under Operation," Nuclear Power Corporation of India Limited, http://www.npcil.nic.in/main/AllProjectOperationDisplay.aspx; and "Projects under Construction," Nuclear Power Corporation of India Limited, http://www.npcil.nic.in/main/ProjectConstructionStatus.aspx.

[37] Ministry of New and Renewable Energy (India), *Annual Report 2014–15* (New Delhi, 2015), section 1.7, http://mnre.gov.in/file-manager/annual-report/2014-2015/EN/Chapter%201/chapter_1.htm.

[38] M. Ramesh, "Wind Power Installations Marginally Up in 2014–15," *Hindu Business Line*, April 7, 2015.

[39] Ajey Lele and Parveen Bhardwaj, *Strategic Materials: A Resource Challenge for India* (New Delhi: Pentagon Press, 2014), 1.

the Maoist insurgency and local objections to extraction (supported by whichever political party happens to be in opposition) have stymied efforts to fully exploit these resources.[40] Rare earth is a specific category of strategic material. India has 3.1 million tons of rare earth reserves and last year produced 3,000 tons.[41] The country's demand for rare earths is increasing, and it plans to triple production by 2017.[42] On the whole, however, the natural resource picture is not pretty, with critical (but at least acknowledged) dependencies in energy stocks and important strategic minerals.

National Performance

The previous section considered the building blocks of Indian power. The country's high economic growth rate is undoubtedly the driver of national power, and India is also strong in some critical technologies. But its general technological capacity, human resources, enterprise capacity, and development of natural resources are encumbered by domestic politics and incompetent state management. This section further assesses the Indian state's capacity to convert national resources into usable forms of power. The first part examines the external pressures to which India must respond. The second part then assesses the ability of the Indian state to generate power domestically through a study of state-society relations.

External Constraints

External constraints comprise the kinds of external threats India faces, the possible expansion of the state's interests in the international arena, and the nature of the state's political objectives in international affairs.

External threats. There can be little doubt about the main sources of India's external security threats: Pakistan and China. Officially, however, India tends to be coy about explicitly identifying external threats. For example, the country's defense secretary recently made the vague statement that the military's operational directive requires it to dominate one country in the case of war and deter another.[43] Though China poses the greater long-term threat, India has generally viewed the threat from Pakistan as more immediate.

---

[40] Lele and Bhardwaj, *Strategic Materials*, 140–49.

[41] U.S. Geological Survey, *Mineral Commodity Summaries 2015* (Reston: U.S. Geological Survey, 2015), 129, http://minerals.usgs.gov/minerals/pubs/mcs/2015/mcs2015.pdf.

[42] Elliot Brennan, "The Next Oil? Rare Earth Metals," *Diplomat*, January 10, 2013, http://thediplomat.com/2013/01/the-new-prize-china-and-indias-rare-earth-scramble.

[43] Ministry of Defence (India), Standing Committee on Defence, "Second Report on Demands for Grants (2014–15) of the Ministry on Defence on General Defence Budget (Demand No. 20, 21 and 27)," December 22, 2014, 19, http://164.100.47.134/lsscommittee/Defence/16_Defence_2.pdf.

But its concerns about China are increasing. Justifying the raising of a mountain strike corps for the Sino-Indian border, the vice chief of army staff informed the Parliamentary Standing Committee "that the way [redacted text] has been getting more aggressive in resolving disputes with neighbors, especially, in view of what we have seen with its maritime disputes in the South China Sea, it was our attempt to make sure that we are fully prepared to deal with this threat if at any time [redacted text] decides to raise the ante and get more aggressive."[44] Although the name of the country was redacted, he was clearly referring to China. Indian officials have recently also begun considering the possibility of a two-front war because of the tacit military partnership between Pakistan and China.[45]

These external threats are heightened by the nexus between India's external adversaries and internal security challenges. Pakistan's continued support of anti-India terrorist groups is a source of significant concern. Although China does not appear to currently support rebellions inside India, the possibility that it may do so again cannot be ruled out by Indian security managers.

India's anxiety is further increased by China's rapid military modernization and by India's apparent inability to keep pace. India seeks to match China's infrastructural development along the border and counter its naval expansion into the Indian Ocean. India's growing missile capability is driven by the need to reach all of China—a capability that India does not yet possess. External threats are thus an important source of pressure to which India must respond.

External state interests. If foreign threats are one driver of national power, another is the possible expansion of the Indian state's interests, determined by where India draws its defensive perimeter, the vulnerability of its natural resources, and its commitment to the Indian diaspora. Although India considers West Asia, Central Asia, and Southeast Asia to be areas of "strategic significance," it has so far defined its immediate defensive perimeter along the country's de facto borders, and there is no indication this will change in the near future. India's defensive strategic culture also focuses more on protecting these de facto borders than on militarily asserting India's claims on disputed territories, such as Pakistan-controlled Kashmir or the Chinese-controlled Aksai Chin region.

This defensive focus is best illustrated by India's inordinate attention to the physical protection of its borders. This is no easy task because the country

---

[44] Ministry of Defence (India), Standing Committee on Defence, "Third Report on Demands for Grants (2014–15) of the Ministry of Defence on Army (Demand No. 22)," December 22, 2014, 23, http://164.100.47.134/lsscommittee/Defence/16_Defence_3.pdf.

[45] "NSA Ajit Doval: India Must Prepare for a Two-Front War," *Hindustan Times*, November 25, 2014.

has some of the longest borders in the world, with its land borders alone totaling over 15,000 kilometers (9,300 miles). The India-Pakistan border itself measures 3,323 kilometers. The threat of terrorist infiltration has led India to fence much of this border: almost 2,000 kilometers are already fenced and floodlit, and 609 border posts have been established to prevent infiltration (with another 90 still to be set up).[46]

The challenge that India faces on the border with China is not so much terrorist infiltration as uncertainty over where the border actually lies, resulting in frequent confrontations between Chinese and Indian troops and accusations from both sides about territorial intrusions. India plans to construct 27 roads in this region, totaling over 800 kilometers, at a cost of about 20 billion rupees ($312 million), but had only completed 5 by late 2014.[47] The Border Roads Organisation, which is in charge of building roads in these areas, faces a number of challenges, including obsolete equipment, outdated technology, and insufficient funds and manpower.[48] The Parliamentary Standing Committee on Defence noted that the infrastructure on the Indian side is so bad that the Chinese army could reach Tawang, an important city in Arunachal Pradesh, much faster than the Indian army could.[49] Briefly stated, India's active defense perimeter has not expanded past its own border.

A second possible source of state interest in the external realm concerns the vulnerability of strategic resources. India's natural resources are not under direct external threat. However, as mentioned in the previous section, India faces serious vulnerabilities because it is dependent on energy imports. India was the fourth-largest energy consumer in the world in 2011, and imported fossil fuels rose to 38% of its total energy makeup in 2012.[50] Thus, India considers the protection of sea lanes of communication (SLOC) to be a priority, albeit a multilateral responsibility rather than a purely national one.

A final possible source of externally focused state interest is India's diaspora. At 25 million strong, the diaspora is the largest in the world and the primary source of large inward remittances (roughly $71 billion

---

[46] Ministry of Home Affairs (India), *Annual Report 2014–2015* (New Delhi, 2015), 33–34, http://mha.nic.in/sites/upload_files/mha/files/AR(E)1415.pdf.

[47] Ibid., 35–36.

[48] Ministry of Defence (India), Standing Committee on Defence, "Sixth Report on Demands for Grants (2015–16) on Civil Expenditure of the Ministry of Defence and Capital Outlay on Defence Services Demand (No. 21, 22 and 28)," April 27, 2015, 81–87, http://164.100.47.134/lsscommittee/Defence/16_Defence_6.pdf.

[49] Ibid.

[50] Data in this section is from U.S. Department of Energy, Energy Information Administration, "India Is Increasingly Dependent on Imported Fossil Fuels as Demand Continues to Rise," August 14, 2014, http://www.eia.gov/todayinenergy/detail.cfm?id=17551.

in 2014).[51] Traditionally, India's policy toward its diaspora had been one of prudence, recognizing the country's insufficient material capacity to protect a community spread around the world. This policy ended around the turn of the century, however, when India realized that its diaspora could be a potential source of both financial and political support. This realization was primarily driven by the wealthy and increasingly politically active Indian diaspora in the United States, which has come to play an important role in U.S.-India relations, as was demonstrated during the negotiation of the U.S.-India civil nuclear deal. Though a limited power-projection capacity reduces its ability to act on behalf of its diaspora, India has been able to intervene *in extremis* to evacuate its citizens from areas of distress, as it did most recently in Yemen in March–April 2015. Thus, India's external interests are gradually expanding in some areas, such as the protection of SLOCs and the diaspora.

Political objectives. In addition to external threats and the pursuit of national interests, the state's political objectives, including revisionist or ideological proselytization tendencies, could also require an expansion of national power. India has pursued a radical vision of international politics since independence, but this has remained more rhetorical than programmatic and has been based on peaceful and institutional means rather than on violence. In the recent past, India has repeatedly called for a new international order that recognizes current balance-of-power realities, yet this appears to be mainly a justification for obtaining a seat on the UN Security Council. India has also repeatedly advocated for a multipolar world order, apparently based on a belief that it would be one of the poles.

All of these objectives represent global aspirations, but New Delhi's primary (and probably only) strategy to pursue them appears to be through diplomatic exhortations. It has also shown little inclination toward ideological proselytization. Though justifiably proud that it has remained a democracy despite great challenges, India has been reluctant to promote democracy as a foreign policy objective, an attitude that is unlikely to change.[52]

Another reason for India to expand national power could be irredentist claims. Yet even though India has significant territorial claims vis-à-vis both Pakistan and China, there is little indication that it will pursue these claims through force. Note, however, that while India has shown no proclivity toward using military force to assert its territorial claims, the country has

---

[51] "Remittances to Developing Countries to Grow by 5 Percent This Year, While Conflict-Related Forced Migration Is at All-Time High, Says WB Report," World Bank, Press Release, October 6, 2014, http://www.worldbank.org/en/news/press-release/2014/10/06/remittances-developing-countries-five-percent-conflict-related-migration-all-time-high-wb-report.

[52] C. Raja Mohan, "Balancing Interests and Values: India's Struggle with Democracy Promotion," *Washington Quarterly* 30, no. 3 (2007): 99–115.

demonstrated great resolve in defending territory that it already holds. As discussed above, most Indian force developments, especially on the Tibet border, are designed to deter or prevent an attempt to take disputed territory that India currently holds. The country might not fight to retake territory that it lost, but it will fight to keep territory it holds.

To summarize, the external constraints India faces provide moderate incentive for expanding national power to address significant external threats and pursue state interests.

Infrastructural Capacity

If the external constraints discussed in the previous section concern the pressures acting on the state from outside, the capacity of the state to respond is the focus of this and the next sections. This section examines the Indian state's capacity vis-à-vis society, which includes the cohesiveness of and consensus among state elites, the autonomy of the state from society, and the state's capacity to penetrate and extract resources from society. India's infrastructural capacity, especially the lack of elite cohesion, represents one of the major obstacles to greater national performance.

Elite cohesion and consensus. Elite cohesion and consensus are important determinants of state power because disunity among elites or disagreement about key national objectives reduces the state's capacity for purposive action.[53] India exhibits a significant lack of elite cohesion even though there is broad elite consensus in major policy areas. India's policy-relevant elite includes two segments: the political elite, made up of electorally significant political parties (especially the elected national government in New Delhi), and the administrative elite, made up of the centralized bureaucracy. Other elite groups—from business, media, labor, and other sections of society—are weaker and play a comparatively small role in policymaking. The dominance of the political and administrative elite has declined over the last two decades owing to a number of reasons: the rise of regional political parties that have redefined the balance of power between the central government and state governments in India's federal political structure, the rise of a new economic elite as a consequence of the liberalization that began in the early 1990s, the relative dilution of the central government's control over the economy as a consequence of the same liberalization, and the rise of a chaotic and boisterous electronic media. Nevertheless, the central elite dominates policymaking, even if other groups have occasionally gained a veto power over some policy initiatives.

---

[53] Randall L. Schweller, "Unanswered Threats: A Neoclassical Realist Theory of Underbalancing," *International Security* 29, no. 2 (2004): 159–201.

Despite this dominance, the political elite is not cohesive because of the fracturing of the Indian political party system. Since the late 1980s, there had not been a single-party government in New Delhi until the BJP won the 2014 national election. This fracturing of the party system—a consequence of the decline of the Congress Party—and the need for coalition-building in the national parliament have made policymaking somewhat more difficult because it involves elaborate negotiations even within coalitions. Political parties while out of power can be expected to fiercely oppose the same policies they had promoted while they were in power. The need to manage disparate coalitions in the face of severe opposition makes ruling parties wary of pursuing any initiative that might risk the coalition, leading to policy gridlock. Although the BJP did gain a single-party majority in 2014, this was likely more a consequence of the lack of unity among opposition parties, given that the BJP received just 31% of the popular vote. It is quite possible, though by no means certain, that the 2014 election was an anomaly and India will return to the gridlock of coalition governments.

Oddly, this lack of cohesion does not mean a lack of elite policy consensus. Fierce political contestations mask the fact that ideological differences among Indian political and administrative elites are not particularly large. On domestic issues as well as foreign and national security, the Indian political elite has shown surprising consistency in views across decades and generations. At least in studies of Indian foreign policy, this consistency of views is well recognized.[54] In essence, then, India appears to have broad elite consensus even when there is no elite cohesion.

State autonomy. The lack of elite cohesion does not appear to affect the Indian state's autonomy from society, a function of the relative strength of the state and its impermeability to social and interest groups. Indian society is extensively and intensively divided, and these divisions have become greater over the decades as the state compromised on linguistic, ethnic, and caste-based demands for recognition, privilege, and state support. This trend is not necessarily negative: the state's capacity for accommodating such ascriptive sectarian demands has been key to both the survival and the deepening of Indian democracy. There has been an unintended side effect as well—the deepening of these divisions has allowed the Indian state to maintain its autonomy from social groups. At independence, India was bequeathed with an administrative and coercive apparatus that was originally designed by Great Britain for colonial extraction, which made it a much stronger state than most newly independent countries. Independent India deepened the roots of control through measures that were ostensibly designed for promoting

---

[54] Vipin Narang and Paul Staniland, "Institutions and Worldviews in Indian Foreign Security Policy," *India Review* 11, no. 2 (2012): 76–94.

economic and social justice and protecting national security but that also effected greater state power over society. Thus, centralizing economic controls, providing social and economic justice to historically marginalized groups, and preventing religious and ethnic differences from leading to violence or separatism all gave the Indian state greater autonomy from social groups.

Penetrative capacity. The state's capacity for social control is also determined by its penetrative capacity, which is usually measured by the ratio of taxes on foreign trade to total revenue. In 2012, India was ranked 23rd in the world with a relatively high ratio of 14.9%, indicating low penetrative capacity.[55] But other measures show a more positive trend: the direct tax to GDP ratio rose from 3.81% in 2003–4 to 5.51% in 2011–12, though it fell from a high of 6.67% in 2007–8. On the other hand, the ratio of indirect tax to GDP has remained relatively steady between 5.39% in 2003–4 and 5.87% in 2007–8.[56] Although traditionally indirect taxes had been much higher than direct taxes in India, this changed around 2006–7 when direct taxes overtook indirect taxes.[57] A greater proportion of direct tax revenue indicates greater penetrative capacity.

Extractive capacity. If penetrative capacity shows a mixed picture, this is equally true of extractive capacity, which is measured as the state's total tax revenue relative to other similarly placed states. India's total tax revenue has gone up from about 8.15 trillion rupees ($127 billion) in 2013–14 to an estimated 9.04 trillion rupees ($130 billion) in 2014–15 and is expected to go up slightly to 9.19 trillion rupees ($140 billion) in 2015–16.[58] Comparing this to other countries, India's tax revenue as a percentage of GDP in 2012 at 10.8% is lower than states such as South Africa (25.5%), Russia (15.1%), and Brazil (14.4%) but akin to others such as China (10.4% in 2011), the United States (10.2%), and Japan (10.1%). Thus, even as the Indian state's extraction capacity is increasing, it still fares poorly compared to the above states. Broadly, however, the Indian state's capacity is reasonably strong or getting stronger.

Ideational Resources

Ideological resources point to less tangible means of converting state resources into power. This requires a populace to have the capacity to

---

[55] "Taxes on International Trade (% of Revenue)," World Bank, World Development Indicators, http://data.worldbank.org/indicator/GC.TAX.INTT.RV.ZS.

[56] Ministry of Finance (India), Department of Revenue, "Direct and Indirect Tax-GDP Ratio," http://dor.gov.in/direct_indirect.

[57] Ministry of Finance (India), Department of Economic Affairs, "Indian Public Finance Statistics 2012–13," 2013, xi–xii, http://finmin.nic.in/reports/IPFStat201213.pdf.

[58] Ministry of Finance (India), "Budget at a Glance: 2015–2016," 2015, http://indiabudget.nic.in/ub2015-16/bag/bag11.pdf.

rationally approach problems (instrumental rationality) and the state to have effective ideological instruments to pursue greater national power (substantive rationality). Because rational problem-solving attitudes are inculcated in secondary schools, enrollment ratios and the quality of secondary school education provide indicators. In Indian secondary schools the gross enrollment ratio increased from 51.7% in 2004–5 to 76.6% in 2013–14, and in higher secondary schools it increased from 27.8% in 2004–5 to 52.2% in 2013–14.[59] But while enrollment is greater, assessing the quality of secondary education in India is hard, especially in comparison with international standards. School education is mostly handled at the level of the state governments rather than by the central government: there are 3 national boards and 34 state and union territory boards (administered by the central government), each with a distinct curriculum.[60] One study concluded that all that can be said of the quality of secondary school education in India is that "we don't really know, but relatively small-scale assessments suggest it is very low."[61]

Although in 2009 India agreed to join the Programme for International Student Assessment (PISA), only two Indian states, Tamil Nadu and Himachal Pradesh, participated, and they both scored at the bottom of the rankings.[62] India refused to join the 2012 and 2015 rounds of PISA. Other small-scale assessments that were administered in Orissa and Rajasthan using modified test items from the Trends in International Mathematics and Science Study (TIMSS) also showed poor results.[63] The reasons for this lie both in the poor standards of teacher pre-service education and in-service training and in the Indian secondary school curriculum's emphasis on rote learning of facts rather than on the development of critical thinking skills.[64]

If efforts at developing instrumental rationality show a mixed picture, India does little better at measures of substantive rationality, indicated by the prevalence of a state ideology and efforts to create national power. Since independence, India has possessed a strong sense of itself as a major global power and a leader of postcolonial societies. Though India is still a

---

[59] Ministry of Human Resource Development (India), *Education for All*, 53.

[60] World Bank, "Secondary Education in India: Universalizing Opportunity," January 2009, http://datatopics.worldbank.org/hnp/files/edstats/INDstu09a.pdf.

[61] Ibid., 34.

[62] Eric A. Hanushek and Ludger Woessmann, *Universal Basic Skills: What Countries Stand to Gain* (Paris: OECD, 2015), 42–43, http://hanushek.stanford.edu/sites/default/files/publications/Universal_Basic_Skills_WEF.pdf.

[63] World Bank, "Secondary Education in India," xix, 34.

[64] Tapas Kumar Sarkar, "Assessment in Education in India," *SA–eDUC Journal* 9, no. 2 (2012), http://www.nwu.ac.za/sites/www.nwu.ac.za/files/files/p-saeduc/New_Folder_1/1_Assessment%20in%20Education%20in%20India.pdf.

poor country, this sense of great-power status continues to generate strong ideological consensus and motivate Indian thinking.

But this desire to be a global power has been mated with decision-making and bureaucratic structures that are far too inefficient to deliver the results needed to realize such ambition.[65] The dominance of the Indian state structure ensures that India's success or failure in realizing its power potential is largely a function of the effectiveness of this state structure. Red tape and the lack of accountability or career consequences, however, have created a bureaucratic structure that is not focused on competence or sensitive to policy failure. This is a general problem across the Indian bureaucracy, affecting everything from infrastructure to poverty-alleviation programs, but it is particularly visible in defense and strategic technology programs.[66] Thus, although the government has directed significant attention and resources to indigenous technology development, with the exception of the space and nuclear programs, which are not managed by the bureaucracy, an inefficient state structure has prevented these programs from succeeding.

The foregoing assessment of national performance shows that while India faces external pressures, these pressures more often are the consequence of foreign actors than driven by domestic political objectives. The country's capacity to respond is also not inconsiderable. Even though India's national performance is hurt by both a lack of elite cohesion and a bureaucracy that is inefficient in converting resources into usable power, the state possesses a reasonable capacity to extract resources from society.

Military Capability

If the Indian state performs reasonably well in extracting resources from society to meet external challenges, how are these resources converted into usable military power? This section examines the strategic resources provided to the Indian military, measures India's capacity for converting these resources into effective military power, and assesses the military's combat proficiency. Broadly, though India's militarily capability is not inconsiderable, it is hurt by inadequate resources and political attention, less than ideal civil-military relations, and poor defense R&D and production.

---

[65] For a relevant argument about the inadequacy of the Indian bureaucracy, though one focused on the failure of India's poverty-alleviation programs, see Akhil Gupta, *Red Tape: Bureaucracy, Structural Violence, and Poverty in India* (Durham: Duke University Press, 2012).

[66] Stephen P. Cohen and Sunil Dasgupta, *Arming without Aiming: India's Military Modernization* (Washington, D.C.: Brookings Institution Press, 2010), 26.

Strategic Resources

Strategic resources include not only a country's defense budget but also manpower, R&D, the defense industrial base, and warfighting inventory. Though India's defense budget has grown in absolute terms, the growth has been inconsistent over the last fifteen years and is inadequate for India's requirements.[67] The budget increased from 542.7 billion rupees ($8.61 billion) in 2001–2 to 2,467 billion rupees ($39 billion) (budget estimate, or BE) in 2015–16, staying between 12% and 16% of total national expenditure and around 2% of GDP. The biggest chunk is allocated to the army, which will receive 52.96% of the total defense budget (BE) in 2015–16, compared with the navy's share at 16.42% and the air force's share at 22.98%.[68] These proportions have not varied by much over the years—a reflection of the fact that India still sees its biggest threats coming across the land borders from Pakistan and China.

Such spending buys a fairly large military force: the army has a sanctioned manpower strength of 1,219,591; the navy, 76,316; and the air force, 147,122 (see **Table 1**).[69] Both the army and the navy suffer significant shortfalls in officers, however, which could affect their combat potential. The air force faces a different problem: its pilot-to-seat ratio for fighter planes is just 0.81 (against a sanctioned ratio of 1.25), compared with 2.5 to 1 in Pakistan and 2 to 1 in the United States.[70] It should also be noted that 50,000 to 55,000 defense personnel from the three services retire every year.[71]

Another measure of military resources is R&D expenditure, which in India's case has been steady over the last five years at around 100–108 billion rupees (approximately $1.5 billion). This has equated to between 5.5% and 6.5% of the defense budget and 0.10% and 0.13% of GDP.[72] Nearly half of this expenditure (46%, or roughly $750 million annually) has gone toward India's

---

[67] The information in this paragraph, unless otherwise noted, is from Ministry of Defence (India), Standing Committee on Defence, "Second Report," 15–17.

[68] All 2015–16 budget figures in this section are from Ministry of Defence (India), *Annual Report 2014–2015* (New Delhi, 2015), 16–17, http://www.mod.nic.in/writereaddata/AR1415.pdf.

[69] The army, navy, and air force statistics are respectively from Ministry of Defence (India), Standing Committee on Defence, "Seventh Report on Demands for Grants (2015–16) of the Ministry of Defence on Army (Demand No. 23)," April 27, 2015, 21; Ministry of Defence (India), Standing Committee on Defence, "Eighth Report on Demands for Grants (2015–16) of the Ministry of Defence on Navy and Air Force (Demand No. 24 and 25)," April 27, 2015, 20–21, http://164.100.47.134/lsscommittee/Defence/16_Defence_8.pdf; and Ministry of Defence (India), Standing Committee on Defence, "Eighth Report," 38–39.

[70] Ministry of Defence (India), Standing Committee on Defence, "Eighth Report," 40.

[71] Lok Sabha (House of the People), "Unstarred Question No. 4427 to Be Answered on the 22nd April, 2013: Resettlement of Defence Personnel," 17, http://mod.gov.in/LokSabha/LokSabha-Q2.pdf.

[72] Ministry of Defence (India), Standing Committee on Defence, "Ninth Report on Ordnance Factories and Defence Research and Development Organisation (Demand No. 26 and 27)," April 27, 2015, 23–24, http://164.100.47.134/lsscommittee/Defence/16_Defence_9.pdf.

TABLE 1   Military force size: India, China, and Pakistan

Service	India	China	Pakistan
Army	1,219,591	1,600,000	550,000
Air force	147,122	398,000	70,000
Navy	76,316	235,000	23,800

SOURCE: Data for India is from Ministry of Defence (India), Standing Committee on Defence, "Seventh Report on Demands for Grants (2015–16) of the Ministry of Defence on Army (Demand No. 23)," April 27, 2015, 21; and Ministry of Defence (India), Standing Committee on Defence, "Eighth Report on Demands for Grants (2015–16) of the Ministry of Defence on Navy and Air Force (Demand No. 24 and 25)," April 27, 2015, 20–21 and 38–39. Data for China and Pakistan is from International Institute for Strategic Studies, *The Military Balance 2015* (London: Routledge, 2015), 237, 276.

strategic programs, according to the Indian defense secretary's submission to the Standing Committee on Defence.[73]

Training is also an important strategic resource that affects military power. The Indian military has 5 interservice establishments, while the army has 27, the navy has 33, and the air force has 7.[74] Frequent accidents in the air force and some in the navy indicate that training is problematic.[75]

Another measure of the resources devoted to the military is the defense industrial base. India's defense ministry includes a separate Department of Defence Production, which manages nine defense public sector units (DPSU) as well as the Ordnance Factory Board (OFB). The OFB itself manages 39 factories, with 2 more being built, all producing battlefield equipment. The total value of production by these DPSUs increased from 415 billion rupees (approximately $6.5 billion) in 2011–12 to 441 billion rupees (about $6.9 billion) in 2013–14.[76] Both the DPSUs and the OFB have been severely criticized for delays in production, cost overruns, poor quality control, and

---

[73] Ministry of Defence (India), Standing Committee on Defence, "Ninth Report," 24.

[74] Indian Army, "Training Establishments," http://indianarmy.nic.in/Site/FormTemplete/ frmTempTrEstablishmentHome.aspx?MnId=b0zNgS4I9Qmd4wwmRxVPdA==&ParentID=sBT0 YTX/sarmtJ+Lw/XNbA==&flag=7FYaOxTF0r9Rj+HgJ0o88Q==; and Ministry of Defence (India), Standing Committee on Defence, "Eighth Report," 21–39.

[75] Air force training is affected not only by a lack of appropriate intermediate trainers but by other, long-standing issues as well. See, for example, George K. Tanham and Marcy Agmon, *The Indian Air Force: Trends and Prospects* (Santa Monica: RAND, 1995), 50–55.

[76] Ministry of Defence (India), *Annual Report 2014–2015*, 55–58.

general incompetence.[77] The most serious indictment of India's defense industrial base—also relevant to the defense R&D establishments—is that India has been one of the world's largest arms importers for several years and apparently will continue to be for years to come.

A final indicator of the resources India expends on the military is its support for the warfighting inventory. The army is divided into fourteen corps, of which four are strike corps and ten are holding corps. Together these corps possess approximately 3,000 main battle tanks, 2,000 other armored vehicles, 3,000 artillery pieces, and 6,500 mortars.[78] However, inadequate resources have led to a "gigantic gap" of between 30% and 70% "in the availability of regular arms, ammunition, [and] equipment" and raised serious questions about the combat readiness of these corps.[79]

The navy currently has 140 warships and 236 aircraft, and according to its Maritime Capability Perspective Plan, it expects to induct an additional 72 ships and submarines and 222 aircraft by 2027.[80] The current inventory includes 14 attack submarines (including a leased Russian nuclear submarine), 2 aircraft carriers, 12 destroyers, 13 frigates, and almost 100 smaller vessels.[81] Resources are a problem for naval modernization, too: India's submarine fleet, in particular, is deteriorating, especially after a Kilo-class submarine was lost in an explosion at port in Mumbai. India has ordered six French-designed Scorpène-class submarines, but they are running years behind schedule, though the first is now undergoing sea trials.[82]

Serious equipment problems afflict the air force as well. The air force informed the Standing Committee on Defence that although it requires at least 45 fighter squadrons "to counter a two-front collusive threat," it actually possesses only 35 active squadrons and the government has sanctioned only 42.[83] The air force has contracted for 272 SU-30MKIs, which are expected

---

[77] Ministry of Defence (India), Standing Committee on Defence, "Sixth Report"; Ministry of Defence (India), Standing Committee on Defence, "Ninth Report"; and Comptroller and Auditor General of India, "Report No. 35 of 2014—Union Government (Defence Services)—Report of the Comptroller and Auditor General of India on Army, Ordnance Factories and Defence Public Sector Undertakings," 2014, http://www.saiindia.gov.in/english/home/Our_Products/Audit_Report/Government_Wise/union_audit/recent_reports/union_compliance/2014/Defence/Report_35/Report_35.html.

[78] International Institute for Strategic Studies (IISS), *The Military Balance 2015* (London: Routledge, 2015), 248–49.

[79] Ministry of Defence (India), Standing Committee on Defence, "Ninth Report," 56.

[80] Ministry of Defence (India), Standing Committee on Defence, "Eighth Report," 10.

[81] IISS, *The Military Balance 2015*, 249–50.

[82] Huma Siddiqui, "Kalvari Adds to Indian Navy's Underwater Stealth," *Financial Express*, April 12, 2015, http://www.financialexpress.com/article/economy/kalvari-adds-to-indian-navys-underwater-stealth/63102.

[83] Ministry of Defence (India), Standing Committee on Defence, "Eighth Report," 29–30.

to be delivered through 2030 and which over the next four to five years will equip 3 additional squadrons.

India also possesses 90–110 nuclear warheads.[84] These are deployed on a mix of aircraft and two dozen Agni-1,-2, -3, and -4 intermediate-range ballistic missiles. None of these missiles have sufficient range to cover all of China from southern India, which would require a missile with a range of approximately seven thousand kilometers. India is building a fleet of nuclear missile submarines, but they too lack missiles with sufficient range to cover China.

All three military services are armed with precision-strike weapons, the most modern and capable of which is the Indo-Russian BrahMos supersonic missile that has a range of several hundred kilometers. In addition, air force and navy inventories include several different types of precision-attack munitions sourced from Russia, Israel, Europe, and the United States. Assuming adequate targeting information, these capabilities—especially the BrahMos—give Indian forces some capacity for stand-off precision strikes.

India does have some reconnaissance, surveillance, and target acquisition technologies, but they are still fairly limited. It currently possesses just three Gulfstream IV surveillance jets, three IL-76 Phalcon airborne warning and control systems, and two Embraer EMB-145 airborne early warning aircraft.[85] India has reportedly decided to buy two more airborne warning and control systems based on the Airbus A330, but it will be years before these are delivered.[86] India has also launched a number of satellites that have military potential, including the IRS (Indian remote-sensing satellite) series, the TES (technology experiment satellite), RISAT-2 (radar imaging satellite), the CARTOSAT-2A (cartographic satellite), and the dedicated GSAT-7 (geosynchronous satellite), which have improved the military's reconnaissance, surveillance, and target acquisition capabilities.

In brief, the resources that India devotes to its military are considerable in absolute terms but low as a proportion of national wealth and less than what the military needs. Thus, there are serious deficiencies in equipment and even in manpower, with the weaknesses of Indian defense R&D and industry being particularly serious. These deficiencies constrain to some extent the amount of military power India could bring to bear in a potential conflict.

---

[84] Hans M. Kristensen and Robert S. Norris, "Worldwide Deployment of Nuclear Weapons, 2014," *Bulletin of Atomic Scientists*, August 26, 2014, http://thebulletin.org/2014/september/worldwide-deployments-nuclear-weapons-20147595.

[85] IISS, *The Military Balance 2015*, 251.

[86] Sudhi Ranjan Sen, "More Eyes in the Sky for Air Force: India to Buy 2 More Radar Mounted Aircraft," NDTV, March 28, 2015, http://www.ndtv.com/india-news/more-eyes-in-the-sky-for-air-force-india-to-buy-2-more-radar-mounted-aircraft-750422.

Conversion Capability

Conversion capability refers to the capacity to convert the resources devoted to the military into an effective fighting force. This includes the strategies to meet the threats facing the country; the kind of civil-military relations that prevail; doctrine, training, and organization; and the military's capacity for innovation.

The Indian government produces no single strategy document that outlines its grand strategic goals or suggests how it intends to meet these goals through the deployment of diplomatic and military tools. No such document is available in the public domain, and it is unclear if one exists within the government either. Perhaps the closest document known to exist is the standing "Raksha Mantri's Operational Directive," which guides the forces and informs the service chiefs on "what sort of war they have to prepare for." Currently, the Indian armed forces prepare for a war where "vis-à-vis [redacted text] they should be able to dominate [redacted text], whereas vis-à-vis [redacted text], the instructions are that they should be able to reach a deterrence level."[87] One can surmise that Pakistan is the country to be dominated, whereas Indian strategy vis-à-vis China is likely defensive, designed to deter China and hold Indian territory. However, as discussed earlier, India's capacity even for a defensive mission is poor primarily because of the weak state of the country's infrastructure in the border region. On the western front, by contrast, the problem India faces is not the lack of military capability but rather limitations on the type of war it can fight, considering Pakistan's threat of nuclear escalation and its acquisition of tactical nuclear weapons.

Another measure of conversion capacity is civil-military relations. India's civil-military relations follow the liberal democratic model of strong civilian control and an obedient military, but this model exhibits its own pathologies. As a young democracy, fear of a coup led the Indian political leadership to downgrade the military's involvement in policymaking below that of the civilian bureaucracy, which is a constant source of angst for the military. Military leaders are not consulted even on matters that might affect national security, such as relations with Pakistan and China. On the other hand, after the disastrous border war in 1962, civilians have also desisted from intervening in matters that are purportedly of purely military concern—such as military doctrine and strategy as well as interservice squabbles—which reduces the military's effectiveness.[88] There is no mechanism for regular

---

[87] Ministry of Defence (India), Standing Committee on Defence, "Second Report," 19.

[88] Anit Mukherjee, "Civil-Military Relations and Military Effectiveness in India," in *India's Military Modernization: Challenges and Prospects*, ed. Rajesh Basrur, Ajaya Kumar Das, and Manjeet Singh Pardesi (New Delhi: Oxford University Press, 2014).

consultations between the political and military leadership, except in crisis situations. Thus, military leaders are uncertain of civilian policy requirements, and civilian leaders remain unaware of military capabilities and potential contributions to strategic policy.

The third measure is doctrine, training, and organization. The Indian military has become much more open, with all three services publishing their military doctrines and some even releasing more than one version. But the doctrinal statements reflect the concerns of the individual services rather than an integrated strategy, even though all pay homage to jointness. On the other hand, the army and air force have conducted a number of exercises to test joint operations.[89]

The Indian Army's doctrine expects future wars to be short, highly intense, and multidimensional.[90] It is not clear why this should be so, considering that the Kargil War in 1999, in a nuclearized environment, was twice as long as the war with Pakistan in 1971 that led to the creation of Bangladesh. The army also expects to fight an offensive war, which is clear from how it has tailored its forces and system as well as from its training.[91] The doctrine calls for mobilizing "in the minimum possible time"; using the "indirect approach" through the turning move, envelopment, and infiltration rather than head-on attack; maintaining a high tempo of operations "to unbalance and paralyze the adversary"; and using whatever forces are available, including holding or "pivot" corps, leaving only the bare minimum for holding operations.[92] This strategy is less ambitious than the army's earlier focus on using its strike corps to carry out all offensive operations and is more viable in a nuclearized environment. But such a rapid standing-start attack (or Cold Start, as it has been termed in the Indian debate) assumes that all forces are prepared and provisioned for transitioning from peacetime to wartime in an extremely short period. It is not clear that the army could carry out this plan successfully at its current levels of readiness. In addition, this plan does not consider the possibility that Pakistan's nuclear red lines might not be so much spatial as consequential: in other words, Pakistan's temptation to use nuclear weapons might increase the closer the Indian Army is to success, even if Pakistan does not lose much territory. Whether Indian political leaders would be willing to undertake such a bold response is also questionable.

---

[89] Gurmeet Kanwal, "Army Doctrine Undergoes Change in Nuclear Era," Observer Research Foundation, June 29, 2006, http://www.orfonline.org/cms/sites/orfonline/modules/analysis/AnalysisDetail.html?cmaid=2322&mmacmaid=267.

[90] Indian Army, *Indian Army Doctrine*, part 3 (Shimla: Headquarters Army Training Command, 2004), 10.

[91] Ibid., 10–12.

[92] Indian Army, *Indian Army Doctrine*, part 2 (Shimla: Headquarters Army Training Command, 2004), 5, 9.

Air power has become increasingly important in Indian strategy because it affords the country a clear area of superiority. As Ashley Tellis has noted, "India's defensive strategy has relied on maintaining superior airpower relative to both China and Pakistan."[93] A recent analysis of the Indian Air Force's experience in the Kargil War showed that if the Pakistan Air Force had joined the fight actively, the war "would have demanded a far more robust and sustainable Indian conventional force posture than that which prevailed well enough over Pakistan in 1999."[94] This points to key problems for the air force's doctrine, which emphasizes above all the primacy of a counter-air campaign. Though the doctrine accepts that other missions can be undertaken, the primacy of the counter-air campaign "means that no other operations be commenced, if they are going to jeopardize the attainment of air superiority, or are going to use up the resources required to attain or maintain air superiority."[95] While this emphasis may be understandable, it is not clear that India's air force currently has the capacity to fulfill such missions, given its deteriorating numbers of combat squadrons and the increasing capacity of Pakistan's air force, and even more so China's air force.

India's naval doctrine also faces capacity issues. The navy is sometimes called the "Cinderella force" because it receives the fewest resources among the three services, which is a consequence of the fact that India's strategic orientation is continental rather than maritime. Even though maritime security has become increasingly important, India's naval assets have not kept pace. Thus, as one analyst noted, the Indian Navy's maritime doctrine is aspirational rather than reflective of the state of the force as it currently is.[96]

India has declared a policy of "no first use" of nuclear weapons but pledges that it would respond with an assured and massive retaliation to a nuclear attack (or an attack with other WMDs), which dilutes somewhat the no-first-use policy. There have been calls in India to review this policy, but so far there is no indication that the government is contemplating any such move. With roughly one hundred warheads, dozens of mobile medium-range missiles, and a nascent submarine-based missile force, along with established procedures for authorizing nuclear launch and alternate command facilities for emergencies, India appears reasonably well-placed

---

[93] Ashley J. Tellis, *Dogfight! India's Medium Multi-Role Combat Aircraft Decision* (Washington, D.C.: Carnegie Endowment for International Peace, 2011), 10, http://carnegieendowment.org/files/dogfight.pdf.

[94] Benjamin S. Lambeth, *Airpower at 18,000': The Indian Air Force in the Kargil War* (Washington, D.C.: Carnegie Endowment for International Peace, 2012), 41.

[95] Indian Air Force, *Basic Doctrine of the Indian Air Force: 2012* (New Delhi, 2012), 42, http://indianairforce.nic.in/pdf/Basic%20Doctrine%20of%20the%20Indian%20Air%20Force.pdf.

[96] Iskander Rehman, "India's Aspirational Naval Doctrine," in *The Rise of the Indian Navy: Internal Vulnerabilities, External Challenges*, ed. Harsh V. Pant (Farnham: Ashgate, 2012), 55–80.

to carry out its stated doctrine. Nevertheless, at least two major deficiencies persist: India has yet to build missiles with sufficient range to cover all of China, and the range of its submarine-launched missiles is extremely limited. But slow improvements are being made in both areas, and these capabilities should become established over the next decade.

A final measure of conversion capability is the capacity for innovation. The Indian military has shown some capacity for innovation in both peacetime and wartime. India's counterinsurgency doctrine, for example, has evolved over several decades to suit the country's unique circumstances as a democratic multiethnic society facing internal armed rebellion. Similarly, since 1998 the army has grappled with the issue of fighting under the tightly circumscribed conditions imposed by nuclearization. The army and the air force also showed considerable innovativeness during the Kargil War, not only in devising an ad hoc protocol for joint operations but also, within each service, in fighting under conditions that had been previously disregarded. This suggests at least a limited capacity for innovation.

Taken together, these indicators show mixed-to-positive conversion capability, with the greatest drawbacks being the state of civil-military relations and some aspects of strategy and doctrine (in particular, weakness in joint warfighting). Inadequate political-military consultations prevent concerted grand strategic planning and the full integration of the military into the strategic tool kit. This will be a drawback if India wants to be a more active military player in the international arena.

Combat Proficiency

Combat proficiency—the final metric—refers to a military service's capability for various types of operations, ranging from irregular infantry warfare to knowledge-based warfare. The Indian Army falls between a basic combined arms force and a full combined arms force. It has demonstrated the capability to conduct sophisticated defensive and offensive operations at the division and corps levels, with some limited capacity for close air support with helicopters and fixed-wing aircraft. The army has long wanted the Army Aviation Corps to have its own attack helicopters. This was finally sanctioned in 2012, and the corps will receive U.S.-built AH-64 Apache Longbow attack helicopters. This gives the army some autonomous capabilities, but the air force would still need to provide fixed-wing close air support. Indeed, the army and air force have conducted joint exercises to develop operational synergy.[97] However, because the air force considers its primary objective to be counter-air missions, such operational cooperation cannot be taken

---

[97] Kanwal, "Army Doctrine Undergoes Change in Nuclear Era."

for granted. For the Indian Army to become a full combined arms force, the army and the air force would need to become a truly seamless joint force, or the army would need to acquire dedicated fixed-wing attack aircraft.

The Indian Navy is best characterized as a naval strike and limited air control force. It has operated at least one aircraft carrier since the 1950s and currently has two carriers, with two squadrons of fighter jets. The navy also deploys long-range maritime patrol and antisubmarine warfare aircraft, including six U.S.-built P-8I Neptune aircraft, with two more on order.[98] In addition, it has its own dedicated communications satellite, the GSAT-7. The navy aspires to become a blue water force but is a long way from achieving that goal.

The Indian Air Force is capable of fixed-wing close air support, basic suppression of enemy air defenses, and basic deep interdiction. It does not possess all these elements in equal measure, however. It gives less emphasis to close air support, whereas its suppression and deep-interdiction capabilities are probably at the higher end of the spectrum. It has some strategic strike capabilities, but these are not dedicated strategic air assets. The Indian Air Force possesses fighter/attack jets such as SU-30s and Mirage-2000s rather than bombers such as the Russian TU-160 Blackjack or the U.S. B-1B Lancer and B-2 Spirit.

Conclusion

This study finds that while India has considerable capabilities to generate national power, they rest on relatively narrow foundations. The most important source of Indian power is the wealth produced by the country's rapid economic growth. This is not surprising because wealth is the most important foundation of power for all countries. India's national resource base includes technological self-sufficiency in some critical areas, developed with strong elite consensus and support. India's access to financial resources is increasing because the country is becoming a more attractive destination for foreign investment as a consequence of more pragmatic economic policies adopted by the Modi government. On the output side, Indian military power remains significant, even if it is not expanding rapidly.

On the other hand, wealth needs to be used efficiently in order to be converted into usable power for the present while laying the foundations for further production of wealth and power. Rapid economic growth is not an indication that India has developed efficient state mechanisms—in fact, in

---

[98] Ridzwan Rahmat, "Boeing Delivers Sixth P-8I Aircraft to Indian Navy," *IHS Jane's 360*, November 26, 2014, http://www.janes.com/article/46318/boeing-delivers-sixth-p-8i-aircraft-to-indian-navy.

India's case a good part of the excess growth over the country's traditional rate of 3.5% is simply the effect of loosening bureaucratic controls on the economy. Indeed, the Indian bureaucracy remains probably the most significant obstacle both to producing the resources needed for generating power and to converting these resources into durable assets for further growth. Despite the post-1991 economic liberalization, the Indian bureaucracy still controls many of India's pathways to power. Without making the bureaucracy more efficient or less dominant—or both—India's capacity to generate national power will continue to suffer. Unfortunately, there is little indication that serious efforts are being contemplated in either of these directions.

The second, but more unpredictable, obstacle is the lack of cohesion among the political elite. Democratic politics is by nature competitive, but the fragmentation of the Indian political system leads to gridlock and policy paralysis. It is difficult to predict whether this problem will grow or diminish over time. Yet even though a lack of elite cohesion might prevent the Indian economy from accelerating much faster, it is also difficult to see the economy slowing down precipitously. Instead, high economic growth rates will likely continue for some time, which gives political leaders a window to carry out urgent reforms, especially of the bureaucratic structure, in order to broaden the foundations of power. This process must start with reforming the bureaucracy to make it better equipped to satisfy India's current and future needs. In particular, India must develop a bureaucracy that has greater domain expertise, including through the lateral intake of personnel who possess the needed expertise. These reforms must include a substantial reduction of the state role in areas such as human resources and scientific research. India also needs a more capable defense research and industrial base, which is another area that could benefit from a reduced state role. By opening up defense production to private industry, India has already begun to do this, but this effort needs to be expanded. One option is to encourage exports so that private defense manufacturers are not just dependent on the Indian defense market. Though the state's role in defense R&D and production cannot be entirely eliminated, it should be confined to strategic technologies. Finally, more effective security policymaking requires much greater interaction between the political and military leadership, which could be done even without creating a single military head such as a chief of defense staff. These measures would begin to provide a broader-based foundation for Indian power and the more effective use of that power.

Continued growth in Indian power could have serious effects on the balance of power in South Asia and Asia more broadly, with implications for U.S. interests. At the regional level, Pakistan's anxieties—at least partly the consequence of the huge imbalance of power with India—will only grow as the power gap widens. For several decades after independence, Pakistan's growth outpaced that of India. Although Pakistan never grew fast or long enough to see this small advantage significantly reduce the natural power gap, the country was at least headed in the right direction. Since the early 1990s, however, India has grown much faster. It is possible that at some point the gap will become so large that Pakistan, like India's other neighbors, will come to accept the natural order in the region. But considering that Pakistan can depend on China's support, this scenario is unlikely.

Faster Indian growth relative to China might also slowly reduce the power gap between India and China. But India is unlikely to grow fast enough (or China slowly enough) for the power balance between the two sides to change significantly in the near to medium term. To the extent that there is any reduction in the power gap, China will have an incentive to balance India more actively by moving closer to Pakistan. Beijing might also be concerned that a faster-growing India could become an even stronger partner for the United States, U.S. allies, and other states that are disturbed by China's rising power.

Finally, the United States has an interest in India's continuing growth because a more powerful India, even one that is not a U.S. ally, can help balance China and divert Beijing's attention. More generally, India could be a force for peace in the region, especially if it continues to maintain a defensive posture. But this assessment also suggests issues of concern for Washington. To the extent that fragmentation in the Indian political party system continues, relations with the United States will always be a sensitive domestic issue. Such public resistance could be overcome through a greater effort by the Indian ruling elite to explain the logic of the partnership, especially considering that most opinion polls point to much higher levels of sympathy and support for the United States than any other country. For U.S. policymakers, this trend suggests the need for both acceptance and a confident patience. Washington must accept that the U.S.-India strategic partnership will follow no existing template—India will neither be an alliance partner like Europe or Japan nor a partner of convenience like China during the Cold War but rather something in between. Likewise, a confident patience is needed because unless China were to collapse suddenly (which is both unlikely and undesirable), the logic of the current balance of power in Asia will keep India and the United States on the same side of the fence.

EXECUTIVE SUMMARY

This chapter examines Indonesia's national resource base and the country's ability to use these resources effectively in meeting its internal and external challenges.

MAIN ARGUMENT

Indonesia has enjoyed four decades of robust economic growth. With little or no external security threat and minimal friction with its neighbors, the country's focus has been exclusively on state- and nation-building in the face of domestic challenges. Indonesian leaders have consequently been unwilling—and perhaps unable—to leverage a rich natural resource base and strategic location to project power externally at a level befitting a country of Indonesia's stature. Yet change is reverberating through Asia at unprecedented speed. Tectonic shifts in the global balance of power are altering Indonesia's perceptions of external threats and opportunities. New challenges now call for a strategic adjustment that gives equal, if not greater, emphasis to external threats to the country's economic security, national sovereignty, and territorial integrity.

POLICY IMPLICATIONS

- To accelerate flagging growth and strengthen economic resilience against external shocks, Indonesia needs to boost the competitiveness of manufacturing and modern services by addressing critical constraints in infrastructure and education and by reducing barriers to competition through trade and regulatory reforms.

- Indonesia will need to boost its military capabilities to meet external threats by more than doubling budgeted defense-related expenditures, reorienting the armed forces from an internal to an external security role, revamping defense procurement, and strengthening defense industries.

- The U.S. needs to respect Indonesia's desire for strategic autonomy, demonstrate its reliability as an all-weather friend, deepen economic and defense relations, and expand cooperation in areas of common interest such as ensuring freedom of navigation in the South China Sea and the Indian Ocean.

Indonesia: The Reluctant Giant

Vikram Nehru

Indonesia is the world's fourth most populous nation, third-largest democracy, and largest archipelagic nation. Comprising thousands of islands, it stretches 3,200 miles (5,150 kilometers) east to west, roughly the distance from Juneau, Alaska, to Miami, Florida. Located at the strategic juncture between the Indian and Pacific Oceans, it commands the eastern and western approaches to the Malacca Strait—the world's second-busiest shipping channel (after the English Channel) and second most popular oil tanker route (after the Strait of Hormuz). Blessed with a cornucopia of natural wealth, replete with oil, hydropower, geothermal power, various minerals, timber, rice, palm oil, cocoa, and coffee, Indonesia has attracted traders in search of raw materials from time immemorial and foreign investors in more recent decades.

Over the last half century, these attributes have made Indonesia resilient in the face of internal and external challenges and a relatively strong economic performer. Robust economic growth, punctuated only by the Asian financial crisis in 1997–98, propelled the country into the ranks of the world's middle-income nations and stoked its ambition to become a high-income economy. After Suharto's departure in 1998, Indonesia successfully transitioned to a decentralized democracy and has since ensured that its many fault lines—regional, religious, ideological, ethnic, and social—have not posed fundamental challenges to its national unity and stability.

Vikram Nehru is a Senior Associate in the Asia Program and Bakrie Chair in Southeast Asian Studies at the Carnegie Endowment for International Peace. He can be reached at <vnehru@ceip.org>.

The author is grateful to two anonymous reviewers for their perceptive comments on an earlier draft and to Louis Ritzinger for his excellent research assistance on Indonesia's defense strategy plan, defense preparedness, and defense industries.

Internationally, Indonesia is *primus inter pares* in the Association of Southeast Asian Nations (ASEAN), Southeast Asia's regional organization created to pursue common economic, security, and sociocultural goals. Indonesia is also a member of the Asia-Pacific Economic Cooperation (APEC) and, in recognition of its economic heft, the only Southeast Asian nation in the Group of Twenty (G-20).

These successes notwithstanding, Indonesia's internal resilience has not been matched by increasing impact in regional and global affairs. Jakarta's focus on managing domestic economic, political, and social challenges has been accompanied by a reluctance to project its newfound power internationally. Indonesia has also been well served by the regional and international economic and security order and has seen no reason to make any fundamental change to the status quo. Since the Sukarno period, Indonesia has faced no existential external threats that warranted international attention or support; its geographic location, together with its low-profile and pragmatic foreign policy, has minimized frictions with both its neighbors and its major trading partners.

Over the next quarter century, however, these dynamics are likely to change, shaped by global megatrends that will affect all countries, including Indonesia. The power of markets and information technologies, for example, will continue to drive the pace of globalization, bringing accentuated volatility and contagion risks that the current global order seems unable or unwilling to contain. Climate change could cause extreme weather events and rising sea levels, posing significant risks to countries like Indonesia that are located in vulnerable regions and with extensive low-lying coastlines. The rise of China and, in its wake, other emerging markets—including Indonesia—is already transforming the global balance of power and is likely to trigger unexpected international dynamics that will create new opportunities for global prosperity. At the same time, these shifts will pose challenges to the existing regional and global economic and security order underwritten by the United States.

Clearly these megatrends will change Indonesia's threat perception significantly over the next quarter century. They raise the question of whether the country's foundations of national power—its resource base, national performance, and military capabilities—will develop in ways that could meet these new threats, strengthen Indonesia's resilience, and project power abroad to advance its long-term strategic interests.

This chapter seeks to answer the above question. The first section examines factors that will sustain Indonesia's economic growth: its resource base, natural and human capital, and technological and innovation potential, as well as the policy environment likely to shape the future pace and pattern of economic development. The next section examines the social and political factors—internal and external—that will shape future national performance. These factors include the evolving range of internal and external threats; the coherence of Indonesia's political, business, and military elite; and the institutional and ideational levers available to the government that help extract and use resources to achieve national strategic goals. The last section focuses on Indonesia's military capabilities, including its readiness to face internal and external security threats, the effectiveness of its armed forces and command structure, the long-term strategic thinking informing its defense strategy, and its efforts to resuscitate its defense industrial base.

The chapter concludes that Indonesia's several and obvious advantages—size, location, and natural resources—have helped create resilience against internal and external challenges. But Indonesia's leadership has been reluctant to use the country's strategic location and newfound economic heft to project power regionally and globally. Power projection in the future is also unlikely to be significant because national performance shows few signs of improving substantially relative to regional competitors, the human capital and technological base is weak, the country's elite is divided, ideational resources have dwindled, the armed forces face huge capacity challenges, and the defense industry has been allowed to wither. While Indonesia's foreign policy, military infrastructure, and defense capabilities are expected to become more outward-oriented in the coming years, its posture will remain predominantly inward-oriented and defensive, and its projection of soft and hard power will still be well below levels expected for a country of Indonesia's physical and economic stature.

Indonesia's National Resource Base

Strategic Location with Rich Natural Resources

Indonesia enjoys a strategic location guarding the eastern and western approaches and the southern banks of the Malacca Strait, which is considered one of the world's most strategic waterways. Some 80,000 ships—accounting for half the world's shipping—passed through the strait in 2014, transporting a third of the world's liquefied natural gas, a quarter of the world's traded goods and seaborne oil, 85% of China's imported oil, 80% of Japan's energy resources, and 60% of Japan's food.[1] Long recognized as one of the world's strategic chokepoints—along with Gibraltar, the Strait of Hormuz, the Suez Canal, and the Panama Canal—the Malacca Strait is only 1.5 nautical miles wide at its narrowest point and provides several facilities for docking, refueling, repair, and warehousing services. Disrupting the flow of trade through this chokepoint would have far-reaching repercussions not just in Asia but throughout the world. The only other seaborne route linking the Indian and Pacific Oceans is thousands of miles longer and hundreds of thousands of dollars more expensive.

Not only is Indonesia strategically located; it is rich in natural resources, with the exception of rare earth minerals.[2] The country is abundant in coal, oil, gas, hydropower, geothermal power, bauxite, copper, tin, nickel, gold, silver, palm oil, rice, wood, and rubber. Indonesia's resource abundance has propelled it to become one of the world's leading commodity exporters, creating a high trade-to-GDP ratio for a country of its size.[3] GDP growth soared in the early 1970s when Indonesia—by then a major oil producer—joined the Organization of the Petroleum Exporting Countries (OPEC) and benefited from the subsequent rise in international oil prices. But it avoided the so-called resource curse that plagued other oil-exporting developing countries (notably Nigeria and Venezuela) by paying attention to agricultural development and food security and investing in health and education, which provided a sound foundation for future growth. Indonesia moved from being the world's largest rice importer in the 1960s to self-sufficiency by the mid-1980s.

By that time, however, oil had ceased to drive growth, putting the country's balance of payments in a parlous state and forcing Indonesian policymakers to liberalize trade and investment in manufacturing. The result was a rapid rise

---

[1] For more on Indonesia's strategic importance, see Noraini Zulkifli, Sharifah Munirah Alatas, and Zarina Othman, "The Importance of the Malacca Straits to Japan: Cooperation and Contributions toward Littoral States," *Malaysian Journal of History, Politics & Strategic Studies* 41, no. 2 (2014): 80–98; Soufan Group, "Maritime Choke Points and Strategic Interruption," TSG IntelBrief, June 6, 2014, http://soufangroup.com/tsg-intelbrief-maritime-choke-points-and-strategic-interruption; "18 Maps That Explain Maritime Security in Asia," Asian Maritime Transparency Initiative, Center for Strategic and International Studies, http://amti.csis.org/atlas; and Merlin Linehan, "The Geopolitics of the Straits of Malacca," Frontier Market Strategy, June 20, 2014, http://frontiermarketstrategy.com/2014/06/20/the-geopolitics-of-the-straits-of-malacca.

[2] Rare earth minerals, such as monazite and xenotime, tend to occur in association with tin ores (cassiterite). The island of Bangka in Indonesia has been a mining site for cassiterite for centuries, but there has been a long-standing issue as to whether the tailings can be exploited cost effectively. A pilot project is being run by state-owned tin producer PT Timah, which, according to one estimate, could yield seven million tons of monazite. For more on this topic, see Linda Yulisman, "Govt to Develop Rare Earth Processing," *Jakarta Post*, July 11, 2014, http://www.thejakartapost.com/news/2014/07/11/govt-develop-rare-earth-processing.html.

[3] Cross-country evidence shows the trade-to-GDP ratio to be inversely proportional to country size (as measured by GDP). Given its level of GDP, Indonesia's trade-to-GDP ratio (which is similar to China's) is above the level statistically predicted by this cross-country relationship.

in the production and export of labor-intensive manufacturing, diversifying growth and foreign exchange earnings away from oil and improving the economy's resilience against the volatility of oil and commodity prices. Such growth was accompanied by rapid structural change, as the industrial sector evolved from the production of simple consumer goods and the processing of basic resources to a wider range of increasingly sophisticated technologies.

Yet, unlike Singapore and the mainland Southeast Asian middle-income economies (Malaysia, Thailand, and recently Vietnam), Indonesia has not quite become an integral part of the East Asian production network with China at its hub. Indonesia's combination of high transportation costs, weak infrastructure, and scarcity of relevant skills has meant that intra-industry trade remained a relatively small proportion of total trade, depriving its economy of the growth benefits of specialization and agglomeration in manufacturing. Indonesia benefited from China's economic expansion, but largely through volume and price increases in commodity exports.

Since the Asian financial crisis of 1997–98, Indonesia's share of manufacturing in GDP, exports, and employment has shrunk. As a result, the economy has become steadily more reliant on natural resources. The proximate cause was a global commodity boom driven by China. At the same time, agriculture and manufacturing were disadvantaged by an appreciating real exchange rate, inadequate investment in infrastructure, a growing shortage of skills, labor market rigidities, and a rise in behind-the-border barriers to trade.[4] The share of raw commodities in Indonesia's exports increased over the last decade, reaching 60% of total exports by 2011. Moreover, Indonesia's industrial base has become increasingly oriented toward the domestic market and processing natural resources, with concentrations in petroleum refining, liquefaction of natural gas, and the production of leather goods, wood products, paper, palm oil, and cement. Labor-intensive exports of manufactures have faced increased competitive pressure from other Asian economies.[5] The termination of the Multi-Fibre Arrangement in 2005 added to these woes as production and employment in textiles and garments declined in the face of competition from other textile-exporting countries, especially Bangladesh and China.[6]

---

[4] Vikram Nehru, "Manufacturing in India and Indonesia: Performance and Policies," *Bulletin of Indonesian Economic Studies* 49, no. 1 (2013): 35–60.

[5] Rajah Rasiah "Expansion and Slowdown in Southeast Asian Electronics Manufacturing," *Journal of the Asia Pacific Economy* 14, no. 2 (2009): 123–37.

[6] The Multi-Fibre Arrangement (1974–2004) was a global arrangement of bilateral agreements that imposed quantitative restrictions on yarn, fabric, and garment exports from developing countries to developed markets. It was eventually replaced by the WTO Agreement on Textiles and Clothing on January 1, 2005. For more information, see Rajah Rasiah, "Beyond the Multi-Fibre Agreement: How Are Workers in East Asia Faring?" *Institutions and Economies* 4, no. 3 (2012): 1–20.

Similarly, Indonesia's global market share in wood products has steadily declined in recent years. Rapid growth of the automotive industry, on the other hand, has been a positive development, driven in part by the scale economies that Indonesia's own large domestic market affords as well as by the integrated ASEAN value chain that has emerged as Japanese automotive companies diversify away from China and Thailand.[7]

Economic Growth

From the perspective of economic growth, the Asian financial crisis proved to be a turning point. In years prior to the crisis, Indonesia's GDP growth rate averaged 7.4% per year over 30 years (1967–97). Since the crisis, it has slowed by 2 percentage points to just 5.4% per year (2000–2013).

Unfortunately, lower growth in the last decade has been accompanied by rising income inequality, weakening the impact on poverty reduction.[8] Although per capita GDP has climbed above $3,500, creating a lower-middle income country (using the World Bank's classification system),[9] 43% of the population still lives on less than $2 a day (in terms of 2005 purchasing power parity).[10] Recent growth has accrued largely to the higher deciles in the income distribution, while those at the lower end have seen their income share fall.[11] Between 2002 and 2013, per capita consumption in the richest 10% of households climbed from 6.6 times to 10.3 times that of the poorest 10%. Nearly one-third of all household consumption in Indonesia accrues to the richest 10% of households, and nearly half to the richest 20%. The poorest 40%, on the other hand, account for only one-fifth of total consumption, and their share has been declining over time.[12] Part of the reason could be that real wages in informal sectors (where the bulk of the poor work) have stagnated or even declined since July 2009, although the evidence is not conclusive.[13]

---

[7] Thomas Farole and Deborah Winkler, "Export Competitiveness in Indonesia's Manufacturing Sector," World Bank, December 2012.

[8] The Gini coefficient climbed from 0.30 in 2000 to 0.42 by 2013. Kunta Nugraha and Phil Lewis, "Toward a Better Measure of Income Inequality in Indonesia," *Bulletin of Indonesian Economic Studies* 49, no. 1 (2013): 103–12.

[9] "New Country Classifications," World Bank, July, 2, 2015, http://data.worldbank.org/news/new-country-classifications-2015.

[10] The latest data is from 2011. For the full breakdown, see "Poverty Headcount Ratio at $2 a Day (PPP) (% of Population)," World Bank, World Development Indicators, http://data.worldbank.org/indicator/SI.POV.2DAY/countries.

[11] Vikram Nehru, "Survey of Recent Developments," *Bulletin of Indonesian Economic Studies* 49, no. 2 (2013): 139–66.

[12] "Indonesia Economic Quarterly: Hard Choices," World Bank, July 22, 2014, http://www.worldbank.org/en/news/feature/2014/07/21/indonesia-economic-quarterly-july-2014.

[13] Nehru, "Survey of Recent Developments."

Indonesia's growth slowdown in this millennium in part reflects lower global growth but was also the result of a deterioration in Indonesia's investment environment, growing shortages in skills, and bottlenecks in infrastructure. The urgency for reforms during the Asian financial crisis faded once the economy recovered and commodity prices soared on the back of China's strong growth, reinforcing the characterization of Indonesia as following "good policies in bad times."[14] Indonesia's traditional openness to foreign trade and investment has become more precarious and under threat from public opinion and pressure from domestic conglomerates.[15] While tariffs have remained low, the increasing use of nontariff barriers has made the trade regime more protectionist. Notwithstanding the 2007 investment reforms that granted national treatment to foreign investors, entry barriers in certain sectors have since climbed to protect incumbent firms.[16] At the same time, local governments have been adding their own opaque restrictions to new foreign investment, increasing investors' perceptions of risk. Reflecting these developments in the private investment environment, some of Indonesia's rankings in the World Bank's Doing Business project show considerable room for improvement (see **Table 1**).

Investment, Growth, and Stability

By developing country standards, Indonesia's savings and investment rates are high. As of 2013, the national savings rate as a share of GDP was a healthy 32% and gross domestic capital formation was 34%.[17] The high investment ratio assures a steady growth rate of 5%–7% per year, depending on the state of the world economy and the health of key foreign commodity markets, especially China. The challenge in Indonesia is usually not the level of investment but the rate of return, which is hampered in part by inadequate public investment in infrastructure, the dearth of skills, and a complex policy environment for private investment that favors incumbent investors and raises barriers for new entrants.

Intermediation between savers and investors is dominated by a banking system that accounts for nearly 80% of the financial sector's total assets. Having learned from the 1997–98 financial crisis, Indonesia's banks are now

[14] Hal Hill, *The Indonesian Economy* (Cambridge: Cambridge University Press, 1996).

[15] Kelly Bird, Hal Hill, and Sandy Cuthbertson, "Making Trade Policy in a New Democracy after a Deep Crisis: Indonesia," *World Economy* 31, no. 7 (2008): 947–68.

[16] Yose R. Damuri and Creina Day, "Recent Economic Developments," *Bulletin of Indonesian Economic Studies* 51, no. 1 (2015): 3–27; and Shiro Armstrong and Sjamsu Rahardja, "Survey of Recent Developments," *Bulletin of Indonesian Economic Studies* 50, no. 1 (2014): 3–28.

[17] World Bank, World Development Indicators Databank, http://databank.worldbank.org/data/views/variableSelection/selectvariables.aspx?source=world-development-indicators.

TABLE 1   Ease of doing business in Indonesia in 2015

Topic	Rank (out of 189 countries)
Overall ease of doing business	114
Starting a business	155*
Dealing with construction permits	153*
Getting electricity	78
Registering property	117
Getting credit	71
Protecting minority investors	43
Paying taxes	160*
Trading across borders	62
Enforcing contracts	172*
Resolving insolvency	75

SOURCE: World Bank, Doing Business project, available at http://www.doingbusiness.org/ data/exploreeconomies/indonesia.

NOTE: Asterisk signifies that Indonesia is in the bottom quartile of all ranked countries.

better capitalized and are on a more solid financial footing as a result of strengthened central bank supervision.

Notwithstanding the country's high savings and investment, an open external capital account makes Indonesia's macroeconomic situation border on instability. The relatively small domestic equity and bond markets render the financial system vulnerable to swings in flows of external short-term capital. A high proportion of the economy's short-term liabilities (debt and equity) is held by nonresidents. As a result, Indonesia's capital and foreign exchange markets remain highly volatile, sensitive to shifts in market sentiments triggered by policies and events at home and abroad.

It is ironic, therefore, that although Indonesia's sovereign debt burden indicators are low by international standards (the government debt-to-GDP ratio is only 26%),[18] Indonesian sovereign debt in secondary markets still commands a relatively high risk premium. This situation exists despite the fact that the country's overall fiscal and balance of payments positions remain within reasonable parameters and the economy is relatively well positioned to withstand economic and financial shocks. The open capital account and

---

[18] International Monetary Fund, "Indonesia: Staff Report for the 2014 Article IV Consultation," IMF Country Report, no. 15/74, 2015, table 5, 39, http://www.imf.org/external/pubs/ft/scr/2015/cr1574.pdf.

sudden reversals in portfolio capital flows tend to amplify small perturbations in the domestic or global economy and magnify minor policy missteps, placing a large premium on the quality of macroeconomic management.

Technology

Whether Indonesia's past growth record can be sustained in the future depends heavily on its technological capabilities.[19] Unfortunately, its record in this sphere leaves much to be desired. In the export-oriented textile, garment, and electronics sectors, technological capability is mostly limited to basic production and operational capabilities. In the export-oriented automotive industry, the relevant technological know-how and intellectual property rights remain firmly in the hands of the foreign companies that dominate the sector.

A World Bank survey concluded that innovation and technological capability in Indonesian firms is well behind comparable countries in East Asia as well as other lower-middle-income economies.[20] On the World Bank Knowledge Economy Index, Indonesia ranks 108th out of 146 countries, surpassing only Laos and Cambodia in the region. In the Global Innovation Index rankings, Indonesia stands 87th out of 143 countries, scoring lower than Bhutan and Guyana. Even so, its innovation score is almost at par for a country with its level of per capita income (see **Figure 1**).

One of the reasons behind Indonesia's low scores in technological and innovation capability is that Jakarta's investments in formal R&D programs have always been very small. Total R&D expenditure as a percentage of GDP has never exceeded 0.2% (the lowest among the G-20) and was only 0.08% a few years ago. Most of this investment has been in the public sector, as domestic private firms have never made any significant commitment to R&D.[21] Moreover, foreign investors do not regard the country as a suitable base for R&D activity, owing to its weak skill base, limited protection of intellectual property rights, and absence of significant public support for R&D.

The low level of R&D expenditure is also reflected in Indonesia's poor score for patent filings. Although the Indonesia Intellectual Property Office recently entered the ranks of the twenty largest patent offices in the world,

---

[19] While future growth in Indonesian productivity can continue to benefit from capital deepening, an increasing amount will need to come from total factor productivity growth, which reflects, among other things, the pace of technological improvements in the economy.

[20] World Bank and International Finance Corporation, "Indonesia Country Profile 2009," Enterprise Surveys, 2009, http://www.enterprisesurveys.org/~/media/GIAWB/EnterpriseSurveys/Documents/Profiles/English/Indonesia-2009.pdf.

[21] Public research institutes (including universities) carry out 96% of all R&D activities, leaving the remaining 4% to the private sector. For more on this topic, see "UNESCO Institute for Statistics Data 2013," Knoema, http://knoema.com/UNESCOISD2013Jul/unesco-institute-for-statistics-data-2013?location=1000920-indonesia.

FIGURE 1   Indonesia on the Global Innovation Index–GDP per capita curve

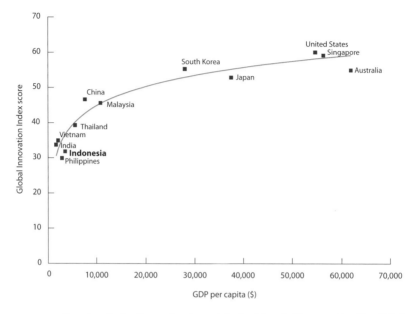

SOURCE: Soumitra Dutta, Bruno Lanvin, and Sacha Wunsch-Vincent, eds., *The Global Innovation Index 2014: The Human Factor in Innovation* (Ithaca, Fontainebleau, and Geneva: Cornell University, INSEAD, and WIPO, 2014), https://www.globalinnovationindex.org/content.aspx?page=data-analysis; and World Bank, World Development Indicators, 2015.

only 663 of the 7,450 patents filed in 2013 were by residents of Indonesia.[22] Further, even Kenya, Bangladesh, and Vietnam produced more articles in scientific journals than Indonesia.[23]

Indonesia's weak technological capabilities affect the country's communications infrastructure. For example, it has one of the slowest Internet connection speeds in the Asia-Pacific. In part, this is because its archipelagic geography makes cable infrastructure difficult and costly. Even so, Indonesia is ranked 64th out of 144 countries in the World

---

[22] For comparison, 825,000 patents were filed in China. World Intellectual Property Organization, *World Intellectual Property Indicators: Economics and Statistics Series* (Geneva: World Intellectual Property Organization, 2014), 48, http://www.wipo.int/edocs/pubdocs/en/wipo_pub_941_2014.pdf.

[23] Data for 2011 is from the National Science Foundation's Science and Engineering Indicators and includes scientific and engineering articles published in the following fields: physics, biology, chemistry, mathematics, clinical medicine, biomedical research, engineering and technology, and earth and space sciences. See also World Bank, World Development Indicators, http://data.worldbank.org/indicator/IP.JRN.ARTC.SC/countries?display=default.

Economic Forum's Networked Readiness Index, which combines measures of environment, readiness, usage, and impact.[24]

These weaknesses in technological capabilities affect other sectors. One example is the energy sector, where Indonesia has gone from being a net exporter to being a net importer of oil and where electricity generation has fallen well below demand. Indonesia currently has few world-class oil and gas R&D centers to develop cutting-edge technologies, and graduates ready to become oil and gas industry professionals are scarce. The lack of domestic technological expertise has severely hampered the upstream exploratory activities of Pertamina (Indonesia's state-owned oil company), which at the same time is unwilling to seek the involvement of foreign oil companies in such work.[25] Another example of this weakness is the aviation sector, which suffers from shortfalls in technological capability that hamper the competitiveness of Indonesian airlines. As a result, all but four Indonesian passenger airlines are currently banned from flying in the European Union because of safety concerns.[26]

Arguably, Indonesia does not need to spend heavily on R&D if it can successfully import and absorb existing technologies from other countries. All studies on diffusion of innovation in Indonesia have found evidence of positive spillovers from trade and foreign investment—of local firms benefiting from the use of foreign goods with embedded technology or the presence of foreign firms within the industry or region. But Indonesian trade and investment policy is trending toward increasing protectionism and higher entry barriers for new investors and appears to be restricting this all-important channel through which foreign technology can be imported and absorbed. Seemingly unable to raise domestic R&D capacity at the same pace as other regional powers and apparently retreating from the path of adopting and adapting global technology through open trade and investment policies, Indonesia will find that technological development could remain its Achilles' heel in projecting national power for decades to come.

---

[24] Beñat Bilbao-Osorio, Soumitra Dutta, and Bruno Lanvin, eds., *The Global Information Technology Report 2014: Rewards and Risks of Big Data* (Geneva: World Economic Forum and INSEAD, 2014), http://www3.weforum.org/docs/WEF_GlobalInformationTechnology_Report_2014.pdf.

[25] Donald I. Hertzmark, "Pertamina: Indonesia's State-Owned Oil Company," James A. Baker III Institute for Public Policy, Rice University, March 2007, http://bakerinstitute.org/media/files/page/9d12f310/noc_pertamina_hertzmark.pdf.

[26] Nadya Natahadibrata, "EU Keeps Partial Ban on Indonesian Airlines," *Jakarta Post*, June 27, 2015, http://www.thejakartapost.com/news/2015/06/27/eu-keeps-partial-ban-indonesian-airlines.html.

Human Resources

Skills shortages present a major obstacle to Indonesia's future development; 84% of employers reported difficulties in filling management positions, and 69% reported problems in sourcing other skilled workers.[27] Following a constitutional amendment in 2002, the share of Indonesia's education budget has climbed steadily, reaching the mandated 20% in 2009. But skills remain scarce and, together with infrastructure deficiencies, persist as a binding constraint to future economic growth, technological development, and by implication the expansion of capabilities essential to Indonesia's national performance over the long term and projection of national power in coming decades.

In its education index, the UN Development Programme ranks Indonesia 112th out of 187 countries.[28] The average Indonesian attained 7.5 years of schooling in 2013, placing it 114th among 187 countries.[29] But the years of schooling is not the only issue; the quality of education is also a concern. In the Programme for International Student Assessment (PISA) scores, Indonesia stands 56th among 65 countries for which data is available.[30] Indeed, the PISA tests found that about a quarter of Indonesian fifteen-year-olds were not proficient at the most basic level of science. The Trends in International Mathematics and Science Study seems to confirm this data.[31] In both math and science, Indonesia performs significantly lower than the mean score of 500 and places lower than many countries in the region (Malaysia, South Korea, Japan, and Hong Kong). Finally, in a study by the Organisation for Economic Co-operation and Development (OECD) ranking the quality of education in 76 countries, Indonesia stood 69th.[32]

Given its per capita income, Indonesia's tertiary education enrollment rate is a reasonable 23% (compared with 42% for the United States).[33] But quality standards are, if anything, a greater concern. A heterogeneous mix of tertiary institutions accommodate this large student population—including

---

[27] Dipak Dasgupta, Julien Courdon, Rabin Hattari, Saurabh Mishra, Nihal Pitigala, and Marinella Yadao, eds., *World Bank South Asia Economic Update 2010: Moving Up, Looking East* (Washington, D.C.: World Bank, 2010).

[28] "Education Index," Human Development Report Office, UN Development Programme, November 15, 2013, http://hdr.undp.org/en/content/education-index.

[29] "Mean Years of Schooling (of Adults) (Years)," Human Development Report Office, UN Development Programme, November 15, 2013, http://hdr.undp.org/en/content/mean-years-schooling-adults-years.

[30] The 2012 PISA results are available from the National Center for Education Statistics at https://nces.ed.gov/surveys/pisa/pisa2012/index.asp.

[31] The results of the Trends in Mathematics and Science Study are available at http://www.timss.org.

[32] See Sean Coughlan, "Asia Tops Biggest Global School Rankings," BBC, May 13, 2015, http://www.bbc.com/news/business-32608772.

[33] See Nehru, "Manufacturing in India and Indonesia," table 1.

central, provincial, public, private, specialist, conventional, multidisciplinary, vocational, professional, and research institutions—but weak regulations and little government oversight have resulted in poor quality control and produced graduates of varying capabilities. Not a single university ranks in the top 500 in the world, and incentives to improve standards are virtually nonexistent. Indonesia's tertiary systems have few links with universities abroad and weak links with international research networks, while peer review of academic work is rare. Low salaries force faculties to shoulder heavy teaching loads or increase administrative assignments to boost salaries, so there is little time for research. Poor incentives contribute to poor performance, and strong vested interests make reform difficult.[34]

Indonesia's National Performance

The previous section examined Indonesia's strong resource base and economic growth record, but at the same time highlighted critical weaknesses: rising inequality, weak technological capacity, serious shortcomings in human capital, and shortages in critical skills. This section analyzes the factors influencing the capacity of the state to transform its rich resource base into national power. It notes the changing nature of external threats to Indonesia's sovereignty and territorial integrity, addresses potential internal flashpoints that constantly threaten domestic stability, and discusses whether the country's political institutions and political elite are capable of overcoming these challenges and exerting national power internally and abroad.

External Threats

Until five years ago, Indonesia felt no compelling reason to project power abroad. It was well served by the prevailing world order and faced few external threats. The country's geography made land invasion unlikely, and until recent concerns arose with China's nine-dashed line, Indonesia had few ongoing disputes over its maritime borders.

Since its confrontation with Malaysia in the 1960s, Indonesia has generally found peaceful ways to manage disputes with neighboring countries. In 2003, it resolved a dispute with Vietnam over their common continental shelf boundary; in 2012, it reached a settlement with Malaysia through adjudication by the International Court of Justice; and in May 2014, it settled a disagreement with the Philippines over the boundary between

---

[34] Hal Hill and Thee Kian Wie, "Indonesian Universities in Transition: Catching Up and Opening Up," *Bulletin of Indonesian Economic Studies* 48, no. 2 (2012): 229–51.

their exclusive economic zones (EEZ) in the Mindanao and Celebes Seas. There is an outstanding border dispute with Malaysia over another tiny island that has yet to be resolved, but even in that case Prime Minister Najib Razak and President Joko Widodo have agreed to negotiate. In addition, Indonesia is engaged in ongoing negotiations with Palau and Timor Leste to clarify their respective maritime boundaries.

The largely benign foreign policy during President Yudhoyono's ten-year administration (2004–14) epitomized Indonesia's nonthreatening posture abroad. The country preferred to solve conflicts between its neighbors (such as the Thai-Cambodia dispute) rather than create conflicts of its own. Being *primus inter pares* among ASEAN member states, Indonesia positioned itself as a mediator and peacemaker. Its foreign policy largely advanced democratic principles and human rights as central political values. Yudhoyono sought to leverage Indonesia's position as a democratic, secular, and majority-Muslim nation to project a moderate voice in the Islamic world. His stance against terrorism and violent Islamic extremism further enhanced the country's reputation regionally and globally and garnered the goodwill of the United States.

Foreign policy actions and announcements in Widodo's young administration contain three strands that appear to signal a departure from the Yudhoyono administration's previous policy of "a thousand friends and zero enemies."[35] The first strand is a more assertive defense of Indonesian sovereignty and interests. The Widodo administration has sunk foreign vessels caught fishing illegally in Indonesian waters, executed foreign drug smugglers despite vociferous opposition from their respective governments, and pursued a nationalistic economic agenda. The second strand is closer ties with Indonesia's giant neighbors, especially China. Widodo has already traveled twice to China seeking investment in transport and energy infrastructure, as well as in manufacturing, and was quick to sign up as a founding member of the Asian Infrastructure Investment Bank, a multilateral financial institution largely created and driven by China. His overtures to China were accompanied by a major foreign policy speech in which he criticized the prevailing international economic order and called on emerging nations to build a new system.[36] The third strand reflects Widodo's desire to transform Indonesia into a maritime power. Internationally, this shift fits neatly with China's initiative to build a maritime Silk Road and the protection of Indonesian waters against

[35] "Indonesia's Foreign Policy: A Thousand Jilted Friends," *Economist*, May 2, 2015, http://www.economist.com/news/asia/21650173-new-president-charts-markedly-different-course-thousand-jilted-friends.

[36] Ting Shi, Yudith Ho, and Rieka Rahadiana, "China, Indonesia Lead Calls for New Order for Developing Countries," Bloomberg Business, April 22, 2015, http://www.bloomberg.com/news/articles/2015-04-22/china-indonesia-lead-calls-for-new-order-for-developing-world.

foreign intruders, while domestically it focuses on increased efficiency of inter-island shipping and reduced economic distance between the major islands in Indonesia's far-flung archipelago.[37]

Perhaps the most important change in Indonesia's threat perception has been caused by recent developments in the South China Sea. The Indonesian military has raised concerns about the implications of China's nine-dashed line for Indonesia's claim to its EEZ near the Natuna Islands, which hold large reserves of natural gas (see **Figure 2**). When the Chinese navy held exercises off Malaysia's James Shoal—only 250 kilometers from Indonesian waters—the armed forces took notice. In 2010, Indonesia sent a letter to the UN Commission on the Limits of the Continental Shelf to contest China's claim on the South China Sea. Then the Indonesian military conducted major exercises on and around Natuna Island starting October 2013. When in early 2014 China unveiled a new official map that appeared to harden its claims in the South China Sea, the Indonesian military announced preparations to strengthen its defense of the Natuna Islands.

FIGURE 2   China's nine-dashed line near Indonesia's Natuna Islands

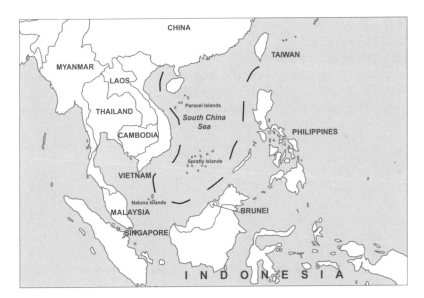

---

[37] Joshua Kurlantzick, "Jokowi's Maritime Doctrine and What It Means," *Diplomat*, November 29, 2014, http://thediplomat.com/2014/11/jokowis-maritime-doctrine-and-what-it-means.

Despite these developments, Indonesian foreign policy has been careful not to antagonize China and has instead promoted the concept of an Indo-Pacific treaty of friendship and cooperation.[38] Indonesia relies on its core principle of "strategic autonomy" in its relationships with larger powers to promote peaceful solutions to overlapping territorial claims in the South China Sea. It has been careful to promote closer ties with both China and the United States, signing a strategic partnership with the former in 2005 and a comprehensive partnership with the latter in 2010. Indonesia has championed the inclusion of the United States in the East Asia Summit, an annual heads-of-state meeting between ASEAN and its eight regional partners (including China).[39] It also has participated actively in other regional and multilateral forums, such as APEC and the Indian Ocean Rim Association, and has built a web of bilateral relationships with regional partners, including Australia, India, Japan, and South Korea.

Internal Threats

Throughout its post-independence history, Indonesia's national security strategy has been largely inward-looking, focusing on numerous domestic fault lines: economic, ethnic, ideological, racial, regional, religious, and social.[40] As would be expected for a country so large and diverse, these intersecting forces are driven by powerful interests and have posed a constant threat to domestic stability. The swollen ranks of the poor, disaffected, and underprivileged have always existed alongside a handful of rich and powerful conglomerates that enjoy a close and symbiotic relationship with the political elite. Racial tensions are fueled by the popular view that the Chinese, though constituting a small minority of the population, own a disproportionate share

---

[38] Marty Natalegawa, "An Indonesian Perspective on the Indo-Pacific" (keynote address at the Conference on Indonesia, Washington, D.C., May 16, 2013), http://csis.org/files/attachments/130516_MartyNatalegawa_Speech.pdf.

[39] The eight regional partners are Australia, China, India, Japan, New Zealand, Russia, South Korea, and the United States.

[40] Bob Lowry, "Key Security Fault Lines—Unresolved Issues and New Challenges," in *Indonesia's Ascent: Power, Leadership, and the Regional Order*, ed. Christopher B. Roberts, Ahmad D. Habir, and Leonard C. Sebastian (London: Palgrave Macmillan, 2015).

of the country's wealth.[41] An economic system favoring Java over the outer islands feeds ethnic and regional tensions. A deep sense of injustice bred by these economic, racial, and regional inequalities initially sparked an Islamic rebellion that was defeated in 1962 and subsequently fostered a Communist movement that was crushed by Suharto in 1965–66. Since then, the search for economic and political empowerment has taken the form of regional separatist movements in Aceh, East Timor, and Papua.

Successive governments have ensured that these fissures within Indonesian society have not challenged the unity or security of the nation. Suppressive actions were justified through references to the centrality of the constitution, the unity of the republic, and the five *pancasila* principles (the official philosophical foundation of the Indonesian state).[42] This was particularly true of the Suharto era, during which national security and unity conveniently justified authoritarian rule and the dominance of the military. The echoes of this period, however, remain very much in evidence today. Although many fault lines appear dormant, they lie just beneath the surface and occasionally erupt when not managed carefully.

Resolving internal tensions has proved difficult because Indonesia's governance institutions remain fragile and are still being tested. Suharto's departure in 1998 caused a tectonic shift in political power relations from which Indonesia has not yet found a new equilibrium. The democracy remains young and has yet to fully settle the balance of power between the central and local governments, the president and parliament, elected officials and big business, civilian institutions and the uniformed services, and religious and secular forces. This section considers each in turn.

Central and local governments. Decentralization shifted significant political and economic power from Jakarta to the provinces. By 2012, one-third of the central budget was transferred to Indonesia's more than

---

[41] The 2010 census shows Chinese Indonesians account for 1.2% of the population. See Central Bureau of Statistics (Indonesia), "Kewarganegaraan suku bangsa, agama, dan bahasa sehari-hari penduduk Indonesia: Hasil sensus Indonesia: 2010" [Race, Ethnicity, Religions, and Languages of the Indonesian People: Results of the Indonesian Census: 2010], October 2011, http://sp2010.bps. go.id/files/ebook/kewarganegaraan%20penduduk%20indonesia/index.htm, 9. There have been no recent studies of the relative wealth of the Chinese Indonesian community. An oft-quoted Australian study in 1995 claimed that Chinese Indonesians controlled over 70% of Indonesia's listed companies by market capitalization. While the numbers may be questionable, the popular perception is that Chinese Indonesians control large swaths of the economy, and as a result they are often targeted for punishment by the government and the public in times of economic hardship. This partly explains the violent anti-Chinese riots at the height of the Asian financial crisis. See East Asia Analytical Unit, Department of Foreign Affairs and Trade (Australia), *Overseas Chinese Business Networks in Asia* (Canberra, 1995); Ignatius Wibowo, "Exit, Voice, and Loyalty: Indonesian Chinese after the Fall of Soeharto," *Sojourn: Journal of Social Issues in Southeast Asia*, no. 1 (2001): 125–46; and Sarah Turner, "Speaking Out: Chinese Indonesians after Suharto," *Asian Ethnicity* 4, no. 3 (2003): 337–52.

[42] The five pancasila principles are unity, justice, monotheism, democracy, and social welfare. See Lowry, "Key Security Fault Lines."

five hundred districts, together with all the responsibility for delivering basic public services.[43] Bank loans followed a similar pattern. The outer islands, which produce the bulk of Indonesia's commodity exports, have seen rapid growth relative to Java (and Jakarta, in particular).

Decentralization also deflated incipient secessionist movements. The prolonged Aceh insurgency, which persevered despite harsh and repressive military action over decades, ultimately ended in the wake of the tragic tsunami in late 2004, but only after a guarantee of significant political and economic autonomy for the region. Papua, which has seen low-level armed resistance against Jakarta's rule since its incorporation into Indonesia in 1969, remains a source of unrest. However, President Widodo's recent release of five political prisoners and promises of press freedoms and new development initiatives have brought fresh hope for peace and reconciliation in the region.

The decision to empower districts rather than provinces was made to ensure that new subnational governments would not be large enough to challenge the center or consider secession.[44] This worked only partially, as Indonesia's urban centers not only are major beneficiaries of decentralization but have proved to be the fastest-growing areas in the country. As a result, cities have created a new generation of leaders that are challenging Indonesia's Jakarta-based elite who represent the status quo. Emblematic of this new dynamic is Joko Widodo, previously a mayor of Solo—a midsized town in Central Java—and then governor of Jakarta. Other second-generation political leaders in local government (such as Ridwan Kamil in Bandung and Tri Rismaharini of Surabaya) are now following his example. Unlike previous Jakarta-centric leaders whose power derived from their proximity to Suharto, these new leaders are earning their political stripes in rapidly growing urban centers, where their competence as leaders and administrators is increasing their electoral appeal.

President and parliament. Indonesian politics since Suharto's departure never really tested the relative powers of the executive and the legislature until Widodo's presidency.[45] Yudhoyono—the only post-Suharto president with

---

[43] Under the decentralized arrangement, subnational governments received 15% of onshore oil revenues, 30% of onshore gas revenues (including offshore gas up to twelve miles off the coast), 70% of forestry revenues, and 100% of fisheries revenues. For more information, see Blane D. Lewis, "Twelve Years of Fiscal Decentralization in Indonesia: A Balance Sheet," in *Regional Dynamics in a Decentralized Indonesia*, ed. Hal Hill (Singapore: Institute of Southeast Asian Studies, 2014).

[44] M. Ryaas Rasyid, "Regional Autonomy and Local Politics in Indonesia," in *Local Power and Politics in Indonesia: Decentralisation and Democratisation*, ed. Edward Aspinall and Greg Fealy (Singapore: Institute of Southeast Asian Studies, 2003), 63–71.

[45] Indonesia continues to be governed by the 1945 Constitution, but four crucial amendments introduced between 1999 and 2002 created a clearer separation of powers between the executive, legislature, and judiciary, together with greater protection for human rights. See Denny Indrayana, *Indonesian Constitutional Reform 1999–2002: An Evaluation of Constitution-Making in Transition* (Jakarta: Kompas Book Publishing, 2008).

several years in office—commanded a ruling coalition with a hefty majority in parliament. Widodo, on the other hand, faces a parliament dominated by an opposing coalition composed of Jakarta's traditional political elite. The parliament's political maneuverings, ironically supported by the president's own political mentor (former president Megawati), highlight the struggle for power in Jakarta. The struggle is centered on domestic issues—notably corruption throughout the entire political system as well as in the police.[46] While the president may have survived thus far, it has not been without cost to his credibility, popularity, and effectiveness. Parliamentary politics suggest that Jakarta's political elite is using the constitutional authority of parliament to regain some of the political power it lost in the recent elections, and that the nature, durability, and stability of Indonesia's political institutions still remain works in progress.

Elected officials and big business. The revival of Jakarta's commercial elite over the last fifteen years since the fall of Suharto is particularly evident in the economy. Severely weakened by the political and economic crisis of 1998–99, Indonesia's large family-owned conglomerates that dominated the economy in years prior to the crisis staged a gradual comeback. Indeed, there is evidence that by 2008, the concentration of family-controlled conglomerates had returned to the levels that existed in 1996.[47] To be sure, some of Suharto's closest associates have yet to restore their earlier fortunes, but others who had previously benefited from their links to Suharto appear to have emerged stronger.

Indonesia's reinvigorated financial and economic elite have also been re-establishing their connections with the political and administrative elite. Such connections help them benefit either from recent policy changes or from favorable implementation of existing laws and regulations.[48] In some instances, conglomerate owners have themselves entered politics formally and assumed important positions of policymaking power and authority. But for the most part, they exercise considerable influence by bankrolling political parties and financing the skyrocketing costs of election campaigns. Recent laws that forbid budgetary financing of campaign costs have helped these owners, forcing political parties to rely on financial support from the conglomerates.

---

[46] Public opinion survey results from Transparency International's Global Corruption Barometer 2013 show that political parties, parliament, and the police are considered the three most corrupt institutions in Indonesia. For more information, see "Corruption by Country: Indonesia," Transparency International, 2013, https://www.transparency.org/country/#IDN_PublicOpinion.

[47] Richard W. Carney and Natasha Hamilton-Hart, "What Do Changes in Corporate Ownership in Indonesia Tell Us?" *Bulletin of Indonesian Economic Studies* 51, no. 1 (2015): 123–45.

[48] Such benefits can accrue in several ways, including the passage of measures that restrict competition by raising trade or nontrade barriers or entry barriers for new investments, the acquisition of bank licenses, preferential access to finance from state-owned banks, and acquisition of concessions or licenses for natural resource extraction.

State subsidies covered a mere 0.4% of election expenses in 2009, compared with 51.7% in 1999.[49] It is no accident that in public opinion surveys political parties are considered among the most corrupt Indonesian institutions.[50]

Civil-military relations. The power of the military has been curtailed significantly since 2000; off-budget activities have gradually been eliminated, which gives the president and parliament greater leverage over the military's strategic and internal management issues. Yet one by-product of the power struggle in Jakarta is that the military appears to be creeping back into civilian affairs. The military, for example, is increasingly called on to undertake operations usually reserved for the police, such as counterterrorism. But it is also being tasked with civilian duties, such as the recent call by the agriculture minister for village-based noncommissioned military officers to act as agricultural extension officers and boost rice production as part of a bid to accelerate the country's progress toward "food sovereignty."[51] There is also some evidence that the military is once again becoming increasingly politicized as senior military appointments are subject to political influence. Such trends, if they hold, will eventually complicate Indonesia's efforts to professionalize the armed forces so that their focus is exclusively on protecting the nation against external threats.

Religious and secular forces. Although predominantly a Muslim nation, the Islamic political parties have consistently failed in their quest to insert Islamic law into the constitution.[52] But since Suharto's departure, Indonesia's religious cleavages are coming into view more and more. Religious intolerance has grown and unmasked Indonesia's professed claim to be a secular nation. Christian, Buddhist, Ahmadi, and Shia communities have been increasingly exposed to discrimination, harassment, intimidation, and violence. Part of the reason has been the spread of Islamic extremist ideologies and the growing prominence of religious hardliners in Indonesia's Islamic parties, but their influence has been facilitated by government laws and regulations that undercut constitutional safeguards for religious freedoms. The "blasphemy law," for example, criminalizes deviant religious behavior, leaving it to nongovernment Muslim clerics to define such behavior.[53] Widodo has vowed

---

[49] Marcus Mietzner, *Money, Power, and Ideology: Political Parties in Post-Authoritarian Indonesia* (Singapore: National University of Singapore Press, 2013).

[50] "Global Corruption Barometer," Transparency International, 2013, http://www.transparency.org/country#IDN_PublicOpinion.

[51] Jonatan A. Lassa and Adhi Priamarizki, "Jokowi's Food Sovereignty Narrative: Military in the Rice Land?" Reliefweb, February 27, 2015, http://reliefweb.int/report/indonesia/jokowi-s-food-sovereignty-narrative-military-rice-land.

[52] Some 90% of Indonesians are Muslim.

[53] The blasphemy law refers to Law Number 1/PNPS/1965 on the Prevention of Religious Abuse and/or Defamation.

to pass legislation to protect religious minorities, but he has so far shown little inclination to expend the political capital necessary to push such laws through a hostile parliament. In the meantime, countering extremist Islamic ideology has become more challenging given the inroads that the Islamic State of Iraq and Syria (ISIS) is making in Indonesian Muslim communities. One senior police officer described ISIS's entry into Indonesia as "fresh oxygen" to extremist groups in the country.[54]

Instruments for Social Control

Since Suharto's departure, many of the traditional levers of power and social control exercised by the central government have been depleted, in some cases dramatically. Democratization and political fragmentation have created national coalition governments with little ability to reach consensus on new strategies. Similarly, decentralization of political and fiscal power has weakened the center's ability to wield these important instruments of social control. Press freedoms and the ubiquity of social media now allow greater scrutiny of the government and give voice to special interests, including religious and civil society groups.[55] Counterbalancing this trend, however, has been the resurrection of large conglomerates, which now exert control over important media outlets that serve the interests of their owners and the political parties and personalities that they support.

To be sure, some of these changes—especially democratization and decentralization—were a reaction to three decades of Suharto's authoritarianism and have made Indonesia a more resilient society.[56] Indonesia is rightfully lauded in the region as a beacon of democracy. Since 2000, the country has witnessed four peaceful and orderly power transitions through the ballot box. But like several other democratic societies, national governments have been formed through coalitions, many with divergent interests. Stability has come at the cost of policy paralysis. Yudhoyono, the

---

[54] Sara Schonhardt, "ISIS in Indonesia," *Wall Street Journal*, Short Answer, March 27, 2015, http://blogs.wsj.com/briefly/2015/03/27/isis-in-indonesia-the-short-answer.

[55] Although Internet penetration is only 30% and smartphone penetration is expected to be 50% in 2015, Indonesia is still considered the social media capital of the world. It has 72 million active Facebook users, and 30 million Twitter users. Jakarta has the largest concentration of Twitter users in the world, putting London and Tokyo in second and third place. See "Jakarta is the World's Largest Twitter Base: Twitter to Open an Office," Indonesia Investments, August 29, 2014, http://www.indonesia-investments.com/news/todays-headlines/jakarta-is-the-world-s-largest-twitter-base-twitter-to-open-an-office/item2364.

[56] As Clifford Geertz, a noted Indonesianist and social scientist, observed, "Archipelagic in geography, eclectic in civilization and heterogeneous in culture, Indonesia flourishes when it accepts and capitalizes on its diversity, and disintegrates when it denies and suppresses it." Clifford Geertz, *A Report to the Ford Foundation Concerning a Program for the Stimulation of the Social Sciences in Indonesia* (Princeton: Institute for Advanced Study, 1971).

only president after Suharto to serve two terms, was widely considered ineffective, especially in his second term, in part because of his inability to win support from members of his own majority coalition. His successor, Widodo, is part of the minority coalition in parliament. Making things even harder, he cannot even be assured of the support of his party's leader, former president Megawati Sukarnoputri. While checks and balances between and among political institutions are hallmarks of a functioning democracy, in Indonesia they have become impediments to collective action in the national interest.

Only fifteen years old, Indonesian democracy has thus still not found the right balance between giving electoral voice to its people and ensuring that the elected government can mobilize collective action and pursue the national interest. In the first few years following Suharto, Indonesia's new leaders drew on the powerful ideas of democracy, human rights, and decentralization. But once these reforms became irreversible, they ceased to be rallying points for unified action. Yudhoyono did not articulate a vision for the country in his two terms, and neither has Widodo in his first months in office. The latter's pragmatism and transactional decision-making lack clear direction. The issues that Widodo has emphasized—a maritime axis, infrastructure development, foreign investment, and a new international economic architecture—appear to be unconnected dots without a common framework, while his drift toward protectionism and his direction of additional resources to state-owned enterprises run the danger of taking the economy down pathways that have been discredited around the world and in Indonesia itself.

In summary, Indonesia's transition to democracy and decentralization have led to greater political resilience. At the same time, national performance—the country's ability to convert national resources into national power—has been weakened by a fractured elite unable to politically reconcile emerging competing interests. The country had pinned its hopes on a political outsider—Widodo—to craft a compelling vision of the national interest, unite the nation, and give credence and credibility to policy reforms and new development initiatives. Unfortunately, this has not happened so far.

Military Capability

The previous section demonstrated how the state's ability to transform the country's rich natural resources and geostrategic location into national power is being hampered by a fractured political elite, weakened executive governance, the depletion of ideational resources and instruments, and fragile governance institutions inherited from the Suharto era. This section examines the impact of these challenging circumstances on the readiness and deployment of military power and its projection internally and abroad.

Inward-Oriented Military

The Indonesian armed forces, the Tentara Nasional Indonesia (TNI), have gone through a transformative change since Suharto's departure. Under Suharto, the military assumed the dual function (*dwifungsi*) of protecting the state against internal and external threats. In the absence of serious external threats, the military focused almost exclusively on internal threats and essentially became an instrument for maintaining political power through domestic surveillance and counterinsurgency (mainly in East Timor, Aceh, and Papua). Moreover, the military enjoyed a large presence in government institutions, including the bureaucracy and local governments as well as parliament, which from 1987 to 1997 reserved a fifth of the seats for the military.[57] Its extensive network of command posts down to the village level ensured nationwide surveillance against potential internal threats. The TNI also held substantial business interests with no governmental oversight, thus giving military leaders substantial off-budget revenues while granting them considerable independence in determining strategy and running the internal affairs of the armed forces.[58]

After Suharto's departure, the newly democratizing Indonesia worked quickly to reduce the independence of the TNI and its role in domestic politics. The most important shifts were to eliminate reservation of unelected seats in parliament and to increasingly finance military expenditures through the budget.[59] In addition, the State Defense Act of 2002 and the Armed Forces Act of 2004 transferred authority for strategic and logistical management to the Ministry of Defense.

Throughout this period, the share of military expenditures financed through the budget never exceeded 1% of GDP, the lowest percentage among all Asian countries (see **Figure 3**). Indonesia's comparatively low defense

---

[57] Suharto reduced the share of unelected parliamentary seats reserved for the military to 15% in 1997, but it was not until 2004, six years after his departure, that the practice of reserving seats for the military was done away with altogether. See Fitri Bintang Timur, "Voting Rights for Indonesian Armed Forces (TNI) Personnel: Yes, No or with Reservation?" Friedrich Ebert Stiftung, Report, http://www.academia.edu/906833/Voting_Rights_for_Indonesian_Armed_Forces_TNI_Personnel_Yes_No_or_with_Reservation.

[58] Even by 2006, well after substantial measures had been taken to reduce the TNI's off-budget revenues, its illegal activities earned an estimated $12–$24 million in gross earnings and "informal activities" earned $7–$21 million. See Lex Rieffel and Jaleswari Pramodhawardani, *Out of Business and on Budget: The Challenge of Military Financing in Indonesia* (Washington, D.C.: Brookings Institution, 2007).

[59] Eliminating the reservation of seats in parliament prevented the TNI from exercising an effective veto over key political decisions. Rieffel and Pramodhawardani discuss the complexity of ending the military's access to off-budget revenues and bringing it fully on budget. In addition to these challenges, the persistence of the territorial command structure allows the armed forces to continue raising off-budget resources from their territorial network. Rieffel and Pramodhawardani, *Out of Business and on Budget*, 60. See also Marcus Mietzner, *The Politics of Military Reform in Post-Suharto Indonesia: Elite Conflict, Nationalism, and Institutional Resistance* (Washington, D.C.: East-West Center Washington, 2006).

FIGURE 3   2014 military budgets as a share of GDP

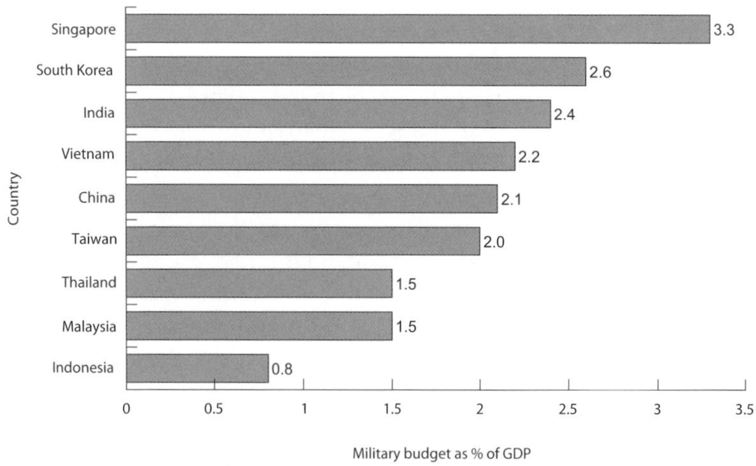

SOURCE: Stockholm International Peace Research Institute, Military Expenditure Database, 2015.

spending reflected an absence of external threats, the low-grade nature of counterinsurgency operations in secessionist provinces, and the inadequate supplies and poor quality of military equipment. Today, military and paramilitary forces exceed 500,000, but (as will be discussed below) weaponry is low-grade and falls well short of meeting Indonesia's evolving threat perception.

With the independence of East Timor and the resolution of the Aceh conflict, counterinsurgency operations declined significantly, and the TNI's focus shifted to dealing with a growing internal terrorist threat. The most recent manifestation of this new focus is operations against ISIS recruiters and recruits. Although these operations have been relatively successful, the armed forces' role in counterterrorism is being increasingly marginalized by nonmilitary law enforcement agencies.

Reorientation and Revitalization

Since 2007, the Indonesian armed forces have engaged in a fundamental reorientation and revitalization. The key driver has been shifts in the TNI's risk and threat perception. Its earlier priorities were the low-grade conflict in Papua and cross-border friction with Papua New Guinea, as well as nontraditional security challenges such as piracy, illegal fishing, and human and drug trafficking. Moreover, the TNI has always prioritized strengthening its disaster-relief capabilities—an objective re-emphasized recently by the defense minister.[60] Unfortunately, however, given the military's (and particularly the army's) historical preoccupation with domestic political stability, limited funding, and low levels of professionalism, these revitalization efforts start from "a very low base."[61] The broad strategic shift is for the military to change its focus from internal order to external defense and deterrence capabilities—most notably the security of the country's EEZs, maritime chokepoints, and land borders. Domestic law and order and counterterrorist activities are expected to increasingly become a police priority.[62]

Indeed, the TNI is beginning to pay more attention to the external security environment. Indonesia's capacity to fully monitor and control its territorial waters, let alone its airspace, is very limited. China's more aggressive stance in the South China Sea since 2007 has prompted the defense establishment to rethink Indonesia's defense strategy and the role of the armed forces more generally. These concerns were exacerbated when China's nine-dashed line began appearing on Chinese passports showing an overlap with Indonesia's EEZ near the Natuna Islands (see Figure 2). In June 2010, these fears were heightened further after Chinese and Indonesian patrol craft were involved in an incident near the islands.

Indonesia sees recent developments in the South China Sea as a dangerous cocktail of distrust between key stakeholders, unresolved territorial claims, and irresistible political and economic transformation.[63] It has sought a "dynamic equilibrium" in the Asia-Pacific "through the promotion of a sense of common responsibility in the endeavor to maintain the region's peace and stability."[64] At other times, Jakarta has expressed concern with the military dimensions of the U.S. rebalancing strategy toward Asia and its implications for regional stability. The government has sought to avoid aggravating tensions in the South China Sea by maintaining an equal distance between Beijing and Washington and has encouraged the United States to adjust its rebalancing strategy by using less confrontational measures.

This emerging security environment in the Asia-Pacific of growing competition and shifts in the balance of power also led to the 2010 Strategic Defense Plan, the most notable goal of which is the creation of a "minimum

---

[60] "Disaster Mitigation among TNI's Top Priorities," Antara News, December 26, 2014, http://www.antaranews.com/en/news/97046/disaster-mitigation-among-tnis-top-priorities.

[61] Benjamin Schreer, *Moving Beyond Ambitions? Indonesia's Military Modernisation* (Barton: Australian Strategic Policy Institute, 2013), 12, https://www.aspi.org.au/publications/moving-beyond-ambitions-indonesias-military-modernisation/Strategy_Moving_beyond_ambitions.pdf.

[62] Ibid., 22.

[63] Natalegawa, "An Indonesian Perspective."

[64] Ibid.

essential force" by 2024 to defend Indonesia from external threats. This force would comprise a 274-ship green water navy, 12 new diesel-electric submarines, an air force consisting of 10 fighter squadrons, upgrades in air combat capability, a more mobile land force, and the development of a capable industrial base.[65] Although then president Yudhoyono pledged to raise defense spending to 1.5% of GDP by 2014 to reach these targets, the share has hardly budged above the historical 0.8% (see Figure 3). Moreover, the bulk of this expenditure is on personnel, not equipment. Even if procurement of military equipment were to rise 40% by 2018, then total annual expenditures on military hardware would still be a paltry $2.4 billion (roughly what the United States spends on defense in one day).[66]

The intention is to provide the TNI with reliable essential capabilities to deal with a wide array of external security challenges with a focus on national sovereignty and territorial integrity, including a worst-case conventional warfare scenario.[67] In addition, the Ministry of Defense has called for the creation of three integrated regional defense commands—west, central, and east—with an emphasis on force integration across the army, navy, and air force.[68] The emphasis will be on revising force structures while updating and replacing aging defense platforms.[69] Finally, as a result of past experience with arms embargos,[70] the plan is to further diversify the pool of arms suppliers by partnering with the United States, the European Union, Russia, China, and South Korea, among others. However, Jakarta has neither explained how it expects to cope with the increased cost that such a strategy implies (especially in the absence of substantially higher defense expenditures) nor examined the operational consequences. By some estimates, Indonesia's armed forces already operate 173 different weapons platforms from seventeen different countries, making maintenance and interoperability a formidable challenge.[71]

---

[65] Schreer, *Moving Beyond Ambitions?* 18.

[66] The U.S. defense budget for fiscal year 2014 amounted to $815.5 billion, which comes to $2.2 billion a day. See "U.S. Defense Spending," http://www.usgovernmentspending.com/us_defense_spending_30.html.

[67] Iis Gindarsah, "Indonesia's Security Review and Defense Development in 2012," in *Security Outlook of the Asia Pacific Countries and Its Implications for the Defense Sector*, NIDS Joint Research Series 9 (Tokyo: National Institute for Defense Studies, 2013), 31, http://www.nids.go.jp/english/publication/joint_research/series9/pdf/02.pdf.

[68] Ibid., 32.

[69] Leonard C. Sebastian and Iis Gindarsah, "Taking Stock of Military Reform in Indonesia," in *The Politics of Military Reform: Experiences from Indonesia and Nigeria*, ed. Jürgen Rüland, Maria-Gabriela Manea, and Hans Born (Berlin: Springer-Verlag, 2013), 37.

[70] Marko Rankovic, "The Resurgence of Indonesia's Defense Industry," *Worldfolio*, December 1, 2014, http://www.theworldfolio.com/news/purnomo-yusgiantoro-minister-of-defense-indonesia/3337.

[71] Prashanth Parameswaran, "Between Aspiration and Reality: Indonesian Foreign Policy after the 2014 Elections," *Washington Quarterly* 37, no. 3 (2014): 156, https://twq.elliott.gwu.edu/sites/twq.elliott.gwu.edu/files/downloads/Parameswaran_Fall2014.pdf.

It thus appears highly unlikely that the TNI will meet its minimum essential force goals by 2024. Rather, its current underfunded and piecemeal approach seems likely to achieve modernization in certain areas (such as fast-attack naval capabilities, amphibious units, and missiles) while remaining deficient in others (including aerial transport, radar technology, and mine warfare). The army, for example, has the explicit goal of operating in various terrains and rapidly deploying across the archipelago.[72] To achieve this, it has begun to decrease unit size for greater mobility and reorient its command structure to focus on border protection.[73] Its fighting capacity is being modernized through the acquisition of 103 Leopard 2A6 battle tanks, 50 Marder 1A3 infantry fighting vehicles, and 10 support vehicles from Germany,[74] as well as 8 U.S. Apache helicopters.[75]

Unfortunately, the TNI's unwieldy bureaucratic practices remain a significant impediment to arms procurement and force restructuring. Poor training and inadequate resources make effective deployment a challenge, and the army's command structure is still built for provincial politics rather than external defense.[76] Finally, military experts have questioned the utility of some armament purchases, arguing that they run the risk of becoming little more than expensive symbols. Battle tanks, for instance, are of little utility across much of Indonesia's terrain, and given their modest range, Apache helicopters would likely only be of use in a relatively limited number of scenarios.[77]

The navy, traditionally ignored, faces an even bigger challenge. Its planned 274-ship green water navy is to consist of 110 surface combatants, 66 patrol vessels, 98 support ships, and 12 diesel-electric submarines.[78] These ships are to be divided into three fleets, each equipped with integrated weapon systems, with a focus on securing Indonesia's sea lanes and chokepoints—the Malacca, Sunda, Lombok, Ombai, and Wetar Straits.[79] On paper, the navy appears formidable: its fleet of 213 ships comprises 11 major surface

---

[72] Law No. 17/2007 on Long-Term National Development Plan, 2005–2025, IV.1.4, cited in Gindarsah, "Indonesia's Security Review," 32.

[73] Gindarsah, "Indonesia's Security Review," 32.

[74] Schreer, *Moving Beyond Ambitions?* 24.

[75] Ristian Atriandi Supriyanto, "Why Does Indonesia Need Apache Gunships?" Australian Strategic Policy Institute, Strategist, September 3, 2013, http://www.aspistrategist.org.au/why-does-indonesia-need-apache-gunships.

[76] For example, the army has thirteen territorial commands, primarily to respond to local threats, gather local intelligence, and ensure political stability. See Schreer, *Moving Beyond Ambitions?* 8.

[77] Schreer, *Moving Beyond Ambitions?* 25; and Supriyanto, "Why Does Indonesia Need Apache Gunships?"

[78] Ristian Atriandi Supriyanto, "Indonesia's Naval Modernization: A Sea Change?" S. Rajaratnam School of International Studies (RSIS), RSIS Commentaries, no. 20, January 27, 2012, http://www.rsis.edu.sg/wp-content/uploads/2014/07/CO12020.pdf.

[79] Kresno Buntoro, "Protecting the Vast Waters of Indonesia," *Jakarta Post*, September 18, 2014, http://www.thejakartapost.com/news/2014/09/18/protecting-vast-waters-indonesia.html.

combatants, 2 submarines, 72 patrol and coastal combatants, 11 mine warfare ships, 5 major amphibious vessels, 54 landing crafts, 26 landing ships, and 32 logistics and support vessels.[80] But fewer than half the ships are seaworthy and the rest are old.[81] For example, the 2 currently operational submarines are almost 35 years old and reaching the end of their lifespans. The largest ships are similarly outmoded and include 6 Dutch frigates constructed in the 1960s. Indeed, one estimate is that the navy has only 25 operational ships to patrol Indonesia's approximately 34,000-mile coastline. Some strategists predict a shift to smaller craft such that the 2025 major surface fleet will consist of only 2–5 light frigates/destroyers and 5–6 corvettes; the rest will be patrol vessels and guided-missile boats likely equipped with Chinese C-705 missile technology.[82] Even if these acquisitions are successful, Indonesia's naval defense will still suffer from major gaps—including in long-range surveillance, antisubmarine warfare, mining/counter-mining, naval aviation, and amphibious capabilities—making it difficult for the navy to exercise full control over its territorial waters.[83]

The predicament of the air force is similar to that of the navy. The Defense Strategy Plan calls for 10 fighter squadrons by 2024, and the air force is looking to Russian Sukhoi fighter jets to help reach that mark.[84] The air force has updated its training fleet with South Korean T-50i Golden Eagle jets and in 2014 received the first of 24 modified U.S.-made F-16 fighters.[85] Here, too, the use of multiple platforms will present significant technical challenges for cost management and operational coordination across different systems. Moreover, investment in fighter aircraft without effective airborne early-warning and control systems and airborne refueling capabilities puts these acquisitions at risk of being merely symbols.[86] Another glaring deficit is tactical airlift capacities to facilitate defense-related transportation between islands. The recent crash of a Hercules C-130 in Medan, the country's third-largest city, only highlights the challenges posed by Indonesia's aging fleet of sixteen C-130s, which will need replacement soon, and the plan to fill the gap with locally produced SN-295 medium-transport aircraft appears unrealistic.[87]

---

[80] International Institute for Strategic Studies, *The Military Balance 2014* (London: Routledge, 2014), 248.

[81] Schreer, *Moving Beyond Ambitions?* 18.

[82] Ibid., 20.

[83] Ibid., 20–21.

[84] "Indonesia's Air Force Adds More Flankers," *Defense Industry Daily*, October 7, 2014, http://www.defenseindustrydaily.com/indonesias-air-force-adds-more-flankers-03691.

[85] Kenneth Conboy and James Hardy, "Indonesia Gets First Three F-16s from U.S.," *IHS Jane's*, July 29, 2014.

[86] Schreer, *Moving Beyond Ambitions?* 22.

[87] Ibid., 23.

Defense Industry

In 2009, President Yudhoyono set the ambitious goal of creating a domestic defense industry that would meet the country's entire defense needs by 2024 and eliminate defense imports. In 2006, only 5% of Indonesia's weapons systems were provided indigenously.[88] To increase that share, the 2012 Law on Defense Industry permits foreign investment in defense production for the first time but requires an Indonesian controlling stake of at least 51%, while also requiring the armed forces to purchase equipment domestically whenever possible.[89] A key element of the strategy is to ensure that all imports and foreign investment in defense production come with technology transfer and capacity building.

Unfortunately, Indonesia's three large defense companies—all fully owned by the government—are in a relatively parlous state, both financially and technically.[90] All were recapitalized to some degree after the 1997–98 financial crisis, although their solvency and financial viability remain precarious. Prior to the crisis, PT Dirgantara (PTDI), the Indonesian aerospace company, had focused on financially disastrous prestige projects, such as the CN-235, but then shifted focus to manufacturing components for large foreign aircraft, such as the Airbus A380 and C295 military transporter, in addition to assembling military aircraft.[91]

More recently, PTDI has entered into partnerships with foreign defense companies, including a joint project with South Korea to develop the KF-X/IF-X, a "generation 4.5" fighter jet designed to match the F-16 in capacity. This leap in PTDI's ambition level will require significant investment, not only in R&D but also in the company's outdated manufacturing capacity.[92] PTDI is also partnering with China, which has agreed to supply C-705 and C-802 subsonic anti-ship missiles with a technology transfer agreement that will enable PTDI to manufacture the missiles indigenously following observation of production in China.[93]

Similarly, PT PAL, the defense-related shipbuilding firm, is partnering with foreign suppliers that agree to transfer technology. For example, the first two of three diesel-powered attack submarines bought from Daewoo

---

[88] Sebastian and Gandarsah, "Taking Stock of Military Reform in Indonesia," 45.

[89] Joe Cochrane, "Indonesian Arms Industry Seeks to Drum Up Business," *New York Times*, February 13, 2014, http://www.nytimes.com/2014/02/14/business/international/indonesian-arms-industry-seeks-to-drum-up-business.html.

[90] The three large defense companies are PTDI (aerospace), PT PAL (shipbuilding), and PT Pindad (armaments).

[91] The CN-235 was the pet project of Vice President B.J. Habibie but was axed during the financial crisis.

[92] Rankovic, "The Resurgence of Indonesia's Defense Industry."

[93] Gindarsah, "Indonesia's Security Review."

Shipbuilding and Marine Engineering Company in 2011 will be constructed by the South Korean company, with PT PAL engineers as observers, but the third is to be constructed in Indonesia.[94] The same model has been followed in the acquisition of Dutch Sigma-class corvettes and South Korean landing platform docks. These agreements notwithstanding, it will be hard for PT PAL to fulfill its prescribed role as the lead contributor to Indonesia's naval fleet. Over 70% of the components PT PAL uses to construct ships, for instance, are still produced overseas,[95] and critics argue that progress in developing indigenous technological capacity has been slow and inconsistent.[96] The plan to build a 274-ship navy by 2024, therefore, may be just too ambitious—something that should worry strategists for the world's largest archipelagic nation.

Indonesia's state-run armaments company, PT Pindad, is the only one of the country's three defense firms that has been profitable over the last decade, with profits in 2016 projected to reach just under $8 million, secured with the help of a $54 million injection of cash.[97] PT Pindad has been a reliable supplier of small arms and ammunition and is now working toward manufacturing larger armored vehicles. Up until now the Indonesian Ministry of Defense has been the principal consumer, but PT Pindad is looking to export its output.[98] It has sought to boost indigenous capacity, such as by developing a new medium tank in partnership with the Turkish contractor FNSS.[99] Like PTDI and PT PAL, however, PT Pindad has significant weaknesses. Perhaps most prominent is its weak capacity to produce larger armaments such as artillery, for which Indonesia still depends on foreign sources.[100]

---

[94] The $1.07 billion contract is subject to a further $250 million injection of funds into PT PAL by the Indonesian government that has yet to take place.

[95] Amir Tejo, "Imported Components Dominate Shipbuilding Industry," *Tempo* (Indonesia), May 14, 2014, http://en.tempo.co/read/news/2014/05/14/056577719/Imported-Components-Dominate-Shipbuilding-Industry.

[96] Vibhanshu Shekhar and Joseph Chinyong Liow, "Indonesia as a Maritime Power: Jokowi's Vision, Strategies, and Obstacles Ahead," Brookings Institution, November 2014, http://www.brookings.edu/research/articles/2014/11/indonesia-maritime-liow-shekhar#_ftn10.

[97] "Self-Defense Is the Best Defense: New Pindad Chief," American Chamber of Commerce in Indonesia, February 13, 2015, http://www.amcham.or.id/nf/features/4886-self-defense-is-the-best-defense-new-pindad-chief.

[98] "A Strong International Presence," *Defence Review Asia*, January 28, 2011, http://www.defencereviewasia.com/articles/73/A-strong-international-presence; and Ina Parlina, "Jokowi Wants RI Military to Be Strongest in Region," *Jakarta Post*, December 31, 2014, http://www.thejakartapost.com/news/2014/12/31/jokowi-wants-ri-military-be-strongest-region.html.

[99] While some observers have questioned the utility of tanks in Indonesia, others have noted the location of urban settings near porous borders where a tank presence may prove useful. See Tiarma Siboro, "Jakarta Gears Up for Indonesian Urban Defense Strategy," *Defense News*, December 10, 2013, http://archive.defensenews.com/article/20131210/DEFREG03/312100020/Jakarta-Gears-Up-Indonesian-Urban-Defense-Strategy.

[100] Sebastian and Gindarsah, "Taking Stock of Military Reform," 45.

The multiple constraints imposed on Indonesia's defense industries and defense equipment acquisition more generally—indigenous ownership, inadequate finance, skills gaps, diseconomies of scale, a domestic procurement bias, and stringent local technology offsets—have done little to enhance the TNI's defense preparedness and have widened the gap between rhetoric and actual capabilities. Thus, despite increased investment, Indonesia still cannot reliably respond to potential challenges to its territorial sovereignty from an external source. Defense policy remains a relatively low priority, the military budget continues to be small by international standards, and the procurement process across the TNI's services still lacks a coherent vision. Although recognition of emerging challenges in Indonesia's regional environment has compelled the government and the military to revisit the country's defensive capacities, military preparedness falls far short of the level expected for a country with its regional and global stature.

Regional and U.S. Implications

This chapter has argued that despite four decades of economic growth and a successful transition to democracy and decentralization, Indonesia is a reluctant giant unwilling—and perhaps unable—to project its power abroad in pursuit of its strategic interests. Since independence, the focus of successive political leaders has been on managing the country's deep internal fault lines and ensuring they do not become threats to its stability and development progress. Over the last few years, however, there has been a discernible shift in strategic thinking, driven in part by tectonic shifts in the balance of power in Asia and the emergence of new external challenges to Indonesia's security and territorial integrity. The country's ability to respond to these challenges is being hampered by a contest for power between competing political interests, which has fractured the political elite and weakened Indonesia's ability to translate its national resource base into national power and then project that power abroad to protect its interests.

Indonesia's Southeast Asian neighbors would like to see the country as an anchor for stability in the region and welcome a more prosperous and stronger Indonesia. They draw comfort from the fact that despite being the largest and most important member of ASEAN, Indonesia is a long-standing supporter of ASEAN's principles of consensus-based decisions and noninterference in others' affairs. Some argue, however, that given its recent strategic shift, Indonesia is already finding ASEAN too limiting and is seeking common cause with other partners, such as Japan and India, which would enable it to play a more active role in Asia.[101] It is quite possible that while Indonesia will continue to support ASEAN's role as a multilateral forum, it may nevertheless choose to play a more active role in the broader regional context outside ASEAN's framework.[102]

Farther afield, U.S.-Indonesia relations were strengthened in the initial years of the post-Suharto era and grew closer still under President Yudhoyono. President Obama, who spent a good deal of his childhood in Indonesia, has drawn attention to the two countries' shared values and interests, including democracy, secularism, and antiterrorism. At the same time, both nations are also driven by common strategic concerns, especially the rise of China, freedom of navigation between the Pacific and Indian Oceans, and the intermediary role Indonesia can play between the West and the Islamic world.

Indonesia's strategic autonomy—a cornerstone of its foreign policy—allows Jakarta to remain equidistant between Beijing and Washington and hedge its bets between the two. Indonesia has benefited enormously from trade and financial integration with China—benefits that could be jeopardized if relations with China were to sour. Yet Indonesia also recognizes that its own virtually nonexistent external security capabilities mean that the presence of the United States in Asia is indispensable as insurance against China's growing assertiveness in the region.

The United States, then, should cultivate Indonesia as a valuable regional partner but cannot expect it to become an ally. Washington will need to understand and respect the pressures that shape Indonesia's ambivalence about the U.S. rebalance toward Asia and recognize that differences in their foreign policy stances on some issues may occasionally arise. Such forbearance by the United States could pay rich dividends. There is a very large regional and global agenda on which Indonesia and the United States see eye to eye and that could form the basis of a strong cooperative partnership. The ongoing U.S.-Indonesia Comprehensive Partnership is already a flagship for both countries. It needs to be used as a foundation to build stronger defense and economic relations and broader cooperation on a range of concerns that would cement the partnership between the two countries, establish the United States as Indonesia's all-weather friend, and provide an effective counterweight to China's growing influence in the region.

---

[101] Vinhanshu Shekhar, "Indonesia's Asian Fulcrum Idea," *Diplomat*, July 24, 2015, http://thediplomat.com/2015/07/indonesias-asian-fulcrum-idea.

[102] Amitav Acharya, *Indonesia Matters: Asia's Emerging Democratic Power* (Singapore: World Scientific, 2014), 54–57.

EXECUTIVE SUMMARY

This chapter assesses U.S. national resources, U.S. competence in converting those resources into national power, and the adequacy of current and future defense budgets and force structures.

MAIN ARGUMENT

The U.S. possesses a large, balanced, dynamic, and adaptive economy. Other major strengths include a rich supply of natural resources, favorable demographic profile, and extensive network of alliances and partnerships. Although the U.S. has the potential to continue world leadership, national performance in recent years has declined. Economic weaknesses include too few skilled workers, obsolete infrastructure, and lack of energy security. In addition, the government has recently been unable to balance budgets, and legislation on immigration reform, energy security, and tax reform has failed. In the area of national security, the U.S. is hampered by an obsolete government structure and has not forged a bipartisan national security strategy supported by the public since the end of the Cold War. Some individual regional strategies—for example, in East Asia and Africa—have been consistent and largely successful, but U.S. policy in other areas—most notably in the Middle East—has fallen short. U.S. military power is still the strongest in the world. However, to meet likely future missions under constrained budgets, its current structure and equipment will have to be adjusted.

POLICY IMPLICATIONS

- U.S. strengths are structural and enduring, while weaknesses can be overcome with the restoration of a political consensus to solve national problems.

- The greatest national security imperatives are updating the national security structure and the development of a bipartisan, publicly supported strategy for the complex future international environment.

- Within that strategy, the most pressing tasks are forging an enduring strategy for the Middle East and East Asia and making hard choices in the defense budget and force structure.

The United States: A Strong Foundation but Weak Blueprint for National Security

Dennis C. Blair

For the decade roughly corresponding to the 1990s, the United States' leading position in the world in political, economic, and military power was historically unprecedented. No observer with any knowledge of history thought such a dominant position would last, and it has not. Success breeds its own counterforces. Formerly powerful and developing competitors like Russia and China, respectively, looked for ways to check U.S. influence, while powerful neutral countries like India and even friends in Europe mistrusted a single dominant power and had no interest in helping sustain it. The sense of urgency and purpose that drove the United States' rise, fueled by the existential challenge first of fascism and later Communism, diminished with victory in the Cold War.

The first decade and a half of the new century saw relative U.S. power and influence slip. The sequence of Middle East involvement beginning with the first Iraq war and expanding with the September 11 attacks, the war in Afghanistan, and the second war in Iraq absorbed large resources without producing decisive results. Meanwhile, China's historically unprecedented economic development, accompanied by a rapid military buildup, contested the U.S. position in Asia. The 2007–8 financial crisis in the United States that spread to much of the world not only stalled GDP growth but also damaged the U.S. reputation for economic prowess. The question this chapter addresses

Dennis C. Blair is the Chairman of the Board and CEO of Sasakawa Peace Foundation USA. He can be reached at <dblair@spfusa.org>.

is whether the United States can or will reverse this trend and maintain its overall leading world position.

The short answer is that the United States can—it has the resources and the competence to do so. However, it is not clear that Washington can muster the national leadership and popular support for a series of difficult programs to overcome current shortcomings. Some improvements will likely happen; others are unlikely without a dramatic crisis.

The structure of the chapter is as follows: First, it assesses U.S. national resources. Economic performance is the most important component of national strength and is addressed at greatest length, but the U.S. network of alliances and partnerships and the habit of world leadership are also important. While these three components are significant U.S. strengths, the assessment discusses the negative trends undermining each and the prospects for reversing them. The second section assesses U.S. competence, or the skill with which American leaders are able to formulate, generate support for, and execute policies and programs for long-term improvements in national strength. With respect to national security, competence is the capacity to pursue consistent and successful policies that support or improve U.S. interests, both in the major regions of the world and on global issues. Although this section identifies some recent successes, readers will find it critical of much of recent U.S. performance. The final section of the chapter addresses the military power of the United States. It measures the currently planned armed forces against the likely missions they will face. The assessment finds that adjustments in the force structure and potentially to the traditional service shares of the defense budget will be required if the United States is to have an armed forces that can handle its most likely future missions.

National Resources

Economic Strength

Economic size and strength generate international influence directly through financial interactions and trade. In addition, the economy provides the tax resources that fund military forces and foreign financial assistance, the primary direct tools for influencing other countries.

The United States has the world's largest economy, measured in exchange rate terms.[1] The U.S. economy is both advanced and balanced, not being dependent on a single sector. The United States possesses a large

---

[1] "The 20 Countries with the Largest Gross Domestic Product (GDP) in 2015 (in Billion U.S. Dollars)," Statista, 2015, http://www.statista.com/statistics/268173/countries-with-the-largest-gross-domestic-product-gdp.

internal market and domestic supplies of raw materials and is roughly half as dependent on foreign trade as the Organisation for Economic Co-operation and Development (OECD) average.[2] Among developed countries, the United States has achieved higher growth rates over the last fourteen years than the Japanese or eurozone economies as well as the OECD average for the last four years.[3] With a slow but steady recovery from the 2007–8 recession, the U.S. economy has stronger growth prospects than other advanced economies.

The dollar is projected to continue to be the world's reserve currency for at least the next several decades. This gives the United States a major line of credit, financed by the savings of other countries. In addition, because almost all international energy transactions and about half of all global trade are denominated in dollars, the United States can use its dollar clearing function to block transactions and put pressure on other countries, as in the case of sanctions on Iran.[4]

The driving and disruptive force for economic development for at least the next several decades will be the digital revolution, and the United States is well positioned to continue to take advantage of it. The U.S. economic system has unique advantages in fostering innovation.[5] U.S. investment in R&D is the largest in the world.[6] In rankings of the world's top colleges and universities, U.S. institutions dominate.[7] American researchers, working primarily at universities, also lead in international prizes in technical subjects.[8] Major U.S. companies dominate or have strong international positions in both the hardware and software domains of the digital industry. In addition, the United States has a unique culture of digital entrepreneurship that provides a steady stream of new ideas and funding for small companies to go to market. As the information technology (IT)

---

[2] "Trade Openness: Average of Total Exports and Imports as a Percentage of GDP, 2000, 2008 and 2009," Organisation for Economic Co-operation and Development (OECD), OECD iLibrary, http://www.oecd-ilibrary.org/sites/sti_scoreboard-2011-en/06/06/index.html?itemId=/content/chapter/sti_scoreboard-2011-60-en.

[3] OECD, *OECD Economic Outlook 2015*, no. 1 (Paris: OECD Publishing, 2015), 14.

[4] Samuel Rines, "King of the World: Why the Almighty U.S. Dollar Dominates," *National Interest*, September 29, 2014, http://nationalinterest.org/blog/the-buzz/king-the-world-why-the-almighty-us-dollar-dominates-11370.

[5] Robert D. Atkinson, "Understanding the U.S. National Innovation System," *Information Technology and Innovation Foundation*, June 2014, http://www2.itif.org/2014-understanding-us-innovation-system.pdf.

[6] "2014 Global R&D Funding Forecast," *R&D Magazine*, December 2013, http://www.battelle.org/docs/tpp/2014_global_rd_funding_forecast.pdf.

[7] "World University Rankings 2014–2015," *Times Higher Education*, 2015, https://www.timeshighereducation.co.uk/world-university-rankings/2014-15/world-ranking.

[8] Henry Williams, "Game of Nobels: The Top 10," *Wall Street Journal*, October 13, 2014, http://graphics.wsj.com/which-country-has-the-most-nobel-prizes.

component of many products increases, large IT companies or even wealthy individuals are mounting challenges to established industries through the development of satellites, rockets, and even automobiles. Whether or not these challenges succeed, they are forcing innovation and efficiency within established industries and creating companies that will ultimately contribute to economic growth.

Ten years ago, the United States was projected to be a major importer of both petroleum and natural gas. Because of the shale revolution, the United States is now projected to be a significant liquefied natural gas exporter and a major producer of oil. Whereas imported hydrocarbons historically have amounted to roughly half of the country's trade deficit, in the future oil and gas exports will make a positive contribution to the trade balance. In addition, the availability of inexpensive and reliable sources of electricity and natural gas give an advantage to locating manufacturing activities in the United States.[9]

The United States has a relatively healthy demographic profile for the next several decades. By contrast, birthrates in East Asia and Europe are below replacement levels. China's one-child policy has already resulted in a decreasing workforce and increasing elderly population, and by 2050 the proportion of the Chinese population over the age of 65 will surpass that of the United States.[10]

Economic Challenges

Despite the United States' overall economic strength, three major negative factors have the potential to hinder growth: shortages of skilled workers for the advanced economy, obsolescence of the national infrastructure, and lack of energy security. Although these factors are widely recognized, the only one for which serious remedial measures are underway is the shortage of skilled workers.

Employers in both the manufacturing and service industries report thousands of skilled job openings that they are unable to fill with qualified

---

[9] Executive Office of the President of the United States, *Economic Report of the President Together with the Annual Report of the Council of Economic Advisers* (Washington, D.C., February 2015), 253–62. Beyond jobs created by the oil and gas sector itself, the Congressional Budget Office (CBO) estimates higher national consumption of natural gas due to the development of shale resources that will generate an additional 0.1% higher GDP in 2020. See CBO, *The Economic and Budgetary Effects of Producing Oil and Natural Gas from Shale* (Washington, D.C., December 2014), 16, https://www.cbo.gov/sites/default/files/113th-congress-2013-2014/reports/49815-Effects_of_Shale_Production.pdf.

[10] Pew Research Center, "Attitudes about Aging: A Global Perspective," January 30, 2014, http://www.pewglobal.org/2014/01/30/attitudes-about-aging-a-global-perspective.

workers. The demand for educated workers will only increase in the future.[11] There are two solutions to this problem: (1) training and education and (2) immigration. The imperative to improve training and education, especially in technical fields, is widely recognized in government, private business, and the philanthropic sector. Although so far all the public and private efforts to improve education have failed to produce dramatic improvements, this is one of the few public issues on which there is currently bipartisan political consensus. These factors make it likely that the United States will discover and implement the right combination of improvements to provide the highly skilled workers needed for its advanced economy to grow.

The second solution to help meet the demand for higher skill levels is immigration. The United States has traditionally benefitted from relatively open immigration, especially for highly skilled workers. Foreign participation in the U.S. digital revolution is no exception. Roughly half of the IT startups in Silicon Valley have foreign-born founders.[12] Likewise, roughly half of those studying for technical degrees in U.S. universities are international students.[13] Currently many of them want to remain in the United States to work but are unable to obtain visas.[14] Increasing the number of green cards for foreign-born graduates of technical courses in the United States would contribute to both GDP growth and job creation.

The last two administrations have attempted unsuccessfully to reform U.S. immigration law. However, the digital revolution will continue, increasing the demand from businesses for higher-skilled workers. It is probable that there will be immigration legislation in the next few years increasing the supply of skilled and entrepreneurial workers.

The second major obstacle to continuing U.S. economic growth is increasingly obsolete economic infrastructure. Increases in U.S. productivity have been driven in recent years by quickly moving people, goods, and data

---

[11] McKinsey research in 2009 estimated that the gap in academic achievement between U.S. students and their counterparts in other countries cost the U.S. economy between $1.3 and $2.3 trillion in 2008. See Byron G. Auguste, Bryan Hancock, and Martha Laboissière, "The Economic Cost of the U.S. Education Gap," McKinsey & Company, June 2009, http://www.mckinsey.com/insights/social_sector/the_economic_cost_of_the_us_education_gap.

[12] "Immigrant Entrepreneurship Has Stalled for the First Time in Decades, Kauffman Foundation Study Shows," Ewing Marion Kauffman Foundation, Press Release, October 2, 2012, http://www.kauffman.org/newsroom/2012/11/immigrant-entrepreneurship-has-stalled-for-the-first-time-in-decades-kauffman-foundation-study-shows.

[13] Stuart Anderson, "The Importance of International Students to America," National Foundation for American Policy, NFAP Policy Brief, July 2013, http://www.nfap.com/pdf/New%20NFAP%20Policy%20Brief%20The%20Importance%20of%20International%20Students%20to%20America,%20July%202013.pdf.

[14] See Neil G. Ruiz, "The Geography of Foreign Students in U.S. Higher Education: Origins and Destinations," Brookings Institution, August 29, 2014, http://www.brookings.edu/research/interactives/2014/geography-of-foreign-students.

around the country—and around the world. U.S. companies have thinned their supply chains, outsourced functions that can be done more efficiently by specialists, and provided their workers with data and analytical tools to operate more efficiently. Efforts to continue and even maintain these trends are hampered by increasingly obsolete seaports, highways, railroads, and air traffic control systems, as well as by inadequate broadband speeds and unsecured digital networks.[15] Failing infrastructure could cost U.S. businesses $958 billion in sales by 2020 and $2.5 trillion by 2040.[16]

Congress has not passed a transportation bill with an authority longer than two years since 2005, and the Department of Transportation's 2013 estimate of the backlog of shovel-ready and economically efficient investments in roads and bridges stands at $649 billion.[17] The Highway Trust Fund, which manages most federal spending on highway and transit infrastructure, has a $13 billion annual deficit that grows, while the fund's primary revenue source (the gas tax) has been eroded by fuel efficiency gains and inflation. Modernizing major U.S. ports to handle the ever-larger container ships coming into the world's transportation fleet is estimated to cost $51 billion through 2040.[18] Likewise, in 2014, airports calculated that they need $33.5 billion to fund capital investments, with the federal government providing $3 billion per year.[19] A replacement air traffic control system that will allow more planes on the same routes has been in development since 2004 and has an estimated future cost of $14 billion.[20] Finally, the United States ranks seventh in the World Economic

---

[15] The United States' digital infrastructure is adequate by some measures and falls short in others; however, it is not world-class in a number of important dimensions. For more, see Steven J. Markovich, "U.S. Broadband Policy and Competitiveness," Council on Foreign Relations, CFR Backgrounders, May 13, 2013, http://www.cfr.org/digital-infrastructure/us-broadband-policy-competitiveness/p30687.

[16] See American Society of Civil Engineers, "Failure to Act: The Impact of Current Infrastructure Investment on America's Economic Future," 2013, 10, http://www.asce.org/uploadedFiles/Issues_and_Advocacy/Our_Initiatives/Infrastructure/Content_Pieces/failure-to-act-economic-impact-summary-report.pdf.

[17] For more information, see U.S. Department of Transportation, *2013 Status of the Nation's Highways, Bridges, and Transit: Conditions and Performance* (Washington, D.C., February 2014), chap. 7, http://www.fhwa.dot.gov/policy/2013cpr/pdfs/chap7.pdf.

[18] American Society of Civil Engineers, "Failure to Act: The Economic Impact of Current Investment Trends in Airports, Inland Waterways, and Marine Ports Infrastructure," 2012, 21, http://www.asce.org/uploadedFiles/Issues_and_Advocacy/Our_Initiatives/Infrastructure/Content_Pieces/failure-to-act-ports-aviation-report.pdf.

[19] Federal Aviation Administration (FAA), *National Plan of Integrated Airport Systems 2015–2019* (Washington, D.C., September 2014), 66, 77, http://www.faa.gov/airports/planning_capacity/npias/reports.

[20] FAA, "NextGen: The Business Case for the Next Generation Air Transportation System," December 2014, https://www.faa.gov/nextgen/media/BusinessCaseForNextGen-2014.pdf.

Forum's Network Readiness Index, but 17% of Americans—and half of rural residents—still lack adequate broadband access.[21]

Lawmakers understand the importance of these projects but differ on priorities and on how they should be funded. The enormous government expenditures required will have to be carved out of already strained local, state, and federal budgets. Moreover, the enabling legislation for public-private partnerships, a possible funding solution besides full government funding, will have to be passed in a difficult political environment against the opposition of those benefitting from the current system. These factors make it unlikely that the U.S. economic infrastructure will improve substantially soon.

The third negative factor in continued U.S. economic growth is the lack of energy security. Although the increase in domestic shale oil and gas production will continue to be a strength of the U.S. economy, it has not provided the United States energy independence or even energy security. A country is energy secure when acts of nature or events in energy-producing countries do not substantially affect its economic or national security interests. According to a careful ranking by the nonprofit organization Securing America's Future Energy, the United States is only the ninth most energy-secure country in the world.[22] Because oil is bought and sold in a worldwide market, U.S. citizens and businesses pay the global price no matter how much the United States produces or from where the rest is imported. The U.S. transportation sector is projected to remain over 90% dependent on oil for decades to come. Demand is inelastic—when prices go up due to supply shortages somewhere in the world, U.S. families and businesses must pay the higher prices and compensate elsewhere in their budgets.[23] As a result, oil price increases have been a major factor in the last six recessions in the U.S. economy.[24]

The current glut of oil and low prices will not continue indefinitely; rather, the balance of global oil supply and demand is projected to be tight

---

[21] "FCC Finds U.S. Broadband Deployment Not Keeping Pace," Federal Communications Commission, Press Release, January 29, 2015, https://transition.fcc.gov/Daily_Releases/Daily_Business/2015/db0129/DOC-331760A1.pdf.

[22] "Secure Energy," Securing America's Future Energy, http://oilembargo40.org.

[23] James D. Hamilton, "Causes and Consequences of the Oil Shock of 2007–08," National Bureau of Economic Research, NBER Working Paper, no. 15002, May 2009, 3.

[24] Commission on Energy and Geopolitics, "Oil Security 2025: U.S. National Security Policy in an Era of Domestic Oil Abundance," Policy Report, January 15, 2014, 84, http://www.secureenergy.org/Oil2025; James D. Hamilton, "Oil and the Macroeconomy Since World War II," *Journal of Political Economy* 91, no. 2 (1983): 228–48; James D. Hamilton, "This Is What Happened to the Oil Price-Macroeconomy Relationship," *Journal of Monetary Economics* 38, no. 2 (1996): 215–20; and Hamilton, "Causes and Consequences of the Oil Shock of 2007–2008," 5–6.

over the long term as larger middle classes emerge in developing countries.[25] The global economy is also still vulnerable to natural or geopolitical supply interruptions. When they occur, U.S. oil companies will enjoy higher profits, but U.S. consumers and businesses will have to pay higher prices, thereby halting or even reversing economic growth. Moreover, the swing producers of oil—the countries that are able within a few months to compensate for oil price spikes caused by supply interruptions—will remain Saudi Arabia and potentially other Gulf countries, including Iraq. Only they can increase production quickly and at low cost. This means that the United States will continue to be heavily involved in the Middle East and will remain in strategic partnerships with countries of antithetical values and uncertain long-range futures.[26]

To achieve energy security, the United States must diversify the fuel sources for its transportation sector away from petroleum. There are some actions already underway. For example, approximately 3.5 million hybrid electric vehicles and 287,000 plug-in electric vehicles were sold and 191 models were on the market through 2014.[27] However, the total car fleet in the United States is about 250 million vehicles, so there is a very long way to go to diversify fuel sources in a significant way. Either inspired government action or another oil crisis will be necessary to make a dent in petroleum's current lock on the transportation sector.[28]

In summary, the continued growth of the U.S. economy is most seriously threatened by three factors: lack of a highly skilled workforce, obsolete infrastructure, and energy insecurity. There are good prospects for improving workforce skills through education reform and new immigration policies. However, the goals of modernizing the country's transportation and digital infrastructure and improving U.S. energy security are very difficult and will only be achieved either by political consensus and leadership of a type not observed recently in the United States or in reaction to a very serious economic crisis. The chances for continued U.S. economic growth still must be considered favorable, but it is unlikely that the country will realize its full economic potential.

---

[25] Projected long-range future energy balances are between 2.0 and 4.5 million barrels per day, with world consumption at roughly 100 million barrels per day. See Commission on Energy and Geopolitics, "Oil Security 2025," 17, 82.

[26] For an extensive discussion of future scenarios, see Commission on Energy and Geopolitics, "Oil Security 2025."

[27] Stacy C. Davis, Susan W. Diegel, Robert G. Boundy, and Sheila Moore, "2014 Vehicle Technologies Market Report," Oak Ridge National Laboratories, 2015, 119, 122; and U.S. Department of Energy, "Alternative Fuels Data Center," http://www.afdc.energy.gov/data.

[28] For a detailed plan for achieving energy security through diversification of the energy sources for the transportation sector, see the Energy Security Leadership Council, "A National Strategy for Energy Security: Harnessing American Resources and Innovation 2013," Securing America's Future Energy, 2012, 31–36.

Alliances and a Tradition of Leadership

There are important components of U.S. national power beyond economic strength. One is the network of alliances and partnerships that the United States has established over the last 70 years. These countries do not follow U.S. direction on all issues, but alliances and partnerships provide a foundational convergence of important interests that the United States can draw on when dealing with a major issue or crisis. Most of these alliances were formed during the Cold War and have endured in modified form. Many Eastern European countries have joined NATO or expanded relations short of NATO membership; the alliance with Japan has been updated; countries in Africa and Latin America that were suspicious of or hostile toward the United States during the Cold War have become friendlier. No other country has the web of alliances and partnerships that the United States enjoys. This group, for example, includes eleven of the twenty wealthiest countries in the world.

In recent years, however, there have been striking instances of a weakening of traditional U.S. alliances. France declined to join the small coalition of countries that the United States led in the second Iraq war, the British Parliament refused in 2013 to join the United States in taking military action against Syria for its use of chemical weapons, and Israel has expressed very public disagreement with the United States over Iran. However, these differences with allies and partners have not resulted in fundamental ruptures of U.S. alliances and partnerships, and there have been counterexamples—for instance, the dramatic recent strengthening of the alliance with Japan, the formation of new strategic partnerships with several countries in Asia, and the restoration of military relations with New Zealand. Thus, the United States' extensive system of alliances and partnerships most likely will continue to be a strong component of U.S. international power and influence.

The final component of U.S. national power is the habit of world leadership. In both the economic and the security areas, the United States has considered itself the world's leader in addressing both long-term structural issues and regional crises and challenges; the rest of the world typically has looked to the United States to take the lead.[29] Although there have been many exceptions, this position of leadership has meant that the United States could shape the international approach to major challenges and issues in a way that favored U.S. interests.

---

[29] This concept was expressed in the phrase "indispensable nation" first used by Secretary of State Madeleine Albright in 1998 and repeated by President Obama as recently as 2012. See Barack Obama, "Remarks by the President at the Air Force Academy Commencement," White House, May 23, 2012, http://www.whitehouse.gov/the-press-office/2012/05/23/remarks-president-air-force-academy-commencement; and "Transcript: Albright Interview on NBC-TV February 19," Federation of American Scientists, http://fas.org/news/iraq/1998/02/19/98021907_tpo.html.

In the world economy, for example, as the wealthiest nation in the world following World War II, the United States took the lead to construct, support, and expand a system that generally favored free trade. World trade in the last 70 years has expanded at one and a half times the rate of global economic growth.[30] In other words, the American-led world trade and financial system has provided an opportunity for developed and developing countries alike to increase their rates of growth beyond what they could have accomplished relying on their domestic markets. The United States itself benefitted greatly from the system, both in gaining markets for its exports, in the availability of lower-priced products for American consumers and businesses, and in the influence deriving from its position of leadership.

Similarly, in international responses to regional crises, the United States has traditionally been the country that led. This habit of leadership, born during World War II and exercised throughout the Cold War, continued after 1990. The United States led the response to the Iraqi invasion of Kuwait; after some delay, led the NATO response to the violence in the Balkans; and more recently has led the international campaign against al Qaeda. As in the case of economic issues and crises, by taking a leadership role, the United States was assured of a solution that was favorable to its own interests.

As will be discussed later in this chapter, the United States has not settled on a broad national security strategy in the post–Cold War era. As a consequence, or perhaps for the same reasons, the U.S. habit of leadership, along with the instinctive expectation of American leadership by much of the rest of the world, has diminished in recent years. Leadership on international economic issues has continued to be strong, with ongoing U.S.-led efforts to negotiate the Trans-Pacific Partnership (TPP) and the Transatlantic Trade and Investment Partnership. However, in the security area the United States has recently assumed a less forceful leadership role. This trend has been most apparent in the Middle East but also can be seen in Eastern Europe. The international coalition for the second Iraq war in 2003 was much smaller than in the first war in 1991. The U.S. role in dealing with Russian aggression in Crimea and Ukraine since February 2014 has been less forceful and comprehensive than it was in dealing with the collapse of the Warsaw Pact in 1991. It is too soon to tell whether the current U.S. tentativeness in world leadership is an aberration. If the trend continues, however, the United States will lose some of its control of the international agenda and will have to settle for outcomes that are less in line with fundamental U.S. interests.

---

[30] Between 1950 and 2007, trade grew at an average rate of 6.2% per year, while GDP grew by 3.8%. World Trade Organization (WTO), *World Trade Report 2008* (Geneva: WTO, 2008), 15.

National Security Performance

Foundational Elements

U.S. overall performance in the area of national security is governed by a number of different factors: basic private sector and governmental competence, including fiscal competence; an effective set of authorities, organizations, and procedures for conducting national security; a competent national security workforce and adequate national security funding; and finally a consistent and effective national security strategy that is supported by Congress and the public and sustained across changes of administration.

For the United States, many of these factors are strong and positive. In general, U.S. national security competence compares favorably to that of other major countries. However, maintaining its leading world position requires several important improvements.

Government Competence

The U.S. government's response to national challenges has deteriorated in recent years. Despite increasing evidence of deep-seated national problems that require legislative solutions along with competent executive branch action—for example, entitlement payments, healthcare, education, national infrastructure, immigration, and energy and disaster response—for the past fifteen years there has been scant government progress on the great majority of these issues. As the political parties have moved away from the center, propelled by the nature of their primary elections, unrestrained campaign contributions, gerrymandering, and the controversy-obsessed media, discussions of solutions to every major national problem degenerate relatively quickly into a stalemate. It has been impossible to fashion practical compromises that blend both public and private action.[31] Beyond their failure to take on big problems, Congress and the executive branch have become less capable of carrying out even the routine functions of government—passing budgets on time and confirming appointees to key positions.

As stated earlier in the chapter, the lack of government action on immigration, national infrastructure, and energy security has directly handicapped U.S. economic growth. The 2007–8 recession and the spectacle of polarized U.S. politics of recent years have had the short-term effect of undercutting U.S. influence and authority. Countries around the world are less inclined to look to the United States as a model and to follow U.S. advice.

---

[31] See Tom Allen, *Dangerous Convictions: What's Really Wrong with the U.S. Congress* (Oxford: Oxford University Press, 2013).

Adversaries or competitors like Russia and China are having an easier time discrediting U.S. ideas.

So far this loss of influence due to the deterioration of government and some private sector competence is recoverable. The United States has recovered from similar periods in the past when it seemed to be losing competence and leadership. When leading on international issues such as the TPP, Iran's nuclear program, or the Islamic State of Iraq and Syria (ISIS), Washington finds ready partners. However, a protracted period of absence from a leadership role or misguided leadership will be difficult to surmount.

Government Fiscal Competence

An important factor in national security performance is fiscal competence. Budgets for defense and other national security departments and agencies must be sustained and adequate. Recent years, however, have raised doubts about the United States' capacity to handle its fiscal affairs.

At the national level, the U.S. government has not balanced a federal budget since 2001,[32] and the national debt has roughly tripled from $6 trillion in 2001 to $18 trillion today.[33] Low interest rates have kept increasing debt service payments manageable, but the liabilities are huge and will likely have an impact on long-term national growth.[34] Federal budgets are projected under the most optimistic forecasts to be in deficit for the next ten years.[35] The current federal debt-to-GDP ratio of the United States is above 100%, having averaged about 60% for the previous 50 years.[36]

All this fiscal pressure does not bode well for sustained and healthy funding for national security programs, from overseas assistance to the State Department's budget to the acquisition accounts of the Department of Defense. While Congress has always funded the current operating expenses

---

[32] Jim Dexter, "CNN Fact Check: The Last President to Balance the Budget," CNN, February 3, 2010, http://politicalticker.blogs.cnn.com/2010/02/03/cnn-fact-check-the-last-president-to-balance-the-budget.

[33] This data comes from "The Debt to the Penny and Who Holds It," U.S. Department of the Treasury, Treasury Direct, http://www.treasurydirect.gov/NP/debt/current.

[34] Carmen M. Reinhart, Vincent R. Reinhart, and Kenneth S. Rogoff, "Public Debt Overhangs: Advanced Economy Episodes Since 1800," *Journal of Economic Perspectives* 26, no. 3 (2012): 69–86. See also the argument that "there is no simple relationship between debt and growth," in International Monetary Fund (IMF), "The Good, the Bad, and the Ugly: 100 Years of Dealing with Public Debt Overhangs," in *World Economic Outlook: Coping with High Debt and Sluggish Growth* (Washington, D.C.: IMF, 2012), 101–27.

[35] According to the White House, deficits will range between 2.2% and 2.7% of GDP through 2025. See Office of Management and Budget, *Fiscal Year 2016 Mid-Session Review, Budget of the U.S. Government* (Washington, D.C., July 14, 2015), 64, https://www.whitehouse.gov/sites/default/files/omb/budget/fy2016/assets/16msr.pdf.

[36] "Federal Debt: Total Public Debt as Percent of Gross Domestic Product," Federal Reserve Bank of St. Louis, FRED Database, https://research.stlouisfed.org/fred2/series/GFDEGDQ188S.

of the armed forces in crisis or conflict, defense procurement accounts have been reduced, equipment has aged, and readiness has suffered during times of budget pressure. This would seem to be the prospect for the future.

The process for passing federal budgets in recent years has been uniquely inconsistent, partisan, and wasteful. Sequester legislation has resulted in heavy pressure on all components of the federal budget and forced stop-and-go funding that is especially damaging to the defense budget. When defense acquisition programs—the purchase of new systems—cannot be planned on a multiyear basis, major additional costs are incurred.[37] Over the last several years, tens of billions of defense dollars have been wasted as the military services have had to continually revise plans for equipment programs based on different possible budgets. Revisions to contracts with defense equipment suppliers have added cost while reducing procurement quantities. Although the worst appears to be over, the sequester process leaves a legacy of deferred funding requirements that will take years to absorb.

In summary, one of the strongest constraints on U.S. armed forces in the future will be the overall tight budget picture at all levels of government as well as the inefficiency of unpredictable annual funding. The potential ramifications of such fiscal pressure will be discussed in the final section of this chapter.

National Security Authorities, Organization, and Procedures

The basic structure of the U.S. national security organization was established following World War II and refined during the Cold War. Authority for directing national security actions was invested in the president, and the chain of command ran directly from the president to the secretaries of the major departments and agencies. The National Security Council was established as a high-level coordinating mechanism to assist the president in providing direction to the national security departments and agencies, but funding and direction flowed through departments.[38] Even during the Cold War, this rigid and stove-piped chain of national security command was often inadequate. For handling complex contingencies with interlinked military, diplomatic, and economic aspects, no established mechanism existed for making decisions in the field to integrate the actions of the different departments. Interagency disputes could not be decided short of presidential

---

[37] A Congressional Research Service (CRS) report cites analysis by the Defense Department that found 2%–8% in savings in multiyear acquisitions. See Ronald O'Rourke and Moshe Schwartz, "Multiyear Procurement (MYP) and Block Buy Contracting in Defense Acquisition: Background and Issues for Congress," CRS, CRS Report for Congress, R41909, June 12, 2015, 3.

[38] For a full discussion of these issues, see the Project on National Security Reform, "Forging a New Shield," November 2008, http://purl.access.gpo.gov/GPO/LPS106470.

action, and the execution of presidential decisions was still transmitted back to the field through separate departmental authorities.

In the complex world that followed the Cold War, such rigid, department-centric authorities and procedures became even more of a handicap. All the major national security challenges, from Iraq to Haiti to Bosnia to Afghanistan, have required tightly integrated diplomatic, military, and economic action in the field. On occasion, largely because of the personalities of senior officials on the scene from the State Department, armed forces, and the U.S. Agency for International Development (USAID), there was tight cooperation and the results were positive. Too often, however, leading officials from different departments and agencies were at odds, and there was no way to settle differences and pursue a consistent policy short of presidential intervention. The result was a great deal of friction in the field, wasting resources, missing opportunities, and jeopardizing the success of national missions.[39]

Successive administrations have noted these problems in interagency coordination in the field, and their solution has generally been to attempt to assert greater control of field actions by the National Security Council staff. The results of this approach, however, have not been uniformly positive. What is needed instead is an updated set of authorities, responsibilities, and procedures that enable the different levels of the national security structure to play their appropriate roles and to work smoothly together. Unfortunately, the unique combinations of circumstances that prompted the Goldwater-Nichols Act of 1986, which was designed to integrate different military services under single operational field commanders, and the Intelligence Reform and Terrorism Prevention Act of 2004 have not occurred to enable or compel wider national security reform. The attempt by the Project on National Security Reform in 2008 to convince the incoming Obama administration to enact these reforms was unsuccessful. The chances for reform are thus dim, and the United States will most likely pay the price of reduced effectiveness in all its important national security actions.

National Security, Human Capital, and Financial Resources

U.S. competence in the middle and lower ranks of national security departments and agencies is greater than it ever has been. The military officer corps performs its duties superbly, and the high tempo of combat operations since the end of the Cold War has produced a generation of combat-tested

---

[39] For examples of the dysfunction of the integrated U.S. effort to rebuild Iraq, see Paul Bremer, *My Year in Iraq: The Struggle to Build a Future of Hope* (New York: Simon and Schuster, 2006); and Ricardo S. Sanchez and Donald T. Phillips, *Wiser in Battle: A Soldier's Story* (New York: HarperCollins, 2008).

field-grade officers. Foreign Service officers have been shifted in large numbers from comfortable embassy assignments in developed countries to difficult and dangerous jobs in developing countries in Asia and Africa and have performed their duties with courage, dedication, and initiative. Intelligence officers have deployed in large numbers to combat zones, where they have gained invaluable experience in providing operational intelligence when lives are on the line. Bright and dedicated young U.S. citizens continue to volunteer in large numbers for military, diplomatic, and intelligence service, so the prospects for the future are positive.

Budget resources for national security departments and agencies have been generally adequate during the 27 years since the end of the Cold War, despite the shortcomings in fiscal competence described earlier in this chapter. Shortages of budget resources have not been responsible for failures during this period in achieving important national security objectives. As shown in **Figure 1**, the budget of the Department of Defense was cut by roughly a third during the 1990s without major damage to U.S. interests. Following September 11, there was a steady and continuous increase in funding,

FIGURE 1   Department of Defense budgetary authority, 1990–2015

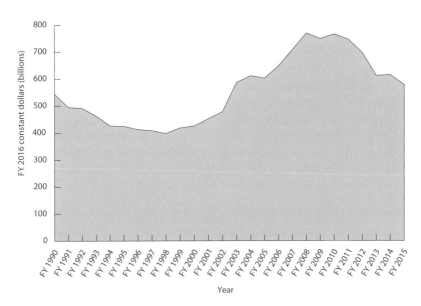

SOURCE: Office of the Under Secretary of Defense (Comptroller), *National Defense Budget Estimates for FY 2016* (Washington, D.C., March 2015), table 6-10, 150–53.

ending in 2010, followed by four years of steady decline to the present.[40] However, during this period, the defense budget process within both the executive branch and Congress has become disconnected from basic policy and strategy.[41] Within Congress there is now an unusual combination of conservative lawmakers determined to reduce total government expenditures no matter what and liberal members who believe that defense spending should be reduced in order to provide more resources for domestic programs without a strong enough offsetting group of senators and congressmen who can make a strong strategic case for an adequate level of funding for the armed forces to carry out a bipartisan national security strategy. As a result, national security budgets have not been determined through a logical process of setting priorities among national interests, relating desired objectives to resources, and assessing the effectiveness of programs. There is great uncertainty about future spending levels with the withdrawal of major U.S. forces from Afghanistan and overall pressure to balance the budget and address domestic priorities.

The State Department and USAID did not enjoy the same budget increases as the defense and intelligence communities following September 11. According to the testimony of successive secretaries of state, and even some secretaries of defense, the State Department is underfunded for its responsibilities.[42] Although highly unlikely, substantial increases would be an important indicator of a new approach to national security.

National Security Strategy

Despite the talented middle ranks of national security professionals and generous funding, especially for the Defense Department and the intelligence community, the United States' national security record since the end of the Cold War is mixed. These results are primarily due to the failure to fashion a consistent national security strategy for the different international environment that emerged following the United States' victory in the Cold

---

[40] U.S. defense spending, including both the Department of Defense base budget and the Overseas Contingency Operations budget, has fallen by 19% since fiscal year 2010. See U.S. Office of the Under Secretary of Defense (Comptroller), *United States Department of Defense FY 2016 Budget Request Overview* (Washington, D.C., February 2015), 1–5, http://comptroller.defense.gov/Portals/45/Documents/defbudget/fy2016/FY2016_Budget_Request_Overview_Book.pdf.

[41] See the memoirs of both Robert Gates and Leon Panetta about their discussions with the president concerning defense requirements. Robert M. Gates, *Duty: Memoirs of a Secretary at War* (New York: Vintage Books, 2015); and Leon Panetta, *Worthy Fights: A Memoir of Leadership in War and Peace* (New York: Penguin Press, 2014).

[42] Thom Shanker, "Defense Secretary Urges More Spending for U.S. Diplomacy," *New York Times*, November 27, 2007; and Ash Carter, "Remarks by Secretary Carter at the Global Chiefs of Mission Conference," U.S. Department of Defense, March 26, 2015, http://www.defense.gov/News/Speeches/Speech-View/Article/606657/remarks-by-secretary-carter-at-the-global-chiefs-of-mission-conference.

War. A country's real national security strategy includes its understanding of the international environment, its vision and goals for the future, and its priorities across regions and functional areas. Since 1988 there have been four administrations—two Republican, two Democrat—and each has written its own national security strategy.[43] Across those 27 years the United States has tried many different approaches to the challenges of the post–Cold War era. Some individual elements have been consistent and largely successful. Several regional strategies, for example, have worked well, including in Africa, Latin America, and the Far East. Relations with Europe have by and large been handled competently during some difficult times. The region in which the United States has most damagingly failed to come up with a good strategy is the Middle East. However, functional global issues—combatting violent Islamic extremists, dealing with issues of global climate change, and building a global rules-based order—have been handled less consistently and with sparse positive results.

There are many reasons for this failure to forge a national security consensus and strategy. The first was the overwhelming military and economic superiority of the United States after the fall of the Soviet Union. With power superiority, Washington had little incentive to develop a clever strategy. Second, and related, was the lack of a single overarching existential threat to compel the United States to set priorities and provide an overall national goal. Third, and also related, the inevitable tensions between individual national interests, whether regional or functional, led to compromise and inconsistency in the absence of an ordering threat or national objective. The fourth factor was the growing polarization of U.S. politics described earlier in this chapter. Although national security issues have been somewhat less partisan than domestic issues, the antipathy between the major political parties has increasingly made the forging of a consensus difficult. Fifth and finally, September 11 played a role. The terrorist attacks by al Qaeda had a shock value that caused a U.S. reaction far in excess of the threat posed by such a small and stateless organization. Elevating the campaign against this group to the country's top strategic objective interfered with the formulation of a strategy that could address the full range of threats and opportunities.

With all these factors thwarting development of an overall strategy that would set priorities, provide principles for action, and guide resource allocation, successive administrations since 1988 have generally handled

---

[43] The last National Security Strategy published by the Obama administration can be accessed through the White House website at https://www.whitehouse.gov/sites/default/files/docs/2015_national_security_strategy.pdf. Past versions can be accessed through the National Security Strategy Archive's website at http://nssarchive.us.

crises in an ad hoc fashion, taking the best short-term action decided on through a series of White House–led meetings.

What would a real national security strategy look like? It would have to deal with the three major strategic challenges that stand out in the future security environment: the rise of China, the breakdown of stability in the Middle East, and the emergence of violent extremist Islamic groups.

The United States has been most successful in developing a strategy for the first of these challenges—the rise of China. The strategy has included engagement across economic, diplomatic, and some military dimensions, seeking to bring China into the world order, along with the hedge of a continued strong military presence in East Asia and maintenance of allied relationships. Successive U.S. administrations have pursued this basic strategy, and it has been largely successful. China's rise in the future will present different challenges from those of the past, requiring adjustments in U.S. strategy, but a solid foundation exists for dealing with these challenges.

The United States has been much less successful in constructing a strategy to handle the remaining two interrelated challenges: instability in the Middle East and Islamic extremism. Developing a consistent strategy, or even a set of strategic principles, for dealing with the Middle East is not simple. U.S. interests often conflict—for example, short-term interests such as cooperation against extremist groups conflict with longer-term interests such as the promotion of democratic governance and human rights. Since the 1970s, the U.S. approach to the region has become heavily militarized. Military campaigns have failed to produce decisive results despite great expenditures of blood and treasure, yet in the Middle East diplomacy without the credible threat of force is generally not effective.

The elements of an effective long-term strategy for the region include several strategic principles and objectives:

- improving U.S. energy security through domestic measures to lessen the importance of Saudi Arabia and other low-cost oil-producing states in the region

- involving other countries from Europe and Asia, including India and China, in maintaining a regional balance of power that checks the ambitions of Iran or any other country seeking a dominant position in the Middle East

- making greater and earlier use of military measures short of the commitment of major combat units, including the allocation of appropriate equipment and sustained training

- shifting much of the campaign against extremist groups in fragile countries from direct military and intelligence action to support for better governance and effective host-nation security capacity

- sustaining support for long-term peaceful democratic change in the region

There will be constant individual crises in the region requiring short-term responses, but the United States needs to make progress on these strategic principles and objectives as it works its way through the crisis of the moment.

Improvements are needed in U.S. strategy to deal with extremist Islamic groups beyond rebalancing operations in fragile states in the Middle East where most of the groups are based. Since September 11, the United States has learned a great deal more about these organizations and the threat they pose even as their names and locations have changed. In addition, the United States has employed a full range of approaches to dealing with them and has the experience to forge a successful strategy in the future. As numerous government officials have testified, the United States is capable of detecting and preventing large terror attacks by multiple teams on the scale of September 11; however, it is not capable of detecting and preventing all attacks by small groups or individuals on the scale of the Boston Marathon bombings. For several years, these attacks, planned and conducted by individuals or small groups living in the United States, have been the most common, and many, but not all, have been thwarted by timely law enforcement action.

An improved strategy to deal with this threat should include the following principles and objectives:

- National leaders persistently and consistently explaining the necessity and legal basis for the programs conducted by intelligence and law enforcement agencies to detect and prevent terrorist attacks. These explanations can be made without compromising classified information.

- Maintaining the FBI- and local law enforcement–led campaign to identify and prosecute terror plots originating within the United States.

- Continuing to improve the Department of Homeland Security–led campaign to prevent members of violent extremist Islamic groups from entering the country. There is still a great deal of work to be done to merge all of the information and intelligence available to identify those who pose a threat.

- Promoting national resilience along the lines of Boston's reaction to the deadly bombs during one of the city's iconic events.

The lack of a consistent strategic approach to the Middle East has been felt not only in that region but also elsewhere. The commitment of large-scale U.S. combat power in Iraq and Afghanistan with inconclusive results has undercut the reputation of the U.S. armed forces throughout the world. Likewise, the setting of red lines in the region that are not enforced when crossed raises doubts among U.S. allies around the world about the reliability of the United States' commitments to global security.

Another lost opportunity concerns the impetus that a robust national security strategy provides for domestic reform. In the past, a broad consensus on national security has driven major domestic programs of substantial and lasting economic impact. For example, the Soviet Union's launch of the *Sputnik* satellite in 1957 caused massive federal investments in scientific, engineering, and language education that propelled subsequent U.S. economic growth.[44] The absence today of a strong national security justification for domestic programs of widespread economic benefit makes it more difficult to overcome the opposition of groups with vested interests in the current system.

It is difficult to foresee whether the United States will be able to forge a national security strategy that will find bipartisan political and public support, lay out a sustained successful approach to the Middle East and Islamic extremism, and provide the rationale for appropriate military budgets. The most realistic positive scenario is that, having tried a series of different national security approaches over the past quarter century, the country's leadership has learned what works and what does not. New administrations would avoid repeating past mistakes while simultaneously building a record of successful actions and gradually improving the process of integrating the actions of the different departments and agencies. This scenario would be an improvement over much U.S. national security performance since the end of the Cold War and would provide the basis for more substantial improvement.

U.S. Values

There is a final intangible, but very important, component of U.S. national security performance that needs repair. One of the great advantages that the United States has traditionally enjoyed is the attractiveness and power of its values. In recent years, however, the United States has fallen short of its ideals in too many instances. At the root of most of these failures has been the so-called war on terrorism. In its zeal to suppress violent extremist terrorist

---

[44] J.R. Minkel, "Sputnik Hype Launched One-Sided Space Race," *Scientific American*, October 5, 2007; and Deborah D. Stine, "U.S. Civilian Space Policy Priorities: Reflections 50 Years after Sputnik," CRS, CRS Report for Congress, RL34263, February 2, 2009, 1–3.

organizations, the United States has cooperated closely with authoritarian regimes from Pakistan to Saudi Arabia to Egypt. In many cases, such cooperation took place directly with the security services of these countries, the very organizations that were the most egregious violators of the freedom and human rights of local populations. Partly as a consequence, the United States failed to anticipate and take advantage of the Arab Spring to bring a measure of democratic reform to these countries, while at the same time undercutting the appeal of radical groups tolerating or advocating terrorism.

In its use of secret detention centers and enhanced interrogation techniques in the first months following the al Qaeda attacks on New York and Washington, D.C., the United States also fell short of its ideals. These measures could perhaps have been justified in the frightening days following September 11, but it was apparent in a matter of months that such actions were no longer necessary. Rather than making a clean break with the past, the U.S. government simply discontinued the use of such measures as secretly as it had started them. This has mired Washington in a debate that continues to this day about whether such actions were necessary, thereby further tarnishing the United States' reputation.

According to the careful and consistent surveys conducted by Freedom House, freedom, democracy, and human rights around the world have deteriorated over the past nine years.[45] The retreat has been due primarily to dictatorships that observe the rituals of democracy—such as elections, the establishment of multiple media outlets, and formal judicial processes—but use their power to rig the results in their favor. However, any instances of diminishment in the perceived commitment to and performance of the United States in democracy and human rights undercut its moral authority, which has been an important component of U.S. influence.

As time passes since September 11, the chances of the United States strengthening the values-based tradition of its national security strategy increase. While some short-term compromises on specific issues will always be necessary, in the future there should be less reason for values to conflict with interests. Although another major attack on the United States could change this calculation, the country is much better protected from major terrorist attacks than it was before September 11, and the experience of the intervening years should help prevent a repetition of the mistakes that were made.

---

[45] For more on this trend, see Freedom House, "Freedom in the World 2015," 2015, https://www.freedomhouse.org/sites/default/files/01152015_FIW_2015_final.pdf.

Overall Assessment of National Competence

This litany of the shortcomings of U.S. national performance in recent years, both in general and in the area of national security, seems overwhelming. It might appear that the United States is in a downward spiral that can only lead to diminished national power and influence.

However, there are two important qualifications to the foregoing analysis. In the first place, national security competence is relative. Virtually all major countries suffer in varying degrees from many of the shortcomings observed in the United States and have their own inherent limitations. None of the United States' allies or partners has developed a real national security strategy following the end of the Cold War. European NATO nations have grown inward-focused and have neglected both their armed forces and other regions of the world; Japan stagnated economically and in its security thinking for twenty years and is only beginning to break out of that period; major authoritarian countries suffer from erratic leadership, corruption, and wasted human capital. All things considered, U.S. national security performance is not markedly worse than the performance of other major powers, though it is also not markedly superior. In the second place, unlike the components of U.S. national power described in the first section of this chapter, which are enduring and difficult to change, the shortcomings in national performance can be addressed and improved relatively quickly.

One of the virtues of U.S. democracy has always been its resilience—its ability to learn from shortcomings, develop initiatives to fix problems, and improve its performance. To formulate an effective and sustainable national security strategy, to rebuild bipartisan political support for and public confidence in that strategy, and to act more in accordance with national values is the work of a few years and of a dedicated group of leaders both inside and outside the government. The human capital for such a positive change is readily available in the United States and needs only a catalyst. There are many distinguished and influential voices in the United States at all levels pointing out the same shortcomings described in this discussion of national performance and recommending general and specific steps to take to remedy them. It remains only for the number of these leaders and supportive citizens to achieve a critical mass and influence.

National Security: The Military Dimension

Assessing U.S. Military Strength

Despite recent budget reductions, U.S. military capabilities are overwhelming compared with those of any other country. The U.S. defense budget equals in size the sum of the next seven countries.[46] At 3.8% of GDP, the United States spends a relatively large proportion of its national income on defense every year.[47] It has officer and senior enlisted leadership with the most recent and sustained combat experience of any major military force, while the U.S. nuclear force is equal by treaty to Russia's and much larger than any other country's. There is no doubt that in a major conflict the armed forces of the United States can defeat those of any other country in the world and will be able to do so for the foreseeable future.

Side-by-side comparisons, however, are largely irrelevant in assessing the adequacy of U.S. military forces. What matters is their ability to perform the missions they are currently assigned and will likely face in the future. The United States, with many treaty allies around the world that it is pledged to defend, is generally satisfied with the status quo. Its most important major military task is to deter cross-border aggression against its allies or other friendly countries, ranging from members of NATO to South Korea and Japan. This mission involves the maintenance of ready conventional force units strong enough, in combination with the armed forces of allies and treaty partners, to convince potential aggressors that a cross-border military attack would not succeed.

The other major U.S. military mission is to deal with violence within states, such as insurgencies and civil wars, when it causes wide-scale suffering or when adversary countries take advantage of instability to increase their power and influence. Examples run from Ukraine to Yemen. U.S. military support in these cases can be for a government defending its authority (e.g., in Iraq and Yemen) or insurgents challenging the government (e.g., in Syria). Such support generally takes the form of equipment, advisers, air strikes, and logistic support.

Finally, specialized military forces are required for operations in a small number of fragile states that are home to violent extremist Islamic organizations that threaten the United States and its friends and allies. Current examples include Afghanistan, Iraq, Yemen, Somalia, Nigeria, Libya, and Syria.

In order to assess the adequacy of U.S. military forces, it is necessary to judge the amount and type of equipment and the skills and number of personnel against the likely range of missions (both in deterring military aggression against friends and allies and in dealing with intrastate violence

---

[46] Sam Perlo-Freeman, Aude Fleurant, Pieter D. Wezeman, and Siemon T. Wezeman, "Trends in World Military Expenditure, 2014," Stockholm International Peace Research Institute (SIPRI), SIPRI Fact Sheet, April 2015, 3, http://books.sipri.org/files/FS/SIPRIFS1504.pdf.

[47] Of the fifteen largest military spenders, only Russia (an estimated 4.5%), Saudi Arabia (10.4%), and the United Arab Emirates (an estimated 5.1%) spend a higher percentage of their GDP on defense. Perlo-Freeman et al., "Trends in World Military Expenditure, 2014," 2.

with wider effects). Finally, it is important to assess the possibility of multiple simultaneous military contingencies and the strategy for addressing them.

Regional Military Assessments[48]

In Latin America and most of Africa the primary missions of the U.S. armed forces are increasing the proficiency of friendly military forces and responding to natural disasters. The U.S. Department of Defense maintains regional command structures, and their prospective missions do not employ significant numbers of combat units. Internal conflicts and violent extremist Islamic groups in Africa potentially threaten U.S. interests—most notably the insurgencies of Boko Haram in western Africa and al Shabab in eastern Africa. However, it is unlikely that U.S. military support for government forces battling these groups would amount to significant conventional force units. More likely, the military component of assistance would be the provision of equipment and advisers to local government forces, along with U.S. Special Forces to conduct raids against the leaders of these groups. As mentioned earlier in this chapter in the discussion on strategy development, one of the strategic challenges in these countries is to develop long-term approaches to improving governance in fragile states where these groups operate. Direct U.S. operations are a short-term measure; over the longer term the United States and its allies and partners need to help countries develop economically and politically to minimize the attractiveness of radical groups and develop the security forces to handle them. For these longer-term goals, an integrated U.S. program of military, political, and economic actions is necessary. Yet as discussed earlier in this chapter, the effective implementation of such a program will require improved national security authorities and procedures.[49]

In Europe, the major military mission is deterring Russia from further armed aggression in Eastern Europe. This mission falls primarily to ground and air forces and is shared by all the members of the NATO alliance. Among its members, NATO has combined ground, naval, and air forces far stronger than those of Russia.[50] NATO also has refined doctrines, communications, and command structures for operating its forces together. The United States is the leader of NATO and is obliged to contribute combat units to the defense

---

[48] These regional and functional assessments are based on the author's experience in government as a senior military officer and as director of national intelligence.

[49] For more on such programs, see Dennis Blair, Ronald Neumann, and Eric Olsen, "Fixing Fragile States," *National Interest*, September–October 2014.

[50] James A. Marshall, "Russia's Struggle for Military Reform: A Breakdown in Conversion Capabilities," *Journal of Slavic Military Studies* 27, no. 2 (2014): 204–9; SIPRI, "Military Spending in Europe in the Wake of the Ukraine Crisis," Media Backgrounder, April 13, 2015, http://www.sipri.org/media/website-photos/milex-media-backgrounder-2015; and International Institute for Strategic Studies, *The Military Balance 2015* (London: Routledge, 2015), chap. 2.

of its European members, including by basing some of the units in Europe. A small number of air wings and army divisions should be adequate for fulfilling U.S. responsibilities in Europe, with reinforcements available from the United States in case of serious crisis or conflict.

The most challenging military missions for the United States lie in the Middle East and in the Far East. Events in the Middle East have been very difficult to anticipate in recent years. However, it is possible to describe the types and qualities of military forces that the United States needs to support its interests in that part of the world and to assess their overall adequacy.

The only conventional force combat operations that seem possible in the Middle East would be directed against Iran. The United States, even with a nuclear agreement with Iran, needs to maintain the capability to heavily degrade Iran's nuclear capability through air and missile strikes. This means continued improvement of U.S. capabilities to penetrate medium-sized but advanced air defense systems and to destroy deeply buried nuclear facilities. The U.S. armed forces have been preparing for these missions and should be able to conduct them effectively indefinitely. The other potential conventional force combat operation against Iran is to protect the Strait of Hormuz against Iranian naval, air, and mining attacks. This operation would involve conventional air and naval forces to destroy Iranian ships, boats, and planes and their support bases within range of the strait. It would also require specialized minesweeping units involving ships and helicopters. The United States should have the support of many allies for this operation, and even of countries like China and India that depend on oil shipments through the strait. U.S. reinforcements may be required to provide assistance to Saudi Arabia and other Gulf states with defenses against Iranian missile and air attacks. Although coalition partners would be needed to provide mine clearance forces to finish clearing operations in a timely fashion, projected U.S. air and naval forces are more than adequate to these missions.

More numerous and likely U.S. military force requirements in the Middle East involve intervention in insurgencies, civil wars, and attacking extremist Islamic groups that threaten U.S. interests. In Afghanistan, the United States will be required to maintain for an unknown period of time a task force to continue to train the Afghan National Army and to support it with intelligence, air strikes, other specialized combat support functions, and special forces to conduct raids to capture or kill leaders of violent extremist Islamic groups. A similar package of capabilities may be required in Iraq and possibly Yemen. In Syria and Libya, military force might be directed to support one of the contending factions in the ongoing civil wars in those countries. The mixture of forces required for this mission is similar to those for support of the governments of Afghanistan, Iraq, and Yemen.

There are many other possibilities for instability and violence in the Middle East and Africa beyond those described here. However, the nature of the required forces would be similar. Note that there is no requirement discussed for the commitment of major conventional ground forces of the size sent to Iraq for the first and second Iraq wars, or even to Afghanistan in 2009–10 at the height of U.S. involvement. With the bad memories of Iraq and Afghanistan fresh, and, more important, without any country likely to take the aggressive actions that played a major role in the decision to invade these two countries, it seems far-fetched, if not out of the question, to project a requirement for major U.S. ground forces in the Middle East.[51]

Air and naval (including Marine Corps) air forces under any reasonable projection will be adequate for their missions in the Middle East. They will be expected to carry out direct-strike and ground-support missions that are in their regular line of training and skills. The adequacy of army and Marine Corps ground forces, however, is not as clear, even without the requirement for multi-division invasion and occupation forces. The Middle East could generate requirements for advisers well beyond the capability of Special Forces Command, currently the Department of Defense organization with the assignment to organize, train, and equip units for the adviser mission. It is conceivable that thousands of such specially trained and experienced personnel would be required in the Middle East and North Africa, well beyond the current supply in the U.S. Army and Marine Corps.

The Far East is the other area where the U.S. armed forces will need to maintain robust capabilities. There are three existing contingency requirements for U.S. military force in this region: the Korean Peninsula, Taiwan, and the Senkaku Islands. It is most likely that these requirements for deterrent forces will continue. For all three contingencies, the United States will need to maintain trained and ready forces strong enough to support the forces of the Republic of Korea, Japan, and Taiwan to defeat North Korean or Chinese aggression and therefore deter it from occurring. In all three cases, the United States has the important advantage of advanced allies with capable armed forces that have an even greater stake than the United States in the successful deterrence and defeat of aggression.

In the event of a North Korean attack across the demilitarized zone, the Republic of Korea has adequate ground forces to stop an attack before it reaches Seoul. However, the United States would need to assist with intelligence collection, air strikes, air defense, and sea control in order to support effective ground operations and minimize damage to South Korea from air and missile strikes and unconventional attacks. U.S. ground forces

---

[51] Thom Shanker, "Warning Against Wars Like Iraq and Afghanistan," *New York Times*, February 25, 2011, http://www.nytimes.com/2011/02/26/world/26gates.html?_r=0.

of corps size might also be required to support a counteroffensive into North Korea after the initial attack is contained. These forces could be the same type as those potentially required for serious confrontations with Russia in Europe.

In the Senkaku Islands, the United States is committed to support a Japanese-led maritime and air operation to repel a Chinese attack or recapture the islands if a surprise Chinese raid occupies them. This would not be a large-scale ground operation; however, the campaign for air and sea superiority over the Senkakus could be fierce because the islands are within close range both of Chinese air and naval bases and of Japanese air and naval bases from which Japanese and U.S. forces would operate. The maintenance of air and sea control is a core mission of the U.S. Navy and Air Force, a mission for which the services continually modernize their equipment and training. Japan is similarly committed to maintaining advanced capabilities, and the combination of Japanese and U.S. air and naval forces should be adequate for deterrence or victory in case of conflict.

For deterrence of a Chinese military attack on or coercion of Taiwan, the Taiwanese armed forces have the responsibility for early defense against a surprise assault. Taiwanese air and maritime forces have the capability to degrade a Chinese assault during its transit across the Taiwan Strait, but in a matter of a few weeks the numerically far superior Chinese air and naval forces would wear them down. To fulfill its obligations to assist Taiwan under the Taiwan Relations Act, the United States needs to maintain the air and maritime capacity for sea and air control around Taiwan. So long as it does so, Chinese forces cannot successfully invade and occupy the island.

The state of military technology offers two advantages to the Chinese armed forces that they have been pursuing steadily and will continue to develop: submarines and missiles. Both submarines and anti-ship missiles threaten the U.S. naval forces that reinforce Taiwan, and ground attack missiles can damage the bases in the Philippines, Guam, and Japan that support U.S. air and naval operations. The United States, Japan, and Taiwan are all developing counters to Chinese submarines and missiles, but the technology leverage is adverse: it is less expensive to build effective submarines and missiles than it is to build effective defenses against them. Although there are potential technological developments that could change this balance, for the immediate future, Japan, Taiwan, and the United States all need to make the investments to maintain and improve robust levels of antisubmarine and missile defenses.

In summary, the currently planned U.S. armed forces appear to have the capability to protect U.S. interests in all major regions of the world with a few additions: greater numbers of trainers and advisers in the army and the Marine Corps, greater joint theater air and missile defense in East Asia, and greater antisubmarine capability in East Asia. If the defense budget is constrained in the future, as is likely, then increases in capability in part of the armed forces will require decreases elsewhere. The consequences of this reality will be explored below.

Functional Military Assessments

In addition to the regional contingencies described above, the U.S. armed forces face three sets of functional force requirements: nuclear modernization, cyberdefense, and space defense.

In the next twenty years virtually the entire current nuclear triad—land-based missiles, submarine-launched missiles, and long-range bombers—will need to be replaced. There is a chance to avoid some replacement costs if the United States were to choose to field two different nuclear attack systems (a dyad) rather than the triad it currently operates. In either case, however, procurement of these very expensive and top-priority systems will leave much less of the defense acquisition budget available for acquiring new and replacement conventional weapons systems. Estimates of the total cost of renewing the triad range from $220 billion to $390 billion over the next 10 years and between $836 billion and $1,082 billion over 30 years in then-year dollars (see **Figure 2**).[52]

In the cyber domain, current technology favors the network attacker over the defender. The United States will have a devastating capacity to attack the computer networks of an enemy. However, even an opponent like North Korea or Iran can pose a formidable threat to U.S. military networks. Both China and Russia devote large resources and skilled personnel to offensive cyberunits. Securing U.S. military networks will require an ongoing major investment by the Department of Defense in technology, highly qualified personnel, and continuous training and exercises. These expenditures will reduce the resources available to spend on other military requirements. The department estimates that it will spend around $5.5 billion on cyberprograms in each of the next five fiscal years.[53] Level funding for cybersecurity will be inadequate to deal with the continually evolving and improving threat to the networks of the Department of Defense, and expenditures will undoubtedly increase.

---

[52] See Todd Harrison and Evan Braden Montgomery, "The Cost of U.S. Nuclear Forces: From BCA to Bow Wave and Beyond," Center for Strategic and Budgetary Assessments, August 4, 2015, 30–34, http://csbaonline.org/publications/2015/08/the-cost-of-u-s-nuclear-forces-from-bca-to-bow-wave-and-beyond.

[53] This estimate is based on budget documents and discussions with department officials in Aliya Sternstein, "The Military's Cybersecurity Budget in 4 Charts," Defense One, March 16, 2015, http://www.defenseone.com/management/2015/03/militarys-cybersecurity-budget-4-charts/107679.

FIGURE 2 Total estimated cost of nuclear forces, 2015–39

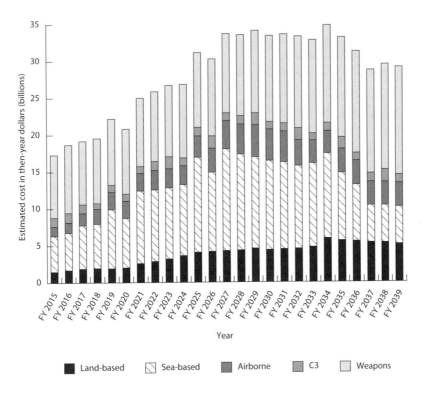

SOURCE: Todd Harrison and Evan Braden Montgomery, "The Cost of U.S. Nuclear Forces: From BCA to Bow Wave and Beyond," Center for Strategic and Budgetary Assessments, August 4, 2015, 30–34, http://csbaonline.org/publications/2015/08/the-cost-of-u-s-nuclear-forces-from-bca-to-bow-wave-and-beyond.

The technology for attacking satellites in orbit, their ground stations, and the networked systems that control them is becoming less expensive and more widespread. With the likely theaters of military operation all far from U.S. shores, the United States depends heavily on space-based intelligence and communications to support military operations. Survivability of satellite systems could be improved by design features, operational maneuvers, and other techniques. The United States will need to spend more resources in the future on its space systems to ensure that they can be effective against attacks from even medium-level threats. The additional $5 billion recently requested by the Department of Defense is a start but is hardly adequate.[54]

In summary, more challenging functional military missions will require increased investment in nuclear force modernization as well as cyber and space defenses. These requirements increase the offsets that must be found elsewhere in a constrained defense budget.

Overall Military Assessment: Strategic Choices by the United States and Its Allies

Besides individual regional contingencies and technological threats, a key consideration in assessing whether U.S. military forces will be adequate to their likely missions is the simultaneity of operational requirements. Virtually all U.S. military forces are flexible and can be moved from one theater to another. Currently planned forces are quite capable of responding to one major threat while continuing to handle several minor threats at the same time. Force shortages could arise, however, in the case of two major simultaneous contingencies occurring along with the usual number of minor threats. For example, should the United States be involved in the aftermath of a strike on Iranian nuclear facilities that included Iranian attacks on U.S. facilities in the Middle East, missile launches against Israel, and a concerted Iranian mining, air, and naval campaign to close the Strait of Hormuz, Washington would be hard-pressed to respond quickly to a contingency in Taiwan. In that case, the United States would have to prioritize, concentrating forces against the more dangerous situation and fighting back later into the other theater. The United States has enormous capacity in the event of a serious crisis to mobilize its reserve and national guard forces, expand defense industrial production, and generate sufficient forces to win several major wars. However, this process takes time. In deciding on the overall level of its forces for the future, the U.S. government will make decisions on the amount of risk it is willing to run that there will be enough time between major contingencies either to shift forces around the world or to rely on its capacity to generate new forces.

The consequences of U.S. strategic defense budget choices will not be felt acutely in dealing with insurgencies, civil wars, and special operations against violent extremist Islamic organizations. These contingencies happen over prolonged periods of time, and there are numerous forms of assistance that the United States can offer that do not strain force structure.

---

[54] Tyrone C. Marshall Jr., "Officials: Space No Longer a Sanctuary; Sequester a Threat," U.S. Department of Defense, DoD News, March 26, 2015, http://www.defense.gov/News/Article/604366.

The U.S. military budgets and force structures have traditionally been roughly balanced among the three major services, with the service shares remaining at approximately one-third each during both the Cold War and the post–Cold War periods.[55] However, the logical approach for the future within constrained budgets would be to reduce and adapt army and Marine Corps ground force structures, while sustaining and adapting the navy and air force with new technology, especially in antisubmarine warfare and missile and space defense capabilities. Spending should be increased for nuclear modernization, cyberdefense, and space defense technology across all services.

However, it is probable that the overall U.S. defense budget will not grow; that increased expenditures for modernization of strategic nuclear forces, cyber defenses, and resiliency of space forces will be necessary; and that the army's and the Marine Corps' shares of the budget will remain roughly what they have been. In this case, navy and air force capabilities will be adequate to handle the air and maritime requirements of a single contingency—either heavy involvement in the Middle East or a major Taiwan or Korean Peninsula contingency—but not both if they are simultaneous or closely spaced. The United States will simply accept the risk of simultaneous major military contingencies.

For the allies on the front lines of aggression, however, the risk calculation looks different. They risk becoming a secondary theater in the event of simultaneous contingencies. It is possible that U.S. allies and partners would increase their own defense expenditures to compensate for any delay in U.S. deployments. However, a combination of continued Chinese military buildup, Russian truculence, North Korean provocations, and Iranian expansion of power and influence in the Middle East would raise the risk for U.S. allies to a very high level. In such a scenario, they could lose confidence in the capability of the United States to come to their assistance in the event of crisis or conflict and could choose to accommodate regional adversaries, severely reducing U.S. influence and power. It is impossible to determine the point at which this spiral would commence. However, continuation of the currently planned reductions in U.S. defense budgets would make it inevitable at some point.

Summing up this review of future U.S. military force requirements, it appears that requirements for air forces, both sea- and ground-based, will remain steady, but forces will need to be modernized. For example, remotely piloted vehicles will displace manned aircraft for some missions. With China's continued building program, naval requirements will grow in both size and

---

[55] U.S. Office of the Under Secretary of Defense (Comptroller), *National Defense Budget Estimates for FY 2016* (Washington, D.C., March 2015), 149–53, http://comptroller.defense.gov/Portals/45/Documents/defbudget/fy2016/FY16_Green_Book.pdf.

required capability. The scale of ground force requirements—of both the army and Marine Corps—will diminish, but the nature of these forces will evolve. Requirements for training and advising deployments will increase. The army and to a lesser extent the Marine Corps need to retain a reserve and national guard structure that can be expanded and brought into active service in case of an unexpected major national threat or convergence of simultaneous threats. Modernizing the strategic nuclear deterrent and improving cyber and space defenses will place heavy demands on the air force budget in particular, and developing new technologies that promise greater effectiveness—from remotely piloted vehicles to new antisubmarine systems—will require additional budget resources. It is clear by any measure that the United States needs to halt the current downward trend in defense budgets and make difficult decisions that will change traditional service organizations and funding shares. The alternative will be a loss of U.S. influence and power as allies and partners fend for themselves in a dangerous and violent future security environment.

Conclusion

As it looks to the future, the United States has very strong and enduring advantages: it has a large, balanced, and dynamic economy; the country's demographic profile is favorable; it possesses many natural resources (especially energy); and the dollar is the world's reserve currency. Challenges to its economic future include a workforce that does not have adequate high-technology skills, economic infrastructure that needs upkeep and modernization, and continued energy insecurity. The United States has a well-established set of wealthy and advanced allies, and both these allies and other countries look to it for leadership on major international issues and global and regional crises. On the other hand, U.S. willingness to form and lead international coalitions has recently declined.

U.S. national performance has deteriorated in recent years. The United States' inept financial leadership brought the recession of 2007–8 on itself and much of the rest of the world, and the government at the national level is gridlocked and postpones solving well-known major problems. The organization, authorities, and processes of the national security structure also need to be updated. The United States has very experienced and dedicated officials in its national security departments and agencies, and it has funded them well in recent years. However, Washington has not developed a coherent, sustained, and bipartisan national security strategy since the end of the Cold War, and its strategy for the Middle East has been especially inconsistent and unsuccessful. Since September 11, U.S. actions have fallen short of the country's ideals for democracy and human rights, diminishing its moral authority. None of these performance shortfalls is fatal, and all can be fixed with fresh leadership that draws on lessons of the last 25 years and takes corrective policies and actions.

The United States' military forces are by far the most advanced and powerful in the world. In the future they will be challenged to meet potential major military requirements in both the Middle East and the Far East simultaneously, while modernizing weapons systems, strengthening cyber and space defenses, and funding strategic nuclear force modernization. To meet all these requirements while maintaining the traditional roughly equal balance among the service budgets will be difficult to achieve in view of other government fiscal pressures. National security budgets might increase quickly if there were bold and successful aggression by another major power against U.S. interests. However, at likely budget levels, and without national security disasters or dire threats, maintaining the military capability to support its strong influence and alliance structure in the Middle East and Far East will require the United States to change the traditionally proportional service shares of the defense budget and adjust the mixture of capabilities within the services.

Although this chapter has identified a series of shortcomings in U.S. performance in recent years and highlighted individual programs that need to be pursued, the challenge to the United States calls for more than simply a checklist of national improvements. Maintaining U.S. security in the future will require mustering a combination of leadership and popular support for a comprehensive and robust national security policy and capability based not on defeating a single hostile threatening country but on dealing with a set of diverse and dynamic enemies and competitors within a complex international security environment. Although China has the potential to be a dominant threat, important aspects of the Sino-U.S. relationship are cooperative and mutually beneficial. It is thus not good strategy to treat China as an enemy. Violent extremist Islamic groups such as al Qaeda and ISIS are actual enemies capable of horrific acts against Americans; however, they do not challenge U.S. power in the fundamental way that another nation can, and the policies and capabilities to defeat these groups are not sufficient to protect other U.S. interests. Global issues such as mitigating climate change, countering the spread of nuclear weapons, and suppressing international people and drug trafficking are important as well, but they do not amount to an ordering principle for U.S. national security strategy.

Most important for the United States is the development of a national security strategy based not simply on threats to its current position and interests but on a positive global vision for the future. Positive national security goals will better inspire the American public and will also better attract support from other countries. A positive strategy provides reasons that threats must be confronted and that important national issues must be faced.

The United States has the potential to play the primary role in bringing about a world that is both safer and more aligned with its ideals and those of most other countries. To do so, Washington needs to develop a realistic and convincing view of that world and the challenges it presents, find a positive objective for the kind of world that the United States would prefer to inhabit, and set sustained policies and programs to achieve such goals. Once a national consensus is forged on these points, the country has plenty of resources to do the job.

About the Contributors

Michael Auslin is a Resident Scholar and the Director of Japan Studies at the American Enterprise Institute (AEI), where he specializes in Asian regional security and political issues. Before joining AEI, Dr. Auslin was an Associate Professor of History at Yale University. He writes a biweekly column on Asia for the *Wall Street Journal*, and his books include *The Asia Bubble: Tracking the Hidden Risks That Threaten the "Asian Century"* (forthcoming) and *Pacific Cosmopolitans: A Cultural History of U.S.-Japan Relations* (2011). Dr. Auslin has advised both the U.S. government and private business on Asian and global security issues. He was named a Young Global Leader by the World Economic Forum, a Marshall Memorial Fellow by the German Marshall Fund, and a Fulbright Scholar, among other awards. Dr. Auslin received his PhD from the University of Illinois at Urbana-Champaign and a BSc from Georgetown University.

Dennis C. Blair is the Chairman of the Board and CEO of Sasakawa Peace Foundation USA. He also serves as a member of the Energy Security Leadership Council and the Aspen Homeland Security Council and is on the boards of Freedom House, The National Bureau of Asian Research (NBR), and the National Committee on U.S.-China Relations. Admiral Blair served as the Director of National Intelligence from January 2009 to May 2010 and provided integrated intelligence support to the president, Congress, and operations in the field. Prior to this appointment, he held the John M. Shalikashvili Chair in National Security Studies with NBR and served as Deputy Director of the Project for National Security Reform. Before retiring from the U.S. Navy in 2002, Admiral Blair served as Commander in Chief of U.S. Pacific Command. From 2003 to 2006, he was President and Chief Executive Officer of the Institute for Defense Analyses. A graduate of the U.S. Naval Academy, Admiral Blair earned a master's degree in history and languages from Oxford University as a Rhodes Scholar and was a White House Fellow at the Department of Housing and Urban Development.

Richard J. Ellings is President and Co-founder of The National Bureau of Asian Research (NBR). He is also Affiliate Professor of International Studies in the Henry M. Jackson School of International Studies at the University of Washington. Dr. Ellings is the author of *Embargoes and World Power: Lessons from American Foreign Policy* (1985); co-author of *Private Property and National Security* (1991); co-editor (with Aaron Friedberg) of *Strategic Asia 2003–04: Fragility and Crisis* (2003), *Strategic Asia 2002–03: Asian Aftershocks* (2002), and *Strategic Asia 2001–02: Power and Purpose* (2001); co-editor of *Korea's Future and the Great Powers* (with Nicholas Eberstadt, 2001) and *Southeast Asian Security in the New Millennium* (with Sheldon Simon, 1996); founding editor of the *NBR Analysis* publication series; and co-chairman of the *Asia Policy* editorial board. He also established the Strategic Asia Program, an annual assessment of the strategic environment in the Asia-Pacific. Previously, he served as Legislative Assistant in the U.S. Senate, office of Senator Slade Gorton. Dr. Ellings earned his BA in Political Science from the University of California–Berkley and his MA and PhD in political science from the University of Washington.

Andrew C. Kuchins is a Senior Fellow in the Edmund A. Walsh School of Foreign Service at Georgetown University. He is an internationally known expert on Russian foreign and domestic policies who publishes widely and is frequently called on by business, government, media, and academic leaders for comment and consultation on Russian and Eurasian affairs. From 2007 to 2015, Dr. Kuchins served as Senior Fellow and Director of the Russia and Eurasia Program at the Center for Strategic and International Studies (CSIS). From 2000 to 2007, he was a Senior Associate at the Carnegie Endowment for International Peace, where he had previously served as Director of the Russian and Eurasian Program in Washington, D.C., from 2000 to 2003 and again in 2006. Dr. Kuchins was Director of the Carnegie Moscow Center in Russia from 2003 to 2005. He has also held senior management and research positions at the John D. and Catherine T. MacArthur Foundation, Stanford University, and the University of California–Berkeley. Dr. Kuchins teaches at the Johns Hopkins University School of Advanced International Studies (SAIS) and has also taught at Stanford University. He holds an MA and PhD from Johns Hopkins SAIS.

Chung Min Lee is a Professor of International Relations in the Graduate School of International Studies at Yonsei University in Seoul and a Nonresident Senior Associate at the Carnegie Endowment for International Peace. Dr. Lee was appointed by President Park Geun-hye as Ambassador for National Security Affairs in June 2013. He previously served as the Dean of the Graduate School of International Studies (2008–12) and the Underwood International College (2010–12), Ambassador for International Security Affairs (2010–11), and as Adjunct Senior Fellow for

Asian Security Affairs at the International Institute for Strategic Studies (2011–14). Prior to joining Yonsei University in 1998, Dr. Lee worked at the RAND Corporation, the Sejong Institute, and the Institute for Foreign Policy Analysis. He has also been a Visiting Research Fellow at the National Institute for Defense Studies and the Graduate Research Institute for Policy Studies in Tokyo and a Visiting Professor in the Lee Kuan Yew School of Public Policy at the National University of Singapore. Dr. Lee is the author of *Fault Lines in a Rising Asia: Political Deficits, Strategic Rivalries, and New Security Dilemmas* (forthcoming, 2016). He holds an MALD and PhD in international security studies from the Fletcher School of Law and Diplomacy at Tufts University.

Vikram Nehru is a Senior Associate in the Asia Program and Bakrie Chair in Southeast Asian Studies at the Carnegie Endowment for International Peace. From 1981 to 2011, he served in the World Bank, including in a number of senior management positions. Most recently, he was chief economist and director for poverty reduction, economic management, and private and financial sector development for East Asia and the Pacific. Previously, Mr. Nehru directed the World Bank's Economic Policy and Debt Department. Prior to joining the World Bank, he worked for the Government of India. Mr. Nehru has written numerous journal articles and contributed to several books. He holds an MA and MPhil from Oxford University.

Rajesh Rajagopalan is a Professor in the Centre for International Politics, Organization and Disarmament at Jawaharlal Nehru University in New Delhi. His publications include three books: *Nuclear South Asia: Keywords and Concepts* (with Atul Mishra, 2014), *Fighting Like A Guerrilla: The Indian Army and Counterinsurgency* (2008), and *Second Strike: Arguments about Nuclear War in South Asia* (2005). His articles (some jointly authored) have appeared in journals such as the *Washington Quarterly*, *Contemporary Security Policy*, *India Review*, *Contemporary South Asia*, *Small Wars & Insurgencies*, *South Asia: Journal of South Asian Studies*, *South Asian Survey*, and *Strategic Analysis*. He holds a PhD in Political Science from the City University of New York.

Nadège Rolland is Senior Project Director for Political and Security Affairs at The National Bureau of Asian Research (NBR). Prior to joining NBR, she served as Senior Adviser to the French Ministry of Defense and was responsible for analyzing diplomatic, military, and domestic political developments across the region. From 2008 to 2014, Ms. Rolland served as Desk Officer for China and Adviser on Northeast Asia in the Ministry of Defense's Directorate for Strategic Affairs. From 2003 to 2005, she was a senior analyst of Asia-Pacific affairs at the French Defense Ministry's Directorate for Strategy, and between 1994 and 1998 she worked in the ministry as a China analyst. In these positions, she wrote reports for the defense minister and other senior government officials, coordinated interagency policy reviews, and directed an external research program on a wide range of topics, including China's military modernization, diplomatic strategy, leadership dynamics, and treatment of ethnic minorities. Ms. Rolland received a master of science in strategic studies from the S. Rajaratnam School of International Studies in Singapore. She also holds a diplôme supérieur on contemporary Asia and a BA in Chinese language with distinction from the National Institute of Oriental Languages and Civilizations in Paris.

Alison Szalwinski is a Project Manager with the Political and Security Affairs Group at The National Bureau of Asian Research (NBR), where she manages the Strategic Asia Program and the Space, Cyberspace, and Strategic Stability project, among others. Prior to joining NBR, Ms. Szalwinski worked at the U.S. Department of State and the Center for Strategic and International Studies (CSIS). Her research interests include the South China Sea disputes and U.S.-China strategic relations. Ms. Szalwinski has lived and worked as an English teacher in Shenzhen, China, where she also continued her language studies in Mandarin Chinese. She holds a BA in foreign affairs and history from the University of Virginia and an MA in Asian studies from Georgetown University's Edmund A. Walsh School of Foreign Service.

Ashley J. Tellis is a Senior Associate at the Carnegie Endowment for International Peace, specializing in international security, defense, and Asian strategic issues. He is also Research Director of the Strategic Asia Program at The National Bureau of Asian Research (NBR) and co-editor of twelve volumes of the annual series. While on assignment to the U.S. Department of State as Senior Adviser to the Undersecretary of State for Political Affairs (2005–8), Dr. Tellis was intimately involved in negotiating the civil nuclear agreement with India. Previously, he was commissioned into the Foreign Service and served as Senior Adviser to the Ambassador at the U.S. embassy in New Delhi. He also served on the National Security Council staff as Special Assistant to the President and Senior Director for Strategic Planning and Southwest Asia. Prior to this government service, Dr. Tellis was a Senior Analyst at the RAND Corporation and Professor of Policy Analysis at the RAND Graduate School. He is the author of *India's*

Emerging Nuclear Posture (2001) and co-author of *Interpreting China's Grand Strategy: Past, Present, and Future* (2000). His academic publications have also appeared in many edited volumes and journals. Dr. Tellis holds a PhD in political science from the University of Chicago.

Michael Wills is Senior Vice President of Research and Operations at The National Bureau of Asian Research (NBR). He coordinates all aspects of NBR's financial, business, research, and programmatic operations and serves as secretary to the Board of Directors. He also manages NBR's publications program, including the *Asia Policy* journal and the *NBR Analysis* series. Mr. Wills was formerly director of NBR's Strategic Asia Program (2001–7) and Southeast Asia Studies Program (2001–6). His research interests include international security and the international relations of Asia, particularly China's relations with Southeast Asia. He is co-editor with Robert M. Hathaway of *New Security Challenges in Asia* (2013) and with Ashley J. Tellis of four prior *Strategic Asia* volumes—*Domestic Political Change and Grand Strategy* (2007), *Trade, Interdependence, and Security* (2006), *Military Modernization in an Era of Uncertainty* (2005), and *Confronting Terrorism in the Pursuit of Power* (2004). He is a contributing editor to three other *Strategic Asia* books and several other edited volumes. Before joining NBR, Mr. Wills worked at the Cambodia Development Resource Institute in Phnom Penh and with Control Risks Group, an international political and security risk management firm, in London. He holds a BA (Honors) in Chinese Studies from the University of Oxford.

About Strategic Asia

The **Strategic Asia Program** at the National Bureau of Asian Research (NBR) is a major ongoing research initiative that draws together top Asia studies specialists and international relations experts to assess the changing strategic environment in the Asia-Pacific. The program combines the rigor of academic analysis with the practicality of contemporary policy analyses by incorporating economic, military, political, and demographic data and by focusing on the trends, strategies, and perceptions that drive geopolitical dynamics in the region. The program's integrated set of products and activities includes:

- an annual edited volume written by leading specialists
- an executive brief tailored for public- and private-sector decision-makers and strategic planners
- briefings and presentations for government, business, and academe that are designed to foster in-depth discussions revolving around major public-policy issues

Special briefings are held for key committees of Congress and the executive branch, other government agencies, and the intelligence community. The principal audiences for the program's research findings are the U.S. policymaking and research communities, the media, the business community, and academe.

To order a book, please visit the Strategic Asia website at http://www.nbr.org/strategicasia.

Previous Strategic Asia Volumes

Now in its fifteenth year, the *Strategic Asia* series has addressed how Asia increasingly functions as a zone of strategic interaction and contends with an uncertain balance of power.

Strategic Asia 2014–15: U.S. Alliances and Partnerships at the Center of Global Power analyzed the trajectories of U.S. alliance and partner relationships in the Asia-Pacific in light of the region's shifting strategic landscape.

Strategic Asia 2013–14: Asia in the Second Nuclear Age examined the role of nuclear weapons in the grand strategies of key Asian states and assessed the impact of these capabilities—both established and latent—on regional and international stability.

Strategic Asia 2012–13: China's Military Challenge assessed China's growing military capabilities and explored their impact on the Asia-Pacific region.

Strategic Asia 2011–12: Asia Responds to Its Rising Powers—China and India explored how key Asian states and regions have responded to the rise of China and India, drawing implications for U.S. interests and leadership in the Asia-Pacific.

Strategic Asia 2010–11: Asia's Rising Power and America's Continued Purpose provided a continent-wide net assessment of the core trends and issues affecting the region by examining Asia's performance in nine key functional areas.

Strategic Asia 2009–10: Economic Meltdown and Geopolitical Stability analyzed the impact of the global economic crisis on key Asian states and explored the strategic implications for the United States.

Strategic Asia 2008–09: Challenges and Choices examined the impact of geopolitical developments on Asia's transformation over the previous eight years and assessed the major strategic choices on Asia facing the incoming U.S. administration.

Strategic Asia 2007–08: Domestic Political Change and Grand Strategy examined the impact of internal and external drivers of grand strategy on Asian foreign policymaking.

Strategic Asia 2006–07: Trade, Interdependence, and Security addressed how changing trade relationships affect the balance of power and security in the region.

Strategic Asia 2005–06: Military Modernization in an Era of Uncertainty appraised the progress of Asian military modernization programs.

Strategic Asia 2004–05: Confronting Terrorism in the Pursuit of Power explored the effect of the U.S.-led war on terrorism on the strategic transformations underway in Asia.

Strategic Asia 2003–04: Fragility and Crisis examined the fragile balance of power in Asia, drawing out the key domestic political and economic trends in Asian states supporting or undermining this tenuous equilibrium.

Strategic Asia 2002–03: Asian Aftershocks drew on the baseline established in the 2001–02 volume to analyze changes in Asian states' grand strategies and relationships in the aftermath of the September 11 terrorist attacks.

Strategic Asia 2001–02: Power and Purpose established a baseline assessment for understanding the strategies and interactions of the major states within the Asia-Pacific.

Research and Management Team

The Strategic Asia research team consists of leading international relations and security specialists from universities and research institutions across the United States and around the world. A new research team is selected each year. The research team for 2015 is led by Ashley J. Tellis (Carnegie Endowment for International Peace). Aaron Friedberg (Princeton University, and Strategic Asia's founding research director) and Richard J. Ellings (the National Bureau of Asian Research, and Strategic Asia's founding program director) serve as senior advisers.

The Strategic Asia Program has historically depended on a diverse base of funding from foundations, government, and corporations, supplemented by income from publication sales. Major support for the program in 2015 comes from the Lynde and Harry Bradley Foundation.

Attribution

Readers of *Strategic Asia* and visitors to the Strategic Asia website may use data, charts, graphs, and quotes from these sources without requesting permission from NBR on the condition that they cite NBR and the appropriate primary source in any published work. No report, chapter, separate study, extensive text, or any other substantial part of the Strategic Asia Program's products may be reproduced without the written permission of NBR. To request permission, please write to:

NBR Publications
The National Bureau of Asian Research
1414 NE 42nd Street, Suite 300
Seattle, Washington 98105
publications@nbr.org

Index